W9-AUI-375

Lehman

H3 '05

The Eyes of **Orion**

The Eyes of
Orion

Five Tank Lieutenants
in the Persian Gulf War

by Alex Vernon

with Neal Creighton Jr., Greg Downey,

Rob Holmes, and Dave Trybula

Foreword by Gen. Barry R. McCaffrey

The Kent State University Press   Kent, Ohio, and London

© 1999 by

The Kent State University Press, Kent, Ohio 44242

All rights reserved

Library of Congress Catalog Card Number 99-21081

ISBN 0-87338-633-7 (cloth)

ISBN 0-87338-715-5 (paper)

Manufactured in the United States of America

First paper edition, 2001

05 04 03 02 01   5 4 3

Library of Congress

Cataloging-in-Publication Data

Vernon, Alex, 1967–

The eyes of Orion : five tank lieutenants in the Persian Gulf

War / by Alex Vernon ; with Neal Creighton Jr. . . . [et al.] ;

foreword by Barry R. McCaffrey.

p.   cm.

Includes bibliographical references (p.   ) and index.

ISBN 0-87338-633-7 (cl. : alk. paper)∞

ISBN 0-87338-715-5 (pa. : alk. paper)∞

1. Persian Gulf War, 1991 Personal narratives, American.

2. Persian Gulf War, 1991—Tank warfare.

DS79.74.V47   1999

956.7044'2'092 — dc21   99-21081

CIP

British Library Cataloging-in-Publication data are available.

This book is dedicated to our fellow 24th Infantry Division soldiers who made the supreme sacrifice while serving in Southwest Asia during Operations Desert Shield and Desert Storm.

3d Battalion, 15th Infantry Regiment
    Spc. Andy Alaniz, Company C
    Pfc. Marty R. Davis, Company B
    Pfc. John W. Hutto, Company C
    Pfc. Corey L. Winkle, Company B
1st Battalion, 18th Infantry Regiment
    S.Sgt. Raymond E. Hatcher, Company D
    Spc. Keven E. Wright, Company D
1st Battalion, 24th Aviation Regiment
    CWO 2 Hal H. Reichle, Company A
    Spc. Michael D. Daniels, Company A
2d Battalion, 159th Aviation Regiment
    Maj. Marie T. Rossi, Company B
    CWO Robert Hughes, Company B
    S.Sgt. Mike A. Garrett, Company B
    Spc. William C. Brace, Company B
Headquarters and Headquarters Battery, Division Artillery
    Capt. Tommie W. Bates
260th Quartermaster Battalion
    Pfc. Cindy D. J. Bridges, 84th Transportation Company
632d Maintenance Company
    Spc. Timothy Hill
724th Support Battalion (Main)
    Pfc. Scott N. Vigrass, Company B

I don't know how many of you have been in the presence of a main battle tank, or, if you have, what you felt. I have an infantryman's view of tanks, which is to say that I've never been exactly comfortable with them. If you're on one side of a village and a tank arrives on the other side, you feel it before you hear it. You feel it in your solar plexus and in the soles of your feet. You would never think that something so massive could be so agile as it smashes through walls and pulverizes brick, the things you thought you could hide behind. And when it slews its gun, the sound of the turret turning is like the sound of death itself.

That's one tank. In the Gulf War, columns of armor rolled across the desert for days and days, so vast and long that the dust they raised could have been seen from the moon.

— MARK HELPRIN, from a lecture at the U.S. Military Academy, West Point, New York, October 1992

Contents

Foreword

On the afternoon of 24 February 1991, I flew at low level by Blackhawk helicopter to link up with the forty soldiers, Bradley fighting vehicles, and a tank platoon that constituted the 24th Infantry Division Command Post (CP). The sky was overcast, eerie, and the weather bitingly cold. The attack aircraft of our powerful air force shrieked overhead. The dull roar of the 101st Airborne Division's massive air assault could be heard off to our west. To the right flank, more than nine thousand armored vehicles of Lt. Gen. Fred Franks's five armored divisions smashed across the frontier in the biggest armor attack since that against Kursk, Russia, in 1943. Up ahead of my Assault CP, in the gathering storm, five armor lieutenants — Alex Vernon, Neal Creighton, Greg Downey, Rob Holmes, and David Trybula — were about to lead their platoons into battle for the first time.

These five lieutenants did not know what to expect. Would they make the right decisions at the right time? Would they perform with honor? Would they even survive? In the words of Gen. Douglas MacArthur, "The soldier, above all other people, prays for peace, for he must suffer and bear the deepest wounds and scars of war."

Unlike most of the green troops of the division, I was one of just a handful of senior leaders who knew from Vietnam the cost of battle — shattered bodies and lost dreams. My exposure to combat as a young infantry officer had left me with the bitter taste of battle. I had been wounded three times. I understood the shock of dragging screaming, mangled, or dead U.S. soldiers onto medical evacuation helicopters. And I was terribly aware that my own son was about to go into this Desert Storm attack as an infantry first lieutenant in the 82d Airborne Division.

We were about to embark upon one of the most violent and rapid military attacks in the history of mankind. I would lead these five lieutenants as well as thousands of other young men and women of our division combat team on a three-hundred-kilometer assault north to the Euphrates River Valley and then through a left-hook, seventy-kilometer exploitation attack down Highway 8 to the outskirts of Basra.

In this book, these young armor lieutenants give a close-up view of battle from the platoon commander's hatch of an M1A1 Abrams tank. They have woven together their experiences: of the deployment of our division from Fort Stewart, Georgia, to the Middle East; of five months of build-up, training, and preparation; and of the subsequent air-ground campaign which destroyed the Iraqi field army that faced us. This is a story of courage, dedication, and agonizing self-doubts as these young officers faced the gut-wrenching responsibility of leading platoons through the enormous confusion, fear, and physical fatigue of high-intensity combat operations.

The authors represent the best of America's youth. U.S. Army armor and infantry lieutenants comprise an impressive group. They are double volunteers: first for army service and then for duty with a direct ground combat force. Lieutenants arrive at their first assignment with a college degree and three to six months of demanding military training. They come with no prior field experience, with fragile tactical judgment, and with novice-level interpersonal skills. But they are vital to tank-infantry company combat leadership.

The newly arrived armor lieutenant takes absolute responsibility for four tanks and sixteen soldiers. In peacetime he learns his trade under the stern supervision of a platoon sergeant with ten or more years of experience in the school of hard knocks. The three other tank commanders in the platoon are staff sergeants, with five or more years of service, who can produce superb results from the high technology of the modern tank.

The 24th Mech Infantry Division tank and mechanized infantry platoon leaders who deployed in August 1990, however, had missed a paced apprenticeship. The new platoon leaders were forced to learn their trade in Saudi Arabia during months of continuous training in defensive operations prior to the Desert Storm assault. The lieutenants either got good at their business or were pulled out of their leadership command positions and replaced. The risk of leaving weak officers in platoon command was too high. The lives of our soldiers and the success of our mission were at stake.

The five young lieutenants who herein recount their experiences in Desert Storm brought to their leadership responsibilities four attributes we value: character, intelligence, strength, and courage. Character is the bedrock of a platoon leader's success. It's a hard commodity to produce, built layer upon layer by attentive parents, caring schoolteachers, and team sports. It's too late for the army to start building character during officer basic training. At West Point/ROTC/OCS, Benning, and Knox we nourish the basic character of these leaders. The army needs them to tell the truth over a radio, even when no one can check on their statements. We want them to to treat young soldiers with dignity and respect; to be without cruelty or guile; to eat and sleep after their soldiers have already done so. We expect good, sober judgment from them, even though they are barely adults. Finally, we want them to have the humility to learn from their sergeants as well as from their own mistakes. As I read this book, I was struck by the depth and sensitivity of the authors, who feared they might not live up to the expectations of their soldiers.

We also need our lieutenants to be intelligent. The army's analysis of tank-mech infantry warfare indicates that sheer intelligence in combat leadership positions wins tactical battles. The battlefield has hundreds of changing variables. If you "lose the bubble," soldiers can be killed horribly and unnecessarily. Tactics are fluid, and visualizing spatial relationships in the AirLand Battle is complex. Being wrong even once can be catastrophic. Mastering the technology of armor warfare requires incredible powers of hand-eye coordination and mental agility for battle drills. The tank platoon leader is enmeshed in a technical cocoon of night vision IR, FM radios, GPS location devices, gunnery controls, and optical target detection, all the while crashing around inside a seventy-two-ton monster moving at forty miles per hour in pitch blackness across broken terrain.

Simultaneously, the lieutenant is tracking his three other tanks and coordinating their movement and battle observation. He is supposed to recognize danger, make split-second decisions, carry out memorized battle drills and procedures, and sound to his soldiers like he knows what he's doing when there's no sure solution. Smart lieutenants do these tasks better and reserve psychic fears for the right problems. Each of these bright young author-lieutenants commanded a platoon of soldiers who valued their leader's intelligence.

To command a tank or infantry platoon successfully, you must have the physical and emotional resiliency of youth. Company-level armor-mech combat is a young man's business. The physical hammering of maneuvering in a tank or Bradley fighting vehicle, the endless twenty-four-hour days of high pressure and intermittent sleep, and the filth, confusion, and responsibility of command combine to pull the lieutenant's thinking away from his platoon and onto his own fatigue. It's easy to make good judgments in a tank turret trainer at Fort Knox. However, by the fourth day of Desert Storm, the physical challenge was immense.

Vernon, Creighton, Downey, Holmes, and Trybula had all been athletes and were physically up to the challenge. I commanded the 24th Mech Division from an Assault CP, riding in a Bradley fighting vehicle with an attached tank platoon as security. By 0330 hours on the last night of the ground war, I was exhausted. Around us for twenty kilometers the sky was lit by the continuous flashes of four brigades of U.S. artillery pounding the Iraqi forces to our east in the Rumaylah oil fields. Though my forty-eight-year-old body was in good shape, it felt like I had been beaten with axe handles for a week. It took cups of bitter coffee and Bufferin to stay alert.

These young officers brought an infusion of personal courage to their tank platoons as well. They were all fearful of failure, personal injury, and of disappointing their soldiers and families at home. However, an armor or mech lieutenant has to be prepared to show his men how to die. A tank platoon leader ought to be fearful in anticipation of combat, but he must have the self-discipline to move aggressively and take calculated risks. The platoon leader must go into combat first. In modern warfare, there are not many people who move into battle staring over a 120-mm tank gun or through the vision blocks of a Bradley fighting vehicle. The 26,000 soldiers of the reinforced 24th Mech Division only included 126 tank, mech, or cavalry-direct combat platoons. Of the 1,800 armored vehicles in this giant divisional battle force, only 241 were Abrams Main Battle Tanks, and 221 were Bradley Infantry Fighting Vehicles. Each of these platoon combat teams of sixteen to forty soldiers prayed that their lieutenant had the character, intelligence, strength, and courage to get the job done and keep them alive. And these five Desert Storm armor leaders certainly met that challenge.

In less than one hundred hours of ground combat, the Victory Division joined twelve other U.S. Army, Marine, and allied divisions to pull apart an enemy force of five hundred thousand troops organized into forty-two divisions. The victory was not without cost. Although losses were lower than our prebattle projections, the 24th Infantry Division lost eight soldiers, and thirty-eight were wounded. A memorial has been erected at Fort Stewart to honor the dead and injured. The free men and women of Kuwait have these brave souls to thank. It was my honor to serve with these soldiers. America should be proud of their service.

Gen. Barry R. McCaffrey, U.S. Army, Ret.

Preface and Acknowledgments

Five former lieutenants in the same tank battalion during the Persian Gulf War wrote this book to provide a more accurate and personal portrait of what it was like to live through Operations Desert Shield and Desert Storm than that painted by the American news industry. This book is not about lessons learned; it is about lives lived. We did not know it when we began, but we also wrote this book for our unit, the 24th Infantry Division (Mechanized), which was deactivated on 25 April 1996 (and then reactivated on 5 June 1999 at Fort Riley, Kansas). Finally, we wrote this book for ourselves.

The vision began with Neal Creighton; he convinced Greg Downey, Rob Holmes, and David Trybula to contribute their stories. Two years later, in the early spring of 1996, Neal passed the responsibility of completing the project to me. I wrote my story, guided the other authors through several revisions, edited all material, and conducted modest research. I then incorporated the other four accounts into my own narrative frame, resulting in what might be described as a commingling of genres, of war memoir and oral history.

In the desert I wrote letters almost daily. My personal account comes from those letters and my memory. Reading the material of the other authors and talking with them certainly refreshed — I dare say revised — my own memory as well. Four of us recorded a conversation about the war the night of 24 August 1996, coincidentally the weekend of our arrival in Saudi Arabia six years earlier. Email enabled me to ask questions of the other authors as they arose during my editing and to receive prompt replies.

Research material consists of relatively easily accessed primary documents, oral histories, official histories and other secondary sources, and inquiries posed to officers who served with us. I relied on these external sources to fill the gaps where our own memories, letters, and awareness of our situation fail to provide the larger view and to address the inevitable discrepancies among our five versions. There are contradictions within the historical record as well as between it and our accounts. The historians who compiled the Eighteenth Airborne Corps's annotated chronology from unit reports acknowledge that "initial reporting contained in the Journals and Journal Files or first daily situation reports (SITREPS) is rarely accurate in matters of detail. The need to pass information quickly takes precedence over the need to be 100% accurate."[1] Fog of war indeed.

The use of the first-person plural pronoun "we" in the text might cause some confusion, as it may refer to groups as small as a vehicle crew or as large as that moment's entire deployed American force, or even the artificial "unit" of we five lieutenant-authors. I have done my best to prevent such confusion; when in doubt, the reader should read into ambiguous first-person plural pronouns the smallest appropriate unit (usually platoon or company, sometimes battalion). It should also be stated that we have changed the names of those few individuals who receive our harshest criticism, as our opinions should not harm their careers or personal lives.

We have many people to acknowledge and thank for their contributions to *The Eyes of Orion*. First, we are grateful to Gen. (Ret.) Barry R. McCaffrey, for his foreword, his enthusiastic support of this book, his historical foresight in directing the publication of official documents and the history of our 24th Infantry Division in the Persian Gulf War shortly after our return home, and, not the least, for his leadership during the war. And thanks, too, to General McCaffrey's current staff for their help and support: Col. Walter Holton, Col. (Ret.) James McDonough, and Francis X. "Pancho" Kinney.

We acknowledge Maj. Gen. (Ret.) Neal Creighton Sr., Lt. Gen. Paul Kern, and Joe Galloway for their support. Col. (Ret.) L. Randall Gordon, Matt Hoagland, Maj. Dave Hubner, Dan Kennedy, Greg Jackson, Bob McCann, and Jon Ulsaker helped to augment our memories. And for their invaluable research assistance, we thank Dale Steinhauer of the Center for Army Lessons Learned (Fort Leavenworth, Kans.); Alecia Bolling of the Gulf War Declassification Project (Alexandria, Va.); Bill Hansen of the Armor School Library (Fort Knox, Ky.); Barbara Christine of the Army Library Program (Alexandria, Va.); Walt Meeks of the Fort Stewart Museum (Fort Stewart, Ga.); and Robert Wright, Richard Hunt, and Stephen Everett of the U.S. Army Center of Military History (Washington, D.C.).

Ned Irvine and Mark Wood provided the graphic artwork. Col. (Ret.) Richard M. Swain, William Donnelly, David Van Hook, and Paul Stillwell offered their insights on different drafts. Col. (Ret.) Pat C. Hoy II thoroughly read the manuscript and recommended revisions; and I thank him as well for his years of friendship, support, and unflagging belief in me as a writer. And, of course, our thanks go to John Hubbell, Joanna Hildebrand Craig, Will Underwood, Susan Cash, and the rest of The Kent State University Press staff.

Mary Creighton, Kelli Holmes, and Jill Trybula, who supplied their observations, read drafts, loved Neal, Rob, and Dave through the war, and struggled

with their own fears and anxieties during that difficult time. Maria Ketner
Garnett Ward inspired and then kept all those damn letters. Michelle Kaem-
merling read drafts and listened to me and counseled me and loved me as I
pulled this thing together; her love, arriving three years after the war, brought
me back from the desert.

List of Maps and Diagrams

Introduction

Books about war were written to be read by God A'mighty, because no one
but God ever saw it that way. A book about war, to be read by men, ought to
tell what each of the twelve of us saw in our own little corner. Then it would
be the way it was — not to God but to us.

— Shelby Foote, *Shiloh*

In *The Soldiers' Tale,* Samuel Hynes characterizes the war narrative as
"something like travel writing, something like autobiography, something like
history," yet something not quite belonging to any of those genres. Hynes con-
cludes that "war is more than actions; it is a *culture.*"[1] Military units have their
own culture, too, and we would argue that military ranks have a kind of culture
as well. This book is about five army lieutenants of the 1st Battalion, 64th Armor
Regiment, 24th Infantry Division (Mechanized) during Operations Desert
Shield and Desert Storm — five young men just out of school and leading soldiers for the first time. It is about leadership at the platoon level, about the men
and women we led as well as the officers who commanded us. It is about the family and friends we left behind.

The Iraqi army invaded Kuwait on 2 August 1990. A light infantry brigade from
the 82d Airborne Division deployed within days to establish and secure the airfield at Dhahran, Saudi Arabia, and to signal the United States's commitment to
the region. The 82d Airborne, the 101st Air Assault, and our 24th Infantry belonged
to the Eighteenth Airborne Corps, the army unit designated to deploy rapidly
abroad. Elements of the Eighteenth had carried out the 1980s' operations in
Grenada and Panama. As the corps's heavy component, however, the 24th had not
participated in those missions. With its 1,600 armored vehicles, 3,500 wheeled
vehicles, and 90 helicopters, the division depended on ships, rather than airplanes,
to deliver its equipment to distant battlefields. But unlike the opposition in
Grenada and Panama, the Iraqis had the fourth-largest army in the world, with an
estimated tank fleet of over five thousand. The defense of Saudi Arabia required
a sizeable armored ground force, and the 24th Infantry was the first armored
division — the first full division of any kind — to arrive in country. The original
mission, the defense of Saudi Arabia, was dubbed Operation Desert Shield.

Based at Fort Stewart, Georgia, the 24th loaded its vehicles and equipment on ships at the Savannah port and flew the bulk of its personnel to Saudi Arabia on civilian aircraft. Ship transit time from Savannah to Saudi Arabia ranged from fifteen to twenty-five days, so air transport was timed to get units in country a day or two ahead of their vehicles. Hussein's decision not to push into Saudi Arabia gave the soldiers of the Eighteenth Airborne Corps six months to acclimate themselves to the desert, establish a logistics system, and plan and train for combat as the rest of the coalition forces poured into the theater.

Operation Desert Storm commenced with an intensive air phase on 17 January 1991, two days after the United Nations' deadline for Iraqi withdrawal had passed. During the air campaign, the Eighteenth Airborne moved to an attack position over three hundred miles to the west. We traveled along Tapline Road, a single two-lane paved road paralleling the Saudi-Iraq border and stretching across the Arabian peninsula. The move, which had to be conducted across the Iraqis' front without their knowledge, was successful thanks to corps planners, the incompetence of Iraqi military intelligence, and most especially the coalition's total air supremacy. When the ground phase of Desert Storm began on 24 February 1991, we found ourselves deep in the desert along the border, on the west side of the diamond-shaped neutral zone between the two countries.

The attack launched into a sandstorm that blinded both the enemy and us. While the marines and Arab forces hit Kuwait from the south, and the American Seventh Corps broke around the end of Hussein's line and into Kuwait from the west, the Eighteenth Airborne swept through Iraq well to the west, then drove east through the Euphrates River Valley to complete the encircling of Iraqi forces in Kuwait. All in one hundred hours. The coalition military force's commander in chief, Gen. H. Norman Schwarzkopf, referred to the corps's attack as a "Hail Mary" play and considers the commander of the 24th Infantry Division, Maj. Gen. Barry McCaffrey — a Vietnam veteran with two Distinguished Service Crosses, two Silver Stars, and three Purple Hearts — his "most aggressive and successful ground commander of the war."[2] Joe Galloway, one of America's best war correspondents, describes our division's portion of the attack thusly: "In four days, the 16,530–man 24th Mech had conducted what one American officer called 'the greatest cavalry charge in history.' It had charged all the way around Hussein's Army, almost 250 miles from the barren Saudi Arabian border to the gates of Basra — farther and with more firepower than General George S. Patton's entire 3rd Army had hauled across France." By war's end, the division had disabled two infantry divisions, four Republican Guard divisions, and the 26th Commando Brigade. It had destroyed 363 armored vehicles and captured over five thousand prisoners.[3]

Casualties suffered by the 24th during the war were amazingly light, eight killed and thirty-six wounded. The number killed in this last campaign before

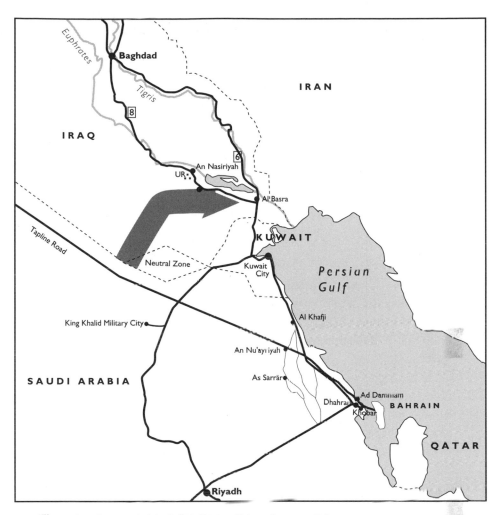

The 24th Infantry Division's "Hail Mary" Attack, 24–28 February 1991

the division's deactivation coincidentally matches the number killed in its first battle, shortly after activation, when its soldiers scrambled out of their barracks to defend Pearl Harbor on 7 December 1941 and brought down five Japanese aircraft. "First to fight" — in World War II, and then again in Korea — the phrase is the division's motto. (Again answering the division's Pearl Harbor ghosts, the 24th in Desert Storm destroyed twenty-five high-performance fighter aircraft and helicopters.) The Desert Storm casualty rate speaks volumes for American tactics, equipment, training, and leadership. But we executed neither Desert Shield nor Desert Storm flawlessly. Another eight division soldiers died during Desert Shield,[4] and this book touches on a number of problems encountered while preparing for and fighting in combat, including the distressing issue of casualties from friendly fire. "This thing was risky as hell," Major General Mc-Caffrey reminded an army historian the day of the cease-fire, "and we're going to forget that very quickly."[5] America's postwar knowledge of the operation's speed and relative bloodlessness should not be allowed to erase the memory of the risks and fears we faced.

■ Writing a book with five narrators poses its own challenges, and we have done our best to create a cohesive narrative. Limiting the authors to lieutenants from the same armor battalion helps unify the book, but confusions and conflicts among our voices and with other accounts and records were bound to emerge, and difficult to avoid. In his history of the Irish Guards, Rudyard Kipling writes that

> a battalion's field is bounded by its own vision. Even within these limits, there is large room for error. Witnesses to phases of fights die and are dispersed; the ground over which they fought is battered out of recognition in a few hours; survivors confuse dates, places and personalities, and in the trenches, the monotony of the waiting days and the repetitious work of repairs breeds false mistakes and false judgments. Men grow doubtful or oversure, and, in all good faith, give directly opposed versions. . . . The shock of an exploded dump, shaking down a firmament upon the landscape, dislocates memory through half a battalion. . . . When to this are added the personal prejudices and misunderstandings of men under heavy strain, carrying clouded memories of orders half given or half heard, amid scenes that pass like nightmares, the only wonder to the compiler of these records has been that any sure fact whatever should be retrieved out of the whirlpools of war.[6]

For us, the speed of our offensive blurred our memory, though our accounts do not diverge as drastically as those collected by Kipling. Doubtless, other members of the 24th during Desert Shield and Desert Storm have still different perspectives and remembrances. Inconsistencies become an accuracy of sorts.

Four of us received our commissions from the U.S. Military Academy; the fifth came from ROTC out of the University of Nebraska-Kearney. We four from West Point had been commissioned in the army slightly over a year and had been with the 24th Infantry a matter of months. We were still learning our jobs, getting to know our soldiers, and trying to become proficient in our profession. Two of us were married. We were all in our early twenties.

Neal Creighton Jr., Chicago, Ill.   Alex Vernon, Chapel Hill, N.C.

The Eyes of **Orion**

1

Operation Desert Shield, Part 1
August and September 1990

Alert and Deployment: Operation Laser Victory

At 0300 hours, Aug. 7, 1990, the 24th Infantry Division (Mechanized) was alerted for deployment to Saudi Arabia. Immediately, the division began to organize itself for combat.

The Victory Division launched into an intensive pre-deployment training program. Every tank crew, Bradley crew, Dragon, AT-4, and aviation door gunner underwent extensive live-fire training. Chemical Protective Overgarments were worn one or two days per week. Classes were conducted on combat lifesaving, host nation customs and courtesies, desert survival, Global Positioning System (GPS) navigation and Iraqi tactics and vehicle identification. . . .

The assumption that drove all pre-deployment decisions was that the division would be engaged in combat operations soon after arrival in Saudi Arabia. Each ship and brigade combat team were task organized to include supporting chemical defense, air defense, medical and fire support elements to meet all possible contingencies. Each combat vehicle was transported fully uploaded with its basic load of ammunition and supplies. . . .

Just six days, nine hours, and 57 minutes following alert, the Fast Sealift Ship (FSS) *Capella,* the first of 10 ships . . . apportioned to deploy the 1,600 armored vehicles, 3,500 wheeled vehicles, and 90 helicopters of the 24th Infantry Division (Mech) commenced her 8,000 mile journey.
— *The Victory Book*

Mike Fadden, an ROTC cadet, had been assigned to my company for his summer training. Mike ran the several miles to work for physical training and often ran the several miles back to shower and dress for the day. He was pre-med and wanted to go infantry. Since I was the company's senior platoon leader and had the most capable platoon sergeant in the company, my platoon was given to Mike by Capt. Jeff Swisher, our company commander, so that he could try his hand at platoon leading.

Then he gave it back.

I believe I was on the walkway between battalion headquarters and the company on the morning of 2 August when Staff Sergeant Kozlowksi told me Iraq had invaded Kuwait. No — I was headed to my car to drive home, and Captain Swisher told me. That feels closer, though I can't be sure.

When I arrived home to the apartment I shared with Rob Holmes, I walked in on him in our combination living room/dining room/den, where he sat back in the large chair, one leg stretched on the ottoman, the other foot on the floor, beer in hand on the armrest. His BDU cap lay in his lap. He was watching CNN.

I can still see the celebrating Iraqi infantry soldiers hitching rides on T-72 tanks headed into Kuwait.

Dave Trybula heard the news over the radio the same evening in his quarters. Until he learned that the 24th would deploy, he felt "appalled and depressed. I had chosen Fort Stewart because I knew we would be the first armored force sent to protect our national interests. But now it seemed that we were never to be used. In December 1989, I had watched as a fellow platoon leader, Al Vernon, sat with his fully uploaded tanks on the runway at Hunter Army Airfield in Savannah for two days waiting for the planes to pick them up for Operation Just Cause in Panama. The planes never came. Now a real threat to a vital interest of the United States existed and we were not even on alert. What would it take for us to go somewhere? Maybe it was time to change our vehicle's paint scheme from desert sand to blue, the army's color for training munitions and equipment.

"I was not a warmonger. Nor did I look forward to putting my life or my men's lives in danger. But I wanted to think my job had a purpose, and with Iraq's invasion of Kuwait and our not deploying, it seemed my job's purpose was gone. I was not sure why I was needed."

Greg Downey learned about the invasion from *CNN Headline News*, which he had fallen into the habit of watching every morning before leaving for a day's work in the battalion scout platoon. "Life was getting pretty predictable and relatively routine early in my military career. Or so I thought. I have heard that when you learn about a significant event, such as John F. Kennedy's assassination, or the *Challenger* space shuttle explosion, you will always remember where you were and what you were doing when you first heard the news. When I saw on the news that morning that Iraq had invaded Kuwait, I felt the 24th Infantry Division would be involved sooner or later. 'We'll be going over there,' I said aloud. I jumped in my car and headed down the street to the company. I didn't notice the heat and humidity of the early Georgia morning. What I had on my mind would occupy it for the many months to follow."

Neal Creighton did not know about Iraq's invasion until the following day. He was at Dugway, Utah, completing the final phase of Ranger School. It was actually his second trip to Ranger School. The first time he had failed the swim test during the initial week. After the instructor indicated that Neal had passed the test and waved him out of the pool, he yelled for him to stop: The LBE belt-and-suspender gear Neal thought he had removed underwater as required still clung to his leg. Failing Ranger School devastated Neal. He swore he would go back. On reporting to Fort Stewart in February 1990, Neal asked our battalion commander for orders for another trip as soon as possible. The commander obliged him; this time Neal passed the swim test easily.

Two months later, having patrolled the densely wooded hills of Georgia, the snake-filled swamps of Florida, and the rocky desert of Utah, waking up on 3 August for Neal meant "another day at Ranger School was over and another one to overcome had just begun. After eight weeks of hell, of carrying one hundred pounds in my ruck, of little or no sleep on missions and sparse rations, I had lost twenty of my 170 pounds. I was emaciated and tired. My body felt like it was running on empty and I thought only about the end of this miserable experience.

"'Rangers, gather round,' yelled an instructor as he waved his huge walking stick in the air. We moved quickly, dreading whatever lay ahead for the day. 'Yesterday, Iraq invaded the sovereign country of Kuwait. Take this desert training to heart, rangers; you could be fighting in one very soon.'

"'Yeah, right,' I muttered to a fellow ranger."

■ Neal Creighton, Rob Holmes, Dave Trybula, and I graduated from West Point on 24 May 1989, two days before my twenty-second birthday. It had rained lightly on the class of 1988's graduation; it poured on ours. From where I sat on the Michie Stadium football field in the second row of graduating cadets, I could see through my classmates' drenched white uniform trousers their colored underwear, plaid boxers and pink panties — visible as they strode across the stage. The legend holds that if it rains on graduation, your class will go to war. Having tossed my white cap up to the nevermore, I walked to the thirty-yard mark on the sideline to meet my family as arranged, wiping my dripping brow, thinking, *knowing*, I was going to war.

Neal, Rob, and I were in the same cadet company. Thirty-three years before we graduated, another cadet from Alpha Company, 1st Regiment, H. Norman "Schwarzie" Schwarzkopf, tossed his cadet cap to the winds and donned the army green. In his day the Academy assigned cadets to companies according to their height so that the plumes of a cadet company on parade formed a seeming plane. Neal, Rob, and I owe our acquaintance in A-1 to a diligent academy administrator, or, more likely, to his or her computer. Of the forty members of A-1 who entered the Academy on 1 July 1985, twenty-six of us graduated.

Though the three of us spent four years in the same company, and though I considered them friends, I had never shared a room with either one and did not know them well. Rob and Neal, however, had been roommates three times at school. When Rob walked into his first cadet room for Cadet Basic Training — what we called Beast Barracks, or simply Beast — his roommate, Neal, who had already shined his shoes and made his bed, was in the process of making Rob's. Neal obviously knew something about military life. His father, as Rob soon discovered, was a 1953 Academy graduate who had commanded a squadron with the 11th Armored Cavalry Regiment in Vietnam and as a major general had commanded the 1st Infantry Division at Fort Riley, Kansas. Neal was born at a U.S. military base in the violent and chaotic Panama Canal Zone in 1965; his parents once narrowly escaped a mob's attempt to light their car on fire. On one of the family's tours in West Germany, Neal was driven around post by his father's driver. Neal stood in the front passenger seat like a general on parade and returned the salutes of the bemused soldiers the jeep passed. At home, in secret, Neal practiced his salute for such occasions.

At West Point, Neal would prove to be one of the most athletic cadets in the company. He excelled in physical education classes, on all his physical fitness tests, and with every intramural team on which he played. He was a natural leader, which everyone recognized; our senior year, Neal was chosen to command our company. He was also something of a prankster, which he disguised under his usual intense demeanor broken only rarely by a devilish, charming smile. You could pick him out at a distance from a pack of walking cadets, identically clad in gray wool uniforms and caps, by his extremely bowed legs. As if he were born to be a tanker, the modern incarnation of the cavalryman. Neal even shared a name with the man after whom our tanks were named, Gen. Creighton Abrams.

Rob also had a military father. A pathologist and retired army colonel, he had received decorations in both World War II and Korea. In World War II he landed at Normandy in June 1944, fought with Patton's Third Army across Europe, and later served for a year in postwar, postbomb Hiroshima as the army's medical representative on the atomic bomb effect research team. He would later become the pathologist for NASA's Able-Baker Project, the first space flight with two monkeys aboard, and won a Legion of Merit — one of three in his career — as the pathologist and ballistics expert on the team that designed the first body armor. But he retired shortly after Rob's birth, so Rob grew up on military stories instead of military posts. Those stories, and his southern upbringing in Atlanta, had much to do with his decision to apply to the Academy. After seeing The Citadel on a South Carolina vacation during high school, then reading about West Point in William Manchester's *American Caesar,* he convinced his parents to take him for a visit. The significance of the school struck Rob. It was old and timeless, rock hard and beautiful. Graceful in its purpose. He watched the cadets around him and saw himself among them.

(I remember reading in my elementary school library a children's biography of Robert E. Lee. I can still see the page where I learned Lee went to West Point. The opposite page pictured him on a horse jumping a log, or was it a stream? with a stately southern home in the background. Naturally I assumed West Point was in Virginia. I did not know better until my junior year in high school, when I wrote for an application. Imagine my surprise: New York state?)

Rob and Neal were fast friends. Rob and I did not grow close until the Armor Officer Basic Course (AOBC) at Fort Knox, Kentucky, where all new second lieutenants assigned to the armor branch spend four months learning to be tankers and leaders of tankers. Once at Fort Stewart, we became pathetic bachelor-apartment mates. Our agent, a beautiful, petite, albeit married brunette, sold us on the place when she told us she lived next door. At Stewart we fancied ourselves something of a Maverick and Goose pair, after the cockpit names of Tom Cruise's and Anthony Edwards's characters in the movie *Top Gun.* Rob's dashing, charming Maverick to my Goose, the lanky, less driven companion.

Dave Trybula was also a West Point classmate, though beyond recognizing his name and face I did not know him at all until the basic course at Fort Knox.

We had been a rude AOBC class. Admonitions by our officer and noncommissioned officer (NCO) instructors that we could see combat sooner than we might imagine fell on deaf ears as a specious ploy for attention. Because of the timing — our basic course started two months after our West Point graduation — less than a dozen of the eighty-something members of our class were not Academy classmates. We spent most of the four-month course in classrooms rather than on tanks, learning useful information about tactics and the threat forces we might meet on some hypothetical battlefield, but also reviewing things we had already learned, and sitting through such useless classes as several days of freshman composition, armystyle ("Words with more than three syllables," the army writing guide decreed, "are *unnecessarily* too long"). And we felt that at the Academy we had heard every possible variation of duty lecture, of calls for professionalism, and of motivational speeches for future combat leaders, by men much more experienced, distinguished, articulate, and inspiring than our instructors at Fort Knox. We passed time in class planning weekends in Louisville, or with girlfriends, and playing "question bingo" by assigning to the squares of our bingo boards the names of other lieutenants in the class. In the end I suspect our attitude had less to do with inadequacies of AOBC than our emotional state: having been cooped up in the gray walls through the gray New York winters at West Point, having behaved ourselves to the nth degree for four years, we were out now, free, released, and together again after two months of vacation, infected by the spirit of juvenility that afflicts young men in groups.

Dave did not have military in his blood. His dad worked in research and development, and the family moved both when his father was laid off and when he left companies for better-seeming opportunities. Unlike Neal, however, Dave did not have the luxury of the military community. No chance of meeting up with an old friend or of making instant friends with others living the same transient lifestyle: "Each time we moved, I had to recarve my identity and sell myself to potential friends. I got used to moving, making new friends, and leaving others behind."

For Dave, outdoing his older brother Mike — they were only seventeen months apart — became a point of pride: he became an Eagle Scout a full year before Mike, and in his high school junior year he earned better grades taking a couple of the same courses as his brother, a senior. Still, outdoing his older brother wasn't enough. It didn't go far enough in defining Dave on his own terms — he was still walking in his brother's footsteps, doing the things his brother was doing. "I felt a real need to break away from the trappings associated with my family and chart new territory. That is why I decided to apply to the U.S. Military Academy."

His decision could not have set him on a more divergent path. As Dave was preparing his application, Mike registered as a conscientious objector. Dave was furious, convinced that his application would not even be considered (his best friend from high school had also applied, and he couldn't imagine both of them receiving admission). His brother's decision makes more sense given their upbringing: Their parents had not allowed toy guns in the house, much less real ones. Still, Dave's mother now believes that had Dave played with toy guns, he would have taken a more peaceful path, his curiosity, or latent aggression, having been sated. She would rather her middle child had not chosen the profession of arms and, as mothers tend to do, has found a way to blame herself. Dave was thrilled when West Point accepted him in March 1985.

Dave Trybula took our training at Knox more seriously than most, certainly more seriously than I did. He wanted an army career. Where I might have been tempted to ask the smart-ass questions, he asked the intelligent, studied ones. He wanted to learn. Our training tank broke a torsion bar on one offensive maneuver, and at the maintenance area Dave helped our NCO instructor repair the tank while Rob and I watched. Dave did not mind the grease, the dirt, and mud; he relished it. Physically, his baby-chubby cheeks belied his fitness; he outran me on every fitness test, always finishing with the leading cluster of runners.

By mid-December 1990, Rob, Dave, and I had reported to Fort Stewart and been assigned as tank platoon leaders in 1-64 Armor, each of us in charge of four M1 tanks and fifteen soldiers. We had all chosen Fort Stewart for similar reasons. First, for the mission. With the recent end of the Cold War, the budget cuts were starting. As the home of part of the army's Rapid Deployment Force, Fort Stewart would likely be spared the worst. Instructors at West Point who had served in the 24th during the militarily plush early and mid-1980s gushed. The 24th had money for training and frequent deployments. The best stateside post, they declared. Tankers have a position of privilege in an infantry division that they do not at a place like Fort Hood, Texas, with its (at the time) two armor divisions. I fully expected to deploy for training; I never expected to deploy for combat. Conflicts of the post–Cold War era would belong, many of us believed, to the light infantry, not armor. So for me, being a tanker represented all the fun and experience without the danger. For others, though, like Dave, the 24th's rapid deployment mission was both significant and real. He didn't want war; he was just professionally minded in a way that I was not, and I think he recognized how much the training and morale of a unit with such a mission would make a difference to his experience.

The other reasons we chose Fort Stewart were personal. For Rob, Georgia was home and he couldn't wait to return to the South after four years in New York. And for Dave and me, Fort Stewart was the closest post with armor units to Columbus, Ohio, and Philadelphia, Pennsylvania, where his Jill and my Maria lived. Dave also wanted to be close to the beach.

Neal joined us at Fort Stewart a few months later. His wife, Mary, was also a new second lieutenant, commissioned through Shippensburg University's ROTC. Her Ordnance Officer Basic Course, at Aberdeen Proving Grounds, Maryland, was a few hundred miles from Fort Knox, where Neal was at the armor course. During the first several months of marriage they flew back and forth on weekends to see one another. The word of Mary's pregnancy came while Neal, Rob, Dave, and I were at Knox. The news was huge and unexpected; they did not think they could have children. Their original orders had assigned them to separate duty stations — Neal going to Korea for a year — but because of the pregnancy Neal and Mary arranged joint orders for the 24th Infantry.

We met Greg Downey at Fort Stewart. He was the senior platoon leader in Delta Company; Rob, newly assigned to Delta, fell under Greg's tutelage. My first months at Fort Stewart I spent more time in the field than any other officer in the battalion, and even when I found myself in garrison, Greg and I somehow never managed to be in the same place at the same time. My recalled first impression:

shock blonde hair, square jaw, tough blue eyes — a soldier's officer. I did not fully appreciate the stature given to him by his demeanor and his reputation as an outstanding officer until we met in Chicago in August 1996, six years after the beginning of Desert Shield: Greg is a short man, and I had never noticed.

Six weeks before Iraq invaded Kuwait, Greg became the battalion's scout platoon leader. The scout platoon is the most autonomous unit in a combat battalion. Working well forward, it provides information on the routes and the enemy to the battalion commander so he can decide how to best employ his four companies; its three sections of two vehicles are often deployed at long ranges from each other, making a command and control nightmare for its platoon leader. The battalion commander picks the most able and trusted among his lieutenants to replace his departing scout platoon leader. In the summer months prior to our deployment, that most able and trusted lieutenant was Greg Downey. Moreover, Greg took the scouts as a second lieutenant over several qualified and eager first lieutenants. This rarely happens.

Rob Holmes recalls their first meeting: "Greg Downey had been the senior platoon leader when I arrived in Delta Company and was in many respects my mentor lieutenant in the battalion. He was a blonde, lean, scrappy, tough as nails Irishman from small-town Nebraska. When I first arrived, he flat out told me that he didn't like West Pointers. Great. Soon enough I overcame this prejudice, and we become very good friends. Greg taught me a lot, and I badly wanted to follow in his footsteps and become the scout platoon leader after him."

In our early twenties, four of us fresh from the irregular social life of the Academy, we concerned ourselves more with the upcoming weekend than any impending crises of international security. So Iraq's invasion surprised us; it caught us with our pants down, as it were. By the summer of 1990, the Soviet Union had collapsed, Germany had unified, and the invasions of Grenada and Panama defined our battle expectations: insertions of light infantry overcoming the enemy through the surprise, swiftness, and efficiency of the operation. Most of us never expected to do anything with our tanks but train. And pull maintenance. Winning the Cold War resulted in a substantially reduced defense budget, and less money meant less training and fewer parts for vehicles broken during training, even for the army's Rapid Deployment Force. Rob became so bored with life in the battalion motor pool at Fort Stewart that he spent several weeks that summer in England taking courses at the London School of Economics.

Fortunately, some members of our chain of command were possessed of a bit more foresight.

Lt. Col. L. Randall Gordon, the man we would nickname "Flash," took command of our armor battalion on Friday, 12 June 1990: "I knew that Iraq would take over Kuwait. I told my wife Debbie the first day I walked into 1-64 as the commander that I knew I would not be at Stewart for long. . . . When McCaffrey came around to visit with battalion commanders right after Internal Look in late July, he and I discussed the probability of Iraq pressing into Kuwait."

Maj. Gen. Barry R. McCaffrey became the 24th Infantry Division's commanding general the third week of June, a week after Lt. Col. Randy Gordon had taken command of 1-64 Armor. McCaffrey and Gordon had both come to Stewart from the operations staff of the Joint Chiefs. Within his first week, McCaffrey assembled his staff for his first war plan update in what they called the "War Room" and declared that the most likely scenario, the one "we will probably see within the next 18 months, is an execution of OPLAN 1002, the Iraqi attack into Saudi Arabia."[1]

The Defense Department's contingency for the Middle East, Operation Plan 1002, had existed for years. Under General Schwarzkopf, Central Command — the organization overseeing military activity in the Middle East, from Kenya to Pakistan — shifted the planning scenario from a USSR invasion of Iran to an Iraqi invasion of Kuwait. From 23 to 28 July 1990, Schwarzkopf conducted Internal Look 90, a command post exercise (CPX) for the leadership of all elements that might participate in the revised OPLAN 1002. The 24th Infantry Division was the main effort in OPLAN 1002, so a month after taking command, Major General McCaffrey and his staff joined the leadership from the rest of the Eighteenth Airborne Corps and other participating organizations in the Internal Look exercise. "As time went on and we approached CPX time," the division intelligence officer relates, "more and more of us became concerned that there was more to this than what met the eye. . . . Gen. Schwarzkopf was instilling a real sense of urgency into the thing. . . . [The exercise scenario] involved Iraq's attack . . . first through Kuwait and then into Saudi Arabia. I remember it was something in the neighborhood of 17–18 divisions. We defended opposite Dhahran, just west of Dhahran, out in the desert. The scenario, in fact, was almost exactly what we later used [for Desert Shield] as our planning scenario to defend Saudi Arabia."[2] The exercise ended some five days before the Iraqi army invaded Kuwait. During the interval, the 24th Infantry's intelligence staff instituted twenty-four-hour shifts, briefed Major General McCaffrey twice a day, and a day or two prior to the invasion submitted a tentative request to corps for an entire division's worth of operational area map sets.[3] The invasion came as no surprise to McCaffrey or his staff. Nor did it surprise Lieutenant Colonel Gordon, though he had expected Iraq would "press the attack to the northern states of Saudi Arabia. There were three states in the north who historically did not support the king and would have likely accepted Iraqi rule."

All of which, six and a half years ago as I write this, now fascinates me to discover. At the time I knew nothing. None of us lieutenants did. Everything was a

surprise, everything a shock. I do remember television news pieces on deterio-
rating OPEC relations over oil prices, and Hussein's presence in the middle of it.
But armored warfare?

Nuts.

After Iraq's invasion but before the actual alert, several NCOs and I were listening to the radio in one of the small offices off the company's front orderly
room. We had gathered, and whatever we heard — I don't remember what —
made us certain we were going. That's why I remember being there.

The alert officially came at 0300 hours on 7 August 1990. We had known for
a couple of days to expect it, though we did not know exactly when. We went
home each evening wondering if we would get a full night's sleep. We also knew
the official alert would be only a formality. We still had to load the division's vehicles and equipment on ships that had yet to arrive, and we would not fly until
two weeks after the loaded ships left port, in order to arrive in Saudi Arabia a day
or two before the ships. Our 2d Brigade would be the first to deploy.[4]

On alerts, Rob's company always called him a few minutes before mine called
me. I would listen to him answer, hang up, and head for the shower, and I lay
there, waiting for the phone to ring for me. Dreading it. So when the phone rang,
waking us both, he answered it.

"Lieutenant Holmes?"

"Speaking."

"Victory Thunder, sir."

"Roger, out."

Rob always talked on the phone as if he were on his tank's radio. Ten minutes
later he was showered, shaved, dressed, and on his way to the office. "As I walked
out the apartment door, I heard Al groaning as he moved toward the shower. Al
was a fine lieutenant, but he hated mornings, especially those that began with a
deployment alert.

"We were used to them. Every six weeks or so in the 24th, the call would come
in the middle of the night, to test our combat readiness. By August 1990, however, I had become bored with these predawn disruptions. I understood the importance of the alerts; I had just become tired of rousing myself for nothing.
Typically during these exercises, NCOs would sit around drinking coffee, half-
heartedly chewing out soldiers who dragged in late. The irony of my cynicism is
that my first alert had been real. Sort of. I had arrived at Fort Stewart two weeks
before the U.S. invasion of Panama in December 1989. My battalion, 1-64 Armor,
was chosen to augment the 82d Airborne's paratroopers sent to capture Manuel
Noriega. Al Vernon's platoon was tapped to deploy. While he prepared his platoon to fly into combat, I spent the alert counseling a soldier who wanted to divorce his wife. I knew the welfare of my men was part of my job and ultimately

contributed to my platoon's combat effectiveness. Nevertheless, while Al was packing his bags to make history, I was trying to fix the marriage of a fellow whose wife had recently shot him because he had impregnated her sister. 'She didn't mean to do it, sir.'

"Deployment alerts had become a predawn portion of my boring sentence at Fort Stewart until early on 7 August 1990, when I walked into Delta Tank ready to go to war. Lights were on all over the barracks area as the enlisted men came hustling in with their field gear. The first sergeant — nicknamed 'Top,' as all first sergeants are — was breathing fire and barking orders left and right. He had two men frantically counting ammunition on the floor; another man scurried in with a box of hand grenades. The supply sergeant was standing at attention explaining to Top why he was short of basically everything. I heard NCOs yelling in the back area as soldiers reported for duty.

"I quickly found my platoon sergeant, the platoon's second in command, who reported the other fourteen soldiers in Second Platoon present for duty. Sfc. Randy Sikes was a large, weathered man with a calm demeanor from eighteen years in the army and four tours in Cold War West Germany. He knew the M1 tank better than anyone but had grown a little cynical about his chances for promotion and continued service beyond twenty years. He had undergone probably a thousand alerts in his career without one of them being real.

"I had never maneuvered my platoon, this man could do it blindfolded, and I was his boss. Nonetheless, we had a good working relationship. I deliberately phrased everything I said to him my first six months as his platoon leader as a question, and I think he liked it. It showed the proper deference.

"Sikes wanted to deploy, but not to save the world, defend democracy, or further his career. He was just bored out of his mind. He wanted to go some place and do what he had trained to do for his entire adult life. He had no malicious desires or Hollywood visions of combat. Yes, Sfc. Sikes had spent those years fighting and winning the Cold War. Still, he was sick of drinking coffee and walking in circles around motor pools.

"A few days before Sfc. Sikes had asked me, 'What's the story with this guy Hussein?'

"'Our country is politically and economically hamstrung to the most volatile region of the world,' I answered Sikes with a stone face. I knew that wasn't the answer he wanted but couldn't help myself. Sikes didn't care about foreign policy, and he didn't need a pep talk or a sugar-coated situation report. He wanted to give his enemy a name and face; beyond that, he only needed clear orders so he knew how to prepare the platoon.

"He smiled and repeated, 'Okay sir, so what's the story with this guy Hussein?'"

■ We watched on television as the 82d Airborne Division's soldiers boarded the planes at Pope Air Force Base and deplaned half a world away. We saw them filling sandbags. Sweating. Drinking water. Sleeping on cots in hangars. My company commander pointed out the bad example set by the 82d soldiers who worked in their brown T-shirts — no uniform top, no helmet, no LBE, no flak jacket. Whatever, sir. I hadn't thought about it. For me, looking at one of them on the television was like gazing into a crystal ball, into a magic fortune-telling mirror: *he is me.*

Mike, the ROTC cadet who for a short while had charge of my platoon, participated with us as he could. He stood in line with us as we prepared our deployment packets, received vaccinations, and underwent quick situation briefings and medical exams. We were *processed* — a perfect use of the passive. Once, at my locker in the company's back area, Mike nearly caught me crying.

Mike's summer training ended prematurely. He did not as acting platoon leader experience the inspections, the vehicle maintenance days, the slight training we could do in garrison. Nonetheless, I cannot imagine a better summer experience for a young man about to enter the profession of arms than to witness volunteer soldiers deploying to war.

We watched a lot of CNN those weeks before we flew out. The news focused on the threat of Hussein's chemical weapons and his long-range SCUD missile delivery capability. Watching journalists detail this scenario, of our violent twitching to death from nerve agent, itself unnerved. Scenes of President Bush golfing at Kennebunkport, refusing to let the crisis interrupt his vacation, showing off his nonplused golf swing to Iraq and America, pissed me off.

Rob and I also shopped. We attacked every store that sold anything we supposed might come in handy. Lord knows what all we bought. How very late-twentieth-century American: two single twenty-somethings striking back at a crisis the only way we knew — MasterCard and Visa. The soldiers struck back, among other ways, by inventing cadences about kicking Hussein's ass.

One early day of the alert I found myself in the office of the battalion chaplain, Father Michael Politt. I didn't know him well; I don't think he knew my name. I told him my fears. Having gone through West Point, through Air Force Survival Training, two trips to the National Training Center at Fort Irwin, California, and several other field and simulation exercises, I knew I did not have the stuff to lead soldiers in combat. Within minutes in the chaplain's office I was bawling. I had myself convinced that soldiers would die because of me, that I would panic, think too much, seize up, make a critical mistake. I did not want to go.

Father Mike said the expected things, about my fears being natural and understandable, and then he said the unexpected: He assured me he could excuse me from deployment due to emotional instability. He sent me away to soul-search, leaving his office door and the option open.

The immediate mundane concern for Greg, Dave, Rob, and me (Neal was still at Ranger School) was our vehicles. Dave's commander promised him one of the division's float tanks, one of the vehicles the division held in reserve to parcel to the most needy units. Dave's tank had been inoperative, or deadlined, for some time due to a bad power cable to the turret. The battalion cannibalized his deadlined tank for parts to fix other tanks. Then, according to Dave, his "initial relief turned to dismay. After my tank had stripped bare, I learned I was not going to get a float tank. Now it needed more than a single cable. It needed several key parts to be operational and dozens more to be in perfect shape. I faced a severe dilemma: I needed to lead my platoon, but my tank would not be fully operational. I could either trade tanks with my wingman, leaving him with the potential for breakdown, or I could keep my tank, trading it only if it became automotively nonfunctional. I decided upon the latter. As long as my tank could move, I could lead my platoon. My wingman needed to shoot more than I did. Though doctrine states the platoon leader must have a fully operational tank, I could not do that to my wingman."

The entire battalion moved shortly after the alert to the National Guard Training Center, a part of the post left vacant unless Guard units were training at Stewart. Dave remembers going the day of the alert. "We had to be prepared to leave everything except what we were actually taking. This included sending the soldiers to their billets with gigantic boxes to inventory and pack all their belongings to be left behind, so the army could store them. For me this problem was exacerbated because my duties allowed me only forty-five minutes to go to my quarters, pack, and return. Needless to say, the packing was anything but neat and orderly. Time was so limited I had to dump the dirty dishes from the sink into a plastic bag." I thought the move to the National Guard Training Center happened a few days later, though. Since Rob and I lived in an apartment off post instead of the on-post bachelor officer quarters where Dave lived, we did not have to pack our belongings before deploying and so were not as rushed during the alert. I do remember driving my tank out the back gate of the motor pool, down a tank trail, across the main entrance road to Stewart, and past the satellite dish–adorned press vans lining the curb, farther down the trail, and into the National Guard area.

Greg, the new scout platoon leader, focused on getting his Bradley Cavalry Fighting Vehicles in working order. He recalls "repair parts coming out of the woodwork, parts we had been waiting on for months. The battalion did more quality maintenance in those four days than we had in the past year. I hoped to repair all six of my vehicles, but we were working against the clock. The trains taking our equipment to the deep water port in Savannah were pulling in a few days. We managed to get every CFV running automotively, but three of them still did not have a working weapon system. I couldn't believe it. I was convinced our first enemy contact would happen immediately upon arrival in Saudi Arabia. This was not the way I envisioned going to war."

Surrounded by soldiers he did not know, and with no nearby lieutenants, Greg felt quite lonely. "I wanted to be back in a tank company," he writes, "where I could always find a fellow platoon leader with whom I could talk and compare notes. Even though I had had the platoon for almost two months, most of my scouts had been elsewhere, doing post support duties at Fort Stewart like picking up trash, or on leave. It was very uncomfortable for me, not knowing the very soldiers I would be going into combat with. I didn't even know most of their names, and these men I didn't know were sizing me up."

From these scouts Greg sensed, as he had from his tankers in his old platoon when he first joined them, a certain animosity. Because he was an officer, it seemed to him, they presumed he was born with a silver spoon. But Greg had struggled for his commission. He hailed from Merna, a small, farming community of 340 people in central Nebraska. The fifth of eight boys, he had four older brothers to better academically and athletically, and three younger brothers always trying to outdo him. He opened a savings account where he stashed every penny he earned for college. (None of his older brothers had earned a four-year degree.) Some of his money came from his monopoly over the town's lawn-mowing business. Greg also worked for the family water well business. His father was a tough, determined Irishman who expected as much from his boys, and who had a temper to make anyone tremble. From him, they learned never to leave a job unfinished. The Downeys worked in hundred-degree temperatures under the hot Nebraska sun and did what they could to keep their hands from freezing during the brutal midwestern winters: "Not once did I ever hear from Dad that the weather was too bad to work."

During his last summer working the wells, Greg was working in a trench about ten feet deep when the walls collapsed. He was trapped under eight feet of sand. The weight of the sand caused his bones to begin to crack; he knew he could only hold his breath for another minute. His brother Steve, who had watched the walls cave in, was digging frantically. Greg remembers feeling against his neck the Saint Christopher's medal he always wore for protection and thinking everything was going to be okay. His brother shoveled more dirt in five minutes than anyone should have been able to in five hours. When Greg emerged from the trench, the Saint Christopher's medal was gone. It had it served its purpose and taken Greg's place in the trench.

Two days later he and his dad were working another site. When the time came to get into the trench, Greg couldn't bring himself to do it. "Dad, the compassionate Irish father, said the best thing he could have said: 'Get your ass down in that hole and deal with it.'"

His junior year at the University of Nebraska-Kearney, when he realized he was running out of money, Greg applied for and won a two-year army ROTC scholarship to finish his degree: "I've asked myself many times if I did it out of financial desperation or because I truly had a desire to serve my country. I think it was a combination."

■ During what I recall as the two days of the lockdown, every battalion soldier moved into the empty National Guard barracks. The lockdown removed soldiers from their families in order to focus their time and attention to the task on hand. We were to don our war faces. We loaded the tanks to the hilt for transport: In addition to the ammunition, we stuffed everything that normally rides on the outside of the tank, including one duffel bag per crew member, in the turret. The gear filled the turret to the hatches; in Saudi, unloading the gear through the commander's and loader's hatches on the top of the tank was no small chore. We would have had a hell of a time driving off the ship straight into combat, as some people envisioned. To help mask our unit identity, we covered all unit information on the vehicles — our bumper numbers — with engineer tape. We also received our first set of desert camouflage uniforms (DCUs).

At the National Guard Training Center I sought out Father Mike again; I didn't know what I would say, didn't know whether or not I would opt out. When I couldn't find him, I learned that he had already flown, with the advance party, to Saudi Arabia. I never spoke to him again. I told myself that the greater evil, the greater threat to the survival of my men than my presence on the battlefield, was my absence. I had worked with the platoon for nine months. We knew one another. Throwing into the platoon a less-prepared lieutenant would not have been fair to either the platoon or that green lieutenant. So I told myself.

I did not remember that one battalion staff officer chose not to deploy. Dave tells the story: "I would like to say that no one cowered in the face of adversary, but this simply is not true. In the first days of the alert, an officer arrived to fill the battalion's vacant chemical officer position. As the unit turned to this young officer for direction and validation of its chemical defense training, he crumbled in fear and failed in his duty by ensuring he was unfit to deploy. This cowardice meant the battalion deployed for war short a capability the army had invested much time and money developing."

One soldier from my platoon also did not deploy. He had himself declared medically unfit due to severe asthma, a condition that had not prevented him from training as a combat-deployable soldier. His failure to deploy severed all friendships with the platoon. Months later, in Saudi Arabia, waiting for the ground war, we heard that he had been arrested at Fort Stewart for shoplifting.

From the lockdown we took the tanks and Bradleys to the railhead, where we loaded them onto long rows of flat rail cars for transport to the Savannah port. Imagine six rows of at least thirty cars; each car fit two tracked vehicles and was perhaps a foot wider than a tank. The first tank on a row of cars had to be guided down the entire row by a soldier keeping one car ahead of the tank. We secured the vehicles to the cars with chains.

Wheeled vehicles moved to the port by convoy. A detail at the port downloaded the tracked vehicles from the train and drove them onto the ships. Ramps reached from the dock to the door on a ship's side. Soldiers who drove our vehicles on board reported the ship's interior resembling an enormous parking garage.

The first ship to depart, the *Capella*, left the Savannah port loaded with 2d Brigade equipment on 13 August. Dave writes that the *Capella* did not embark on schedule. With the tide out and the equipment weighing it down, the ship rested on the bottom of the Savannah River. The *Altair*, the ship I remember as carrying my company's equipment, sailed out on the fourteenth.[5] For security, and in case any vehicles had to be moved, each ship carried a small contingent of soldiers. I lost one soldier to the ship detail; the executive officer of Charlie Company was named the officer in charge of the complement on the *Capella*, leaving Dave Trybula, Charlie's senior platoon leader, as both platoon leader and acting executive officer (XO).

There had been rumors of our being locked down for the two weeks between the ships' departure and our own, leaving us to wonder whether we would move into the barracks, spending all time not training or preparing there, or continue to live at home and spend time with loved ones. We were fortunately not locked down. Dave called his girlfriend, Jill, and asked her to come and spend some time. They had been dating for several years and he wanted to see her prior to deploying.

"Training focused on the threats we were about to face," Dave writes. "We had classes on the Iraqi army's weapon systems, organization, and capabilities; and on chemical weapons defensive procedures, Arabic customs, and techniques to cope with the heat." I remember classes as well on navigating in the desert, and the Rules of Engagement, Rules of Conduct, Conduct Rules, and Rules of Combat: We received official, laminated cards for each of these sets of rules, and were ordered to carry them in our BDU breast pocket at all times (to which I added a pocket *Webster's Dictionary,* inscribed by my granddad, and a photo of my girlfriend, Maria). The Rules of Conduct amounted to the following list of dos and don'ts:

DOS

1. RESPECT ALL HOLY SHRINES, TEMPLES, AND MOSQUES.

2. REMOVE FOOTGEAR WHEN ENTERING A HOME OR MOSQUE.

3. REMAIN RESPECTFUL TO ALL LOCAL PERSONNEL.

4. PAY OR TIP (10–15%) FOR ALL SERVICES RENDERED.

5. BARGAIN FOR ALL PURCHASES.

6. ACCEPT TEA OR OTHER REFRESHMENTS OFFERED IN A BUSINESS OR SHOPPING ENVIRONMENT.

7. EXPECT AND ACCEPT PHYSICAL CLOSENESS WHEN IN PERSONAL CONVERSATIONS.

8. LEARN AS MUCH AS POSSIBLE ABOUT ISLAMIC CULTURE.

9. BE AWARE OF LOCAL RELIGIOUS PRACTICES.

10. PROTECT YOURSELF AND YOUR BUDDIES BY KEEPING THE CIVILIAN POPULATION FRIENDLY TO YOU.

11. ADHERE TO THESE DOS AND DON'TS.

DON'TS

1. MESS AROUND OR INSULT THE WOMEN.

2. ARGUE ABOUT RELIGION.

3. DRINK IN PUBLIC.

4. EAT WITH OR OTHERWISE MAKE EXCESSIVE USE OF THE LEFT HAND IN PUBLIC.

5. DISCUSS LOCAL POLITICS.

6. ACCEPT AN OFFER OR INVITATION THE FIRST OR SECOND TIME.

7. POINT THE SOLES OF FEET TOWARDS ANYONE.

8. USE THE "THUMBS-UP" HAND SIGNAL.

9. WEAR SHORTS, CUT-OFFS, ETC. IN PUBLIC.

10. ENTER ANY MOSQUE UNLESS SPECIFICALLY INVITED TO DO SO.

11. OFFER ANY PORK PRODUCT TO THE POPULACE.

After the tanks shipped, a number of new soldiers sent from Fort Knox flooded the battalion to augment its strength to over 100 percent. I heard that none of them had wives or families — the army was notorious for discriminating against the single soldier. The company first sergeant introduced one of these men, Sfc. Thomas P. Freight, to me and Staff Sergeant Rivera, my platoon sergeant, behind closed doors. The platoon's second in command, the platoon sergeant position on paper calls for a sergeant first class. As Rivera was only a staff sergeant, the army deemed it necessary to disrupt a cohesive platoon by replacing its platoon sergeant, one of the battalion's best, on the eve of combat.

A new lieutenant on his way to his platoon leader assignment prays especially for a solid platoon sergeant, the most senior NCO in a platoon usually with ten years or more under his LBE. Though technically the platoon sergeant is second in command, he and his platoon leader actually exercise joint leadership. In the field, while the platoon leader is away conducting route recons and planning battle positions, the platoon sergeant ensures the platoon is ready to fight: weapons cleaned, tank equipped, maintenance conducted, main gun boresighted, soldiers informed, practiced, fed, rested, and ready. The lieutenant can't be in two places at once, and both jobs must be done. This translates in garrison activities to the platoon leader planning and conducting platoon and section level training, and the platoon sergeant planning and conducting individual skills training. Soldiers often speak of "NCO business," in which the platoon sergeant has the final word. The phrase indicates the leadership space the lieutenant allows his sergeants in deference to their experience and closer relationship with the soldiers. NCO business can include the assigning of soldiers to various support and guard details to the handling of some personnel conflicts and issues. A competent platoon sergeant is clearly a critical part of a well-run, high-spirited, successful unit.

The best platoon sergeants, however, become something a little more to that new lieutenant. These are the officer's formative years, years spent as much learning as leading. Indeed, when I arrived at Fort Stewart, I believed — I think most new second lieutenants believed — the eighteen to twenty-four months as a platoon leader to be a period for learning how to tank and how to lead, by practicing and by observing and listening to experienced officers and NCOs. One's platoon sergeant in particular. The platoon sergeant has an obvious vested interest in training his lieutenant well; his life could someday be in the other's hands. Put yourself in his boots: a strapping thirty-two-year-old man who has been in the army since turning eighteen having to train a twenty-two-year-old kid who spent a few summers soldiering and who knows his way around beach towels, college bars, and library books better than he knows his way around tanks, woods, and troops. Yes, sometimes the older man's pride and cynicism get in the way, but no more than the younger man's presumption and naïveté (I say older man: The wear and tear of soldiering takes its toll, and platoon sergeants often look older than their years — fortunately they are wiser, too — and anyway, to a twenty-two-year-old kid, anybody over twenty-five looks old). The better platoon sergeant finds a way to train his lieutenant without undermining the officer's authority. Naturally the relationship between the two depends largely on their particular personalities and talents.

Efrain Rivera, a tall, lean, strikingly handsome, thinly mustached Puerto Rican, had served as Second Platoon's platoon sergeant for over a year. During that time the platoon had won nearly every gunnery table and had led 2d Brigade on every offensive mission during its most recent trip to the National Training Center, the army's foremost tactical armored warfare training area, at Fort Irwin, California. The previous platoon leader left the platoon to become the aide to the division's assistant commander for maneuver. This was the platoon I had inherited, the platoon our previous battalion commander had chosen as the only Abrams platoon in the army to be on standby for Operation Just Cause. Rivera had earned the respect and trust of the battalion and company commander, the other platoon leaders and platoon sergeants in the company, and most important, the soldiers of Second Platoon. If he resented my ignorance or position of power over him, he did not show it; from him I only felt respect and goodwill. Then I had to give him up for an incompetent.

From Lumberton, North Carolina, Thomas Freight had been in the army over twenty years. For the several years prior to August 1990, he had served as a basic training drill instructor at Knox. Meeting him I thought: goofy, out of shape, and not very bright. An aged country bumpkin. But no, I reasoned, against my instincts; the man deserves a chance. He is a professional NCO. He cannot be dismissed.

I resisted the transition only a little. At twenty-three, I didn't yet understand my ability — my duty — to contend unwise command decisions. I protested slightly to the company commander and first sergeant, and abundantly to my powerless sympathizers, the other lieutenants and my girlfriend Maria. Not protesting further was my first mistake; to this day I do not know what other mistakes I made, what other actions I could have taken over the course of Desert Shield, to prevent the immorality of willfully sending a platoon into battle under a platoon sergeant not fit to lead a thirsty dog to water.

Two of my soldiers cornered me on a break during chemical training. They would follow Rivera anywhere, they said, but already did not trust Freight. While verbally assuring them everything would work out, I gestured my powerlessness in a way that tacitly communicated my agreement. I probably should not have indicated my empathy; as a sergeant first class, Freight deserved more initial support from his platoon leader. I couldn't help myself.

My company flew on the battalion's last sortie. Neal, Rob, Greg, and Dave left before me. Neal had returned to Stewart straight from Ranger School graduation: "I hopped in my red Firebird and swore that the last time I would see the home of Ranger School would be in my rearview mirror. My platoon was waiting." His platoon had loaded his equipment on the ships without him; he arrived one week before deploying and almost missed seeing Mary altogether. Her commander had ordered her support unit locked down at their warehouse for days, fearing the soldiers would talk to the press corps swarming around the post's front gate. Neal's company commander raised hell with her commander so Neal and Mary could spend time together, with their infant daughter Katherine, before deploying. They had two days.

Neal had met Mary, another army brat, in junior high school in Germany. The shy and studious Mary Faley had a crush on him, but he had his eye on other girls. Their mothers connived for Neal to take Mary to the junior high prom. He eventually did, only after teasing her by waiting until three days before the prom to ask. All the while Mary knew he had already bought two tickets and was convinced he had asked someone else. They had a great time — "she was the brightest kid in our school and just plain nice" — and Neal was glad to have gone with her. Two days later the Creightons moved again. During high school at Fort Riley, Kansas, Neal was visiting in Germany and ran into Mary again. This time he couldn't keep his eyes off her. But she had a boyfriend and did not appear at all interested in him. Several summers later, before Neal's junior year at West Point, Mary paid him a visit. They connected, never dating anyone else, and married shortly after graduation.

Mary's possible deployment for Desert Shield caused more than one debate in the battalion. Volunteer soldiers in deployable units have trained in those assignments for the express purpose of deploying. In the case of Neal and Mary, however, I felt — and argued with a few peers — that the army could show some sympathy. With a four-month-old baby, theirs was a rare case, and as a member of a support battalion, Mary would not have deployed for some weeks after the combat units, allowing the unit time to adjust for her absence.

Convincing the chain of command to be allowed to stay with her daughter had not been easy for Mary. Neal's company commander, Capt. Eric Schwartz, and our battalion commander, Lieutenant Colonel Gordon, fought for the Creightons and took the situation before the division commander. Major General McCaffrey decided that either Neal or Mary could stay with Katherine but would have to resign his or her commission. Mary wanted to stay in the military, wanted to do her duty and deploy with her unit, and could have: Katherine could have lived with her grandparents. But Mary would not let Katherine spend her first year without at least one of her parents, much less risk losing both parents in a war. She submitted her resignation. In addition to losing her career, she faced losing the respect of some of her seniors, peers, and soldiers.

Ironically, the army had activated its Stop-Loss policy, which prevented all officers from leaving active service during a period of international crisis. Mary's resignation was denied. Instead of deploying with her 724th Support Battalion, she served in the Family Support Group Coordination Office, an organization created by McCaffrey. The FSGCO worked directly with volunteer members of the soldiers' wives' community, together forming the "chain of concern" paralleling the division's chain of command. One deployment story Mary remembers from her time at FSGCO: A local trailer park manager had noticed that one of his tenants, a soldier, had not been around for several weeks. Nor had his wife. The manager went to check on his trailer, where he found the woman locked inside. She had been there a month. The soldier had assumed he would return before too long and had left her with two weeks' worth of groceries. No checkbook, no money, no key. The manager had the woman taken to the Fort Stewart's Family Service Center.

For Rob, "the getaway from Fort Stewart had been a blur. Tank parts, unavailable for months, seemed to fall from Heaven. Little booklets on Iraqi weaponry and doctrine were in our hands within days. We went through an assembly line–like immunization for all kinds of crazy diseases. People have always joked about military intelligence, but somebody, a whole bunch of somebodies, had planned for this. The night before we actually deployed, I got absolutely plastered with Bob McCann, a platoon leader in Bravo Company with Al Vernon. When we got back to the car, I took a leak and Bob threw up. We reclined our seats, opened all the windows and the sunroof, and passed out. We woke at 0600 and drove home to deploy. What an idiot I was."

Greg finds it difficult "to describe the feelings prior to leaving for war. Everything was shrouded in uncertainty. You had no idea when you might come home, if you'll come home. I looked around the house and took note of everything. Staying focused on anything was extremely difficult. When we had our wills done by the Judge Advocate General's office, well, solemn doesn't begin to describe it. Wills were for old people, I had always thought. There was no laughter, no smiling, no joking. Very unusual for a group of soldiers.

"August 22, 1990, was the next milestone. The battalion mustered at Newman Gym and waited for the buses. The day sped by. Final good-byes were said. After the emotional roller coaster of the last two weeks, I was ready to go and get this over."

■ On 22 August, both my brothers called. Walt promised to write often. "I remember my *M*A*S*H*," he said. "Come back, all right?" Eric, a Coast Guard officer, told me he thought our parents might arrive in the morning: "Promise me that when you're hot and sweaty and itchy in that rubber chemical suit, you won't take the fucker off."

Mom and Dad did arrive the next day. We ate dinner that night in a second-floor Hinesville restaurant, above a bar. I had stir-fry steak and shrimp, and apple pie à la mode. Under the impression that we would see each other the next day, we parted cheerfully. The restaurant, along with a number of other local businesses, went under while the division was away.

Bravo Company reported to work at 0700 on the twenty-fourth. Dad had an early flight back to Kansas City; Mom's flight was later, if not the next day, and after taking him to the airport she drove down to Hinesville to see me again. Only that morning our manifest time came. I dashed home to leave a note for Mom, on the small whiteboard Rob and I used for messages by the kitchen phone. I left it where Mom would see it when she opened the door, on the staircase: "Mom and Dad — Sorry I missed you. I've already left. Thanks for coming down. See you soon. Love you, Always, Alex."

The company processed through Newman and Jordan gyms. Wives brought fried chicken and sub sandwiches for us while we waited for the bus ride to Hunter Army Airfield in Savannah. We rode at dusk. I remember an old staff sergeant up front shouting to another NCO in the back, "You know you're going to find your wife just like you left her, don't you? — freshly fucked." His own laugh overpowered the chuckles and moans his joke had drawn from the rest of us.

Several hangars at the airfield served as a holding area for deployment sorties — rows and rows and rows of army cots. Soldiers played cards, slept, wrote letters, tuned into headsets, read newspapers, made last phone calls. Every few hours buses dropped off units from Fort Stewart; every few hours, buses picked units up to take them to the plane. For some soldiers the fence around the airfield became a last place to camp with loved ones. A lot of kissing and finger-squeezing took place through those cold steel links.

For me, and for many others it seemed, the sadness and anxiety had been suspended. For the first time in weeks we could stop wondering when, we could stop worrying about preparations, we could simply stop. Even play a little. Bravo Company's lieutenants — Bob McCann, Greg Jackson, Matt Hoagland, and I — played Frisbee and paddleball between hangars.

One of my platoon's tank gunners broke out his electric clippers and shaved the heads of several soldiers in the platoon; the gunner's own tank commander had his slight widow's peak shaped into a prominent V to match the Vs all of us, as soldiers of the Victory Division, wore on the side of our helmets. The division had been given its nickname by liberated citizens after Gen. Douglas MacArthur announced the end of the Philippines campaign on 5 July 1945. Thereafter, the Victory Division has marked its vehicles and helmets with the V symbol. In our generation, a soldier of the division saluting a ranking officer greeted the superior with the division motto, "First to Fight, sir," the latter returned the salute with "Victory."

In the center of our hangar, by the command center of the support unit in charge of the operation, stood a table piled with books. A sign above limited one per soldier. Greg Jackson, the company executive officer, already had a book, *Brazen Chariots,* on desert tank warfare during WWII — something we all should have been reading. I didn't see anything I wanted but at the table met a woman lieutenant from the support unit running the hangar operation. She had majored in English also, and I talked her into allowing me into her office to look through the boxes of books waiting for table space. Later the lieutenant — Jeannie Novak, from Boston, graciously spared the accent — found me at my cot and gave me four other books. She sat on the concrete hangar floor beside my cot and we talked a little, about books and writing. Matt Hoagland, a single father eager to change his status, exchanged unit addresses with Lieutenant Novak. He was, I later discovered, neither the first nor the last to do so. Jeannie Novak was an attractive woman, voluptuously so, and one of those rare people with whom strangers feel completely at ease, to whom they relieve their souls. Something nurturing, genuine, and utterly generous about her. Something that brought soldiers on their way to combat to tears in her hangar office; something that heartened them.

We left the hangar at 1400 hours on the twenty-fifth. Soldiers from the support unit, including Lieutenant Novak, gathered around the buses to wave goodbye. The buses took us to another hangar, almost an amphitheater, opening onto the runway. We sat there for a moment; then Top called our names off a roster, and with a "Here, first sergeant," each soldier stood and filed into either the smoking or nonsmoking line. For each line a staff sergeant handed out pocket *New Testaments* to takers (I took); a civilian woman gave each soldier a plastic bag with a water bottle, sunscreen, and other small necessities; and another civilian woman passed out small American flags, the handheld variety you buy at K-Mart for the Fourth of July with a wooden pole and a gold-painted tip.

We walked to the Pan Am 747. Several hundred meters to our right, a crowd of about twenty five waved. The bleachers set up for farewell-wishers were empty. As the plane taxied to its takeoff position, the pilot announced that a soldier had stuck a flag out a hatch at the top of the aircraft.

Neal, Greg, Rob, and Dave had flown out a day or two before me. Neal's company commander, Capt. Eric Schwartz, handed him some in-flight reading, documents stamped SECRET in red on the cover. He had never before seen classified documents. They contained information on the kind and numbers of equipment fielded by Iraq's Republican Guard. Greg sat next to a company first sergeant from the brigade's infantry battalion: "I noticed he wore a combat patch from the 173d Airborne, a unit that had fought in Vietnam. We talked a lot during the flight. I was after any knowledge he could give me. He had been an infantryman his whole army career, just over twenty-one years.

"'LT, there's nothing I can tell you that you don't already know. Every second lieutenant I ever served with always knew the right thing to do. The difference between the ones who lived and the ones who died is that the latter went out looking for a fight.'

"'You were in an infantry platoon in Vietnam. Wasn't it your job to fight?'

"'Yes, sir,' he replied. 'But it wasn't our job to go looking for one. There is a difference.' I could tell he was finished with that subject. It was time to soak up the last few comforts the plane had to offer before arriving in Saudi Arabia."[6]

Rob sat next to 2d Lt. Jeff White, the platoon leader of Delta Tank's Third Platoon. Jeff was the newest lieutenant in the battalion, having arrived at Fort Stewart a month before the alert. From Florence, Alabama, Jeff had just received his commission through ROTC at the University of Alabama, and had married his college sweetheart.

"The first day I met him," Rob writes, "I gave him my sarcastic job description about our being mechanics and marital counselors and told him we would likely never go to the field. He was thrilled — it was football season, and like most Crimson Tide fans, his alma mater loyalty reached another dimension. Jeff and I quickly became good friends. His love of football and his familiar drawl made him the perfect companion. He was also one of the nicest guys I have ever met. His platoon sergeant nicknamed him 'Bambi.'"

Across the aisle from Rob and Jeff sat 2d Lt. Jon Ulsaker, Delta Company's First Platoon leader. A West Point classmate and the son of a graduate and retired colonel decorated in WWII, Korea, and Vietnam, Jon, according to Rob, "was thrilled to deploy and carry on the family tradition.

"Jon had married a darling girl from South Carolina a month after graduation. He openly revealed that he had tried to get Becky pregnant before we left Fort Stewart so he had a namesake in case he were killed in action. Al and I thought he was being a little overly dramatic, if not borderline crazy. Then again, just the word 'pregnant' about made us break out in hives. Jon even showed us this instruction book that guaranteed he would produce a son. Even crazier, I remember standing at the port in Savannah listening to Jon try to convince Jeff to impregnate his wife Kim. What really scared me was how open Jeff was to the idea. If Kim gave birth in nine months, the baby would be old enough to cart to Alabama games the following season. Frankly, it was the most compelling argument.

"One would think we had more important issues on our minds. We were each twenty-three years old, getting ready to land in a combat-eminent environment, with sixteen soldiers whose lives depended on us. Jon was studying intelligence reports on Saddam, but I was scanning the lead stories in *The Economist* and Jeff was buried in *Lindy's Southeast Conference* preseason picks, focused on the upcoming game against Tennessee. We were three bright men, albeit naïve goofballs, leading men into the unknown."

What Rob doesn't write: Of the several hundred men on his flight headed to the desert for an indeterminate stretch of time, possibly for eternity, only he walked off the plane "leading men into the unknown" after having secured a postwar date with the bombshell blonde flight attendant. As he dutifully reports, "She came up to me while I was standing in the aisle, we talked, and she asked for my address, which I happily gave her." She, he is quick to point out, approached him. Rob is undeniably a glib and handsome man. I don't know how many people I have heard predict, wrongly, that he would become a politician. Dark hair, dark eyes, and dark skin — I have seen women plow through crowds like fullbacks through the defensive line to plant themselves in the end zone of his presence. Having as quarterback led his high school football team to the North Georgia championship, Rob will appreciate the football simile.

■ Other than the claustrophobia — we jammed all our personal gear, our helmets, gas masks, and small arms, under the seats and in the overhead compartments — my flight over was unremarkable. My audio headset was broken, so I only looked up for glimpses of the two inflight movies, *The Hunt for Red October* and *Pretty Woman*, of long submarine interiors and even longer legs. We refueled in Bangor, Maine, and then in Rome. That amuses me still: how this largely Christian force passed through Rome on a Sunday morning on its way to fight the army of an Arab and predominately Muslim nation; how one of the division's major maneuver units, its vanguard cavalry squadron, was commanded by Lt. Col. Glynn *Pope;* and how the first American soldiers to deploy for Saudi, from the 82d Airborne Division, had flown out of Pope Air Force Base. (Six months later our allied armies would attack on a Sunday.)

At the airfield in Rome, a blue armored car circled the plane. Sergeant Rivera gave his American flag to one of the Italians resupplying the plane with meals. The crews changed; the departing crew took our mail.

Arrival in Saudi Arabia

The division's 18,000 soldiers deployed in 57 aircraft sorties. Their first aircraft departed Hunter Army Airfield on Aug. 20, just 13 days after alert. By August 24, the majority of the Victory Division soldiers had closed into the Saudi Arabian theater of operations. . . .

By Sept. 7, the Victory Division had 10,000 soldiers representing two brigade combat teams in the field deployed in initial tactical assembly areas. Shortly thereafter, the division moved to occupy assigned General Defense Plan (GDP) positions, just 94 miles from the Kuwait–Saudi Arabia border. The "line in the sand" had been drawn.

— *The Victory Book*

Notions of why soldiers fight: for king and country and an *ism,* to protect the homeland, to defend a way of life, or for the buddy hunkered beside. For me, soldiers fight because they are there. Taking the oath merely gets them in uniform and on the battlefield. They fight; they recover a wounded man they do not know, whether ally or enemy; they clear a lane through a minefield because they, the wounded man, and the minefield are there. I am reminded of the passage in Michael Shaara's novel of Gettysburg, *The Killer Angels,* when Colonel Chamberlain on Little Round Top, his 20th Maine out of ammunition and facing another Confederate assault, orders a bayonet charge: "One recourse: Can't go back. Can't stay where we are. Result: inevitable."[7]

Sunday evening, 26 August. The plane descended with the Persian Gulf on the right, the coast of Saudi Arabia on the left. From my seat in the middle aisle, looking over two bodies, across the aisle, over three more bodies, and out the small window, I could see the sand beneath the water crawl gradually out of the water and become the unending wispy khaki nothing that is the Arabian peninsula. When we disembarked at Dammam airport, three stewardesses (two of them easily over six feet tall) stood at the airplane door, crying and forcing smiles through their tears.

We soldiers were in good spirits, were genuinely smiling and joking. The stewardesses' tears made some of us chuckle. What else could we do?

■ Sunday evening, 26 August: the second anniversary of the evening I received my West Point class ring during a ceremony in Washington Hall, the cadet mess. Raising her three sons, our mother jibed that she would send us to military schools if we didn't behave. Two of us went anyway. When people ask why I went to West Point, I answer in hindsight: I chose West Point out of a child's foggy romantic and ambitious sensibilities — it was about being a cadet, not a soldier — and out of a youngest son's competition with his two older brothers.

If only she and Dad had had more money, our mother believes, my middle brother and I would not have gone to the tuition-free academies. She has always struggled with notions of money and class, and it did not help that our parents raised us in a Kansas City, Kansas, suburb where, during the Gulf War, kids from our high school trying to paint a peace sign on the water tower mistakenly painted a Mercedes-Benz symbol. By using her middle-class income as the reason I went to the Academy, she could by extension six years later blame herself for my going to war. The only grounds she has for self-indictment: She had three sons.

The oldest, who as a boy had made a hobby on family trips of insisting we visit every Civil War battlefield in range of our route, attended Vanderbilt on a full academic scholarship, where he earned three majors with only one additional semester. The middle son went to the Coast Guard Academy in New London, Connecticut. I went to West Point. I don't think I would have considered a military academy if Eric had not gone to the Coast Guard.

Sunday evening, 26 August, was also the second anniversary of my first date with Maria. We had met a month or so before our first date, at a birthday party for the girlfriend of one of my classmates. Maria was a petite brunette with a tan and, beneath her brown bangs, dazzling blue eyes. We talked about Kate Chopin's novel *The Awakening;* we drank together; I made my move with a peck to her head, then we found a vacant room with a couch where we kissed for several hours and managed what denim dissatisfactions we could. I apologized two or three times for whatever lack in my talents she might be feeling: "It's been a while." She was a senior at the University of Virginia, and we spent almost every other weekend that year traveling to each other's school, or to her home in Philadelphia, conveniently located between West Point and Charlottesville. The following year we loved at an even longer distance, with her in Philadelphia and me at Fort Knox and then Fort Stewart, seeing each other much less frequently.

Maria had called one night shortly after the alert asking to visit. I refused her. I hated good-byes, and I did not want to face a potentially final one with the woman I loved. The next day she called to tell me her flight arrival information. She had pluck. We spent my last stateside weekend together, and I am glad for it. At the airport when I saw her off, I slipped an envelope into her purse with a note and my class ring. I told her not to open her purse until the plane had taken off.

Sunday evening, 26 August: Was this the weekend that, according to the division intelligence officer, "other intelligence people, to include the Israelis, were saying the enemy will attack"?[8]

At about 1700, I stepped off the mobile staircase and onto Saudi Arabia. One hundred and five degrees, the copilot had told us; one hundred five and degrees at five o'clock in the evening. Stepping out of the plane, describes Dave, was "like walking into a sauna. Just taking a breath seemed different. I was not accustomed to breathing hot air. It took a conscious effort. As soon as I inhaled, the heat seemed to suck the oxygen from my lungs." The humidity surprised Greg as well, who had imagined Saudi Arabia lacking the humidity of the coastal lowlands of Fort Stewart, Georgia. "Bullshit!" the Vietnam veteran first sergeant who sat next to him on the plane had responded to his speculation. "Of course," Greg writes, "first sergeants are always right." The humidity slapped him in the face as he stepped out the door.

My planeload of troops was herded to a spot of sand just off the tarmac. A few reporters arrived and snapped shots; two majors gave our commander conflicting instructions on speaking with the reporters. Saudi Tornadoes and somebody's F-15s taking off and landing from a nearby runway thundered overhead. A photograph shows Bravo Company's three platoon leaders on our first day in the desert. From our bodies still dangle the manila tags we used to mark our gear, and on the ground lay several red and white plastic bags from the woman at Hunter.

In a similar scene a day or two before, while Dave rested on the ground sipping from a plastic water bottle, "a Saudi man got out of his truck, squatted, and relieved himself in front of everyone."

Eventually three Saudi double-decker busses arrived, white ugly things with orange and blue stripes that always looked about to tip over. Nearly a year later, and home, I heard from a former West Point English instructor who had served in Gen. Schwarzkopf's transportation command group that those three ratty buses were the division's only source of transportation. The area at the back of the bus, shielded from the rest by a *purdah* of metal dividers and having its own entrance, belonged to the women. Or the women belonged to it.

The buses took us to a cantonment area in enormous covered bays on one of the port's piers. A captain briefed us on Saudi culture, then we set up cots and went to sleep.

The next day we moved to the tent city, still under construction. We raised our tents among the others in the middle of the afternoon, filling and moving sandbags to support the tents. "Mad dogs and Englishmen," another platoon leader quoted. I believe the tent city built by the 24th as its elements passed through became the Tent City that housed all future incoming units.

At five in the morning, the sun had risen enough to give light to this world without the heat: the most orange sun I had ever seen, so low in the sky and so near, over blue, blue gulf waters with their dancing orange tips. The breeze still blew. By six, the heat encroached. By seven, it should have been siesta time. Heat and humidity — the words do not suffice. Imagine Hollywood beautiful people Richard Gere and Julia Roberts as a climate; even they do not suffice.

Across the road, three rows of plywood toilets had been built. Though most of the doors had already fallen off, the plywood latrines were nicer than the indoor Saudi toilets back on the pier — nothing more than holes in the floor (for squatting) and not cleaned for days. I saw Dave Trybula my first day in Tent City, leading his platoon in PT — leg squats with a buddy on the back. While they exercised a white Mercedes passed in the background, and I remember wishing I had a camera.

Like me, like all of us, Rob spent his first night in Saudi Arabia "lying on the concrete floor of a warehouse in the port city of Ad Dammam, packed in like cord wood. I remember looking at my watch at midnight and then the thermometer clipped to my field pack: 112 degrees. It was absolutely oppressive. It was so hot we couldn't sleep.

"We were trapped in this furnace waiting for the ships to arrive with our beloved tanks. Armor soldiers are the modern day cavalrymen; tanks have simply replaced horses. I missed my four M1s. I landed in Saudi with nothing but my .45-caliber pistol. I couldn't imagine Jeb Stuart *walking* into battle *waving* his saber. We were a terrorist's dream: five hundred American soldiers packed into one warehouse. One truck bomb would have done us in and made a huge media pool splash." The division intelligence officer shared Rob's concern, adding in an oral history interview that "we were on a pier where there was several hundred thousand pounds of explosives [where] the ammunition ships were unloading. We estimated that if it was to be detonated, the kill area would be 5 kilometers in radius."[9]

The personnel unloading the ammo and hauling it about the pier were third country nationals — in other words, not even Saudis. Rob trusted neither these workers nor the Saudi forces helping us secure the pier. "We posted our own guards, but we also had Saudi soldiers and police to filter the traffic around the port. Our allied friends were rarely in complete uniforms, nor went anywhere in an organized manner. Often we found them asleep. Even this young lieutenant could tell they lacked discipline. I surveyed these Saudi guards for signs of organization, discipline, and tenacity. They were a bad joke. As far as I was concerned, my platoon would rely on itself.

"It was a glorious sight when the ship arrived a couple days later. I couldn't wait to get out of the port. Tankers prefer open terrain where you can take advantage of the tank's night vision and the weapon system's range. I hated the port. And had Hussein attacked before the tanks came, we would have had to move into the cities of Dhahran and Dammam and fight as dismounted infantry. That was not something any of us wanted to do.

"The press was everywhere when we rolled our tanks off the ship. The brass wanted Saddam to see those M1 tanks in country. But we knew, had Saddam continued his invasion into the Saudi oil fields, our battalion would have been just a speed bump. We had been trained to fight outnumbered by three to one, in case the Soviets invaded Europe. We were good, and had the air force and navy jets above us, but with fifty-five hundred Iraqi tanks to our fifty-eight, we would eventually run out of ammunition.

"Nevertheless, President Bush had upped the ante considerably by deploying 1-64. If Saddam invaded Saudi now, we would make him pay dearly, and more important, he would have to kill a bunch of Americans to do it — not good politics. We were poker chips, but relatively happy poker chips. We had our tanks and were leaving that awful, sweltering port."

Rob exaggerates a bit: The 1st of the 64th wasn't the sole unit shoved into the breach. Yes, one of Dave's tanks was the first M1 tank to ever set track in the Kingdom of Saudi Arabia. But 1-64 deployed with the entire 2d Brigade, and with such other division assets as elements from division artillery — artillery historically the largest volume killer among all the army's branches, the "King of Battle" — not to mention those portions of the 82d Airborne with their handful of M551 Sheridan light tanks and the miscellany of other American military forces in theater.[10] But Rob is correct insofar as any of us in the division's initial sorties were aware: We knew we were on the ground, but besides the 82d, we could hardly hazard a guess as to who else was in theater.

Dave Trybula also recorded his memories of our short life at the port:

"I was sure Saddam was no idiot. He had to know that the 82d Airborne Division, the first American unit to deploy, could not stop him, even with the help of the air force. Seizing the Saudi oil fields could be costly for him, but he would suffer less if he struck before our tanks arrived. I continued to worry about this [throughout] the two days we waited for our equipment ship. We received no current information on Saddam's forces. We were living in an information void, and we desperately wanted to know when and where we'd fight.

"The division supplemented our meals with Saudi brown-bag lunches. These meals consisted of a sandwich made of mystery meat, mango juice, maybe a piece of overly ripe fruit, and a couple of forgettable sides. Luckily, water was in abundant supply to wash down every meal. The lunches were certainly an interesting change from the MREs, or Meals Ready to Eat, which we nicknamed 'Meals Rejected for Ethiopians.' We ate them for every breakfast and dinner. Vacuum-packed to last forever in tough brown plastic, the MRE came in twelve varieties, each its own complete meal, the same awful entrees morning, noon, and night. A dehydrated beef patty for breakfast is not appetizing."

("Luckily," adds Rob, "every MRE included a small bottle of Tabasco sauce which could fix anything. Once we had our tanks and moved into the desert, we would be able to use the tank engine to heat the MRE food, making it much more palatable.")

Dave continues: "Back in Georgia, we had begun to prehydrate ourselves, something I had learned from reading accounts of the Arab-Israeli wars, and we continued to enforce water consumption in Saudi Arabia. Fort Stewart had been hot, but it was nothing compared to the 120-plus-degree days we were now experiencing.

"Added to the anxiety of war was the concern for our loved ones. Whenever time was available, my thoughts turned to my family and to my girlfriend Jill. Did the news provide them with an accurate picture of what we were going through? How were they dealing with the stress of separation? There was no mail system, no telephones, so we could not answer their questions or reassure them that they were, at this point anyway, worrying over nothing.

"Our ship finally reached the port. We immediately began unloading it, a process that would take a day and a half. Not long after the equipment started rolling off, I saw one of my M1 tanks, bumper number C13, exit the gang plank, the first M1 tank ever on Saudi soil. The presence of our equipment let me breathe easier. He could attack, but he would not win; he would now pay an extremely high price just for trying. His window of opportunity had slammed shut. Iraq would now start playing by our rules."

But underlying Dave's confidence was his recognition of the enemy's capabilities. "Throughout all of my training, at West Point, at Fort Knox for the Armor Officer Basic Course, at Fort Stewart, and during Desert Shield," he continues, "the lethality of the Soviet bloc tanks had been stressed. Their larger guns and hyperkinetic rounds were an enormous concern. Not only did the Soviet-equipped Iraqi army have tanks very likely superior to ours, they also outnumbered us. Finally, the Iraqi army had leaders and soldiers tried and proven in a protracted war with Iran. They had shot and been shot at, and knew from experience how they would and should react in the chaos of combat. This was what I thought about during deployment, and at the port in August, and during the first months of Desert Shield."

Additionally, Dave's own tank's turret was not fully operational. The majority of the fourteen tanks in Neal Creighton's Alpha Company could not transfer fuel from the rear to the front tanks from where the engine drew, halving the distance the M1s could travel before running out of gas. Three of Greg Downey's six Bradley CFVs could not shoot. Since we had not received the parts to repair these vehicles in the States, we hardly expected them to fortuitously appear in Saudi Arabia — the division had in fact exhausted its supply of spare parts getting its vehicles ready for shipping. When the alert for deployment hit, the 24th did not have a single brigade's basic load of ammunition and had to scrounge from depots across the country to arm itself.[11] From where would the next load come? Rob Holmes did not have either a gunner or loader on his tank, effectively rendering it weaponless as well. These are the problems we can remember. Mary Creighton had probably told Neal a story I have only just heard, of how she watched a company commander in the division's main support battalion order his lieutenants not to pack spare M1 tank track for early transport because it took up too much of his allotted space and weight and would do *his* unit no good. I did learn, sitting in the port, that one of the ships carrying division equipment had been rushed out of Savannah insufficiently repaired, had broken down, and was expected to be two additional weeks in coming.[12] Our supply lines, our medical evacuation plan, our ability to survive and fight amid chemical warfare, were all tenuous. The larger portion of the division's firepower had not arrived.

Greg had not had a chance to attend the army's Scout Platoon Leader Course at Fort Knox nor conduct any scout training with his platoon. He had more experience leading soldiers than Neal, Rob, Dave, or I did — more "troop time," we called it — but he would have to learn his new job, his boss, the equipment, and his soldiers, in the saddle. At Fort Stewart nine months as a platoon leader, Rob had never maneuvered his platoon in the field at all; nor had Neal, who had been at Ranger School. And while I had significantly more experience leading armored platoons on training missions than Neal or Rob, I had never, beyond one brief spring gunnery, taken to the field the platoon I was about to take to war. Dave had spent six months in and out of the field with his platoon, though imitating Soviet tactics on Opposing Force missions with 2-4 Cav instead of practicing American tactics with our 1-64 Armor, and beating his tanks into the ground. We had a flock of new platoon leaders, more green even than ourselves, and several new platoon sergeants. Our battalion commander and all four line company commanders were new and had not yet maneuvered as a team. Nor with us, their lieutenants. We had never, in other words, practiced. Not together anyway. And the Iraqi army, the fourth largest in the world, had years of experience engaged in war. While none of us believed an Iraqi invasion would overwhelm us as the invading North Koreans had the 24th Infantry Division's Task Force Smith forty years earlier in the first action of the Korean War, especially given the might of our air forces, we had our worries.

Major General McCaffrey would later characterize his deploying division as the "opposite end of the spectrum from Task Force Smith," with the best equipment, training, leaders, and soldiers of any armed force in the world.[13] Looking back, I can't disagree. Still (and conveniently), neither the American public, with its post-Vietnam need for reassurance, nor Saddam Hussein, with our need for his discouragement from attacking, was aware of our not insignificant vulnerabilities and limitations.

■ Task organization is a fundamental part of modern mechanized warfare's combined arms principle. A combined arms force integrates units from various branches of the army, notably armor and infantry, to take advantage of each branch's strengths and minimize its weaknesses. Tanks attached to an infantry unit provide it with the tank's firepower, mobility, and protection; infantry attached to a tank unit give it necessary security from the enemy's dismounted infantry threat and the ability to clear trenches, bunkers, and buildings and to guard prisoners of war. A task-organized battalion is designated a task force.

Before 2d Brigade's first companies moved out to the desert, the commander, Col. Paul Kern, made an initial task organization, ordering our 1-64 Armor to cross-attach one company with 3-15 Infantry. Lieutenant Colonel Gordon, our armor battalion commander, chose to swap my Bravo Company (which we then called *Bravo Tank* to distinguish it from 3-15's Bravo Company); in exchange, Gordon received 3-15's Alpha Company (Alpha Mech). At the time I believed Gordon had chosen us because we were his only company with tanks on the as-yet-unarrived second ship. He has since written to me that he chose us because my company commander, Capt. Jeff Swisher, "had the best company and best command team, so I sent him and you on to 3-15 because that was the way I did things."

On 28 August, the day after the *Capella* had begun unloading, Task Force 1-64 Armor, dubbed Rogue Force, departed for the desert with Neal, Greg, Rob, and Dave. It was the division's first maneuver unit to leave the port.

The *Altair,* with Bravo Tank's vehicles, arrived the next day. A detail unloaded and drove them to a fenced-in staging area about a kilometer from Tent City. We walked back and forth between the two, preparing the tanks for our movement into the desert. On the twenty-ninth I heard the first rumors: 82d Airborne soldiers had clashed with Bedouins, and several from each side were dead; a C-5 military transport plane on the way to Saudi had crashed, killing ten to twenty soldiers; and a two-star general was relieved for failing to logistically support the deployment. And on the thirtieth, our first official intelligence update: Hussein had reported he cannot feed his troops, was considering withdrawal from Kuwait, and had promised to release women and children from the West held hostage in Iraq and Kuwait.

In the staging area with the tanks, Captain Swisher told me that my platoon would be attached to Delta Company, 3-15 Infantry. Within a battalion task force, companies may also be task organized. In this case, platoons are attached or cross-attached among the companies. A task organized company is referred to as a company-team. Swisher felt obliged, he explained, to give another commander his senior platoon leader. I had been attached to a 3-15 Infantry company during my trip to the NTC in March and so had some experience training with them as well. There was more. My new company, Delta Mech, would be attached to the division's cavalry squadron, and that unit, 2-4 Cav, would shortly move to occupy a screen position for the entire theater — the most forward American unit. In a defensive posture such as Desert Shield, a cavalry squadron on a screen acts like a battalion's scout platoon, serving as the major unit's early warning for an attack, buying valuable time by delaying the enemy's advance through tactical skirmishes and withdrawals. A combination speed-bump and trip wire, the Cav screen slows the enemy while sending up an early warning flare. The 24th Infantry Division's cavalry squadron did not normally have tanks and so had minimal ability to sustain tanks in the field. My four Abrams would be the Cav's only tanks, and not a spare part for miles. When I met Delta Mech's commander, Capt. Rick Baillergeon, and his executive officer, the latter — 1st Lt. Brian Sneddon, a wiry fellow with a high-n-tight haircut, mustache, and ice-blue eyes — upon learning I would have the only tanks in 2-4 Cav, sympathized with me, army style: "You're fucked."

On one of my trips from the tank holding area to Tent City another classmate, John Wildermuth, a Multiple Launch Rocket System (MLRS) platoon leader in the division artillery, gave me a ride in his Humvee.[14] John's MLRS platoon was assigned in direct support of 2-4 Cav. Seeing him, and hearing that, comforted me. Throughout Desert Shield and Desert Storm, the knowledge of friends in units around me, be it in the company on my left or the division on my right, comforted. Placing faces on units gives one the confidence of the known.

Into the Desert

There is satisfaction in the feeling that here is something to be defeated and mastered, nature at her worst. I suppose Kipling would call it a man's life. And for hundreds of miles around there is one occupation — war. War in surroundings that cannot suffer, where there can be no distractions. I feel that I'm "getting down to it."
— Christopher Seton-Watson, British soldier, North Africa campaign,
   World War II

The Second Brigade's destination, according to its commander, "was a Division directed assembly area located about 130 km west of Dammam, 30 km north of the Dammam-Riyadh Expressway. The Brigade's mission was to establish a hasty defense while waiting for the rest of the division to clear the port."[15]

The move into the desert served a number of other purposes. It decreased the terrorist threat to the unit substantially and prevented the unit from becoming caught at the port or in the city during an Iraqi invasion. Armor units need space to effectively move, see, and shoot. The move also began the process of desert acclimatization and the establishment of the American deliberate defense of Saudi Arabia. The line in the sand couldn't be drawn by soldiers stewing on a pier. Finally, our moving into the desert freed room at the port for the arriving soldiers and equipment as they streamed into the theater behind us.

On 28 August, Greg writes, "we drove our vehicles off the ship and onto the trucks. I took one last look at the port facility at Dammam, not knowing when I would see it again. With nine MREs and a case of bottled water per man, we headed off into the desert."

"After loading the tanks on Heavy Equipment Transport System (HET) trucks," adds Dave, "we clambered aboard Saudi double-deckers for the trip to the desert. We only knew we were going into the desert to set up a defense. I did not know where, nor how far from the border; still, I was getting used to ignorance and was happy to be away from the port and doing my job. We departed the port

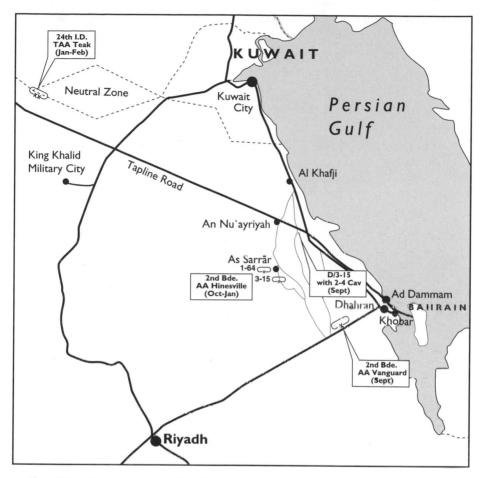

The 2d Brigade, 24th Infantry Division, in Saudi Arabia, 24 August 1990–24 February 1991

in the late afternoon and arrived at the HET download site in the early morning. We had to travel at night because the HETs could not handle the combined pressure of the M1's weight and the desert heat — under these conditions, the HETs' tires sometimes exploded. The number of vehicles moving in such a small area in the dark demanded much care. Despite our best precautions, the movement brought my first brush with death: A Saudi HET driver had dismounted his truck after off-loading its cargo and had decided to sleep on the ground beside his truck. Another HET, driving past his vehicle, ran over his head."

Neal, with Alpha Tank, would lead the battalion's road march from the HET off-load site to the assembly area. "Unbelievable, the stories I later heard from my soldiers who rode as passengers in the Saudi trucks," writes Neal. "Some of them stopped whenever they felt like it. Many got lost, and some tried to off-load the tanks in the middle of nowhere. My driver, Spc. Forbes Watkins, who rode shotgun in the truck carrying my tank, had to argue for an hour with the truck driver not to unload our tank about fifty miles short of its destination. Other trucks had blowouts and without spare tires they sat for a day before receiving assistance. I was thankful that night to have all four of my tanks off-load at the right place.

"The company commander assembled his three platoon leaders: 'We are going on a leaders' recon in a few minutes because tonight we are executing a tactical road march twenty kilometers north. Neal, you just got out of Ranger School, so you should know how to navigate. You take lead. Don't get us lost. We don't want to look like idiots.'

"'Yes sir,' I replied. Navigating was one skill in which I had complete confidence. I likened navigating in the open desert with navigating in the ocean: Even if you had no terrain features that appeared on your map to orient yourself, as long as you knew your azimuth and tracked your distance, you could not get lost. Unequipped with any advanced navigation aids like the Global Positioning System (GPS) or the Loran, I had only a compass and my tank's odometer, and a few hours to figure out how to make a lensatic compass read accurately while my seventy-ton steel tank was interfering with the magnetic field. I started to get a little nervous." Neal had never before maneuvered his tank platoon, much less led an entire battalion on a road march.

"The two other platoon leaders and I went back to our platoons, issued warning orders about the upcoming movement, grabbed our maps, and hopped in the commander's Humvee. As we drove north, I paid close attention to my map, marking down the location of the Bedouin camps we passed to use as landmarks. At the halfway point, I jumped out of the commander's vehicle and planted a picket firmly to the ground, then attached to it a VS-17 panel — a plastic tarp, orange on one side, green on the other — orange side visible.

"'You think you'll find that panel at night, with 40 percent illumination, lieutenant?' Captain Schwartz asked with a slight smile.

"'Yes, sir, or I would not stick it in the ground,' I replied. *I will probably never see that panel again in my life,* I thought as I climbed back into his Humvee.

"When we reached our future assembly area, I placed one more picket in the spot Captain Schwartz told me my platoon would occupy. Afterward, we headed back to the company and had two hours before the road march.

"I issued a movement order to the platoon, then Sfc. Wilson conducted a premovement inspection of the soldiers and the tanks. I had one hell of a platoon sergeant in Wilson. A large black man with a booming voice to match his size, he led by competence and obvious goodwill. He never complained in front of the soldiers and managed to give orders with an encouraging wide-open, full-tooth smile.

"As he conducted the inspection, I had a few minutes to think. Tonight was critical. If the platoon did well, we would win the confidence of the commander. If we did not do well, another platoon would lead the next time.

"I pulled out my compass, stood on the ground centered on my tank's front slope. I shot an azimuth at a stationary vehicle in the distance.

"'Forbes,' I told my driver, 'crank up the tank and have Sergeant Davis turn the turret power on.'

"I quickly mounted the tank and sat on the rim surrounding the tank commander's hatch. Holding the compass above the .50-caliber machine gun, I shot an azimuth to the same distant vehicle. The difference in the two azimuths was fifteen degrees.

"Now I had a formula for shooting and adjusting azimuths on the move. I had learned at West Point and Ranger School to trust my compass; a working compass never lies, and I always carried two. I marked the azimuth and distance for each leg of the road march on my map. We would have to change azimuths six times during the night, so the distances were critical. Forbes could track the distances on his odometer and tell me when to change direction. I wrote the distances on two index cards and gave one card to Forbes. Another factor in my favor: We were going generally north most of the night, and the Big Dipper would be visible. If the stars were clear, I would not end up going the wrong way.

"Many of the constellations seemed to shine more brightly in this part of the world. I found the constellation Orion the most easily recognizable. Orion, the warrior, with his sword commanding the night sky, would watch over us every night. His presence comforted; for me Orion represented God's eternal monument to soldiers. We would move under his omnipotent eyes during the night's road march.

"As the sun went down, the company lined up in platoon columns and waited for the order to move. A lone tank darted in front of mine, directly in my path north. 'Who is that bastard? What's his bumper number?' Sergeant Davis, my gunner, pointed the main gun at the other tank and looked in the thermal night sight.

"'Sir, I dare you to call him a bastard over the net,' Sergeant Davis chuckled over the intercom. 'It's the battalion commander.' Lieutenant Colonel Gordon. The lieutenants called him Flash.

"A transmission from Captain Schwartz interrupted our laughter.

"'White Six, this is Black Six, move now, over.'

"I keyed the mike. 'Roger, Black Six. It's going to be slow at first. I have to maneuver around Rogue Six, over.' All commander vehicles bear the 66 bumper number, and the commanders all have 'six' in their radio call sign: either 'Black Six,' or 'six' preceded by their unit's nickname. Captain Schwartz was Black Six. Lieutenant Colonel Gordon, commander of the 1-64 Desert Rogues, was Rogue Six.

"'This is Black Six,' Captain Schwartz acknowledged, 'roger, out.'

"We moved out into the darkness, the company's thirteen other tanks lined up behind us, every tank commander hoping we were going the right way. The stars were out in full desert sky splendor and every few minutes I'd look up at the Big Dipper and check my compass.

"'Sir, we've finished the first leg,' said Forbes.

"'Okay, come right a quarter turn . . . steady . . . you're on. Start keeping the distance for the second leg.' I double-checked the initial compass reading with my second compass. Both compasses read the same and the fifteen-degree differential seemed to be working. We finished the second leg and adjusted our azimuth again.

"'Sir, there is a picket about two hundred meters ahead stuck in the ground,' said Sergeant Davis as he scanned through the gunner's thermal sight.

"'Thanks.' I keyed the radio, 'Black Six, this is White Six, can you have the picket and VS-17 panel recovered as the last tank passes? I don't want to lose my property, over.'

"'This is Black Six, I'll believe it when I see it! We'll get it, White Six.'

"We continued to move and a small dune I remembered from the recon being just south of our final destination became visible through my PVS-7 handheld night vision device. The company closed in on the march objective as I used the second picket to guide my platoon into position. Captain Schwartz instructed me to develop and execute a security plan, then to get some rest. After Sfc. Wilson straightened the platoon into position, I grabbed an MRE and lay down on the front slope of the tank.

"I didn't know it at the time, but my platoon would lead the company from then on, and the company would become the lead element for a 750-man task force. We had built a reputation as navigators that night. As the noise of tanks and personnel carriers still finding their positions in the night rumbled around me, I fell asleep."

When Neal woke the next morning, "there were these Bedouins camped out in front of us. We hadn't noticed them the night before. One of them drives up in his jeep, Datsun pickup, whatever it was, drives right up to one of my tanks, and he starts yelling at my guys in Arabic. I sent Carrol over there, because he spoke Arabic. Carroll was fresh out of basic training. His family was from the Philippines and as a child he had learned Arabic from workers who migrated back and forth to Saudi Arabia. I kept his valuable talent a secret during deployment at Fort Stewart — I could see division pulling him as an interpreter, and I intended the company to benefit. So Carroll hopped off my tank and trotted over barefoot to talk to the guy. He came back and told me the guy is a Bedouin chieftain, he was missing some camels, and he thought we had stolen his camels and were hiding them inside our tanks. The chieftain was still over at the other tank going nuts. I'm sitting on my tank with 'Big Daddy' Wilson, my 240-pound platoon sergeant.

"'Sergeant Wilson, can you take care of this?' I asked him.

"'Roger, sir,' he boomed, with one of those grins that took over his face.

"He gets off my tank and starts walking over to the Bedouin. This guy had probably never seen such a huge black man in his entire life. Sergeant Wilson wasn't halfway to the other tank when the chieftain turned around, jumped back in his truck, and hauled ass out of there. We never saw him again."

■ "We had built a reputation as navigators that night." Neal is being modest here, sharing with his entire platoon the credit and praise he earned and deserved. Such modesty may come partly from having no brothers to outboast, or partly from being a general officer's son. I've known other sons of generals with a similar tendency. It's as if growing up they had daily lessons, taught by example, of how success speaks for itself. The phrase "Deeds, not Words" had been the platoon motto in cadet basic training for Neal, Rob, and me.

Neal's modesty also comes from a full and warranted confidence in his abilities. But as personal as his reticence is, it is also a quality of our profession. A Vietnam veteran friend of mine, reflecting on a draft of this book, remarked that good combat leaders are "so busy thinking about others and the mission that they almost erase themselves." Feelings do not absolutely get in the way of soldiering, but a certain amount and kind of self-reflection — the amount and kind I was guilty of in the desert — certainly detracts focus and energies from warmaking (if focusing solely on the mission bears its own dangers). Soldiering and leading soldiers require a selflessness more complicated than merely spending time away from home, suffering miserable conditions, and risking life and limb.

Dave Trybula and Rob Holmes remember their first day in the desert. I had not yet left the port.

"We deployed in a defensive line and set up camouflage nets over our tanks," writes Dave about his Charlie Tank platoon. "The sun kept getting higher and the air hotter. It's hard to explain how hot it was, even under the net's shade. If you drank before going to sleep, you still awoke dehydrated. The sweat rapidly saturated your clothes. Exposed flesh felt like it was on fire. Even the sand was too hot to touch or walk on without protection. My eyes became narrow slits against the sun's reflection off the sand.

"That first day in the desert, I checked my entire platoon to feel out their morale and to ensure my tank commanders were forcing their people to drink water. The heat drains energy and makes the MREs much less appetizing. Some days later I ran across my platoon sergeant standing at his wingman's tank forcing an overwhelmed soldier to drink. The soldier kept saying that he was going to die from dehydration. We were able to calm him down and inject him with a bag of intravenous fluid to replenish his body. On each of my tanks at least one soldier had been trained as a combat lifesaver, which meant every crew had someone who could apply proper first aid techniques until a medic arrived. A tank company of sixty-five men had only two medics, both of whom rode in the same M113. Combat lifesavers could administer CPR, IVs, splints, and attend to eye injuries, sucking chest wounds, etc. Every tank carried a combat lifesaver bag with the necessary medical supplies. Given the chance of a vehicle's combat lifesaver becoming seriously wounded, I had tried to get at least two per vehicle.

"The first day in the desert brought a lot of confidence to my platoon. As I walked from vehicle to vehicle and talked to my soldiers, it was apparent that each day would be easier than the last. My soldiers' questions that day, which were also my own, I had to answer as best I could. Where were we? How close was the Iraqi border? What was our mission? Was Iraq going to attack us, or we Iraq? I told them what I could: Our mission was to bolster the American presence in Saudi Arabia to deter an Iraqi attack, and if deterrence failed, the mission became the defense of Saudi Arabia. I didn't tell them where we would defend because I couldn't. I had no idea where in Saudi Arabia we were."

That first day in the desert, Rob remembers the temperature reaching 135 degrees. He and his tank crew "baked on the blistering sand beneath a tarp that we had thrown over our tank's main gun to shade us from the scorching sun. We sat silently and stared vacantly, not quite believing the heat. A slight breeze blew, as if God were giving us hope. We guzzled bottled water and sweated our asses off.

"Our orders were to set up a hasty defensive position quickly and prepare for an enemy attack. My priority was determining, for each of my four tanks, sectors of fire that supported each other and the adjacent platoons. That done, the manual reads, we would continue to improve our fighting positions with cover and concealment as time and engineering assets became available. I looked out from beneath my tarp at my other three tanks. Each had its tarp similarly draped over the gun tube and showed no sign of life. Although not far from the Kuwait-Saudi border and the Iraqi army, our overriding concern was surviving the damn heat. We couldn't even touch the machine guns, let alone fire them, because they were so hot.

"Occasionally the radio crackled with traffic, but nobody was any more active than we were. As ordered, Task Force 1-64 Armor had spread out across two thousand meters, a cluster of steel muffins baking in an oven. We may not have been combat effective on that August day, but we had accomplished and were continuing to accomplish our mission. We had deployed around the world a few fast weeks after Saddam had invaded Kuwait the first M1 tank unit in country, and we now sat between the elite Iraqi Republican Guard and the Saudi oil fields. If the enemy attacked, they would have to fight American soldiers.

"As I baked under that tarp, drinking my umpteenth bottle of water, I considered my tank crew. Like any small team, a tank crew must function as one well-oiled unit. As a basketball point guard must 'just know' when to look for a back door pass, a tank driver must 'just know' when to steady his maneuvering before the gunner takes a shot. My crew was a long way from the NCAA Final Four.

"I had received my gunner right before we left the port. He had been a clerk back at Fort Stewart counting the days until his enlistment ran out in another year. I am usually a very lucky person, but somehow this dud landed with me. We faced fifty-five hundred enemy tanks one hundred miles to the north, and my gunner had spent the last two years pulling out desk drawers and pushing paper instead of pulling triggers and popping caps.

"My loader, Spc. Russ Underberg, had also joined my platoon at the port, having been transferred directly from Germany. From Pismo Beach, California, he had a wild look in his eyes, and boasted that he had been a star on his high school surf team. We didn't have one of those in Georgia. I could tell Underberg was intelligent. He saw through my new gunner immediately. Field soldiers always know a fraud. I worried how Underberg's assessment would affect the discipline on the tank.

"My driver, Pfc. Chris Bell, was nineteen, a high school state champion wrestler still in peak physical condition. Bell sat under the tarp with his usually fair complexion red as a tomato. He was probably in better shape than anyone in my platoon, and the heat was killing him.

"There we lay: a twenty-three-year-old lieutenant on his first field exercise, a clerk masquerading as a gunner, a surfer listening to the Beach Boys through his Walkman radio, and a nineteen-year-old heat casualty. Had Saddam had an accurate impression of the 24th Infantry Division, he would have been firing up his tanks. The bottled water we drank was room temperature, our room being the Saudi desert. The water burned our mouths until invention followed necessity: Underberg figured out that if we put the bottles of water in a wet sock or wrapped it in a wet rag and hung it so that it could blow in the breeze, the water temperature would drop significantly, making it, if not exactly cool, at least drinkable.

"So let's finish this portrait of our fearsome hasty defense: a battalion of tanks in the middle of a big beach, each with their gun tubes swung over the side supporting a tarp, and a dozen swinging socks holding water bottles hanging from the turrets.

"Late that afternoon on our first day the breeze picked up. It refreshed us, and I began to think that we were going to survive. I praised it as a Godsend. Then the wind strengthened. In a matter of fifteen minutes, I felt like I was in a tornado. Sand whipped our faces. We clambered onto the tank, burning our hands on the hot steel, as we headed for the interior. I sat in my seat and pulled my hatch closed. Looking out my periscopes, I saw only a wall of sand enclosing the tank. I couldn't see either of the tanks beside me.

"The storm lasted about two hours. When we finally climbed out of our stifling tank turrets, our tarps were scattered all over the place and the cases of water stowed under them were covered with sand. My .50-caliber machine gun was so clogged with sand I couldn't cock back the charging handle to chamber a round, let alone fire. Even after hiding inside the turret, I was covered with gritty sand. I felt like I had sat in the dentist's chair as he scrubbed my whole body with fluoride. I was not enjoying my first day in the desert.

"The sun set about 2100. I hadn't left my tank all day, but I was exhausted and caked in a salty sand mixture. I stripped down and dumped a canteen over me. It felt terrific, easily the best moment of that lousy day. The temperature was still almost 100 degrees, but it felt much cooler. I dumped another canteen over me and lathered up with a bar of soap. The moon was full and visibility was excellent. I paused again to look around, taking in the desert for the first time. And I found it beautiful. Clean. The white sand, the deep, rich, black sky sparkling with a million stars, and the largest full moon I had ever seen. There I stood, naked as the day I was born, enjoying, appreciating, the Saudi desert for the first time, when the unmistakable sound of a .45-caliber pistol cracked the tranquil air. I wheeled around; charging at me full speed a threat I had never faced before—a grunting, galloping camel.

"This huge animal charged by and disappeared over a dune. One of my trigger-happy soldiers had fired at the animal and missed. I couldn't blame him for missing; his .45-caliber pistol had probably been in the army inventory since D-Day. My loader Underberg doubled over with laughter on top of the tank as I stood there dripping.

"'Hey sir, that camel must have really liked what he saw!' Underberg cackled.

"I put on a fresh uniform and sat on the turret to clean my pistol before going to sleep. My crew had already crashed. Underberg and Bell would have guard duty later that night. I laughed a little at how we were in a rather dangerous situation, but nobody seemed all that concerned. We were simply glad to have survived our first day in the desert.

"I looked up and saw a shooting star. As I considered several wishes — returning home safely, a cold front tomorrow, a Braves World Series — I saw another star race by. Over the next thirty minutes, I probably counted a half dozen such marvels. The night was so clear I thought that I could see forever. The white sand rolled out like a carpet in every direction. It was hypnotic.

"On the horizon I saw some movement. A column of Bedouin-bearing camels made their way slowly from my left to right. To my right, I heard the turret move on Sfc. Sikes's tank; he and his gunner were tracking the Bedouin column in their sights. It was their turn for guard watch, and I felt good with them observing our perimeter. The M1 tank is equipped with a thermal night sight that detects different heat signatures and illustrates the picture with the resolution of an old black and white television. For example, tanks are hotter than people so they display as different shades of black and white. I flipped my radio. 'White Four, this is White One, watch for enemy camels attacking in our sector.'

"'This is White Four Golf — acknowledged. It's just a column of rags at 1600 meters.'" (*Rag* was short for *raghead,* which was soldier-speak for Arabs, the Gulf theater's equivalent of Korea's and Vietnam's *gook.*)

"White Four was my platoon sergeant, Sfc. Sikes; White Four Golf was his gunner, who was pulling watch on their tank. At 1600 meters told me he had lased the Bedouins. The tank's fire system included a laser range finder that worked something like sonic radar by bouncing a beam off the target, then calculating the distance to it by multiplying the beam's travel time by its rate of travel and dividing this round-trip distance by two. We weren't supposed to lase people, not even the enemy, because it could burn the retina.

"I walked about twenty meters away to relieve myself before turning in, and while doing so I glanced over in the distance and stared down the gun tube of Sikes's tank about 150 meters away. The gunner looking through his sights must have been getting a big kick watching his platoon leader take a leak. I had been quite an exhibitionist that night — I wondered what my stream looked like in the thermal sights.

"As I walked back to my tank, I considered my sleeping location. My gunner looked pretty comfortable curled up on the sand. I took off my shirt and began to untie my boots while surveying a soft place of my own. Then my worst nightmare slithered by. As if the scorching heat, relentless sandstorms, and raging camels weren't bad enough. I hate snakes. I really, really, really hate snakes. I don't know why; I've never been bitten or had a bad experience with one. The several-foot-long serpent disappeared into the sand about ten meters away. Decision made: Forget the sand, I'm sleeping on the tank. I woke my sleeping sergeant, told him of my snake sighting, and recommended that he join Bell, Underberg, and me on our seventy-ton steel mattress. He whined and whimpered as he crawled aboard the tank. Part of me wished I hadn't bothered the fat slug.

"I lay down next to my .50-caliber machine gun and within reach of my radio microphone. A second lieutenant can do a lot of things wrong and get away with them, but the fastest way to trouble is not answering the radio when called.

"I gazed up at the stars. *What the hell is going to happen to us?* I remembered asking a similar question my first night at West Point. I thought about my Beast roommate, Neal Creighton, rolling around in his bed that first night mumbling in his sleep. Somewhere in this desert Neal was probably doing the very same thing atop his tank. He was a platoon leader in Alpha Tank about fifteen-hundred meters to my east. I thought about my Savannah roommate, Al Vernon, also not far away in Bravo Tank. Our life of shrimp and beer sure had changed. I couldn't help but smile as I recounted my day and how badly I had wanted to leave the Fort Stewart motor pool. So much for the grass always being greener — hell, on this side of the globe I didn't even have grass.

"I had an eerie feeling I better get used to this desert. Today my enemy had been the sun, wind, and sand. Tomorrow it could be T-72 tanks. I had to adapt to the desert quickly so I could concentrate on the enemy. In a few hours, it would be 135 degrees again. I figured I ought to catch some sleep."

■ Bravo Tank, less my Second Platoon, left King Abdul Azziz Port two days before we did. My platoon left with Delta Mech on 31 August, at 1800; the soldiers on the orange Saudi double-decker buses, the vehicles on the Saudi HETs. Our convoy consisted of Delta Mech with two Bradley infantry platoons and my Abrams tank platoon, two MLRS artillery-rocket delivery systems, and two Fox NBC Reconnaissance vehicles. The Foxes, manufactured in Germany, were prototypes still undergoing testing at Fort Knox a month before.

We were told to be ready to fight as soon as we arrived at our destination. Also to be prepared to download en route. Just in case.

The trip lasted nine hours. We had been instructed, because the buses would not stop, to take empty water bottles to use as individual portable toilets. No one around me had used theirs when at sundown the Saudi drivers stopped the buses, dismounted, unrolled their prayer mats, and dropped to their knees toward Mecca. We poured out, lined up, and had a group pee, the praying Saudis like bookends flanking our golden scribbling in the sand. We were a pack of dogs, American mutts, marking our new turf.

We arrived at the 2-4 Cav Tactical Operations Center at 0300 on 1 September. A few hours later the HETs with the company-team's tanks and Bradleys caught up to us. Late that afternoon, Captain Baillergeon took his four lieutenants in his Humvee to perform a recon of our new destination, a hasty defense about eight kilometers to the northeast. We returned to the Cav's TOC, mounted up, and moved out.

It felt good to be back on my tank. Less vulnerable, for one thing. But also because the M1 main battle tank is a thing of beauty. A machine meant to move: I have never enjoyed a smoother ride in a tracked vehicle. Abrams tankers commonly joke that their ride suffers more breakdowns while sitting unused in the motor pool than during field operations. The M1 was designed to support the army's doctrine of AirLand Battle, which was developed in the seventies and eighties to defeat the much larger forces fielded by the Soviet-led Warsaw Pact in Europe or China in Asia. AirLand Battle calls for fast, fluid, mobile battles — even in the defense, by means of shifting positions and rapid counterattacks. The goal is to throw the enemy off balance with rapid and aggressive strikes from unexpected directions. Thus the mobility and firepower of the M1 tank, which could shoot on the move (an inspiring vision, the tank flying in one direction, the turret spinning in another, the gun tube floating still when it suddenly fires, the air exploding with the shot while the tank, seemingly oblivious to the recoil absorbed inside the turret, drives on). Greg Downey describes the M1 as "a combination of a heavyweight and a lightweight boxer. It has the brute power to destroy you in one lightning quick punch, and the finesse and precision to dance around the ring in circles until you show your chin just enough to take a blow. It is a work of art."

My introduction to the vehicle to which my military career would be wed happened at maintenance training during the Armor Officer Basic Course at Fort Knox. We spanking new second lieutenants stepped into a building that housed more than a company's worth of tanks; four of us were assigned an NCO instructor and a tank. Packed in among the others like horses in stalls, my tank loomed leviathan. We spent the next two days becoming familiar with its nooks and crannies and secrets   to return to the marriage trope, taking our first nervous gropes toward learning to be intimate with her.

When I left the army two years later, I had domesticated my perception of the tank: I had grown to marvel over its compactness. So much power, so many memories, bundled in such a svelte package.

A single armored tracked vehicle moving in the dry desert kicks back enough dust to obscure an entire company of vehicles on the other side of the cloud. Those of us who rode out of the hatches wore goggles beneath our CVC helmets and used green linen field dressings borrowed from first aid field splints as bandannas, which we tucked under the goggles' face pad and into our shirts. Those of us who wore glasses enjoyed that extra bit of discomfort jammed under the goggles against the bridge of the nose. A lot of soldiers would learn to wrap a field dressing over their heads, pulling it tight and knotting the loose ends in the back. They wore these "do-rags" under their helmets to keep the sand out of their hair. When they weren't riding, when they were

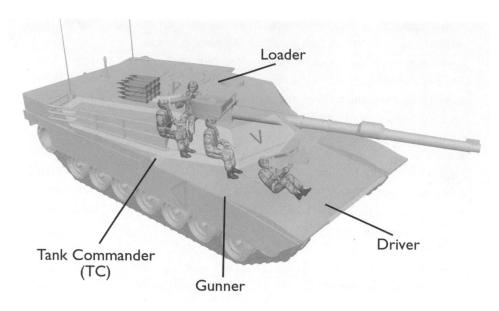

M1 Abrams Tank Crew Positions

relaxing and not wearing headgear, they wore the do-rags to protect their scalp from the sun (and to look cool). I would learn to carry in my sponson box — the long storage bin welded to my side of the turret within reach of the hatch — a plastic container of Wet Ones for a quick postmission face cleaning. Because the sand always won. After dismounting from a mission, I still had dust buried in my ears and ringing my face where my goggles had been. And Neal, Greg, Rob, Dave, and I were the lucky ones: In our respective company's lead vehicle, we did not have to eat somebody else's dust. Everybody behind us ate ours, and their vision was that much worse.

Delta Mech moved a few kilometers east and north. My platoon had the left side of three-platoon horseshoe position; the company-team's engagement area, where all three platoons' fires as well as planned artillery fires would converge, was an opening in the road from between flanking high ground, where an approaching enemy, having been forced by the steep inclines of the high ground to travel in a column down the road, would emerge one or two vehicles at a time. I moved the platoon back again and again, trying to find what I called the military horizon, that point where a slight crest in the ground between us and the engagement area would hide from his sight all but our turrets. But denied by the flatness of the terrain, I settled for placing the platoon as far back as we could while still ranging the engagement area. I placed the tanks on line about seventy-five meters apart, far enough that an enemy could not have two in his sights at once, far enough that an artillery round could not hit two, close enough for vocal communication.

That night I saw my first camel, a white silhouette in the tank gun's thermal sights. We ran 50 percent security that night: two soldiers per tank, two tanks with turret power on, scanning for the enemy. The next afternoon we moved again, north up the road, to our final position.

The evening before Staff Sergeant Rivera, my displaced platoon sergeant, had mumbled to me, "Jesus Christ, sir, there's nothing to do here but die." His comment foreshadowed something of our short journey that afternoon to Tapline Road. Carcasses populated the roadside like lost mile markers: camels, goats, vehicles, and equipment. The sight of abandoned carcasses would become very familiar, both in Saudi Arabia and Iraq.

My platoon took up a reverse slope position behind a ridge overlooking the intersection of our north-south road and Tapline Road. I did not know the name of Tapline Road, much less its significance as the only paved Saudi road crossing the Arabian peninsula and paralleling the Iraqi border. I didn't have a map of the area I was to defend; like Dave Trybula, I had no idea where in Saudi I was. The road to me was the two-lane hardball (paved road) about nine hundred meters to my direct front. Friendly aircraft considered any military vehicles north of Tapline Road as hostile. My commander had explained that the north-south dirt road we had come up continued north to Kuwait and represented a major potential Iraqi avenue of approach.

A small service station and general store to the platoon's front left occupied the southwest corner of the intersection. One of Delta Mech's infantry platoons covered our left flank to the west; the other platoon with the commander's and executive officer's Bradleys sat in the flat east of the north-south road. The company headquarters platoon camped a kilometer or so behind my tanks. Several kilometers south of the Bradleys in the flats, just before the area rose into the hills that became the rock quarry, was an MLRS platoon.

Twenty miles west was the town of An Nu'ayriyah, which rhymes with *diarrhea;* ninety miles north was the Saudi-Kuwait border, and the Iraqi army.

S.Sgt. Joey Yocum, one of my tank commanders, turned twenty-eight that day. To me at twenty-three, Sergeant Yocum looked thirty-five. To me at twenty-nine as I write this, Yocum then remains so much older than I am now. His blonde hair had begun to disappear from both the bottom up and the top down. He had a small blonde mustache, a slight potbelly, and ruddy everything. Yocum had walked out of the script of *Kelly's Heroes:* Keeping him and his crew in uniform and on task was hell, although he was one of the best tankers I have known. Few soldiers in the battalion had not heard of his four thousand-meter kill during their last live-fire maneuver exercises at the NTC.

In the bowl behind the ridge my tanks occupied, a flock of black sheep, tended by Saudi men in two trucks, watched us settle in. They "grazed" the area every day I can remember. Thick, black wool, in the desert: I theorized that to warrant this fate these creatures' forbears must have committed a sin worse than the serpent's in the Garden of Eden, a sin biblically unmentionable.[16]

The Longest Month: September 1990

The division's Operation Desert Shield mission was to:

   *Defend in sector to defeat Iraqi forces;

   *On order, counterattack to destroy the enemy's lead division of the second operational echelon forces in zone, and;

   *Be prepared to continue offensive operations and complete the destruction of the enemy's capability to resist.

The 24th Infantry Division's defensive sector was 63 miles wide by 7 miles deep. During the succeeding months, the division would work to fine tune the plan while aggressively confronting the myriad of logistical and sustainment challenges posed by the austere desert environment.

— *The Victory Book*

Neal, Rob, Greg, and Dave passed their first month in the desert with Task Force 1-64 Armor in the 2d Brigade's Assembly Area Augusta. Serving in different companies, however, they had little to no contact with one another. That first month the 24th Infantry Division constituted the main ground force defending Saudi Arabia, waiting as other units mustered for deployment and the logistical system geared up. In that first month the unanswered questions hovered new and dangerous. Our desert homes (I was at Tapline Road; the others were at Augusta) would be temporary, although none of us knew it. We didn't know much at all, although we certainly knew more than our families back home. I never cease wondering how they managed. We didn't know about the world, about our region of the world, but we knew about ourselves. They had the world at their fingertips through television and remote controls but couldn't learn about us to save their lives.

While at Augusta, Greg Downey's scout platoon was "in survival mode. The intense heat and raging sandstorms made everything difficult. Weapons were nearly impossible to keep clean and what training we did was done at night. The only map we had was a 1:250,000 scale map, the scale used for planning division and corps level operations, and not much use for navigating locally.

"Constant focus on the chemical threat required us to conduct two hours of chemical training per day. This consisted of wearing our chemical overgarments while performing other tasks. Wearing the entire ensemble was called MOPP IV, for Mission Oriented Protective Posture Level IV. MOPP IV increased our water consumption considerably, as you could lose a gallon of body fluid from sweating during one hour of wearing the charcoal-lined suit and impermeable black rubber gloves, boots, and facemask. Chemical training was 90 percent physical and 10 percent mental. We had to learn to tolerate the uncomfortable conditions before practicing ordinary battle skills as well as tasks related to wearing MOPP IV, such as changing protective filters, drinking water, and performing MOPP gear exchange and decontamination procedures, all those tasks I had despised doing back at Fort Stewart. Now the very real possibility of fighting in a chemically contaminated environment had me paying close attention to every step.

"I was also getting to know my soldiers, many of whose names I hadn't known upon deployment. Going to the field is a bonding experience for soldiers. You never feel part of a unit until you've completed a field exercise with it. In the desert, we had no choice but to get to know each other. I started to notice more differences between these scouts and the tankers I had before.

"First, most of these scouts had to be told to do everything. My tankers generally did things with little supervision. Second, the majority of the scouts could not have cared less about their vehicles. For a tanker, the condition of his machine is his pride. Third, and most perplexing, my scouts appeared lazy as hell. I could not understand why, whenever I left the area, every one of them would crash for sleep. Getting one of them to answer the radio was impossible. Things would have to change. I was waiting for my platoon sergeant to crack down and tighten things up. Daily discipline and operations are his job, after all; the lieutenant only intercedes when the platoon sergeant fails or otherwise proves himself not up to the task.

"In Desert Shield, I waited much too long.

"Despite my bad platoon sergeant, the maintenance posture of the scout platoon had improved. I now had four of six CFVs fully operational. The other two could not fire the 25 mm chain gun due to inoperable cables. Needless to say, this was an enormous concern. The ship carrying the repair parts for the division would not arrive for a few weeks.

"It appeared that the Iraqi army would not attack into Saudi Arabia. This was to our advantage and a great relief, considering our maintenance and logistics challenges. I took the next few weeks to get familiar with my vehicle and weapon system."

Not as luxe as the Abrams, the Bradley nonetheless got the job done. The Bradley is AirLand Battle's companion to the M1, Robin to the Abrams's Batman. The Vietnam-era M113 Armored Personnel Carriers could not match the new tank's speed; its thin aluminum skin could be pierced with relatively small caliber munitions; and its own standard .50-caliber armament could hardly defeat the armor of the new generation of Soviet-brand infantry vehicles. With the

Bradley, the army abandoned the personnel carrier concept in favor of the fighting vehicle.

The Bradley sports as its main armament a 25-m chain and a two-tube TOW antitank missile weapons system. Its diesel engine rides forward of the turret, allowing the back of the hull to carry soldiers who can dismount the vehicle either after the entire back end is lowered as a ramp or through a hatch in the closed ramp. Because mechanized infantry soldiers travel to the battlefield in vehicles and dismount to fight (much in the fashion of nineteenth-century dragoons), ground troops are called "dismounts." But despite the number of personnel a Bradley carries, it is not nearly as accommodating as the Abrams. Soldiers in the back compete with one another, weapons, munitions, and other equipment for space; the ride is tight, bumpy, jerky, and blind. They cannot possibly all sleep inside or on top of their Bradley, which has a rising, craggy top, is difficult to stand on, and impossible to lie on. This silhouette rises nearly a meter taller than the Abrams's, making the Bradley a more easily spotted target. It lacks the M1's armor and the M1A1's overpressure NBC defense system. The Bradley is still a tremendous advance from the M113 PC. It keeps pace with the M1 and gets better gas mileage. It has the firepower to destroy or disable any armored vehicle on the modern battlefield; the chain gun can even take out some older tanks.

Greg's gunner, Spc. Rick Lowther, taught him the turret and the weapon systems. Lowther, Greg writes, "was not your typical GI, having been in the U.S. Navy for four years where he worked as a ship hydraulics mechanic, then getting out and joining the army as a scout. We were the same age and had similar backgrounds, but the similarities stopped there. He acted like a kid, not having a direction in life, barely knowing where he was at or where he had been. But he never, ever complained. He just smiled. About everything. He was a good guy to have in the turret with me. When I got my Irish up and heated the turret with my temper, he could drop a line to cool me down. I delegated to him a great amount of responsibility for a specialist, but I had no choice. He was my gunner. Our track and the scouts on it were as much his as they were mine.

"Scouts in the field talk about three things: sex, sex, and sex. Specialist Lowther was the master. He could talk about it for hours, driving all of us crazy. He immediately related every conversational tidbit to some fantasy or actual experience he claimed to have had. I quickly numbed to his *Penthouse Forum* talk.

"The battalion's Unit Maintenance Collection Point, the UMCP, was filling up fast. The desert heat and sand were causing problems for the M1 tanks and other combat vehicles. We did as much maintenance as possible without the needed repair parts. Eventually, to avoid further breakdowns, we were ordered to limit tracked vehicle movement. The next day the engine on my CFV blew. There were of course no Bradley engines in theater. I could not get an estimate of when I could expect one. The mechanics towed my CFV to the UMCP. It would not be returned to me for another forty-five days. My driver, Pfc. West, was devastated. Unlike the other scouts, he was very fond of his vehicle. From Omaha, a fellow Cornhusker, his only goal in life was to own a restaurant. He talked for hours about recipes, cooking, and eating. Lowther would ride him hard about the eating part. West's appetite for food was matched by his appetite for comfort and for stuff. He was a pack rat. You could open an auto parts store with what he kept down in the driver's compartment. Very seldom did anyone see him out of his driver's seat. He slept in it, ate in it, lived in it. He truly loved his vehicle; I often heard him talking to it.

"I couldn't help but like West. He was devoted to his wife and his religion. Lowther was the only target of West's anger. I guess everyone is entitled to hate something. West was pudgy and clumsy, but very smart. He possessed a great sense of direction, always knowing which way we were headed. This is very useful for a driver, especially in the open desert. I could turn the vehicle around in circles, tell him to take me east and off he'd go, east. Amazing.

"When our CFV disappeared to the UMCP, West accompanied it and lived with it at the UMCP, to help the mechanics. I would go to the UMCP to check on him and the repair status. I always found him hunkered in the driver's seat. He was depressed and grieving. He hadn't spoken to Spc. Lowther since the engine had gone belly-up. Lowther had been driving when the engine blew; he might as well have shot West's dog.

"'Don't worry, West, we'll get it fixed,' I tried to assure him.

"'Sir, it will never be the same.'

"'You're right; it'll be better. I figure we were due for a new engine anyway. I would rather have it blow now than in battle. We'd be up shit creek if that happened.'

"'I guess you're right, sir.'

"'You talked to Lowther lately?' I asked, knowing the answer.

"'No, sir.'

"'I tell you what,' I started. 'You keep looking down there in your driver's compartment for an engine and I'll see if I can make a deal with these mechanics to borrow one for awhile.'

"I did my best to appease West, knowing we would not see an engine anytime soon. I always thought supplies would be abundant during wartime operations. I had not counted on an eight thousand-mile logistics line. During a daily command and staff meeting, Lieutenant Colonel Gordon, the battalion commander, mentioned a fuel shortage in process. I couldn't believe my ears. A fuel shortage in Saudi Arabia? The next shortage to come was bottled water. This was not good news. With no potable water available, we were totally dependent on bottled water. A contract dispute with our local suppliers was causing us to ration our water.

"Restricted track movement for fear of breakdowns, fuel shortage, water shortage: It was all we could do to survive and preserve our morale, much less train, recon, and maintain in preparation for war. That was life those first weeks of Desert Shield."

For Dave Trybula's platoon, "the days in the desert did seem to get easier. The confidence gained during the first days in the desert relieved the majority of our anxiety. On 1 September 1990, we received our first news update. The company commander, Capt. Greg Hadjis, returned from battalion with a paper copy of headlines from around the world. Getting linked back into the world boosted morale considerably. We no longer felt as isolated and disconnected. At roughly the same time, the mail started trickling in.

"We stayed a very brief time at our initial desert location. Our move was not prompted by military necessity or insight; instead, as it was explained to me by my commander, the Saudi prince who owned the land we were on had paid us a visit to see what we were doing and had felt the earth rumble beneath the tracks of our moving vehicles. Fearing we would destabilize his oil fields, he told us to leave. In the name of diplomacy, we obeyed. In the new positions, the terrain was barren sand dunes as far as the eye could see. My map of the area had no contour lines, and a note at the bottom commented that the topography changed with the wind. My company's defensive line was spread over fourteen kilometers, my platoon spread over five. I could not see all of my own tanks. My twice-daily ritual of checking on each of my crews and their vehicles became a real chore as one round trip equaled almost six miles.

"One of our biggest concerns was how the desert would affect our tanks. I had great confidence in the M1's ability to withstand anything the desert could bring to bear, as long as the crews took care of their tanks. Taking care of a multifuel capable turbine engine and a computer-integrated fire control system amid blowing sand and temperatures consistently exceeding 120 degrees demanded significantly more preventive maintenance that we had done at Fort Stewart. For one thing, it meant cleaning out the turbine engine's air filters at a minimum after every six to eight hours of operation, and once daily on days the tank engine did not fire up. Concern about the effects of the new environment on our tanks culminated in what my company termed "Operation Sand Still," which went into effect in early September. Operation Sand Still called for an unequivocal order not to operate our equipment during the afternoon, and to focus all maneuver training at night when the desert cooled considerably. Incredibly, my tanks continued to perform excellently in the harsh environment.

"The one major problem with my tanks stemmed from changing from diesel to jet fuel. After eight years of wear, my tanks had considerable diesel deposit build-up in the engine's combustion chamber. The jet fuel increased the combustion chamber's temperature substantially, enough to break away the diesel deposits, which could and did damage the turbine as chunks from the combustion chamber were thrown through the recuperator. During the first two months in the desert, two of my four tanks had their engines replaced.

"Stress manifested itself in everybody in different forms. After one week in country my platoon sergeant and I had to submit a list of those personnel who had not had a single bowel movement since we arrived. Five of my sixteen soldiers made the list. A week later we still had one name on the list, so we started the soldier on constipation medicine. Another week passed before he met success at the slit trench. He never quite recovered; during maneuvers in January and throughout the war, he kept several trash bags by his side so he could relieve himself within the tank, without interrupting the maneuver. Needless to say, the rest of his crew did not appreciate his problem.

"I rapidly established a routine for the platoon. By the fifteenth of September, our days pretty much ran the same. We held stand-to in MOPP II, chemical suit and boots, at 0430. At stand-to, conducted every morning, all soldiers are awake and at their positions in the tank. Accountability reports for personnel and sensitive items are sent to the company, after which we would stand down and move to the company area for physical training. Initially PT consisted of light stretching and calisthenics, though it grew into a full program as our stay became more permanent. Personal hygiene followed PT. From 0700 until 1000 we turned to maintenance. Each day's maintenance focus changed to ensure every piece of equipment received thorough attention on a regular basis. Between 1000 and 1200, then between 1500 and 1600, we held classes on maintaining the tanks and enhancing our war-fighting skills. The three hours from 1200 to 1500 we spent on weapons maintenance and sleep. The arid climate coupled with the blowing sand was extremely harsh on the weapons. Because of the sand, we could not use oil to lubricate the weapons else the sand would stick to the lubrication. Eventually the army purchased a dry graphite lubricant to keep the weapons functioning properly. From 1600–1800 we received our logistics package, or LOGPAC, when battalion sent around food, fuel, water, mail, and other supplies. After LOGPAC we played recreational sports, which changed daily. And throughout the day personnel on guard manned weapons for security.

"After an hour of personal and preparation time, we conducted mounted training from 2100 to 0100 when the desert had cooled off. Our spot of desert area had no nearby towns or cities, so when the moon was not out our only light source was the stars. We trained in complete blackout mode, using no vehicle lights, which might give away our positions. On one of the first night road marches, the platoon sergeant of Second Platoon drove his tank into another when a company crossed our column. Fortunately no one was injured and the tank damage was minimal. That this happened to a platoon sergeant reinforced to all the need for extra caution as we learned to fight in the desert at night. I learned the location of a few essential constellations and how they moved throughout the night. The Southern Cross, for instance, rose in the southeast, peaked in the south, and then fell in the southwest. The entire process took six to eight hours. After I learned the stars, navigating in the desert at night became easier than during the day."

Writes Rob Holmes: "The next four weeks, while the rest of the division continued to arrive in Saudi, Task Force 1–64 Armor began to acclimate to the heat and sandstorms, to shaving and bathing out of canteens and sleeping under the brilliant desert sky on seventy-ton steel mattresses.

"At night, we maneuvered more and more each week. We started with dismounted patrols around our company's perimeter for security. Although we weren't far from the border, the most likely threat in hindsight was probably only a curious Bedouin. We watched them at night traipsing across the horizon on their camels. Then, no lie, a Mercedes would race across the sand. Here we were in the middle of nowhere, and a beautiful new Mercedes full of Arabs would cruise past. Saudi Arabia was clearly the most bizarre place I had ever been. Usually the luxury cars had two men in the front and two women in the back, all four in full Arab garb. As they sped by, the women might glance over their shoulder and 'flash' us by unhooking and pulling back their veils to shoot a smile through the window and over the sand, then just as quickly reattach the veil and snap to face front.

"We also observed little Nissan pickup trucks, which caused more serious concern. Division Intelligence reported that Iraqi scouts dressed in Saudi garb and mounted in commercial pickups were crossing the border to reconnoiter the location and composition of our defenses. As fuel and spare tank equipment arrived in country, we shifted our hasty defenses every several nights. If these trucks were enemy operatives, we didn't want to make it too easy on them to plot our locations. Regardless of our moves, the day after we always saw more trucks; let's be realistic, they knew this desert a lot better than we did. The curious Nissan trucks on our horizon made for a tough call, however, if one of my gunners acquired one in his sights. Does he blast him? Our Rules of Engagement, or ROE, allowed us to fire only in self-defense, but an enemy scout's eyes and radio are also weapons. A truck in the distance could have been an Iraqi recon patrol calling in our position or an innocent, curious Saudi Arabian or Bedouin. The ROE probably sounded simple two hundred kilometers south when some REMF — *rear echelon motherfucker* — wrote them, much less some Yale grad in the State Department.

"My platoon sergeant and I talked through several such scenarios so we could provide clear guidance to our men. First, we would observe and report all activity in our sector. Most often the trucks stayed about twenty-five hundred meters away, but if the vehicle approached within five hundred meters we would fire a machine-gun burst as a warning. If the vehicle retreated, we would report it and let our battalion scouts track him. If the vehicle kept coming, we would blast him.

"Sfc. Sikes and I also talked about the possibility of our attacking Saddam. We had been in country several weeks, and the likelihood of Iraq pressing its offensive into Saudi Arabia had lessened significantly. Our mission remained defensive, but there had already been talk among the men about our attacking Saddam. I didn't think this likely, but I wasn't home witnessing the president's resolve on CNN. Remember also, I had never imagined leaving our Fort Stewart motor pool.

"Tanks have simple missions: They attack or defend; they kill people and break things. When your ride is the most advanced direct-fire killing machine in the world, one that can travel almost fifty miles per hour and shoot accurately on the move, you don't spend much time talking about defending. To Sikes, the scenario was simple. 'Lieutenant, if we attack them, I'm blasting anything in our path that's not sand.'

"He didn't say it with bravado or malice. He said it as someone who had trained as a warrior for eighteen years and who was responsible for bringing home the men of our platoon. I had no problem with his paradigm. This might have been my first field exercise, but I knew my responsibilities: mission first and men always. Still, with all the hustle and bustle of deploying and then occupying in the desert, I hadn't thought a lot about shooting and being shot at. Now that things had settled down, I guess I became a little more introspective.

"As early as mid-September, as more soldiers arrived in theater daily, I had begun to wonder after President Bush's plan. The men referred to attacking Saddam as 'going north.' I didn't believe we would go north, though if we did, I knew exactly what my responsibilities would be. The written mission of the armor branch is *to destroy the enemy using fire, maneuver, and shock effect.* Put into Sikes's language: Blast everything in our path and bring these guys home.

"Our first month in the desert was over. We had beaten the desert; it was time to prepare ourselves to meet and beat Saddam. Whether that day would come I did not know, but I knew we weren't ready. I had work to do. I had to grow up, learn my job, and bring my men home."

■ To talk about sand in America conjures the texture of a beach. The desert sand at our screen line position with the Cav was rock and dust. The dust clung, you felt it weigh you down and fight your efforts to pick up your feet to walk. Trudging the one hundred meters between tanks, loaded with gas mask, a .45, rounds, flak jacket, helmet, water bottle, and other gear, was exhausting.

The wind against the camouflage nets snapped the fiberglass support poles, and so we became increasingly accomplished at keeping the nets over the tanks with fewer and fewer long poles, and more and more short ones. Though enemy spotters would have had no trouble seeing the green nets, the nets at least disguised the type, even the presence, of equipment beneath. The dry air gave some of us regular nosebleeds. Windstorms that we called *shamals* drove us into a huddle against the lee side of the tank, where we covered ourselves in bandannas, hats, and blankets to fight off sand. We battled flies constantly, using empty plastic water bottles as swatters. I became an ace my first day. More than once I wrote home about my imperiled sanity; the flies drove us all a little crazy.

Camels ambled by sporadically. We assumed them wild: They moved untended, single file through the desert in groups of ten to twenty. Having no shoulders, a camel is so thin that it seems two-dimensional and verily disappears when it faces you; a pack of camels in single file is also two-dimensional. At least one albino per herd.

Scarab beetles, spiders, scorpions, and ticks shared our spot of earth, as did horned snakes we called sand vipers.

In mid-September I read an article in *Stars and Stripes* describing the deployed lifestyles of the 82d and 101st Airborne Divisions, the other two divisions in Eighteenth Airborne Corps. The first paper I had seen since deployment, it reported that the other two divisions enjoyed air-conditioned buildings, free cold drinks, movies, and popcorn. I never saw this purported luxury, but the paper made it sound as if those elite light-division combat soldiers might as well have been sailors living on floating apartment complexes.[17] Our 24th Mechanized lived in the desert because we could hardly defend Saudi Arabia from an attack by sitting in motor pools over three hundred kilometers from the Iraqi-held Kuwaiti border and the enemy's avenues of approach. Our tanks and Bradleys had to be where theirs might dare go — which happened to be in the middle of nowhere.

I immediately wrote home to correct any false impressions of life in what Delta Mech's Lt. Wayne Seal called "The 24th Dimension: the division in need of an enema." We still expected to live on an entirely MRE diet for another two weeks, after which we might taste one hot meal a day. These T-Rations, or "T-Rats," were frozen dinners for twenty prepared by dropping the sealed tin in a pot of boiling water. We lived on our tanks in the dappled shade provided by the camouflage netting. We ate, slept, wrote letters, swatted flies, played chess or cards (everyone wanted a piece of the LT), joked, bathed, swatted flies, listened to music on headphones, sweated, drank water, swatted flies, shaved, cleaned our weapons, swatted flies, and bitched, either on our tanks or within the radius of the gun tube. Some of my soldiers shot dice. By swinging the gun tube to one side of the tank, we could create shade on that side by throwing a tarp over the tube and on the other side beneath the overhanging rear of the turret.

It is a cliché among grunts — infantry soldiers — that tankers avoid the ground like the plague. With its sleek, flat design, the M1 Abrams tank's surface area could likely sleep ten soldiers more or less comfortably. Soldiers woken up by their bladders in the middle of the night often relieved themselves off the side of the tank, a practice discouraged for hygiene. In cold weather the back deck remained warm throughout the night from the day's operation of the tank's turbine engine, so we would gather there like homeless on city grates. We could also use the engine exhaust's back grill both to dry wet clothing and blankets and to heat food and water, a practice discouraged for reasons of fuel conservation and noise discipline. At any given time two of my four tanks' interior heaters worked, though the contortion required to sleep inside the turret demanded miserable weather and utter exhaustion. The heater system leeched fuel and its constant rattle owned the turret, preventing a soldier inside from detecting any exterior sound, so its use too was discouraged.

On 21 September I saw my first Arabian cloud, hanging like a shred of white cotton candy, seemingly in arm's reach as I walked across the road to meet with my Delta Mech commander, Captain Baillergeon. I experienced my first Arabian rain four days later. We would back the tanks out from under the nets at night to prevent scorpions, spiders, and other night crawlers from climbing the nets and dropping on us. That morning I walked under the net to guide the tank in for the day, and the condensation from the night before dripped on my head. My crew joined me for a modest sprinkle and a laugh under the net.

After the initial threat of a preemptive ground attack by Hussein, our primary security concerns were SCUD missiles, Iraq's long-range ballistic missiles capable of delivering chemical or biological warfare agents; Iraqi special forces working in Arab garb; and Bedouins. The Bedouins had been a hot issue during predeployment briefings at Fort Stewart. They did not recognize national sovereignty; they belonged to their tribes and lived as they had been living for thousands of years. The diamond-shaped neutral zone between Iraq and Saudi, I was told, existed as a passage lane across the border for the nomads. They did not speak English, would consider any encroachment on their temporary ground as cause for a violent response, and were said to survive by traditional tribal warfare methods of thieving and murdering.

My platoon began with 50 percent security: two men alert per tank at all times during the night. The company headquarters section conducted hourly radio checks with the three line platoons to ensure we hadn't fallen asleep on watch. For the threat of SCUD-delivered chemical agents, we deployed two chemical detection alarms for each platoon. After a few days I reduced security to 25 percent with one tank per section at the ready, turret power on, and scanning. A tank platoon is organized into two sections of two tanks, led by the platoon leader and platoon sergeant. The platoon leader uses this sectional organization to control platoon fire and movement. In the offense, for example, one section may move while the other provides covering fire. The other tank in a section is called the wingman — a concept popularized in such aerial warfare movies as *Top Gun*. The wing tank guides his movement and fires off his lead tank. In defensive positions, sectors of responsibility for scanning and firing are often assigned by section. These sectors overlap to ensure no enemy vehicles eke through the crack between the sections' scanned areas. My platoon's defensive plan was to engage the enemy in cross fires by having each section cover the area in front of the other. This guaranteed overlapping fires and gave gunners shots at the vulnerable side of an attacking vehicle instead of its heavily armored and sloped front.

On 13 September, Captain Baillergeon began having his platoon leaders submit schedules. We were to sleep from 1000–1700 hours and fill the remaining seventeen hours of the day with maintenance and training. I objected. We simply could not sleep from 1000 to 1700 — the heat was too intense. Even the Saudis at the gas station laughed when they heard of our plan to sleep during the day. Baillergeon eventually signed off on my platoon schedule, of training and working in the morning and evening, with some late night training.

Because of our limited ability to do maneuver training, I focused on cross-training my crews to ensure that tank crewmen learned the basics of all four tank positions. Cross-training allowed the soldiers to train one another, sometimes privates teaching sergeants; it bolstered each man's confidence, reinforced his knowledge, and increased each crew's ability to communicate and work as a team. And in combat, soldiers would often have to do another's job. We also cross-trained with Lt. Brian Luke's infantry platoon and with the artillery fire support team assigned to the company. The fire support officer (FSO) in charge of the team was 2d Lt. Bill Lockard. After the war, Bill coauthored an article for other artillerymen on what they had learned as FSOs for maneuver companies. They describe training their host unit's grunts and tankers to call for artillery fire by tracing a map "grid system on the ground. Then we simulated artillery rounds by throwing rocks at various 'targets.' We complemented this training by using AN/PRC-77 radios to give the soldier the feeling of talking to a fire direction center." I vaguely remember participating in such field-expedient training with Bill and his team.[18]

A few times the company's officers conducted reconnaissance, first of the quarry area behind us, which would serve as our first fallback position. We planned routes back, individual positions, and routes out. I later took my tank commanders on a recon of the position. The quarry was a beautiful defensive position, the high ground commanding the flat area, though not so high that an enemy, from a map reconnaissance, would target it for preparatory artillery. Its scraped pits made for excellent dug-in individual tank positions, and its hard, rocky contours provided cover and concealment from artillery and for our escape route (though we would have to have planned our withdrawal carefully, and executed it swiftly, else get trapped in the quarry as the enemy bypassed us down the road). I would like to have defended a training mission there.

We also reconnoitered an alternative position in a flat, dusty area south of Nu'ayriyah. We planted engineer stakes to mark vehicle positions and hoped we would never have to move the platoons to this unfamiliar place to defend such a wide-open, infinitely flankable position. In places between the intersection where we lived and Nu'ayriyah, the Trans-Arabian Pipeline (which Tapline Road paralleled) emerged from the ground and ran on supports several feet aboveground. The pipeline had tactical implications for us. It potentially restricted Iraqi movement. And we wondered what might happen if either side launched a few high-explosive rounds into the enormous oil pipe. Mostly, though, I remember fighting the boredom and pulling maintenance on the tanks.

The Cav squadron had a show-of-force defensive mission. The idea: Let Hussein see an armored American unit that far forward, with M1 tanks, and make him size us at least as a regiment if not a division. For the first weeks, my four tanks constituted this division-sized fleet. Actually my two or three, since beginning around 8 September I had at least one and often two tanks back at the Cav's squadron maintenance area. At some point another tank platoon joined the Cav, which we discovered when it got lost one day and drove through our position from the northwest. Imagine our reaction when we heard tanks coming, saw the dust signature their tracks threw up, *from the direction of Kuwait,* before we saw the tanks (though we could all identify an Abrams and a Bradley by sound).

Around 8 September a Saudi unit and elements of our 101st Airborne (Air Assault) Infantry Division assumed positions north of us. No longer the most forward unit, we remained the most forward armored unit and continued our screen line, show-of-force mission.

We did several things to deceive the Iraqis about our size. First, we maneuvered. Not extensively, because of maintenance worries, but the company's three platoons moved, kicked up dust, made themselves known. I think the company-team's two Bradley platoons did more of this than my platoon, since the all-Bradley Cav squadron had trouble supporting even our tanks' most mild maintenance problems. Not that the Bradleys didn't have maintenance worries: Lt. Brian Luke's First Platoon blamed their deadlined vehicles on "Frankie," the ghost of an Arab skeleton they had unearthed.

The division also sent a Humvee around with a speaker mounted in its bed that blared sounds of heavy-tracked vehicle movement. And on 23 September, the company emplaced four decoy tanks, flat screen, life-sized, photographic silhouettes of a tank's front, supported by a grid of plastic poles. Like the Mona Lisa's eyes, the gaze of its gun followed the viewer. We erected camouflage nets over and behind the decoys and spread some trash around them. At night we drove a tank around them to make tracks; during the day, soldiers from the headquarters' platoon hung around them, posing. Hard as hell to make those things not look like tank gunnery targets. We also incorporated the decoy unit into our radio transmissions. Standard radio call signs are Red, White, and Blue for First, Second, and Third Platoons, respectively, though 3–15 calls attached tank platoons Gold. Since I was Gold Six, we called the decoy unit Silver. The infantry company's first sergeant gave that fictional platoon leader a molasses of a southern accent. I did my best to invent my contemporary, Silver Six (inspired by the *M*A*S*H* episode in which Hawkeye and B. J. invent Captain Tuttle), but no one else felt like playing. I got as far as making Silver Six a graduated cadet from Texas A&M.

The arrival of Silver Six was a nice morale boost. The soldiers had fun — each platoon set up one decoy tank, and I let my most excited soldiers and junior sergeants choose the position of ours and build it. Sports also helped. We played stickball (a version of softball using a ball made of tape and an ax handle as bat) and football. Haircuts, too, proved a boost, especially when one of my sergeants had me in his "chair," and I let him buzz the lieutenant's head. The platoon gathered around, taking pictures, laughing at my expense.

Trips to the store at the intersection were more problematic. Initially these were forbidden, yet my platoon began to pester me after catching wind that one of the company's infantry platoon leaders had several times led a group of his soldiers on dismounted patrols to the store. A classic leader quandary: allow the trip and you become either rebel hero bucking the commander or weak lieutenant giving in; refuse the soldiers and become either weak lieutenant without the balls to buck the commander or strong lieutenant holding firm. I chose the latter, though soon enough occasional trips were authorized. Captain Baillergeon may well have been bucking his commander; I do not know. At the store we bought soda, pita bread (to save our palates from the MRE meat), and hygiene products. These trips supplemented the rare visits of an army goodies truck.

On 13 September, three of my privates were taken to the town of Qabar to spend twenty-four hours with American families working in the oil industry. Twenty-four hours of phones, cooked food, showers, T.V., and A.C. They left at 0530. That afternoon I was sitting on the tank's front slope, my back against the glacis, when my gunner Sergeant Dock tapped my foot. "Sir, what's that?" A four-wheeler had materialized from the desert. It parked beside my tank, and two civilian men popped out, Dick Schneider and Tom H-something. They worked for ARAMCO, a joint Saudi-American oil refinery. Dick had lived in Saudi thirteen years. They had been driving around the desert since before daylight, stopping at any units they saw. They gave us sodas, snacks, and ice, and took Polaroids. A second ARAMCO group showed up on the twentieth; this group had a woman and so was a huge hit. A lone man came the next day, passing out books. A third group that afternoon. Another bunch came on the twenty-seventh with two women, causing Dock to scamper for his razor and my driver Vanderwerker to bemoan an untimely zit. Our most attractive female visitor was an army Medevac UH-60 Blackhawk pilot who touched her bird down one scorching afternoon to drop off ice-cold water: thick, wavy brown hair, dark eyes, a face both strong and soft, her figure accented by the snuggly gripping flight suit — there's something about a woman in a flight suit.

The civilians visited on Thursdays and Fridays, the days of the Saudi weekend. One group came the morning of 4 October with grills and cooked marinated meat and omelets. They also brought softballs, gloves, bats, and bases, and played with us. Three people from the second ARAMCO group — including the woman — also dropped by but did not stay long. One of the men had called my girlfriend, Maria, to tell her I was okay and had fallen for her after hearing her voice. Driving away, he shouted he would marry her himself, since "in Saudi we can have more than one wife!" They also brought McBryde, my loader, word of his son's birth on 28 September. Sean James, eight-pounds-something. His third child. McBryde was twenty-five, I believe; a black man, bright, with a baby face, he hated the army because it opposed his gentle nature but had signed up at a time in his life when he felt directionless. He and I understood each other, and in that longest month when I had no friends nearby, no fellow lieutenants with whom I could commiserate, when I had always to be the lieutenant, I was grateful to have someone on my tank with whom I could share my feelings by a glance. With the news of his new son he spent the next few days understandably happy and demonstratively sad.

The rest of us had our low moments as well, as a platoon and as individuals. The first ARAMCO civilians could not have come at a better time. Morale had bottomed out. Mail had been incoming for four days, but several soldiers had received nothing. Sergeant Freight's wingman refused to keep his tank crew in uniform, and at night the crew neither made its nightly radio checks nor monitored the radio; to stay awake they had hooked a Walkman portable radio up to the external speaker of the tank's radio. Over some childish Kool-Aid dispute the day before, one private would not speak with anyone on his tank except the other private. And that night I had chastised two of my gunners over the radio. They were chewing up the company radio net, gabbing about the dinner and mail they were anticipating, when I stepped in and yelled them off the radio. One of them became pissy and decided not to speak with me even after I apologized, which I should not have done.

No mail that night took an additional toll. The next afternoon I was sitting on the tank's front slope, my back against the glacis, considering how I might report to Captain Baillergeon and ask to be relieved — because I felt I had lost control — when Sergeant Dock tapped my foot. "Sir, what's that?"

Thank you, Dick Schneider and Tom H-something. Thanks also to the others who visited and lightened our lives, some of whose names I have on business cards and paper scraps: Chuck Peterson, Saudi Petrochemical Company; Michael Oliver, Petromin Shell; and Mike Willis, fire chief.

I attribute the platoon's other worst moment during our time with the Cav less to ebbing spirits than erupting stress. On 16 September, Captain Baillergeon reported that Iraq had opened part of the Kuwait-Saudi border, and we expected Iraqi spies to join the Kuwaiti exodus. Around this time we also received two reports of drive-by shootings against soldiers from Arabs in a white sedan. To improve security, the platoon would construct an observation post (OP) on the forward slope of our ridge to watch our sector while keeping our tanks hidden behind the ridge. A forward-slope OP would also be less visible than one positioned near the top of the ridge, where the sandbags and the guards' bodies would break the horizon.

Sergeants Dock and Boss took charge, organizing a group of soldiers to dig a small trench, fill sandbags, and build the OP. Dock and Boss, a pair of stout, strong-shouldered men, were happiest when sweating. Building or destroying didn't matter, as long as their bodies sweated and ached. Late in the afternoon on the seventeenth, Sergeant Miller joined them. He and Boss began to argue — I guessed because they had different notions of how to work, which led to a clash when instructing the soldiers. Miller and Boss argued, then Boss pulled a knife. "Honestly, sir," Boss told me later when I asked for his side of the story, "I wanted to stick the motherfucker."

I spoke with Miller, Boss, then Freight and Rivera, and some of the witnessing soldiers, before deciding that night to remove Boss from the platoon. I called Captain Baillergeon, asked him to drive over to meet me, explained what happened, and told him my decision. I asked him to contact Captain Swisher, my commander in Bravo Tank, and pass along my request to switch Boss with a gunner from one of the company's other tank platoons. Baillergeon agreed but reminded me that Swisher or any of the three battalion commanders to whom we belonged (2-4 Cav, 3-15 Infantry, and 1-64 Armor) might insist on more formal disciplinary action.

After passing the night and the next morning hearing various pleas from my NCOs, none of which changed my mind, I explained my decision to the gathered platoon: Boss would go, and I would convey his crew's request that they go with him. I concluded with a brief speech about "driving on."

I blamed myself for the environment in which such a thing might happen. Part of me also felt good. I had made a hard decision, and the platoon, even those who disagreed with it, supported me. I felt the platoon's respect. I was in charge, the soldiers trusted me and followed my command. The next time I felt anything similar and so powerful was in battle five months later, when my platoon reacted to my maneuvers and commands without hesitation and with absolute confidence.

Then the army stole my thunder. The next day the 2-4 Cav squadron commander demanded written statements. Several days later Captain Baillergeon reported that the commander had passed the situation to either Barrett or Gordon, whoever had punitive jurisdiction. There may have been some confusion about which battalion had jurisdiction. Nearly three weeks after the incident, when Delta Mech was reattached to Task Force 3-15, nothing had happened.

I wonder now, for the first time since the event nearly six years ago, if, had I been there, not as the leader, but just there, helping dig sand and fill sandbags, my presence would have prevented the event.

A week and a half after the incident, the Cav squadron commander summoned me to his daily command and staff meeting. Riding to the meeting in the back of a cargo Humvee, I suspected that he either wanted to speak with me about the incident or to tell me bad news about my grandfather, who had suffered several strokes and could no longer speak. Why else would the squadron commander send for me? Because, it turned out, he wanted to scream at me — this silver-haired man who towered above me, whose face turned artery red as he "spoke" — because my soldiers with their broken tank at the UMCP were not staying in complete uniform — despite the fact that I had no means of visiting and supervising my soldiers at the UMCP, located several kilometers to the rear and in the squadron maintenance officer's charge. Not that I would have required my crew to wear helmet, LBE, mask, weapon, and ten-pound flak vest while manhandling a several-hundred-pound tank track in the afternoon desert sun anyway. But I know, and half knew at the time, that in fancying some dire news about my grandfather, my melodramatic imagination was simply reaching for a way home.

■ The 3d Armored Cavalry Regiment out of Fort Bliss, Texas, relieved 2-4 Cav on 6 October. In the preceding days we had watched as the regiment's vehicles on HETs crossed our front on Tapline Road, and I couldn't help but think of Tom Sands and Bob Notch, two good friends from West Point serving in the 3d ACR. Once again Delta Mech loaded our vehicles on HETs, our soldiers on Saudi double-deckers, this time to rejoin Task Force 3-15 in an encampment just southeast of As Sarrar. Before leaving that day, at our last LOGPAC with the Cav, we received our first free cigarette packs: *Camels.* I can still see the bemused face of the Pentagon supply officer who chose that brand.

Nine days earlier, I had taken my tank to 2-4's TOC as part of a static demonstration for the secretary of the army, the Honorable Michael P. W. Stone. Before the secretary arrived, we received a briefing by the squadron's command sergeant major. He reported that because of our fame at the Pentagon, the squadron — known as Task Force Pope, after its commander — was the only unit smaller than a division visited by the secretary. It seems the Pentagon had fully expected Iraq to attack within forty-eight hours of our arrival at the screen line after the nine-hour bus ride; someone at the Pentagon had assigned the squadron a 1:150 chance of success. I don't know how they defined the term. The sergeant major believed that Iraq had not attacked those first forty-eight hours because the squadron had fooled Hussein into believing it was a division, a unit some twenty times its own size.

Regardless of the accuracy of the sergeant major's evaluation, Hussein had not attacked; we had survived him, the desert, and ourselves, and our immediate future promised to be a bit more civilized.

2

Desert Shield, Part 2
October 1990 through 16 January 1991

> We are in for the long haul. Guard against building any false expectations by your soldiers.
> — Maj. Gen. Barry McCaffrey, Commanding General's Note No. 1,
>   12 September 1990

Assembly Area (AA) Hinesville: Our New Home

As additional units rolled into the desert to bolster the defense of Saudi Arabia, the 24th Infantry Division shifted its positions to make room. On 26 September 1990, according to Dave Trybula, leaders from Task Force 1-64 Armor reconnoitered new positions to the north of AA Augusta, around the town of As Sarrar.

The company commander and all three platoon leaders in Charlie Tank went on the recon. But with only one Humvee allowed for each company, Dave recalls, "the platoon leaders rode in the back of an open-top cargo Humvee. Even with our sleeves down, the sun still managed to find flesh to burn around our hands and faces. It was the hottest day yet. We drank water continuously for the two-hour ride. As we rode north, the desert changed from the vast empty sand dunes without relief, to terrain with mountains, wadis, cliffs, towns, and farms. I was shocked to see bright green crops, in perfect circles, in the middle of the desert. One of the other lieutenants explained how the farmers used center pivot irrigators to water their plants; at the edge of the irrigated circular area, the desert abruptly resumed.

"The homes and buildings of the towns we passed through were almost all one story cinder-block structures. Nobody was out during the day. Most houses had several trucks and a couple of cars. Acres of heaped and strewn trash and junk. Vehicles abandoned where they had broken down. Why would anyone risk life and limb for this place?"

Rob Holmes also went on the recon. From the outskirts of As Sarrar, looking through his binoculars, he spotted an unmistakable sign of civilization: "a Coca-Cola logo on the side of a building. From about eight hundred meters, I identified a dozen camels, several Nissan pickup trucks, and Arab children dotting the rooftops, watching us. In a matter of minutes, a flock of them ran out to welcome us. Cute as they were, a reasonable level of paranoia filled us as they ran our way. For all we knew, one of them had a bomb under his robe. Their smiles allayed our concerns; these kids just couldn't be repressed. They soon surrounded us, laughing and jumping up and down."

Rob's flit of paranoia was not without cause. The Gulf War's younger generations of soldiers had grown up with the images of Vietnam tattooed over our military corneas. We had seen the movies and the television shows of preadolescent Vietnamese civilian girls throwing their bomb-strapped bodies at U.S. soldiers. And *jihad* was in the air.

"I had brought with me my tank's loader, the cocky Californian Specialist Underberg, and the Arab kids loved him. He taught them how to high five. He broke out his Walkman and played the Beach Boys for them, and passed out Jolly Ranchers candy and Wrigley's gum to his new friends. These kids might not celebrate Christmas, but they had just met the next best thing to Santa Claus.

"'Hey sir, I'm just doing a little PR with the rags,' Underberg cackled. He reached into our Humvee and pulled out a Frisbee. The whole flock of them chased it as it sailed over the sand.

"It wasn't long before the city fathers came walking our way. The ranking officer on site, Maj. Jim Diehl, walked over to meet them. Major Diehl, our battalion operations officer, had finished sixteenth in his class at West Point. He was a large man with rusty red hair and a dry, caustic wit. As the operations officer, he was always on the move making the battalion's business happen, so we were familiar with the sand mask caked on Diehl's face, neck, and hands, and on those huge, sepia-tinted goggles he wore. He looked like a character from the movie *Road Warrior*. His brief meeting with the city fathers broke up, and he strolled to my Humvee.

"'Hey, sir, what'd they have to say?' Underberg asked the major before I could greet him. Underberg had been on his battalion commander's tank crew in Germany. Soldiers don't fall into the battalion commander's track by accident, and having been around a lieutenant colonel, Underberg wasn't one bit shy in front of a major.

"'*Hey, sir?*' Major Diehl repeated sarcastically. '*Hey, troop*, do you think I know how to speak their language?' He looked my way. 'Holmes, this clown belong to you?'

"Underberg had his Walkman hooked to his pistol belt, the headphones slung around his neck. He was twirling the Frisbee in one hand and holding a Mountain Dew in the other — I had no idea where the drink had come from. It wasn't like we had stopped at a Seven-Eleven.

"'Sir, this is Specialist Underberg. He just joined us from Germany,' I answered.

"'He looks like he just came from Malibu,' Major Diehl retorted, sticking up his nose.

"'Pismo Beach, sir. You're not far off.' Underberg was enjoying his new officer friend.

"'What do you think of Saudi Arabia, soldier?' Diehl asked.

"'It's okay, but it doesn't have any waves, bikinis, or beer, so I'm not sure how long we should hang with this scene,' Underberg quipped. I had to smile.

"Back in our Humvee, we followed Major Diehl and surveyed the outskirts of As Sarrar. The town straddled a two-lane north-south road. An oasis with green trees, flowers, and running water, just like in the movies, disrupted the horizon about three kilometers to the east. Between the road and this little Eden, the sand was soft, with a darker complexion from absorbed moisture. A *septka*. Even our light Humvees made deep tracks, so we knew this was not a place to drive tanks. To the town's west a wadi complex rose up into a hilly, solid range that also ran north-south, parallel to the road. In the north the terrain was open, but the range on the west and the soft sand to the east channeled southbound traffic down the road through As Sarrar.

"Our reason for moving here was now very clear. If Saddam attacked south, this road offered a major avenue of approach. Bounded by the range to the west and the soft sand to the east, 1-64 Armor could construct a beautiful engagement area, or kill sack, with intersecting direct fires and indirect fire. If the Iraqis traveled south down the road, we could massacre them.

"Major Diehl told us that this would be home 'for a while.' His tone suggested a very long time. We camped that evening hidden in the wadis beneath the range to the west. The rest of the battalion would arrive the next day. Delta Tank would occupy a company assembly area tucked in this range, overlooking the wadis. Our new home had a beautiful view of As Sarrar and the oasis on the far side. We were several hundred feet above the desert floor and would wake each morning looking east across the desert at a spectacular sunrise.

"At the conclusion of the advance mission, Underberg and I fell asleep listening to the lingering whisper of 'Little Surfer Girl.'"

■ After the recon, most of the other officers returned to Assembly Area Augusta to bring the task force forward. Explains Dave, "This meant another HET and bus operation. As we consolidated to load the tanks on the HETs, a shot rang out. One of the guards from the forward supply battalion had failed to clear his M16 after going off duty during the night and managed to shoot himself. Fortunately, he was quickly attended to and not seriously injured." Throughout Desert Shield, movements with non-American HETs caused small nightmares. Rob Holmes remembers other incidents: "almost drawing my .45 on an Arab HET driver because the SOB didn't want to drive any farther, somebody's tank crew having to fix the engine on a HET, and somebody almost flipping a tank off a HET because the driver and TC had never loaded one before."

Task Force 1-64's tanks downloaded from the HETs on the northern outskirts of As Sarrar, Saudi Arabia, in an area its company officers nicknamed the "Pet Cemetery" for its litter of goat and camel carcasses. During the downloading, some of the officers sneaked across the road to an Arab food stand where they ate chicken and rice while the locals toked on a *hookah* pipe.

The remains of a camel marked the site where Rob's company, Delta Tank, made its home. Someone named the dead camel *Elvis;* the company assembly area was thus dubbed *Graceland.*

By 1640 hours on 29 September, Second Brigade had closed on its new home, AA Hinesville, an area encompassing the town of As Sarrar. The brigade named its assembly area after the small Georgia town outside Fort Stewart's main gate. Because of poor HET availability and road restrictions, the 140-kilometer move had taken seven days.[1] Task Force 1-64 Armor set up to the west of As Sarrar; south of town, Task Force 3-15 Infantry straddled the north-south road into Sarrar. The 24th Infantry Division's main tactical headquarters, DMAIN, sat atop a large flat hill — a small mountain, or *jebel* — in 3-15's area. For the move to Hinesville, the brigade completed task organization by swapping Neal Creighton's Alpha Tank for 3-15's Charlie Mech. Each battalion task force now had two tank companies and two Bradley companies. Neal and I were attached to 3-15 Infantry, while Rob, Greg, and Dave remained in 1-64 Armor.

Downloading my tanks from the HETs after the trip from the 2-4 Cav screen line on 6 October, I saw my first face from Bravo Tank. First Lt. Greg Jackson, the company executive officer, was peering out from the commander's Humvee. I beamed. As a new platoon leader at Fort Stewart, I had clung to Greg's experience and maturity. First lieutenants enjoy a position of privilege in a battalion. Having spent eighteen to twenty-four months as a second lieutenant and line company platoon leader, they have learned the business of taking care of troops and fighting the enemy. Enlisted soldiers and higher ranking officers grant them a respect not given to the untested "butterbar" second lieutenant. Captains treat first lieutenants nearly as peers; indeed, a company commander's second in command and primary adviser is his executive officer, a first lieutenant; the

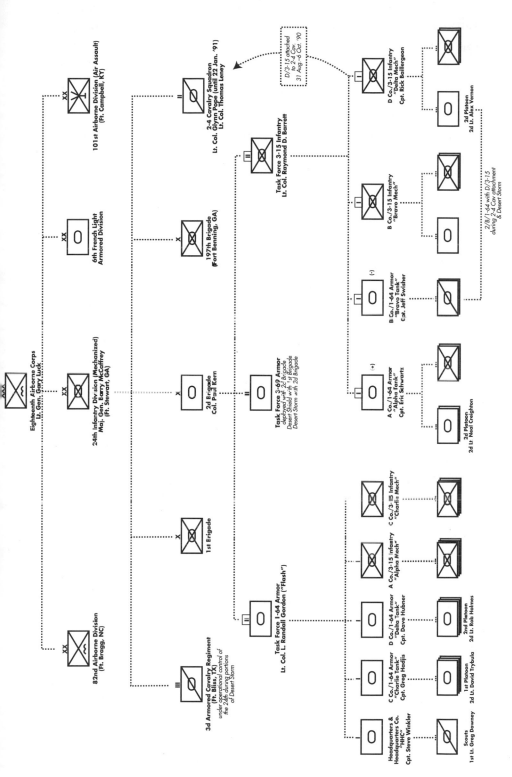

Organizational Chart, Eighteenth Airborne Corps

battalion's critical specialty platoons are commanded by first lieutenants; many captain slots on battalion headquarters staff are held by first lieutenants; and having been platoon leaders for up to two years, first lieutenants have generally spent more time in the battalion than any of its other officers.

At West Point, Greg Jackson's deep, resonant voice had earned him a spot as a parade announcer. During cadet parades, he addressed the audience over loudspeakers, giving them information, instructing them when to sit and stand, and naming the companies, their commanders and the commanders' hometowns as they passed the reviewing stand. His voice seemed tuned to some biofrequency in me; his talking calmed me. When at the HET site I saw Greg's grinning face, when he spoke my name, I wanted to hug him. I settled for a handshake and a pat on the back. I had never in my life been so happy to see a person.

The next day my platoon rejoined Bravo Tank. The 3-15 commander, Lt. Col. Raymond Barrett, had decided that logistic and training operations would be much more efficiently conducted in pure units — though living with the unit with which we were to fight would have had its advantages: my tankers and Delta Mech's grunts would get to know one another, and the company would learn to better logistically support tanks as the battalion learned to support mixed companies (God forbid a Bradley mechanic learn a thing or two about an M1). That evening Captain Swisher, my Bravo Tank company commander, walked my platoon position with me. He assured me that he would resolve the Miller-Boss knife incident promptly. Then he told me he had heard great things about my platoon during its time with the Cav; he would square me against any platoon leader in the brigade as the best. I thought he exaggerated, as he had no firsthand knowledge of my performance and so was in no position to judge. Thinking back, I should have savored those remarks; they are the last deeply encouraging, personal words I recall Captain Swisher tendering me. He was a good man and a good commander, but like a lot of soldiers, he had trouble articulating anything beyond accomplishing the mission. A few days later he had me personally count every piece of ammunition in my platoon: some 45,600 rounds of 7.62 mm; 1,600 rounds of .50 caliber; 268 rounds of .45 caliber; and 220 main gun 105-mm rounds. The task occupied my entire day and would be repeated monthly.

The terrain of Assembly Area Hinesville was much rougher than the terrain on the Cav screen line. There you could see for kilometers, sometimes tens of kilometers. Here, there was more high ground — more plateaus, rises and ridges, small jebels, and cliffs. More severe slopes, wadis, and rocky berms (none of which appeared on the map) broke the low ground. You could drive by a entire company area not ten meters away, on the other side of a rise, and not notice it. The area reminded me of some parts of the National Training Center in the Mojave Desert, where I had fought my tank in a number of wadi dogfights.

The number of high-terrain features eased general navigation, as you could locate yourself on a map relative to these easily identified masses. Finding your way on the smaller scale proved more difficult. Sometimes the wadis and the berms hid the high features; it was easy to get turned around in the broken terrain.

When my platoon rejoined Bravo Tank on 7 October, the company had already occupied its position for nearly a week. Bravo Tank's spot of desert was, like the brigade's assembly area, also called Hinesville. The company's three tank platoons formed a large circle around the area, with the headquarters platoon — the commander, XO, and their tank crews, and the first sergeant, the Humvee drivers, the mechanics, and the medics — encamped in the center. On my platoon's arrival, the company had three latrines, a handful of small Arabic tents, and a cot for every soldier. The latrines were of the two-seater, plywood and mesh variety we had used back at the port's Tent City. Before the latrines (and later, when we abandoned Hinesville), we made do behind rocks and sometimes bushes, with shovel and toilet paper. Dave's Charlie Tank platoon had at first dug a slit trench, but its walls tended to cave in while being used. Once the company commander got his Humvee stuck in the trench, much to his displeasure.

At Hinesville, each Bravo Tank platoon had one latrine to use and maintain. Daily, two soldiers pulled the metal buckets out from under the latrines and burned the waste, stirring as it burned. Third Platoon decorated its latrine's interior with pictures cut from magazines more raw than *Penthouse*. My soldiers had higher standards. They covered our latrine's walls with enemy vehicle identification training posters as well as tasteful *Playboy* clippings.

The three platoons also had one small Arab tent per tank. Approximately ten square feet, they were made of a white fabric exterior with a color patchwork pattern inside. A lot of orange. The tents blocked enough of the cooling desert breeze to diminish the effect of their shade without blocking much of the sand. My platoon chose to erect the tents separately, one per tank crew; other platoons used all four tents to make a single large platoon tent. Initially my crew joined me in our tent, though it did not take long for them to move back to the tank and its camouflage net. So for the first time, for a brief time — mid- to late October — I had some private space.

Greg Downey's scout platoon did not receive enough cots in the initial October issue for everyone. "I had learned long ago that a leader does not accept any luxury until every soldier in the platoon has been taken care of. I lived by that rule and did not receive a cot until mid-November. Besides, I had grown accustomed to sleeping on the vehicle, close to the radios where I could stay abreast of any information."

We received army tents on 24 November, one General Purpose Medium tent per platoon. I heard a rumor claiming that the U.S. Government had been leasing the Arab tents and was in a rush to return them to save money. Rob Holmes believes we received the tents to combat the "drastic change in weather. It got bitter cold at night, even down in the teens, and pretty brisk even during the day." My company's XO, Greg Jackson, received a GP Small and suggested all the company lieutenants live together — himself, the platoon leaders, and the attached artillery fire support officer. The other platoon leaders and I appreciated the offer but promptly and unanimously declined. We belonged with our platoons.

The single army tent gave the platoon less room than the four Arab tents, so each of us had less space and privacy. My space was my army cot and the area underneath it, on the sand, where I stashed my books, papers, and the foodstuffs sent from home. When my cot didn't have me on it, it lay with sleeping bag open for airing out — no way to wash it in the desert, its odor gathering over the months — and a small travel pillow at the head. I replaced the pillowcase monthly as it turned from white to brown. I remember times sitting on my cot, leaning over to tie or untie my boots, smelling myself.

Something was always happening in the tent. A radio or cassette player playing; a card game; a ribbing; a row; a belching or farting contest; at night, the changing of the guards. My Walkman cassette player helped, but I missed silence. Sometimes I loitered alone on my tank, sometimes I found a rock just on the company area boundary where I could put the others behind me and enjoy the desert breeze and the desert calm.

Rob's platoon didn't take to tent living and returned to their tanks. The night of the first rain, in late November, it was about thirty degrees. Rob describes having "three blankets around me and was reasonably warm as I drifted off. Contentment and tranquillity never last in the field. I woke in disbelief as rain poured down. My blankets were soaked. My crew scrambled inside the tank and closed the hatches.

"All three of us in the turret were freezing, wet, and almost naked. We yelled down to Bell in the driver's hatch to turn on the heater. Within minutes, hot air was blasting throughout the turret. Unfortunately for Bell, the driver sits right next to the heater vent. He was getting fried in his compartment. Once the three of us in the turret were warm, we told Bell to kill the heater.

"Now I had another problem. The hot air inside the turret was making water condense on my cold steel hatch. Icy cold droplets began dripping on my naked neck and back. It wasn't long before this drove me crazy. I popped my hatch open to let some hot air out and check the weather. Bad decision: I got a bucketful of rain and was soaked and freezing again in a matter of seconds. I yelled down to Bell to turn on the damn heater again.

"The cycle continued throughout the night: cold, hot, Saudi water torture, and cold again. Needless to say, we all spent the next week with head and chest colds."

Bravo Tank's company dining area underwent the most marked evolution. It began as the area outside the first sergeant's white Arab tent where our daily hot meal was served. Soldiers carried their meals elsewhere, usually to their tanks, to eat their by-then sand-covered meals. The lieutenants sometimes dined on the hood of Captain Swisher's Humvee, he and the first sergeant eating with us as they were inclined. Sergeants Miller and Boss, as their disciplinary extra duty for the knife fight they nearly had filling sandbags, built a low, L-shaped table of sandbags, with seats of three to four sandbags on either side. Miller and Boss joked about the irony of their bonding over this sandbag chore. I did not believe them, not completely. On 1 December we received plywood picnic tables with metal legs, which we covered with a camouflage net. The tables kept plates from falling off the sandbags to the ground, their height kept sand off the food, and they gave a convenient place for meeting, working, writing home, playing, or talking. Finally, some industrious soldier built a mailbox from spare wood, painting it red and blue to look like the real McCoy. It stood outside Top's tent. Letters fell into the orange postal bag inside.

About the same time as the delivery of the GP Mediums, each platoon received a gas stove. Greg Downey calls the tents and potbelly stoves "an early Christmas present. Having a roof over our heads during the cold, blustery nights was a luxury. After living in the desert for the last four months, it seemed like the Hilton." My men rigged our stove to fit inside the fiberglass water tank atop our platoon shower. Hot showers meant more to us that an unevenly heated, flammable tent. Some of the headquarters soldiers used our shower, and we let them go first, to use the scorching water in direct contact with the stove at the tank's bottom. Water and fuel trucks from battalion visited daily to top off our tanks, showers, water buffalo, and stoves.

But the hot shower luxury was late in coming and did not last. We conducted a lot of training in December away from the company area, then in early January we broke camp to move in preparation for the offensive into Iraq. We had the wooden showers for maybe a month before the gas heaters arrived. The showers were as crudely constructed as the latrines: a two-by-four frame and plywood walls, mounted on a slotted pallet floor. Before and after the showers, and during all training away from them, we took bitch baths, or whore baths, which — whatever the person's preferred variation — involved standing buck naked to the universe. My tank crew helped one another. The bathing soldier stood on a tarp on the ground by the tank, and the facilitating soldier stood on the tank pouring water from a five-gallon plastic jug over the other, once to wet him down, then to rinse him off. Dave Trybula's platoon hung a canvas bucket with an oversized shower head at its bottom from the end of the gun tube; Rob Holmes and his soldiers rigged showers by punching holes in garbage bags, draping them over the gun tube, and filling them with water. "When I really needed to relax," he writes, "a shower was my relief valve. I would usually take one just after sunset when not too much was going on."

The bitch bath worked fine through October. During those first months the sun kept the jug water warm enough to bear. When the weather turned, however, showering became a more significant ordeal and a less frequent event. And how the weather turned. We spent much of November through February shivering in an unusually cold and wet Saudi winter.

Generally, though, personal hygiene did not present the severity of problems it had presented to American soldiers in other wars. The essentially dry, sterile desert did not breed the bacteria, diseases, and trenchfoot of winters in European forests and rain seasons in Southeast Asian jungles. Our clothing and gear dried quickly; when it did not, we dried it using the hot air blazing from the tank's turbine engine exhaust. I established something of a routine, showering twice a week, donning the clean uniform (we only had two sets of DCUs) and washing the nasty, just-removed one in a bucket. Dave describes "some people scrubbing their dirty clothes with soap and a brush on the tank front slope. Others washed their clothes while they showered and took them off to finish bathing themselves."

Local food proved the larger threat to our health. We did not eat this often. In camp, we usually had one hot meal a day and MREs for all other meals. Many days I only ate the hot meal, supplemented by snacks from home. Sfc. Sikes, Rob's platoon sergeant, forbade Arab food. For Rob, "after more than a month of eating dehydrated beef patty or cold corned beef hash, I would have loved some barbecue and pecan pie, but my platoon sergeant was right. These rations were critical to keeping our platoon healthy. Soldiers sometimes ventured into As Sarrar and found a little hut that served chicken dinners, rationalizing that a hot, fresh meal was good for morale. Behind these 'restaurants' chickens darted about, ready for that evening's clientele. I never saw the Arab kitchen operation, thank God. I supposed the reason Arabs don't shake hands: toilet paper doesn't exist in Saudi. Arabs use their hands and wash themselves with sand. Those little diners could not have gained FDA approval. MREs were fine by me. MRE peanut butter even came from Stone Mountain, Georgia, outside my Atlanta home. When the men complained, Sfc. Sikes answered by saying he never knew a soldier with high morale and diarrhea. They still complained, but they stayed healthy."

Those of us without the insight and discipline of Sfc. Sikes suffered for it. According to Neal Creighton, "Our first meal that did not come from an airtight plastic brown bar or a tin can" had come from the Saudi government. The meal's lettuce was for Greg Downey. "The most attractive item served. It was the first green vegetable I had seen since leaving Fort Stewart in August. I devoured it as if there were no tomorrow."

All five Bravo Tank officers and half the company's soldiers went down from the bad lettuce, bad chicken, or the bad ice from nonpotable water. I don't know that anyone ever determined the cause. I woke the morning of 25 October feeling ill and weak and spent much of the morning on the toilet. Shortly after our arrival at the battalion's Recreation Site for our day of relaxation, I was half-carried to an ambulance, stuck with an IV, and hauled to the brigade field hospital.

I passed a delirious twenty-four hours there. The IV was pinned to the tent roof where it angled toward the ground above my head. Nurses changed it whenever its fluid ran low. The aim of the IV was to keep me hydrated and to flush the poison out of my system: Must flush now, must hydrate, must flush more now, must hydrate — the meanest cycle. Had IVs existed in Italy during the fourteenth century, Dante would surely have figured them into his *Inferno*. When I recognized that my body needed a latrine, it was too late. I would stand, unpin my IV, and work my way through the tent and up the fifty yard slope to the latrine. Twice I did not make it. When that happened, I rerouted to the shower, where I washed myself and my clothes as best I could while also managing the IV still stuck in my arm, and, dressed and dripping, returned to my cot. Repinned the IV to the tent roof. Passed out until the next time.

I remember half-hearing Neal Creighton's arrival, 1st Sergeant McKinney's flirting with one of the enlisted nurses, and one man and two women from Savannah, Georgia, civilians, passing out cookies. I don't recall their offering me any. Likely my stench kept them away. Neal and his company commander, Captain Schwartz, were both transported to the field hospital. "At the hospital I received ten bags of intravenous fluid. I lost a lot of body fluid from uncontrollable diarrhea. A scout entered the hospital tent without trousers. He had passed out from dehydration due to diarrhea and had no clue what had happened to his clothes. What a miserable experience. Never had I lost control of my body. Our stomachs were not used to the same things as the natives. A parasite had rendered Task Force 3-15 combat ineffective for days."

The food poisoning, or parasite, whatever it was, stayed longest with Greg Downey. "Twenty-four hours after consuming the meal, I fell sick. After a week, I was out of commission. Several soldiers in my scout platoon became violently ill. Sixty percent of the division was afflicted by dysentery. Some were affected worse than others. A scale at the Battalion Aid Station showed my weight had dropped from 145 to 112 pounds. I fought dysentery for seven weeks, received countless IVs, and drank gallons of water. If I could walk one hundred feet without getting dizzy, I considered it a good day."

General Defense Plan for Saudi Arabia

We are right now essentially four and a half U.S. Army divisions. We've got a Marine Division on our right flank. We've assembled the biggest artillery force I've ever seen, including in Command and General Staff or Army War College war games. The 101st Airborne Division with the 3rd ACR attached is to our front. The 1st Cavalry Division is behind us. If attacked, I will gain operational control of the 3rd ACR and defend in sector on a frontage of about 80 kilometers wide and 120 kilometers deep.

People ask me what I am concerned about. I'm not concerned about anything. We are working a whole bunch of problems and a whole bunch of issues. We didn't have any logistics infrastructure at all when we started. Now supplies and repair parts are starting to pour in. Defending Saudi Arabia is not something I wake up in the morning and worry about. If the Iraqis cross the border with six, eight, up to fourteen divisions, in my professional judgment, we would turn this into the biggest junk pile of armor ever seen in the Middle East.

— Maj. Gen. Barry McCaffrey, Oral History Interview, 24 October 1990

"Our mission," as Dave Trybula defines it, "was to deter Iraq. This meant if nothing happened, we were successful. The nothingness criteria of our success proved a hard concept to sell to the soldiers. As the 1st Cavalry Division moved into theater, we were finally able to solidify our defensive plans. Commanders and platoon leaders reconnoitered areas, picked positions, and rehearsed engagement areas. In addition to our primary defensive position around As Sarrar, we had to develop alternate and subsequent battle positions."

How we organized and trained for the GDP was, our leaders doubtless considered, how we would prepare for and fight either a defensive or offensive operation — especially given the likelihood of the division's defense turning into a counterattack. Lt. Col. Raymond Barrett, the Task Force 3-15 commander, chose to task organize by mixing armor and infantry platoons within his companies, the way most of us were accustomed to fighting our training battles. Neal's Alpha Tank, with two tank platoons and two Bradley platoons, had been assigned to lead the task force on all maneuvers. The combined arms task force inevitably places a tank company up front, to optimize the firepower, speed, armor protection, and shock effect of the first element to meet the enemy. Alpha Tank's Third Platoon leader was cross-attached to Bravo Mech, as my platoon was from Bravo Tank to Delta Mech. In Task Force 1-64, Lieutenant Colonel Gordon decided to fight pure. Keeping his armor and infantry in their separate companies he believed would maximize speed of resupply efforts and optimize company effectiveness: "I wanted thirty M1A1 tanks to deal with the enemy when the time came. I wanted the maximum number of dismounts to deal with trench clearing. The volume of fire from the two Brad companies could suppress any position while the two tank companies moved to assault."[2]

As scout platoon leader, Greg spent more time than the other lieutenants in Task Force 1-64 with Lieutenant Colonel Gordon and the battalion staff working on the General Defense Plan.

"The area of our new GDP position was not as austere as our staging area at Augusta had been and possessed a great deal of tactical advantage for whomever held it due to the high ground overlooking the lower desert plain to the north. An ideal engagement area. We were pretty confident the Iraqi army would not attack into Saudi Arabia, but if they did, we wanted the most defensible terrain possible.

"Finding great observation posts for my three scout sections was not hard. A desert plateau on the left, and flat, open terrain on the right flanked the battalion sector. The trick was figuring out how to mutually observe the entire low desert plain with my scouts in the high ground. I opted to establish OPs in depth, along the direction of attack, as opposed to in a screen line perpendicular to the attack; in doing this I hoped to pass the observation responsibility of each attacking element off to the next scout section as the enemy progressed through my sector. The in-depth deployment also gave me coverage of two main enemy avenues of approach, one on the desert floor and one coming across the higher desert. The rockier terrain of our high ground afforded each scout section OP highly survivable terrain, with excellent concealed routes in and out of the positions. I was confident we could fight and win from these OPs — if we had to fight, that is. Scouts avoid engaging in direct firefights. Often, after reporting enemy activity, we call for indirect fire (artillery and mortars) to destroy or disrupt the enemy. We engage the enemy directly only as a means of reconnaissance, as a delaying action to give the battalion time to act, or as a last resort. A scout's best weapon is his FM radio.

"The task force engagement area was flanked on the left by a steep plateau, and a large, muddy lake bed on the right flank. All the deliberate obstacles, such as mines, wire, and tank ditches, would be tied into the natural terrain obstacles, canalizing the enemy into our engagement area (though we couldn't emplace our obstacles in peaceful Saudi Arabia until Iraq attacked). Alternate battle positions were planned to react to any lateral movements of the enemy. Furthermore, a linear defense perpendicular to the direction of attack spells defeat, as it can be easily penetrated, so depth is required to kill the enemy throughout the unit's sector. At the same time, you must mass all possible weapon systems on the enemy. Lieutenant Colonel Gordon managed to build all of these considerations into our plan. When the task force GDP preparation was complete, I felt confident we could kill at least two regiments from this battle position.

"Then someone changed the plan and gave the task force an additional enemy avenue of approach to cover. Rob's commander Captain Hubner, Lieutenant Colonel Gordon, and I recon'd the new area: very channeling, without enough space for a large mechanized force. Slow-going, if traversable at all. A mechanized force on this route would be a turkey shoot for our air force and army aviation. Someone had not done his homework. Colonel Gordon took the issue to his commanders; they let him move his GDP position back north.

"The other part of our GDP was a counterattack into the flank of the enemy if they chose an avenue to the brigade's east. Although I saw the graphics for this operation, I did not truly appreciate the complexity of the movement until we rehearsed it in November."

■ I remember during our three months at AA Hinesville conducting only two or three recons of the immediate area, one recon of an area on the other side of DMAIN, and two recons of an area further south — a crescent-shaped plateau that I think was to have been a brigade alternative position, the bowl in the crescent below forming the engagement area where we would mass our fires. Out of expediency, most of these recons I did with Captain Swisher and the other Bravo Tank lieutenants instead of with Delta Mech, the company with which I would fight. And because track movement was limited for maintenance purposes, and because I had no access to the company's wheeled vehicles, only twice did my tank commanders have the opportunity to recon any of the positions.

I did not treat this defensive planning as seriously as I should have. An Iraqi offensive into Saudi Arabia no longer felt probable. I believe most other soldiers shared my opinion. Three rumored scenarios: a prolonged standoff, with another division replacing our 24th Infantry after an interval of maybe twelve months (we may or may not leave our equipment for the new unit); a prolonged standoff, the division remaining in theater while individuals rotated back to the States; or an allied offensive into Kuwait and Iraq. (Rumors about when we would return home had begun before we ever left home: in sixty days. By Christmas. In six months. Eight months. Twelve months. We eventually became desensitized to them and continued to entertain them only as another way to counter the boredom. Mary Creighton reports that it didn't take long before some frustrated stateside soul removed "Home of the 24th Infantry Division" from the Fort Stewart main gate welcome sign.)

The daily component of our defense was local security, or force protection, from Iraqi operatives infiltrating Saudi Arabia, Arabs sympathetic with Iraq, and scavenging Bedouins. Of the three, I considered the sympathetic Arabs the most probable source of danger. Iraqi operatives would more than likely only gather intelligence, and the long-ballyhooed Bedouin threat had not manifested.

Twenty-four-hour armed guards; single-strand concertina wire tied into berm walls; entrenched, sandbagged guard posts at the entrances to assembly areas; and passwords for admittance constituted the main of this self-defense effort.

Security at Bravo Tank's assembly area gradually felt less and less critical. From one soldier per tank we downgraded to one per section, and at times one per platoon. But we increased security on certain occasions: for Muslim holy days, which might bring jihad-inspired Iraqis, and when the platoons failed Captain Swisher's standards. The latter happened more than it should have. Every few nights he or the first sergeant would patrol the area, waiting to be challenged by the guard. Inevitably he found the guard asleep, smoking, tuned into a Walkman or electronic game, or otherwise not paying attention, such as when Swisher caught one of my younger soldiers with his pants down, self-involved. The company resisted Swisher because there seemed to be no real threat. Here the three Bravo Tank platoon leaders failed our commander. I know I could have more aggressively enforced the security in my platoon. And the three platoons could have worked together, testing each other's security, perhaps making a game of it. One night the company did organize a game of capture the flag, all three tank platoons and the headquarters platoon playing against one another. Captain Swisher even listed it on the weekly training schedule. The event proved great for morale, but, in the end, was just a game.

Dave Trybula describes force protection in Task Force 1-64. In addition to the guard posts and obstacles, "the task force rotated a mounted patrol mission among its companies. Mounted patrol involved a fire team of four to six soldiers and two machine guns in a Humvee checking the perimeter at irregular intervals. The final element in the task force security plan was the rapid reaction force, an assignment that rotated daily among the tank and infantry platoons. Within fifteen minutes from notification, regardless of time of day or distance to travel, the rapid reaction force had to arrive at the location specified by the alerting body. The rapid reaction force status did not release a platoon from its normal duties; it simply became an additional tasking.

"My tanks were spread out over a mile, and their crews pulling maintenance, the day in late October when we had the rapid reaction force mission and an alert came. I alerted the platoon over the radio. Everyone scrambled to retighten loose parts, return tool bags to the sponson boxes, and close track skirts. When I received word from my tank commanders that everyone was mounted, I issued the short count for all the tanks to fire up their engines. The short count is a technique for ensuring all vehicles start their engines simultaneously so the enemy cannot determine the size of the unit by counting individual engine start-ups. Once the turbine engine wound up, I pulled out. When I passed my wingman, he would follow my lead.

"I expected to see my platoon sergeant's section's dust trail approaching from the south. Instead, to my amazement, as I passed my wingman, my platoon sergeant and his wingman appeared beside me. I told my driver to floor it and then keyed the radio to let the platoon know what I knew: We had been alerted to respond immediately to the task force TOC, threat unspecified, probably a drill, but to be ready to lock and load weapons at my command. My tank commanders acknowledged in turn with a 'Roger.' I radioed the company executive officer that we were en route and would arrive in three to four minutes.

"The guards at the TOC stood well back from the encircling berms and concertina wire. We raced through the zigzag of berms that formed the entrance to the TOC and popped out in front of the main operations tent. I had my platoon coil, forming a small cross with vehicles back to back, stopped my tank, and hopped off the tank. I reached Captain Hadjis, who glanced at his watch after returning my salute. 'Thirteen minutes. Not bad, Red Six.' He informed me that Lieutenant Colonel Gordon had called the alert as a test. He then dismissed me, ordered me back to the company, and then, obviously pleased by his lieutenant's performance, returned with the other company commanders to the task force command and staff meeting."

Mail Call and Phone Calls

My primary spiritual salvation was mail. For me, a letter from home was worth more than a hymn, a package more than a religious service. Mail was everything. To juggle metaphors, it was the lifeline, the heart and lung machine, the umbilical cord to the motherland. If getting mail boosted the spirit, not getting mail bashed it. Dave Trybula calls it "a mixed blessing from the start." The first day his company received mail, he had thirteen of the company's twenty-one pieces. "Others joked I had been writing myself." Imagine the attitude of the soldiers who did not get mail that day toward the young college-brat of an officer who got most of it. Rob cites initial irregularity of the mail on theater logistical demands: "The priority items for the supply planes those early weeks were ammunition, fuel, food, and more soldiers. By mid-October, mail usually came every day." But travel time for a single piece still took from ten to fourteen days, sometimes longer, making replies lag by a month or more.

Mail included packages of junk food, batteries, flashlight bulbs, film, paper, underwear, and razor blades; cassette tapes with music, both albums and personally mixed tapes, and recorded letters; and books, magazines, pictures, good-luck charms, love, and hope.

When my platoon was with 2-4 Cav, we were told the Saudis censored our mail. Occasional pieces and packages had obviously been opened and resealed with tape. The exposed torso skin of models in magazine pictures was covered by black markers, though I don't know whether cautious senders or Saudi censors did this. My soldiers' friends quickly found ways of smuggling smut mags in country, normally by hiding them in food containers. As more troops entered the theater, however, and the volume of mail soared, the Saudis either quit inspecting our mail or spot-checked with such infrequency that we no longer saw signs of tampering, and *Playboy* and *Penthouse* required no camouflage.

My stats: I received my first mail when I was with 2-4 Cav on 6 September. My documented record for a single mail call: twenty-two pieces on 1 October, the day I returned to Delta Mech from my static demonstration for Secretary Stone at 2-4 Cav's Squadron TOC. At that time a number of soldiers had not yet received any mail.

"After a month or so," Dave writes, "incoming mail stopped. One story purported that some ten or fifteen tons of mail was backed up at the division's rear supply base, overwhelming the system. Then came the legend that the officer in charge had ordered some soldiers to police up trash and burn it. Unfortunately, before lighting the trash pile, no one checked the wind direction. The embers were blown onto one of the mail tents, one of the white cotton Bedouin tents, extremely flammable. The officer in charge rushed over and rescued the soldier inside but could not save all the mail. The brave young officer, the fable ends, was awarded a Commendation Medal for saving the mail. Two days after I heard the story, we began receiving charred mail. One of my letters had been burned around the edges, so I couldn't read the beginning or end of each line. Neal Creighton received a burnt bit of envelope with only his name and address."

The Eighteenth Airborne Corps's "Annotated Chronology" reports that two tents of the 129th Postal Company (attached to the Second Brigade) caught fire on 8 October. Rob recalls hearing that a soldier had fallen asleep in the mail tent while smoking a cigarette, thereby "torching letters to our whole battalion. I got one letter with part of it, including the girl's signature, burned away. As I read what remained of this mystery letter, I could tell the author knew me and my family extremely well. She talked about visiting with my parents, and about how she would be there when I came home. Before leaving for Saudi, I had asked just about every girl I knew to write me, so I was a little concerned about who exactly was planning to be at my family's side when I got back, and what she had in mind. Later I learned the letter had come from my brother Randy's girlfriend, my future sister-in-law."

A few weeks later Dave's company received its first care packages sent from the labor union at the M1 tank plant in Lima, Ohio, which Dave had visited every time he had visited his girlfriend Jill in nearby Elida. Dave was the only person the workers knew in the desert, and a tanker to boot, so they adopted him. Each shipment consisted of sixty large boxes of food, razors, books, gum, other sundry supplies, and letters, nearly a box for each man in the company.

A lot of soldiers complained, with Rob, about the "soldiers down south in the support units who rummaged though our stuff before it got to us, taking what they wanted and leaving the remains for us, the rightful recipients, in a beat-up and obviously opened and retaped box. After six months in the desert, I had determined one irrefutable fact: the closer a soldier is to the enemy, the higher his discipline, competency, and morale. Okay, so there were probably only a few rotten eggs giving the entire support network a bad name; but damned if those rotten few didn't inevitably handle the packages for my platoon. If a soldier did not get a package his honey claimed to have sent, he blamed the 'fucking REMFs.'"

For a very short while, until they both insisted I stop, I tallied how many letters my mother and my girlfriend, Maria, had written me and let them know who was "winning." Mom took the opportunity to write about her family history and my childhood. I did not know her parents; both died before my birth. Those letters are a personal treasure. In October or November I received a letter from her about her deployment, with Rob's mother, to Fort Stewart, to pack our belongings and clean the Hinesville apartment for the landlords. Rob and I had kept the apartment upon deployment; we were under the influence of hope. When our lease expiration approached, our mothers took care of it. Years after the war, at Rob's wedding, his mom described mine that weekend: "I've never seen anything like it, the way she took out all her anger and anxieties on those poor kitchen and bathroom floors, and that tub. Her hands were red and swollen long before she finished. She just kept going. Hardly said a word."

High school friends and their parents sent me mail. West Point classmates who did not deploy, and some classmates in theater, wrote me. Wives from the battalion wrote. Several of my instructors at the Academy sent letters. Maria's family and friends wrote. For Maria's discovery that she could send faxes through AT&T's "Operation Desert Fax," with someone in Saudi sticking the fax in an envelope and delivering it with the mail, she was dubbed "the Desert Faxtress."

From a former West Point English professor, I received a box of books insured for sixty-five dollars; he was apparently optimistic enough about my future to start my graduate degree a few years early. From a friend working for the CIA, I received sketches depicting what he knew of Iraqi defensive tactics.

My brother Eric, at the time Coast Guard lieutenant junior grade stationed in St. Louis, wrote that he wanted to request duty in the Gulf. Navy ships needed volunteer temporary duty Coast Guard officers for possible boarding missions. Eric wrote that he couldn't bear the thought of his kid brother "over there" and him unable to protect me; Eric, though, is also the most adventurous of the Vernon children, who I knew would rather be at sea than docked deskside. In my letter back I told him he better not dare do that to our mother. One son facing war was already one too many.

Eric also sent me a buckeye. Growing up, the three of us were often given buckeyes bought at roadside tourist traps by our parents as we drove east from Kansas on vacations. Buckeyes, Mom and Dad claimed, were good-luck charms. I didn't realize Eric had sent me one until, as the presumed empty envelope spun across the Arab tent toward my trash box, the dark blur dropped out and plopped into the sand. How lucky for me.

I received mail from college girls, high school girls, elementary school classes, and one letter from a cadet who worked on *The Pointer* magazine, largely a lampoon of academy life, which I had edited my senior year at West Point. I still have no idea how some of these people acquired my name and address.

In a number of pictures of me in the desert I am writing. At times I could not reply to all the mail I received.

I took very few letters addressed "To Any Soldier." We distributed these letters among those who did not have any mail of their own on a particular day. Writes Rob Holmes, "This spawned some rather interesting correspondence. Men and women, strangers, can get pretty bold in letters. Though more often it was just between a gracious and grateful American and a lonely soldier far from home. My wingman's gunner became pen pals with a seventy-year-old widow who had written her husband in WWII." Similarly my gunner, Sgt. Randy Dock, struck a correspondence with a peculiar old woman with some 140 pen pals. She wrote each of the names on a wall poster, attaching to each a colored star: silver star for soldiers successfully returned home, gold for those killed in action. To Dock she gave a green star, without explanation; perhaps all her pals received a green star until its color needed to change?

The recorded letter was especially popular for soldiers with families. Neal received his first such letter in October, in a box with a microrecorder and a tape from his wife Mary and their infant daughter Katherine. "Listening to her speak was very hard for me," Neal writes. "It was depressing. It wasn't like talking on a phone. I could not respond, could not say I love you, could not say I miss you. One night I took the recorder and sat down by my platoon's tent. As I began to speak, a mild sandstorm pushed its way into the assembly area. I spoke slowly, describing life for me and my soldiers. After a half an hour of rambling, I listened to the tape. It was awful. All I could hear was the sandstorm. I sent the tape, but decided to correspond by writing from that point on." My girlfriend Maria also sent me one recorded letter, and I sent her one back. Like Neal and Mary, we didn't do it again.

(Typically me, on the cassette I sent her I recorded myself reading an essay I had recently read from Paul Theroux's *Sunrise with Seamonsters*. I found a lonely hillock of rock beyond the company's perimeter, just outside our circle of tanks. The essay, "Being a Man," challenges America's notion of the manly and characterizes "the Hemingway personality" as "tedious." Theroux's book also contains an essay on "Cowardice," initially published in 1967, the year of my birth; I circled the date beneath the title in my dog-eared paperback. A pacifist and Vietnam protester, Theroux was an interesting companion for a young lieutenant facing the mother of all battles. His was a voice I had to simultaneously appreciate and deny.)

Rob and his platoon sergeant, Sfc. Sikes, withheld mail from soldiers as a disciplinary measure. "In the desert we didn't have the same discipline mechanisms we had had in garrison. If a soldier misbehaved, we couldn't confine him to the barracks or suspend his privilege. Nor could we give him extra duty — every day was a twenty-four-hour workday. The standard line from a misbehaving soldier was, 'What are you going to do, send me to Saudi Arabia?' Putting a man on radio watch at 0200, or having him pull an extra shift, only led to his falling asleep. Making him burn the waste in the latrines worked fairly well. Of our various disciplinary actions, though, holding a man's mail got the fastest response."

Rob continues: "When a package came from home, the tank crews divided everything in it. Rank didn't matter. We maintained the appropriate protocol, but when you eat, sleep, and bathe together for six months, you either work as a team or kill each other. While at times the latter option was tempting, the only real choice was to share and sacrifice together. One of the most important lessons taught by military service is joining in a common cause with people from diverse backgrounds whom you might not like.

"My mother wrote a letter almost every day. She never mentioned the danger or what Bush and Saddam were saying those days. She instead wrote about my dad or brother, or how my high school football team was doing. I learned later that she could hardly watch the news. Proud as she was that I had gone to West Point, this was the awful part of the diploma.

"My father, on the other hand, wrote me about once every two weeks, but his letters were long, complex, and beautifully written, full of well-articulated deep thoughts and inspiring lessons. Later, I learned that unlike my mother, he had watched CNN practically twenty-four hours a day from the time I left to when I returned. He read every article and watched every news story about the Gulf conflict.

"My brother wrote often as well. He was a senior at the University of Georgia that fall. Although we had chosen different paths after high school, we were big fans of one another, and I enjoyed his letters. Nevertheless, we had something of a 'professional' relationship, like the one I had with my dad. It was easier to say *I love you* in a letter.

"After the mail came one evening, Jon Ulsaker shared with me and Delta Tank's other platoon leader, Jeff White, an unforgettable surprise: a box of bourbon balls from his wife. As I walked over, I smelled them one hundred meters away. I immediately forgot Sfc. Sikes's MRE-only rule. The three of us ate so fast we almost got sick. Not that we cared. We thought we'd come as close to Heaven as we ever could in Saudi."

(My mom sent me a tin of bourbon balls as well. The alcohol had been cooked out, but they tasted strong nonetheless. I shared a few with my crew and rationed the rest, taking one a day with my scurvy-preventing Vitamin C tablet.)

Rob also received letters more and more frequently from Kelli Barker, an attractive North Carolinian he had met on leave in a London pub. "Six months after the night I met her, I still remembered her honest eyes and quick wit. While I maintained committed to no commitments, her well-written letters and generous packages full of supplies and sweets had the desired effect. So when we traveled to the phones, I would call either my parents, my brother, or Kelli."

According to the "Annotated Chronology of the Eighteenth Airborne Corps," "2nd Brigade, 24th Infantry Division, open[ed] a 48-unit AT&T telephone bank in the town of As Sarrar" on 31 October 1990. Before the phone bank, our only means of phoning home was the telephone in the Saudi roadside gas station–general stores. I believe these were declared off-limits at some level in the chain of command for reasons of equity — because only soldiers buzzing around in Humvees had access to them, though my company commander and first sergeant did slip into town when a soldier had real cause. Greg Downey recalls that "the Saudi shop owner with an eye for capitalism charged ten dollars for two minutes. He could have retired in a few months from the GI phone business."

Except for the occasional critical case, we traveled to the phone banks in groups. A company would load the back of its supply truck with the soldiers each platoon had elected to send and would inevitably make the ten- to twenty-kilometer trip in the middle of the night or the very early morning. The phone bank was a set of four tents erected on the edge of Sarrar. Humvees and trucks parked where they could among the others and as close as possible to the entrance in the concertina wire enclosure. Only side arms were allowed inside; soldiers with rifles stacked arms outside. After waiting in line outside the wire, we were led inside one of the four tents to a cluster of twelve phones in carrel-like plywood booths where you stood to talk. The NCO in charge of the tent shuffled us through in fifteen-minute intervals. An operator connected you to whatever number you requested. If no one answered or the line was busy, you could ask for another number, but your fifteen minutes had started when you walked into the tent. Collect calls only. Every few minutes the NCO in charge barked out the time remaining.

Delta Tank, Rob Holmes remembers, made a weekly trip to the phones: "For some army reason, we could only go in the middle of the night. Not only would we get no sleep as we bounced across the desert in the back of a truck, but most of our friends and relatives back in the States would be at work or school. Not that the possibility of talking to an answering machine stopped us. Since we couldn't take the entire platoon at once and leave our position unattended, we rotated the soldiers so that at least every two weeks each had a chance to call. My platoon sergeant and I flip-flopped; he went one week, I would go the next.

"In November the desert turned pretty cold at night, so I always grabbed a blanket for the trip. I loved calling home. Like everyone else, I missed my family, and I always tried to call them. I reread their letters on the truck ride south so I could answer their questions in the limited time we had on the phone. Once my mother told me that she had seen soldiers playing volleyball on the *Today Show* and being entertained by Jay Leno and Brooke Shields. She innocently asked if I had been there. God bless her, but my mom didn't have a very clear a picture of a tank battalion's mission. The clowns on the *Today Show* were well south of us, probably the same fellows who were eating her cookies. I had not seen anything like Brooke Shields for months.

"While the trips to the phone bank were always fun, the excitement growing as the distance shrank, the ride back was usually more sober. Some of the men were obviously replaying in their heads the conversations they had just had. Others were mad or sad. Some had been told of problems at home, maybe with their children, maybe that their wife was leaving them. The loader on my wingman's tank, Spc. Brian Ressdorf, learned on one trip that his wife had a rare form of cancer. She was twenty-five. Unfortunately, we could not send Ressdorf home unless she died. I sat next to him on the way back to Graceland that night as he cried his eyes out. I might have been cynical back at Fort Stewart when that pathetic private came to me after his wife had shot him for knocking up her sister, but by now I had learned to care about the family life of my soldiers. It was part of my job. For the next three months, Ressdorf waited on pins and needles each time a letter came or during each trip to the phones. It drove him crazy. His wife hung on.

"About four hours after leaving for the phones, we arrived back at Graceland right before dawn. Even with no sleep, the next day would often be the best day all week for my men."

Dave Trybula also knew he had to be prepared for the phone call that would hurt a soldier's morale instead of help it. He and his platoon sergeant, Sfc. Ron Ruff, "prioritized phone trips among soldiers based upon personal situations, and ensured all of our soldiers were able to make a phone call before we did. Our own turn did not come until late November, a few days before Thanksgiving."

Mary Creighton found that the phones were a mixed blessing for the soldiers' families as well. The rumor mill's production increased exponentially. And "soldiers in the rear with easy access to the phone banks called home almost nightly. Their wives received phone bills for hundreds of dollars, which they could not afford on an enlisted soldier's salary. Meanwhile, I received only three calls from Neal over the entire eight months of his deployment."

■ I called Maria once from the gas station and once from the phone bank. From the gas station the morning of 30 October I woke her, catching her completely by surprise: "Al? . . . . Al? . . . . I love you . . . I love you" — her first words to me. *I still feel them,* I wrote to her the next day. I still feel them as I write this sentence today. Outside the store an Arab civilian sat against the corner of the building with an automatic rifle, magazine inserted, and a magazine belt slung over his shoulder. Some American GIs drove by in a Mazda 626.

I reached Maria from the phone bank on Christmas Day; except for that trip, I gave my spot on the truck to the phone bank to one of my soldiers because it meant more to them. However much hearing Maria's voice palpitated my nerves, it also thrashed my mind, as for the next couple of days I could not give anything else its due attention. Anyway, I had my letters.

The one poem I wrote in the desert was about mail. I had a rough version of it in December, when one of Captain Swisher's daily updates announced a Department of Defense-sponsored Desert Shield writing contest. The contest's April deadline was not encouraging. I finished the poem and sent it off and after the war discovered I had lost to a poem about a tank turret's whining and the soul of a tank being the people inside.[3] My poem I titled "A Desert Shield soldier, to his mistress":

> Arabia offers a paucity of pulchritudinous pleasures:
> No bikinied bunnies on beaches,
> No glossy 2-D festal virgins.
>
> I receive a *Playboy* in a Pringles can:
> Americans cannot live without America,
> So my friends send this piece of her.
>
> Peace — her peace, her salaciously splayed solicitude:
> Packages pour from her;
> She delivers.
>
> Only she slakes me:
> My odalisque, my Madonna;
> America, the beautiful.

Arab Culture

I have done a good deal of business with Arabs and can advise you that their cultural weakness is "ego." Gail [his wife] calls it a "toxic level of testosterone." They absolutely cannot admit that there is anything they do not know. The Arab male will set upon a plan and will never deviate even when he knows that he is wrong. I do not know what good this might do you in a tank except to tell you that Arabs are easily beaten in business when you structure the situation such that they must make quick decisions, because they just can't do it. They have to be able to explain a change of direction before they can change that direction. So much for the advice of a silly old guy who never drove a tank.

— Bryant Jensen, letter to his nephew, Alex Vernon, 30 August 1990

According to Col. Paul J. Kern's history of his 2d Brigade in Desert Shield and Desert Storm, "while the Brigade occupied the desert near As Sarrar, each battalion sponsored towns to maintain good relations with the Saudi Arabians in the area. . . . This allowed for a beneficial cultural exchange and a development of mutual trust between soldiers and the local people." Task Force 1–64 Armor sponsored As Sarrar, and Task Force 3-15 Infantry sponsored the towns of As Sahaf, Am Sawat, and Az Zughayn. To my memory I was unaware of this program. The names of the three towns my task force sponsored do not ring a bell. Rob, however, participated in one of these cultural exchange events in late November.

"I was sent on an 'urgent mission,'" he writes. "My orders were to take my tank and my wing tank to an Arab village immediately and await further instruction. Tankers hate towns, veritable viper dens of snipers and antitank missiles. My two tanks cruised down the main street until I saw a Humvee with a major sitting in it. I dismounted and reported to him, but before he could describe my mission, a dozen Arabs appeared, one prominently in the lead.

"The major introduced the lead man as the emir, or village mayor. The emir had been a Saudi armor officer years ago. Oh no, I thought; I knew why I was here. Next thing I know, this guy had commandeered my wingman's tank and rode off into the sunset.

"The emir returned like he had just defeated Patton. His minions showered him with reverence. About this time, I heard Spc. Arthur Howard yelling. A flock of kids surrounded him. Howard was short with huge arms, a handsome, dark-as-night twenty-one year old from Baton Rouge, Louisiana. Howard had adjusted to Saudi reasonably well, but he missed his mother's gumbo terribly. He was one of eight kids, so mama could surely cook. He was always yelling about something, which got old, but I guess growing up in a ghetto with seven brothers and sisters and only one pot of gumbo makes you scream for what you want.

"Some Arab kid had absconded with Howard's sunglasses. Howard was going wild yelling at kids trying to find them. The emir joined in, shouting orders and clapping his hands, sending his underlings scampering. Great. Now some poor kid will get his hand chopped off in swift desert justice. Then there appeared two Arabs with Howard's sunglasses and two cases of Pepsi-Colas! The country never ceased to amaze me. Although the Saudis were some of the most irrational and undisciplined people I had ever met, they were also among the most generous. The emir walked to Howard and presented him the Pepsis. We returned to Graceland with the case of Pepsis and pictures of us drinking with the emir and his flunkies. This place was crazy."

■ My own interactions with Saudi men were limited — they ran the stores where we sometimes stopped to make a call or buy some pita. I heard that one of these As Sarrar gas station–general store owners had a degree from an American university. I had no interaction with Saudi women. We did see them on occasion. Peeking beneath their solid-colored *abha* robe hems, and out their sleeves, I caught glimpses of brightly colored Western clothes. I heard that the Saudi women visiting Bahrain — the Persian Gulf island nation off the Saudi coast, connected by causeway to Dharhan — would lose their robes and veils as soon as they passed out of Arabia, stuffing them into bags and revealing fashionable Western clothes and painted faces. Bahrain, needless to say, is considerably less orthodox Muslim than Saudi Arabia. I heard, too, that Saudis drink up a storm whenever they visit Bahrain, and a fair number of them have personal caches of liquor at home.

The bus driver for our trip from the Cav screen line to rejoin Task Force 3-15 at AA Hinesville, a handsome, dark-skinned, blue-eyed, blonde army specialist, had been assigned to the 24th's Military Intelligence group from his permanent unit, a Special Forces outfit at Fort Campbell, Kentucky, because he spoke fluent Arabic. He was raised in the United States and knew Arabic because his father was Syrian. And with a mother from the Philippines, he spoke Filipino as well, and, as he told me, used it in Saudi more than he used his Arabic. Filipinos comprised most of the labor force in Saudi Arabia, and at our level we had more dealings with these men. It sickened Rob "to see how people were treated over there. I have never seen anyone abused worse than a Phillipino in Saudi Arabia. They were used for cheap labor and literally kicked around and spat on." Jeannie Novak, the lieutenant I met in the hangar during deployment who then deployed herself, reported meeting a number of black Africans working in Saudi. One of these men told her that the dream of most Third World blacks is to emigrate to America.

From Jeannie I recall two other stories: one, when an Arab man approached the male captain with whom she stood and tried to horse-trade two fine camels for the beautiful American woman; and another time when she had a meal in a Bedouin tent. All the rumors we hear of Arab men running only the world outside the tent flap, she remarked, are absolutely true. Inside, the Arab woman issues the orders.

Saudi men also drive horribly fast. For them, the left turn indicator communicates to the trailing vehicle that it is okay to pass. Americans trying to turn left had a number of accidents with Saudi's attempting to pass them. The women are not permitted to drive.

A billboard outside Nu'ayriyah advertised Zit cola.

My Saudi road experiences also revealed the utility of the Arab dress; twice outside Nu'ayriyah on an Delta Mech officers' recon in Captain Baillergeon's Humvee we drove past a Saudi family, its car pulled over, and while the others waited at least one member squatted, more or less casually, his white cotton *thaub* or her abha hiding the nether business.

The colors and pattern of an Arab man's headgear — *kafia,* or *keffiyah* — I was told, signified his tribal affiliation.

On any day I spent traveling away from my tank position, I saw carcasses of animals dropped dead by that unforgiving sun. In the evening, I stared at that same sun in awe of its sheer orange beauty. And it seemed to me that the desert sun explained something about desert people and the gods they have produced. This sun that kills without discrimination and without blinking also provides the sole aesthetic thrill of desert living. It struck me as perfectly fitting that the world's three monotheistic faiths have their origin beneath the omnipresent, omnipotent desert sun.

A few kilometers away from Bravo Tank's camp at AA Hinesville, in the middle of the nowhere that was our home, sat an active, walled mosque. Five times a day the recorded call to prayer sounded across the desert through loudspeakers mounted on the lone minaret, and, when the wind blew our way, to our hearing.

Recreation

Recreation is training. Soldiers must have some fun. Stand down each company on a scheduled basis (recommended one day/week). Ensure: Sports, VCR, Religious services, BN PX, showers, fresh uniforms, relaxed/sleep uniform rules, horseplay. Do physical stuff; hikes, boxing, wrestling, camel riding. Let soldiers be non-serious. No booze. No pornagraphy [sic]. Only cultural contact with Saudis.

— Maj. Gen. Barry McCaffrey, Command Training Guidance, 7 October 1990

Soldiers always find a way to play during downtime — cards, dice, chess, handheld electronic games, sports. Whiskey and whores in earlier wars; near-beer and Gameboys in ours.

Once or twice one of my platoon's radios caught an Iraqi radio station broadcasting in English. Baghdad Betty lectured us about the tenuous moral justification of our operation and warned us about the pain and death we would suffer if we pressed the fight. Neal Creighton listened to her all the time. "She was a scream. She once said something like, 'go home! Your women are running around with Tom Cruise, Burt Reynolds, and Bart Simpson.' Obviously Iraq's psychological operations folk didn't know Bart was a preteen cartoon character. My guys joked that maybe we should worry about cheating wives and girlfriends because the cartoonist could draw Bart's penis as big as he wanted."

For more formal relaxation, our battalion constructed a Recreation Site co-located with the battalion trains, the unit's internal maintenance, supply, and support area. Initially the site had little more than several sleeping tents, picnic tables, a tent with benches and a generator-powered VCR, and a volleyball net. White engineer tape on metal stakes cordoned the area off to make it a privileged space. The battalion's PX truck, with its scant supply of junk food and hygiene supplies, usually sat right outside the entrance. Weekly the truck visited each company assembly area, and each company visited the Rec Site every seven to ten days.

Both battalion and brigade staged talent shows. I don't remember either very well, except that battalion's had two separate renditions of Lee Greenwood's "God Bless the USA," the show closing with the second one. The commander had us stand for it, giving this pop culture national anthem stand-in more privilege than I felt it deserved. He finished his closing remarks with a quotation from Shakespeare's *Henry V*, from the famous "band of brothers" speech rallying the troops at Agincourt. Kenneth Branaugh's film version had recently been released, and a friend from home had sent the commander the quotation on a snippet of paper. This was the second time I had heard the colonel quote the speech; he would do it at least twice more before the ground war. It was difficult to squelch my cynicism as he quoted a play I arrogantly presumed he did not know. By quoting capital-L *Literature*, wasn't he trespassing on *my* turf?

Bravo Tank also took a day trip to Half Moon Bay, a resort of sorts on the Gulf, where we relaxed in an air-conditioned movie theater, ate free food, swam in a pool, floated effortlessly in the Gulf, walked about in shorts with the fresh air on our legs for the first time, and bought Desert Shield T-shirts. Americans can't host anything without souvenir T-shirts.

For Thanksgiving on 22 November the companies rotated through the battalion trains for a dinner of four shrimp, potatoes, stuffing, turkey, roast beef, ham, and ice cream. The prospect of a traditional Thanksgiving meal thrilled Rob Holmes: "Beautiful green peas, mashed potatoes, sweet potatoes, cranberry sauce, turkey — everything! I held my plate in my hands before diving in, to admire the gorgeous picture before grabbing my fork and scooping up my first bite.

"*Crunch.*

"Oh God. *Crunch, crunch.* The food was full of sand. Everyone had the same expression on their face: *I hate Saudi Arabia.*"

The breeze that coated Rob's food did not find my corner of the world. Though we had to travel to the battalion trains for it, it was the best meal I had in the desert.

The next evening Task Force 3-15's officers held a dining-in. In peacetime, the dining-in is a formal social for battalion officers and senior NCOs to eat, drink, and tell "war" stories from their training exercises. Major General McCaffrey joined us for our Desert Shield dining-in. At the dining-in, after each company's officers presented some bit of entertainment, the division commander addressed the group. Combat leaders, he said, need three qualities: competence, confidence, and the heart for their job. (*Three strikes against me,* I wrote Maria the next day.) McCaffrey expected combat in 90 to 180 days, sometime in the winter, after the arrival of Seventh Corps. He also discussed the 4.6 percent of deployable soldiers the division had left behind. "I made it perfectly clear," he told us, that he would not bring those "who had emotional difficulties, whose hearts weren't in it." I thought about my visit to Father Mike before we deployed, and his offer, now confirmed, to permit me to not deploy. According to my letters, I still gave occasional thought to approaching the unit chaplain and asking to go home.

Comedian Jay Leno and his wife visited the battalion on 24 November. Leno used the trim vanes on the front of two side-by-side Bradleys as his stage. Leno wore DCUs. He cracked us up, his risqué humor catching us off guard in our politically correct army. His introduction of his wife, a small, slender woman sporting very dark long hair, sunglasses, and a camera, begat a lot of approving whistles and yelps from the assembled soldiers.

I heard a rumor that Gary Trudeau, the *Doonesbury* political cartoonist, had volunteered to visit the troops, but President Bush refused him permission. Bush found Trudeau's political criticism inappropriate to acknowledge. This peeved a number of us and diminished our commander in chief a little in our eyes — this after his golfing at Kennebunkport while we readied for war and then his refusal (so the rumor ran) to accept King Fahd's offer to pay each soldier defending his kingdom one thousand dollars per month as a gesture of gratitude. If the man couldn't take mercenary money, couldn't he at least take a joke? Because Trudeau got it. His strips, which we saw both in the few papers that found their way to us and in clippings sent from home, captured our desert life more accurately than anything else. His satire of the politics of our situation echoed some of our own feelings. His cartoon soldiers did and said things we did and said. One soldier grabbing his umpteenth bottled water and telling his buddy, "Cover me while I drink." Another soldier saying that dirty word, "sailors," followed by a ship scene with beer-swilling, card-playing, air-conditioned sailors. A group of soldiers betting on the outcome of a gladiatorial bout between a scorpion and a snake. And a wounded soldier asking the medic if he would be on CNN, the medic replying, "How do you think we found you?" We heard a soldier in country fed Trudeau his material. It made sense. One of Trudeau's strips featured a wooden semaphore with arrows pointing the direction to such places as England, New York, and the great coincidence: Philadelphia, Pennsylvania, Maria's home, and Prairie Village, Kansas, mine. After the war I learned that Trudeau's colorist lived in Prairie Village.

The Army-Navy game is traditionally played the first weekend in December. I didn't know to tune in. About a dozen Academy alumni in Task Force 1-64, however, gathered that night on a sand dune in Delta Tank's Graceland with a radio that could pick up the game on Armed Forces Radio Network. The game kicked off around midnight, Saudi time. "Even though none of us lived more than fifteen hundred meters apart," recalls Rob, "I hadn't had much time to spend with any of my West Point friends except Jon Ulsaker, another platoon leader in my company. We laughed together all night, reliving stories of cadet life. It was bitter cold and well past midnight when the game ended, but it had been great to see my friends.

"Afterward we went our separate ways, disappearing into the night back to our platoons. I suspect the other guys, as I did, slept a little easier the next few nights. I took great comfort knowing the people on my right and left flank. That's not to slight any of the fine ROTC or OCS officers in the battalion. None of us had been tested with our platoons, but having gone through West Point together, my classmates and I knew what one another could withstand and deliver. It's not to say that I feel the same way about every West Pointer, either. But I had worked with everyone in that particular group before. I knew from personal observation that they could handle themselves and their soldiers. When I looked around our circle as we listened to the game, I saw young men with whom I would go to war any day."

With the approach of Christmas, cards and packages began streaming in. I had some catalogues sent from home, so with the one credit card I took to the desert was able to order presents for loved ones. Greg Downey "wanted to get December twenty-fifth over with as fast as possible"; thoughts of home and family naturally peaked as Christmas loomed. He wanted to get on the far side of the sadness. Rob complained when he heard that Christmas cards might be prohibited out of respect for our host nation's religion. "Here we were defending them, and they were going to tell my mother she couldn't send her son a Christmas card."

Rob continues: "My North Carolina pen pal, Kelli Barker, sent me a fabulous package, which I received just before Christmas. In Saudi Arabia, I needed razors, shaving cream, toothpaste, boots, socks, batteries, and Chapstick. That stuff was gold, and Kelli was the mother lode. For Christmas she was a little less practical: She sent a little tree decorated with cinnamon lollipops shaped like huge red lips. Licking those lips was the most erotic thing I had done since leaving Savannah six months before."

Christmas Eve day was gorgeous. That night we had a small party in the company dining area. The battalion's wives had organized and sent stockings, each a wool army sock full of goodies, the sock's partner stuffed into the toe. The first sergeant's driver burst out of their tent in full Santa regalia, his huge plastic, tinted glasses hiding his jolly eyes, his own blonde mustache competing for space with Santa's cottony white one, his slight paunch needing little costumed augmentation. I posed for a photo on Santa's lap with my platoon sergeant. The company ate and laughed. Our high spirits amazed me.

Rob spent the last hours of Christmas Eve with Jeff White, the Delta platoon leader from Alabama. They walked together to the battalion headquarters, where Chaplain Tim Bedsole was giving a midnight service. "We walked into a tent full of soldiers. It was a simple sermon, typical Tim: very sincere, and full of music. Jeff and I slipped out right as the service ended. We returned up the hill back to Graceland. The night was absolutely spectacular. The white sand rolled before us illumed by a blazing full moon and a million stars. I would have much rather been in Atlanta with my family, but we certainly didn't lack for a beautiful sanctuary. Jeff and I shook hands, wished each other a Merry Christmas, and turned in."

On Christmas, the sandstorm that had hit Rob on Thanksgiving made a second holiday pass to catch what its first sweep had missed. The day-long *shamal* relegated us to our platoon tents. In the afternoon about half the company braved the wind and sand for a decent meal at the task force TOC's mess, the meal not as impressive as the one at Thanksgiving. By 1630 hours the wind had let up and the evening chill set in.

Two days after Christmas a small contingency from the company left for an excursion aboard *The Princess,* the *QE2*'s sister cruise ship, at port at Bahrain. When the group returned on the thirtieth, they told us of dancing women, a magician, and a mess of drunk soldiers. Some of them spent a night in a Bahrain hotel. Prostitutes, they reported, ran $180. Our 24th Infantry Division soldiers spent sixty thousand dollars on alcohol on the ship, beating the 101st Airborne

(Air Assault) Division by three to four thousand. So our proudly returned soldiers boasted, anyway.

We did not know it, but Bravo Tank's 28 December trip to the Rec Site would be our last. By this time the site had evolved considerably; it now had a Ping-Pong and a foosball table, and a basketball court with hoops and backboards on either end of a marked rectangle of sand that I never saw anyone use, two volleyball courts, a weight room tent, and, under construction, a nine-hole miniature golf course complete with green indoor/outdoor carpeting. The VCR tent had gained flooring and folding chairs. I remember our collective bitching because, in spite of its many luxuries, the Rec Site did not have stove heaters in the tents. Nor did the shower have warm water — I feared mine would throw me into shock. Most of us would have preferred to have taken a day off in the company area, where we had recently received heaters and where we had built our own volleyball court. The truck ride to the site alone was so miserably cold as to belie the trip's purpose of comfort and respite.

The evident energy being poured into the Rec Site in late December indicated a long stay. I prayed for as much, as I would have rather lingered in the desert than go to war. Still, the effort going into the Rec Site felt a bit misplaced.

My most discouraging Rec Site visit had occurred a month earlier. On that other wet Saudi winter day, 24 November, I watched the movie *Pretty Woman* with sound for the first time. It was the day after the dining-in with Major General McCaffrey. After the movie, after everyone else had left the VCR tent, I stayed. Bob McCann, the First Platoon leader, sat with me. I was crying. What struck me to tears was the difference between what fate did for Julia Roberts's and Richard Gere's characters, bringing them together, and what fate had done to me. What struck me was the beauty of Roberts. What struck me was the resemblance I perceived in nose and smile between her and Maria. What struck me was that the story had ended, and had ended happily, as we knew it would, as we knew it should, while as for how our story was to end, only God or Allah knew.

Official news of the Rec Site's closure came to me on 9 January.

Training

The tank platoon can survive and win in battle, however, only if it is well trained, effectively led, and highly motivated. Crews must be aggressive, and their tactics must reflect the tempo and intensity of maneuver warfare. Platoon training must prepare them to operate in hostile territory with the enemy to their front, flanks, and rear.
— FM 17–15, *Tank Platoon* manual

Training for Operations Desert Shield and Desert Storm began in the army's post-Vietnam era of rebuilding, when it committed itself to a new standard of professionalism, and organized, outfitted, and trained itself to fight outnumbered and win against Soviet bloc equipment, tactics, and doctrine. The junior officers of Desert Shield and Desert Storm had gone through college prior to 1989, prior to the end of the Cold War. The classroom terrain boards on which we moved our miniature tanks and Bradleys matched the terrain of the Fulda Gap, the fastest and most likely avenue of approach for an attack into Western Europe from the east. Career soldiers in the seventies and eighties counted on several tours in West Germany. Even if we did not directly fight the Soviets or its Eastern European allies, most of the Third World countries we might find ourselves fighting used Soviet equipment, tactics, and doctrine (with some variation). Countries like Iraq.

To train American units to wage battle against this threat, the army created the National Training Center (NTC) at Fort Irwin, California, in the middle of the Mojave Desert. At the NTC, units from stateside divisions fought against a permanent Opposing Force (OPFOR) employing Soviet tactics and in terrain spacious enough to accommodate brigade maneuver and live-fire maneuver training. A number of commentators have attested to the excellent training provided by the NTC, especially as it prepared us for armored desert warfare against Iraq. The NTC OPFOR brags that it is the best fighting unit in the world. It is the only unit that fights nearly every day and night of the year on the same terrain, with the same equipment, and with the same people. Every "friendly" unit participating in an NTC rotation against the OPFOR, every platoon, company, battalion, even the brigade, has an evaluator assigned to observe its performance. At the conclusion of each mission, this observer/controller (OC) sits down with the entire platoon, or the staff, to critique it.

Of the five authors of this book, only Greg Downey and I had the benefit of training at the NTC prior to Desert Shield, though other officers in the battalion and noncommissioned officers in our platoons had made at least one trip. During Greg's two weeks in the desert around Irwin, the sun reached 120 degrees. Greg's OC was Sfc. Ramirez, "an old, crusty NCO who had been a tanker in Vietnam." After the first battle, Greg was thrilled to have only lost one tank to enemy fire. Ramirez checked Greg's joy. "Think about the four men in the tank, lieutenant. Imagine all four missing their arms and legs, imagine them burned to a crisp by the fire. Now imagine yourself going inside to pull out the bodies of the people you knew, these soldiers who trusted their safety to you, whose faces you can no longer distinguish. Hear one of them moan as you pull him out, feel him try to move, watch him die knowing you can do nothing. Picture yourself telling his family, and having flashbacks. You think about that, LT, the next time the OPFOR kills one of your tanks."

During my junior year as a cadet, I spent six weeks in the mechanized infantry battalion that was part of the permanent OPFOR at Fort Irwin. I led an infantry platoon in that unit; and given the unit translation, I acted in the field as a Soviet rifle company commander with nine mock-Soviet infantry fighting vehicles (old Sheridan tanks rigged with fiberglass to look like Soviet BMPs). At twenty, I was the youngest man in my platoon. I was immature and overwhelmed. I most assuredly did not learn how to fight a platoon, but I learned how to ride and drive from the tank commander's position, and how to steer in the desert leading a formation of armored vehicles. I began, as it were, to break in my saddle.

A few months into my assignment at Fort Stewart, our battalion commander sent me to the field with the other armor battalion in 2d Brigade in preparation for its trip to the NTC. So in March 1990 I found myself for a second time in the Fort Irwin dustbowl, this time fighting in the Mojave Desert on the American side. The army could not have done anything more to better prepare me for war in the Persian Gulf. Though I admittedly had not taken full advantage of some of my training opportunities — I was young, remember — I felt comfortable in my hatch and with my platoon. However afraid of combat I was, however excruciatingly diffident of my abilities to lead men in battle, I possessed at some base physical level with the tanks and with the men a familiarity and ease that my soldiers perceived as confidence. God bless their optimism — I am thankful for it.

■ Dave Trybula succinctly sums the value of Operation Desert Shield: "The six months prior to Desert Storm allowed us plenty of time to acclimate ourselves and our equipment to the desert, and to train. Training was accomplished at all levels. Soldiers learned at an ever-increasing rate. Unlike at Fort Stewart, in Saudi we did not have months of post support duties between training cycles interrupting the process and forcing us to repeat the basics. We were able to train more frequently and on a larger scale than ever before. The personnel stability also allowed us not to have to retrain the basics for newcomers. While I did have some personality conflicts, stability permitted everyone in the platoon and company to learn each other's strengths and weaknesses in detail. We became able to anticipate each other's actions during maneuvers; I could direct my platoon by merely changing my tank's direction or speed. Having deployed as a group of soldiers *thinking* we were ready to fight, by the end of December we *knew* we were ready. We had learned what we had to do to survive and win."

Desert Shield was a luxury. In our post–Cold War army, we hardly believed in such a protracted period of preparation. The contingency operations in Grenada and Panama were our models: deploy and fight, not deploy and sit. Historically Desert Shield had precedents: A fair portion of soldiers in the world wars, after the initial operations anyway, had somewhat similar experiences, traveling to

England and Africa to train, or sitting in fairly stable defenses, while the generals planned and prepared for the upcoming campaign.

We could only do so much training. We had limited resources and much boredom. How many times can you practice injecting yourself with the chemical nerve agent antidote followed by the antidote's antidote? Arguably never enough. At Valley Forge the Continental army drilled endlessly at manual of arms; in Saudi Arabia, we drilled endlessly at NBC warfare.

Bravo Tank's most ingenious training methods were devised by Staff Sergeant Sebastio. As the company's master gunner, Sebastio was in charge of tank gunnery training. He built a miniature tank gunnery range on the eastern edge of the company area to sharpen each tank crew's skills. The first component of his course simulated a defensive position. A tank would begin down a small slope as if in a turret-down position (behind cover or dug-in so that the tank is hidden from the top of the turret, down — except for the sight system housing, the doghouse, which has to "see" so the crew can scan for targets). The evaluator, seated on the ground a few yards from the tank and communicating with the crew by a PRC-1 field radio, would yank a string to pop up targets. Iraqi tanks and BMPs, which were armored infantry vehicles akin to our Bradleys, and troops. The targets were small cardboard silhouettes Sebastio had fashioned, roughly scaled to their range from the tank to appear a reasonable size in the tank's gun sights. The tank commander would then issue the fire command and take his crew through the drill, from driving forward to a hull-down position to expose the main gun, through the engagement, to backing back down into the turret-down position. Crew members keyed the radio to speak with one another, instead of using the tank's intercom system, so the evaluator outside could listen.

The offensive component of Sebastio's course ran similarly, except that the tank drove a course through a small wadi and berm complex, reacting to whatever targets it found as it rounded turns. The final component of the course was a static snake board, which we had brought with us from Fort Stewart. The snake board consists of a number of horizontal and vertical lines of varying curves and zigzags. It exercises the gunner's and tank commander's ability to track moving targets by tracing the snaky lines with the sight reticle. The tank commander's gun control, a single joystick manipulated with one hand, is much more difficult to manage than the gunner's two-handled control.

We boresighted daily, both for the necessity and the practice. The tank's optical system peers out from a "doghouse" on top of the turret in front of the tank commander, several feet at a diagonal from the main gun. The process of boresighting ensures that at some optimal distance the bore of the cannon points exactly where the sight looks. (To optimize sight adjustments, the main gun's computer combines the boresight data with the range to target provided by the sight system's laser range finder; wind data from an exterior sensor; and manually input weather data, gun tube wear data, and round type specified to production lot number.) Also, as Rob Holmes notes, gravity, ambient temperature, and firing cause the tank gun to droop: "This, in an all male unit, led to predictable jokes." A boresight in combat would have to be done quickly and accurately, and it would have to last. The other two platoons in Bravo Tank would send out one tank to sit for the others to use as a boresight target. My platoon was luckier: The division's main headquarters sat on a small, flat-topped jebel in Task Force 3-15's area. One of the TOC's plywood latrines was almost precisely three thousand meters from my platoon position; the upper corners of the latrine, at that distance, made for a perfect boresight target, convenient and fun as we imagined the unsuspecting brass, maybe McCaffrey himself, dropping trou as we took aim.

I most enjoyed the platoon maneuver training conducted by my platoon NCOs and me. We did these exercises as often as we could — given fuel and maintenance constraints, maybe once every seven to ten days — leaving the company area late morning and returning early evening. We worked individual tank drills, such as reaction to indirect fire or to antitank missiles, with unexpected announcements from me over the radio, and we practiced platoon formations, movement techniques, and battle drills. I have heard the battle drill compared to an audible play called by a football quarterback upon reading the defense's setup. When contact with the enemy is made or immediately expected, the platoon leader issues a battle drill command: action front, action right, action left, or action rear. The platoon changes its traveling formation to an attack formation in the indicated direction, its four tanks coming on line to direct the platoon's entire firepower against the enemy. Platoons, companies, battalions, brigades, and divisions all have battle drills, and we practiced them at all levels — if at the platoon and company level (and sometimes even battalion), we could mount up in our tracks and really run the drills, at brigade and division our commanders could only talk and walk through them. Greg Downey writes, "Flexibility is the name of the game."

Greg similarly devoted the majority of his training to maneuver. Maneuvering the scout platoon, however, is an entirely different proposition from maneuvering a tank platoon. Whereas a tank platoon can get away with a kind of tactical follow-the-leader, the scout platoon operates in three independently moving sections of two Bradleys each reconing separate areas or screening different parts of the battalion. Greg therefore "wanted to make sure the scout section leader could tactically employ his vehicles. This is not difficult to do, provided you can read a map, and the map shows sufficient terrain features for you to locate yourself relative to the terrain around you. That was the problem. The map contour interval was twenty meters; a hill would have to be at least

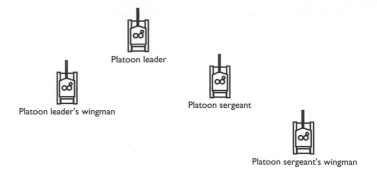

Tank Platoon in Wedge Formation

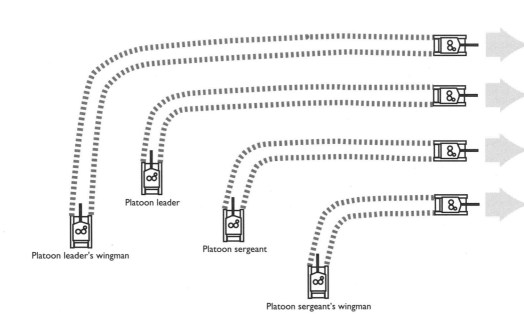

Platoon "Action Right" Battle Drill

sixty-six-feet high to appear on the map." So Greg did as Neal Creighton had done, and turned to "the old fashioned method. I used a compass."

On 20 October, Task Force 3-15 subjected its companies to a mass casualty exercise. The companies were to be hit with artillery, and we were to pretend that the chemical alarms sounded. Several soldiers from each platoon were to be evacuated. I volunteered in order to spare one of my soldiers from having to do yet another such task, and to see for myself how the evacuation process worked. Beyond buddy first aid, casualty care and evacuation had never been trained well, in my opinion, even at the National Training Center.

At the company level, the exercise went smoothly for Bravo Tank. My crew and the medics evacuated me fairly quickly after performing preliminary aid on my wounds and filling out the necessary tags and papers. I had a leg wound; I believe my gunner Sergeant Dock dressed it with a loose tourniquet. We wounded were placed on a truck. Actually, we were helped as we climbed onto the truck mostly under our own power. We were artificially crowded, sitting upright in shock with our splintered limbs and sucking chest wounds on the side benches in the back. The truck then drove around the desert searching for the hasty aid station and evacuation point. And drove around. And drove around. When we did find it, the task force medics on site had us first do a MOPP chemical suit exchange. This procedure is accomplished in pairs, the two soldiers taking turns assisting each other in removing a contaminated suit and donning a clean one. The medics, who did not want to risk contamination, stood back and watched. I had to remove my tourniquet to change suits, helped by a partner suffering from a projectile lodged in his eye. Right.

From the time the artillery fell on the company and the chemical alarms sounded to the time a medical specialist attended me, four and one-half hours passed. I wondered how many of us would have survived the wait. I was not encouraged. The army's general problem with medics manifested that day in the desert: In peace, each unit has too many, and they have too little to do; in war, each unit has too few. One medic track with two medics is not enough to handle a company of one hundred men that sustains serious casualties, especially when that track is a Vietnam vintage M113, with skin thinner than any of the company's other vehicles, and penetrable by a .50-caliber shell. A single hit could take out both medics. Nor did I completely trust the Medevac helicopter evacuation plan, which may have worked in Vietnam over short distances and relatively contained infantry firefights but would be much more stretched by the distances and the casualty potential of armored divisions battling over immense desert tracts. (Though I was impressed to learn that when the appendix of one of Bravo Tank's soldiers burst in early October, the system had him on a hospital ship in the Gulf and under the knife in less than two hours.)

The brigade built a primitive small arms range, Rock Range, through which all its companies rotated in November. Task Force 1-64 moved to the division-established Faisal Range for vehicle maneuver and live-fire training in mid-November. Greg Downey had never fired his Bradley Cavalry Fighting Vehicle:

"The whole scout platoon was looking forward to it. I wanted to use the live-fire exercise as a confidence builder for my crews and as a check on my vehicles' weapon systems. Prior to deployment, five of the six CFVs were not mission capable; by our arrival in Saudi, we had three with inoperational weapons systems. By the end of October, I had a platoon of six fully mission capable CFVs. My driver, Pfc. West, was back with us smiling ear to ear, having spent the month with our broken vehicle at the UMCP. I was glad to have him back. I think even our gunner, Specialist Lowther, had missed him.

"Unlike the gunnery ranges back at Fort Stewart, this range lacked targets that pop up to surprise the crew, electronically sense a hit, and automatically fall. The targets which populated this stretch of open desert were simple plywood silhouettes supported by wood poles. West pulled the vehicle up to the firing line while Lowther and I fed the 25-mm ammunition belt into the chain gun. The Bradley belt-fed chain gun works much like a machine gun, pulling the rounds into the firing chamber one after another. The rounds keep firing until the gunner releases the trigger.

"Crew coordination was a must, whether in a Bradley CFV or an M1 tank. Everybody had a job to do. As the Bradley Commander, or BC, I looked for targets, my head and shoulders outside the turret, using the naked eye or binoculars. Once I saw a target, I reached down and grabbed the BC's override, a joystick that took control of the turret and weapon systems from my gunner. I would then without getting down on my sights quickly lay the gun barrel in the general direction of the target and release the override, relinquishing control back to the gunner so he could scan to identify the target. Once the gunner started to fire, I helped him observe where the 25-mm rounds were landing and walked him on to the target — the Bradley's chain gun does not, like the Abrams's weapon system, sport a laser range finder, so you have to estimate the distance and adjust on the fly. We could see the rounds, day or night, by the glowing red phosphorous embedded in the back of the tracer rounds. In addition to helping my gunner, I would also tell the driver where and how I wanted him to maneuver the vehicle, though often he steered the vehicle to the best cover and concealment without my commands. On a mission, I would also be directing the movement and fires of the other five Bradleys, which I could not necessarily see; navigating; monitoring two radio nets; sending reports to battalion; and possibly calling for indirect fire. It can get pretty hairy.

"The gunner scans until either he or the BC identifies a target. He then selects the correct round to fire depending on the target. Armor-piercing AP rounds are used on hard targets, such as the enemy BMP, the Soviet-built version of our

Bradley. The AP rounds do not explode on contact; they pierce or cut right through the target. High explosive HE rounds explode on impact, spraying shrapnel like grenades, and are designed for soft targets, like trucks. Both ammunition types are most effective between 100 to 2,500 meters. The CFV also has a TOW missile launcher for destroying tanks, though it requires a few seconds to raise the TOW into its firing position. The Tube-launched, Optically-tracked, Wire-guided missile has a range of 3,750 meters — over two miles. The vehicle has to be stationary to fire the TOW; once fired, the missile is guided by signals sent through a wire that unspools as the missile flies down range — the gunner has to keep his reticle on the target for the duration of the missile's flight. The TOW launcher holds two missiles. A 7.62-mm machine gun, used for such soft targets as trucks and personnel, is coaxially mounted with the 25-mm chain gun. The coax can effectively range to eight hundred meters.

"On Faisal Range, Spc. Lowther and I concluded the prefire checklist. 'Well, let's see what this war pig can do,' I said.

"'Lowther, I bet you miss every target,' came West's voice over the intercom from the driver's station.

"'Kiss my ass, fat boy, you non-drivin' bitch!' Lowther retorted.

"I watched with excitement as the rounds started flying down range. The smell of the gunpowder inside the turret was sweet in its own way. As the chain gun rotated through the rounds, Spc. Lowther was yelling, cursing, and laughing up a storm. He seemed to let off a few extra rounds every time I gave the cease-fire command. He would have fired every round we had if I had let him. For all that, I did not get the rush from firing the 25 mm like I did when I fired the M1's 105-mm main gun. The 25 mm was like firing a .22-caliber semi-automatic rifle, continually squeezing off every round in the magazine. The M1 tank was like shooting a double-row, twelve-gauge shotgun, pulling both triggers at once. Big difference. When an M1 fires, the earth quakes.

"All six of my CFVs fired and hit. No maintenance problems. No surprises. This was a great confidence and morale boost for the soldiers. They were finally convinced that if we had to fight, we could depend on our vehicles. The crews had developed a bond with their vehicles. It was their home, their transportation, their lifeline. I was happy to see them performing maintenance without being told. We had come a long way from the Fort Stewart motor pool."

■ It sprinkled on 27 November, the area's first rainfall, as a postscript from one of my letters claims, in three years. The next day Captain Swisher, my company commander, evaluated Neal Creighton's platoon. Each tank platoon in the battalion would be evaluated conducting the same mission, against either another tank platoon or the battalion scout platoon in Humvees. I rode with Swisher in his Humvee to observe Neal's run. Because the mission called for a simulated chemical attack, the platoon had to wear gas masks and button-up, locking down all the hatches. Navigation is much more difficult when you are looking through the scratched plastic of your gas mask's eyepieces and then through the small rectangular vision blocks around the base of the tank commander's hatch. And because you aren't out of your hatch looking down on both the turret and the hull, you have to struggle to know where the parts of your own tank are in relation to one another — you can't tell the driver to turn right when he is in the hull facing one way and you are in the turret facing another. All this while leading four other tanks across unfamiliar ground, reading maps, talking on the radio, and looking for the enemy.

Once again, as he had done for his first move in the desert, Neal figured out the difference between magnetic north and the north his compass read when distorted by the tank's magnetic field. This time, though, the compass was mounted inside the driver's compartment in the hull, and Neal relied on his driver Forbes to steer the tank on the right azimuth and track the distance on the odometer for each leg of the route.

I watched Neal lead his platoon exactly to his objective. Remarkable. Moving with any speed in the open desert, you can locate yourself easily within a couple hundred meters, but it's extremely difficult to do with much more precision — even without being buttoned-up. That evening I wrote home for compasses. I initially received from my parents two brands made for automobile dashboards, and later Maria sent a pair of expensive aviation gyrocompasses used in small planes. Every time my platoon tried to determine a consistent magnetic deviation, we failed. My brother Eric still admonishes me for not having known better. But Neal had done it. Neal remembers that the task force, following his example, locally purchased several gyrocompasses, only to meet with the same lack of success I did.

The exercise included a mission to test section maneuver in addition to platoon maneuver. When my platoon was evaluated, Sfc. Freight got his section lost in a lane less than one kilometer long. My section did not get lost, but we had our own problems. As I rounded a berm, Sergeant Rivera's tank behind me, I spied an antenna and a .50-caliber machine gun poking up from behind a berm a few hundred meters to my front. The antenna and Ma Deuce could have belonged to either another M1 or a scout Humvee. We backed behind our berm. I conducted a recon by fire by shooting my .50 at the enemy's — really by announcing "caliber .50" over the radio followed by a bit of "rat-tat-rat-tat-tat" onomatopoeia — to make him move. Then I called a mortar mission on his location. Finally I decided to assault: I ordered Rivera to provide overwatching fires, then follow me as I bounded forward into the open against the enemy. As I left the cover of the berm, I saw an M1 to my direct front and had my gunner blast it with a main gun round. Swisher radioed that we had a kill, then that we had killed Rivera, who had assaulted from around the other side of the berm. He was supposed to have been behind me. In war, at thirty meters, I could hardly mistake an M1 for anything else. But the event illustrates the ease of confusion, even in the most controlled training environment, even at the smallest tactical level.

The first week of December, all leader tracks in 2d Brigade down to platoon leaders executed a four-day rehearsal of our counterattack against an Iraqi offensive into Saudi. Rehearsing the GDP's counterattack was the exercise's express purpose. "At the time," writes Col. Paul Kern, the brigade commander, only he and his executive and operations officers "knew the exercise was also a rehearsal for our upcoming attack into Iraq."[4] While the rest of us in his brigade may not have had the official word, we certainly talked among ourselves.

Neal Creighton was to lead Task Force 3-15, and Rob Holmes was to lead Task Force 1-64. Occasionally Task Force 3-15 would maneuver in two columns, Neal leading the left column while I led the right.

The attack, a movement to contact, commenced the night of 4 December. The brigade maneuvered against combat elements of the 3d ACR, the cavalry regiment from Fort Bliss, Texas, that in early October had relieved 2-4 Cav on the American Forward Line of Troops. We considered them, and they considered us, Iraqi forces.

With 91 percent illumination — no need for night vision devices — and less than one-quarter of the brigade's vehicles, we still had trouble navigating and sustaining formation. Eventually that night we ran into another unit of M1s. I saw them first, checking fire until we could identify them. They could have been the enemy 3d ACR or a friendly 24th unit. We sat on their flank and watched them drive by, ducks in a row. With a single command from me to fire, my platoon could have destroyed what looked like an entire company. After several minutes the other tanks opened fire on us — in these mock battles, we simulated fire by flashing our headlights. The firefight lasted some ten minutes, at which time both sides tired of flashing lights over and over again. Baillergeon then informed us that we had just engaged Task Force 3-69, the third task force in 2d Brigade. Friendlies.

Granted, the Soviet brand of tanks used by Iraq, with their rounded turrets, looks nothing like the angular M1 Abrams. Nonetheless, two friendly units found one another unexpectedly in each other's sights and at a greater distance could have mistaken the other for the enemy. The round turrets of American M60 tanks, which some U.S. Marine units employed, the French AMX tank series, and Arab coalition Soviet brand tanks could also have easily been misidentified. If the American military were ever to battle the angular tanks of other Western countries, such as West

Germany's Leopard, Great Britain's Chieftain and Challenger, or Israel's Merkava, vehicle identification would be that much more difficult.

Do you fire on vehicles you can't squarely identify? If you wait, they may fire on you — because they are the enemy, or because they are friendly and believe you are the enemy, or because they are friendly and not sure about you but unwilling to take the chance that you are an enemy, that you are a friendly believing them to be enemy, or that you are a friendly unsure and unwilling to take the chance. Kill or be killed. Indeed the very violence and speed of our AirLand Battle tactics seemed to invite friendly fire incidents. But I also knew that this same violence and speed can shock opponents into paralysis and bring the battle to a quick end, preventing the loss of even more American lives from a protracted fight against a less-dazed enemy.

Greg Downey considered the event "a waste of time" as a counterattacking exercise, "since the likelihood of the Iraqi army attacking was slim to none. Throughout November training continued to focus on defensive operations, even though we all knew our focus should have shifted to offensive operations. Publicly discussing purely offensive maneuvers was taboo. I don't know why; after all, we were reading about the different scenarios for a coalition attack into Iraq in newspapers and magazines. Nonetheless, Lieutenant Colonel Gordon was very clear in his guidance: No discussion of purely offensive maneuver was allowed.

"The counterattack consisted of a flanking maneuver to the north and east, a little over one hundred kilometers. My scout platoon would conduct a moving flank guard mission on the brigade's left flank. This is an extremely difficult mission to execute. My original plan was to have my sections bound, or leap-frog, essentially establishing a series of mobile security posts to guard the task force's flank. But I knew that splitting the platoon into sections would spell disaster. I trusted only two other scouts to navigate at night, Staff Sergeant Deem and Corporal Thornton. I decided we could bound as long the sections maintained visual contact with one another. The section bounding forward would stop as soon as the others lost sight of it.

"This worked well initially. But since my scout platoon was ten kilometers from the main body on the outer curve of the route, we kept falling behind the task force, and I finally abandoned that concept. I ordered my six scout vehicles into a column formation and raced the rest of the way, averaging about twenty miles per hour. At the time I thought to myself, How can you recon anything when you're moving this fast? The rehearsal proved to be great preparation for what was to be the fastest zone recon in the history of land warfare."

The mission ended at 0400 on the fifth. At 1500, Task Force 3–15 moved to the gunnery range, where I returned to Bravo Tank. The rest of company did not join us until the night of 7 December. Over the next exhausting two and a half days, my platoon conducted five evaluated maneuver missions, one day and one night live-fire gunnery exercise, and four missions as the Opposing Force against another platoon under evaluation. The furious training pace was really the only kind of training that could prepare you for the pace of AirLand Battle.

Tank firing startled me awake the night of the twelfth — my platoon had completed all of its missions, and for the instant of my waking I forgot my whereabouts and panicked, fearing Hussein had launched an offensive against us. It took me a while to fall back asleep.

We returned to our camp at Hinesville on 14 December. I had been away for two weeks, and the next day we boarded buses for a trip to the Dammam port for training on the new M1A1 tanks we had been scheduled to receive. "By this time," writes Greg Downey, "the 15 January Iraqi withdrawal deadline had been established and Seventh Corps was coming to Saudi Arabia from Germany. The tide was turning from a coalition defense to a coalition offense. There was still an abundance of rumors circulating about going home soon, but you were either overly optimistic or undeniably ignorant to believe them. We could talk openly about pure offensive maneuver now."

Task Force 3-15's last large training exercise before the decamping of Assembly Area Hinesville started on the evening of 6 January. The next day we practiced task force battle drills. The principle is the same as the platoon battle drill; the task force has set plays to execute on contact with the enemy. Only instead of drills to the front, rear, right, and left, Task Force 3-15 used a quadrant system to enable it to respond diagonally from its axis of advance: to the front left (Quadrant I), front right (Quadrant II), rear left (Quadrant III), and rear right (Quadrant IV).

That night I had a dream. I remember it vividly because when I woke the next day, I was crying. The dream began with the back of the head of a boyish figure whom I knew to be Russian in the way you simply know things in dreams, and who turned around to reveal himself as a herself, and we fell ecstatically in love. Her dad didn't want us to be together, and he was a spitting image of my dud platoon sergeant. The dream ended after I punched "Freight" in the left eye and floored him. I woke up in tears because the dream felt more real to me than the desert; because I didn't want to be awake; because I wanted to be back there, with the boyish Russian girl, loving ecstatically.

On 9 January the task force conducted an obstacle breach. The officers had gathered the previous afternoon to discuss the operation. I remember our commander, Lieutenant Colonel Barrett, calling our immediate future a time of "high adventure" and resenting him for it. For the exercise, engineers from division had built a single-belt obstacle, to include a tank ditch, concertina wire, and a fake minefield, with an Iraqi trench line behind it. Iraqi defensive lines

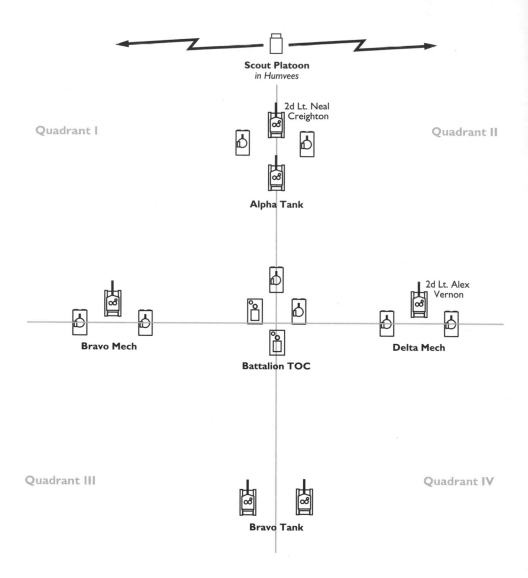

Task Force 3-15 in Diamond Formation

Note: vehicle icons in company formations represent platoons.

typically had two or three obstacle belts in front of the trenches. After we breached the obstacle, the infantry would dismount from the Bradleys and practice clearing an occupied trench.

Battalion simulated a preparatory artillery strike followed by an intensive "smoke mission," during which artillery fired smoke rounds simulated on the ground by smoke grenades to cover the engineers while they laid bridges across the tank ditch and cleared lanes through the minefield behind it. The operation was well synchronized; from when my company began its move at 1000 hours, it did not stop and we hit the obstacle belt in stride. My platoon fell into a line formation as we approached the right side of the ditch, and when we turned left toward the bridge we blew smoke on my command to provide additional cover to the company's Bradleys following us. A switch in the driver's compartment sprays fuel onto the turbine engine; the resultant steam cloud tumbles and swells thickly white behind the Abrams and hangs, drifts, shrouding the forces on the other side until the unimpeded desert breeze dissipates the cloud first to a smoky gray haze, then to wisps, then to nothingness. When the tank is long gone.

I hit the bridge and led the platoon over the ditch, then through the lanes made by the engineer's MICLIC ("mick-lick") device — a single-shot mine-clearing line charge that blasts a one hundred-meter path by shooting the line charge across the obstacle with a rocket-propelled explosive — and sped toward the Iraqi trench. My gunner continuously sprayed the trench with the coax, the 7.62-mm machine gun coaxially mounted beside the tank's main gun. I drove over the trench and made a sharp right to find where it ended on the right side, so the infantry behind me knew where to enter. I had the last tank in my platoon column blow smoke as soon as it was over the trench; then, after I found the edge and turned again in the direction of the attack, it stopped blowing smoke when it made its turn. The smoke thus marked where we crossed the trench and where the trench began, and it provided cover for the infantry from enemy forces beyond the trench. I took the platoon to a position about two hundred meters beyond the trench, where my tanks and those from Bravo Mech and Alpha Tank joined to protect against a counterattack, while the grunts dismounted from their Bradleys and did their job in the trenches.

That mission gave me more confidence in our combined arms ability, in our ability to deliver a blow so violent and swift and overwhelming, than any other training we conducted during Desert Shield. The other remarkable event of that day, really a sequence of events, began the night before. I dreamed I saw Maria, and she was pregnant. I touched her belly's swell. Then, about thirty minutes into the mission, while traveling toward the obstacle belt, I saw a sheep's head behind a bush in the center of my axis of advance. I swerved to miss it, wondering why it did not move. As I passed, I looked back. A tiny white fur ball next to the sheep's rear end stood, shakily, and shook off liquid goo. The sheep had just given birth (later in the day I learned from another soldier in the company that she gave birth to a second shortly after). Five minutes later, still attacking toward the obstacle, we passed a small Bedouin camp, probably belonging to a single family. A Bedouin woman outside the tent and several children watched us.

Traversing the gun to scan for the enemy, Sergeant Dock broke across the intercom: "She has kids, sir, she must like to fuck. I see tit! She's breast-feeding her kid! Tit! Tit!" I saw the bundle clutched to her, and it was all I could do to keep Pfc. Reynolds from steering the tank — and the half of the task force following me — in her direction.

The pregnant dream, the birthing sheep, the breast-feeding Badawiyah: How could I not find this awesome coincidence, its elements even appearing to me in natural sequence, auspicious? U.S. Secretary of State James Baker and his Iraqi counterpart Tariq Aziz were that day scheduled to talk; I so wanted to believe I had witnessed something greater than the sum of its happenstance.

The hope would hang with me until the day the division invaded Iraq.

Soldiers and Soldiering

Soldiers don't really fight for ideals, or for country, or for God. We fight for each other. After six months in the desert together, it's my buddies, my NCOs, my lieutenant, I'm willing to die for! . . . Okay, maybe not the lieutenant.

— Soldier in *Doonesbury* comic strip

One night during our first month in the desert, the month my platoon spent along Tapline Road with the cavalry, the two enlisted on my tank, Vanderwerker and McBryde, asked me to point out constellations to them. I showed them what I knew, the dippers and the lazy "W" of Cassiopeia. Sergeant Dock hadn't paid attention to my brief class. When I concluded, he mapped his version of the starry night for us. He had picked one star as his wife, another as his toddling daughter, still another his dog. "Every night I look up, and there they are looking back." Vanderwerker thrilled at the idea, immediately picking a star for his twin sister and another for Tina, Dock's sister-in-law whom Vanderwerker had yet to meet but was wooing in letters. Vanderwerker and Tina fell in love through their letters, or fell in love with the idea of falling in love through wartime letters, and married shortly after meeting for the first time upon redeployment. The new bride was pregnant within two months.

For Neal and Mary Creighton, the constellation they looked to was Orion. "Because even though we were not together with our new baby," Mary has shared with me, "Orion was watching over the three of us. Even though we were separated, we could both look up to the same night sky and share the view together of Orion." Neal wrote and told her about a song that he wanted her to listen to, that he wanted both of them to think about when looking up at Orion and feeling for the other across the earth's arc. In the song, two lovers are separated, and the lonesome singer doesn't know where in the world the other is. The "I" of the song finds comfort in the stars: "Orion's heart is bright enough" and "Orion's arms are wide enough" to hold both of them, despite the distance, in a single, glowing embrace.[5]

Like a lot of American soldiers, Greg, Neal, and Rob grew up playing football. Dave participated in track and field in high school, then played intramural football at West Point. I played soccer and have not yet figured out how to get my hand around that oblong, pointed "ball."

For Greg, growing up in Nebraska, playing for the University of Nebraska Cornhusker football team meant everything to a young boy. The dream ended when he stopped growing at five feet seven inches, and 140 pounds.

Neal became something of a local hero as the high school's varsity quarterback at Fort Riley, Kansas. This success came despite his size, only 175 pounds at six feet. His size had also been an issue when he first started playing tackle football at seven. Then, at sixty-five pounds, he was the smallest player on the team. Those first teammates joked that he needed a diaper pin to hold up his jockstrap. Over the years of playing sports, he broke an elbow, dislocated a shoulder, and separated a knee. These injuries, and the innumerable bumps and bruises, he says, fostered both physical and mental toughness and the discipline he would need to be a leader. Neal's hopes of playing college ball abruptly ended his senior year when his dislocated shoulder caused him to be sent to the bench. The next time he took the field he was rusty and fumbled the ball. The entire student body booed. But he rebounded at West Point, where he quarterbacked our cadet company intramural team to a regimental championship and went on to play for the Academy's intercollegiate 150-lb football team, a club sport whose members, like wrestlers, must make weight before each contest.

Rob also credits football with helping develop his discipline and physical and mental tenacity. Like Neal, Rob started playing football young, and he too played quarterback. It's hard for boys growing up in Georgia to escape football; it's their cultural kudzu. If a young man isn't on the field on a fall Friday night, he's in the stands. Rob wasn't tall and had only an average throwing arm, but he decided to play quarterback anyway because it "fit his personality" as "the most visible, fun venue" he could find for being a leader. What Rob lacked in physical talent he made up for by reading defenses quickly and adjusting plays accordingly. "I don't believe there is a better way for a young man to grow up than with sports," he writes, "especially team contact sports. I learned to sacrifice, and I became comfortable leading people under pressure.

"One lesson I learned from high school football was how to judge people under pressure. Everyone reacts to stress differently. Some of my soldiers needed exercise and athletics to blow off steam, so we played baseball. Underberg's Frisbee helped also; another man had a football. Soldiers were always wrestling. A lieutenant from one of the infantry companies even had a golf club and balls shipped to him.

"Some people just wanted to be left alone. They would write letters or read. Others slept at every opportunity. Sometimes a soldier would yell and scream to vent. Everyone needed to release pressure somehow. For each individual in my platoon, I tried to identify how they did it, when they needed to do it, and let them.

"I enjoyed walking around and talking with my soldiers in Second Platoon. I genuinely liked most of them. I wanted to know their needs and let them see that I was sentenced to this desert with them. Soldiers hate elitists, but if you treat them like human beings and show them that you are human too, they will most likely support you.

"Since I was also human, I had to defuse every so often just like my men. When I needed to relax, I took a shower and read *The Economist* magazine. When I renewed my subscription from the desert, the magazine's London editor wrote me a personal note wishing me luck in his concise, British way."

When Rob arrived in Saudi, he had neither a loader nor a gunner on his tank. Underberg and the incompetent clerk-turned-gunner joined the crew at the port. That gunner lasted all of a week. Rob did not receive another gunner until Delta Tank's first day at Graceland, some three weeks later.

From the ridge overlooking Sarrar where he had slept in his Humvee the night before Task Force 1-64 rolled into the area for the first time, Rob watched the battalion closing in. "An armor battalion moving across the desert leaves quite a cloud of sand in its wake. Delta's tanks pulled in south of the wadis. I met the company, and as soon as my platoon was in position, I sought out my platoon sergeant. Sfc. Sikes gave me a quick report on the maintenance of our four tanks, made a couple comments on personnel, and was halfway into his next sentence when my driver, Pfc. Bell, came running up and interrupted.

"'Sir, we got a new gunner!' Sikes scowled at the impetuous private for spoiling his surprise.

"Sikes began, 'I don't know exactly what to think of this guy yet, lieutenant, but he's better than your old one, and if he is half as good as he says he is, you'll be fine.'

"The platoon leader should have the best gunner in the platoon — not necessarily the best marksman, but the best sergeant in terms of caring for the tank and crew so the lieutenant can focus on the whole platoon. He also helps take care of his lieutenant, ensuring the busy officer keeps his individual skills up, maintains his gear, and gets enough sleep. I looked toward my tank and saw my newest gunner approaching. A five-foot-five-inch, very-well-built black man with dark sunglasses and an olive-drab bandanna around his neck.

He positively strutted, and with his new Beretta 9-mm pistol on his hip, he looked like a short gunslinger. Bell had dashed back to him, bouncing around him like a puppy.

"'Are you my new lieutenant?' the new man asked when he stood in front of me, hands on hips.

"'Are you always this formal when reporting for duty?" In the field army protocol differed than in garrison, but I was not yet sold on my new gunner's quite evident opinion of himself.

"'Sir, I am Sgt. Kurt Downing, formerly of the 2d Armored Cavalry Regiment, and you are the luckiest officer in Saudi Arabia.' He flashed a beautiful smile beneath his dark shades.

"'I'm Lt. Rob Holmes, and why don't you tell me why I am so lucky?' At least my other gunner had been quiet.

"'Because I am the best gunner in Saudi Arabia, sir. I can knock the wings off a mosquito at three thousand meters. I'm taking you home to mama.' Sergeant Downing let loose a wild laugh, took off his sunglasses, and extended his hand for me to shake. If Major Diehl had liked Underberg, wait until he met this character.

"I shook his hand, and Downing returned to the tank with Bell bouncing behind. I gave Underberg a quick glance. Beach Boys and all, Underberg was a sharp soldier. He couldn't get away with his goofball antics without knowing his job.

"'What do you think of our new gunner?' I asked him.

"'He's full of shit.'

"Sfc. Sikes tried to allay our fears. He told us Downing had been decorated with a Meritorious Service Medal when he left Germany, which was extremely uncommon for a soldier his rank. That, coupled with his training in the 2d ACR, gave me hope. Sikes was proud of being an NCO, and had less tolerance for bad NCOs than I did. My old gunner was now the first sergeant's driver.

"My new man Downing had Bell crawling all around the tank's track, checking the tension and road wheels, and he was down on the sand with Bell showing him where to look for problems. He got dirty with the soldiers. This was a very good sign. My platoon sergeant knew within about sixty seconds when someone didn't know the technical aspects of the tank, so if Downing passed his first meeting with my platoon sergeant, I felt pretty confident in my new gunner. As I watched the rejuvenated crew, Sikes continued with Downing's biography. 'He was the battalion master gunner in his old unit and has a chest full of medals for gunnery scores.' The master gunner meant he had been sent to an elite army school to learn how to train other tankers to shoot. Like his Meritorious Service Medal, it was an unusual attribute for a man of his rank.

"'Hey! Are you Underberg?' Sergeant Downing barked over at my loader, who was still standing with me and Sikes.

"'Yes, sergeant! And I'm the best loader in this division! I'm going to bring you home to your mama!' If my tank crew didn't yet have cohesion, it definitely had attitude.

"Sergeant Downing laughed and yelled back, 'Then quit kissing the lieutenant's butt and get over here and help Bell!' Another good sign. Downing's predecessor had been scared to give orders to Underberg.

"After Underberg left, Sfc. Sikes added that Sergeant Downing had been busted from staff sergeant about six months ago for messing around with a married woman.

"'He got busted and still got an MSM when he left?' I asked Sikes.

"'Listen sir, the man made a mistake, but he looks like a good NCO. There's not a woman within one hundred kilometers — Sergeant Downing will do just fine.' I had plenty on my mind enough without having to worry about my soldiers' sex drives. We were not far from the Iraqi army, I had sixteen men to return home, and at some point I might get shot at. I was happy that I didn't also have to manage love triangles. I looked over at Sergeant Downing working with Bell and Underberg getting our tank squared away. Over in the first sergeant's Humvee my last gunner was asleep behind the wheel, his mouth wide open. He missed his clerk's desk back at Stewart.

"'Yes, Sergeant Sikes, Sergeant Downing will be just fine.'"

"At times in the desert Sergeant Downing drove me absolutely crazy and I wanted to kill him. Other times I honestly thought he was an angel from heaven. I'm serious about that: the guy appeared in my life when none of us knew what was going to happen after I had been in the desert three weeks without a gunner. We did have to grow on each other — it wasn't love at first sight. Downing was one of the most generous and compassionate people I have ever met, with a great sense of humor.

"He had a Gameboy, one of those electronic games, and he played it incessantly. It made me nuts. I hated the little bleeps and chirps and tunes that thing made. Downing told me he did it to keep his reflexes fast. Whatever. As I got to know him better, I learned that his son had sent him the Gameboy. Kurt Jr. had one back home. It was his favorite toy. So I concluded that Downing's playing the Gameboy was how he thought about his son, how he missed his son, how he stayed connected.

"Downing somehow rigged his gunner's station in the tank so that the gun tube actually traversed back and forth as if he were scanning. He and Underberg were in cahoots. Underberg was a little genius. I found out when one day their contraption broke, and the gun tube hit maximum elevation, pointing up in the air. I dropped down in my seat to look through my commander's sight extension to see what was going on. I called to him over the intercom.

"'Negative contact, sir,' he came back.

"'Is that the moon, Sergeant Downing?' I asked. He woke up completely and realized where the gun pointed. He was able to go on movements and training missions, crammed in that seat in front of me with my feet and knees bumping into his back, and sleep like a baby.

"But when it came down to business, Sergeant Downing could use his weapon system. If he wasn't the best gunner in Saudi Arabia, I am convinced that he was among the best."

■ Two months before the war I submitted two of my soldiers for Army Commendation Medals for heroism. The event happened on the return from our four-day mid-December platoon gunnery. Six tank-bearing HETs and one bus carrying the six crews made the first convoy and were to make a second trip for the remainder of the company. The first five HETs pulled off the north-south hardball east of Assembly Area Hinesville to download the tanks. The brakes locked on the sixth HET, the one with my tank; it got as far off the road as it could and stopped, some five hundred meters short of the others. Brunner and Vanderwerker, the loader and driver on my tank, stepped off the bus with me, and we started walking the half kilometer back to our tank. Sergeant Dock had ridden shotgun in the HET carrying our tank. He had it downloaded by the time the three of us had another two hundred meters to walk.

When it happened. The HET driver dashed off the road. A metallic crunch. Black smoke billowed from behind the HET. My mother always said that most wrecks happen within two miles of home.

Our MP escorts scrambled for their Humvees and raced to the accident. Dock flew out of the driver's hatch and sprinted to the HET, disappearing behind it. Greg Jackson joined Vanderwerker, Brunner, and me as we hurried to the scene, where we found an Arab flatbed truck loaded with pallets of bottled water rammed alongside the right rear of the HET and a semi plowed directly into the rear of the Arab flatbed. The Arab driver emerged unscathed; fuel and water poured beneath his truck. We arrived to find Dock and the MPs wielding tools from our tank to pry into the bright yellow cab of the semi.

As I closed on the crushed cab I heard the high-pitched screams. My stomach somersaulted. I executed an about-face and stood still, catching myself. When I turned back to the cab, a few more soldiers and some Arabs had materialized and joined Dock's and the MPs' efforts to free two trapped GIs. My first thought, watching Arabs and Americans piling atop one another to get inside the cab — what a photograph.

Greg and I let the others continue the work and established a Landing Zone for the Medevac Blackhawk helicopter. We anchored the bright orange VS-17 panel from my tank with the tank's heavy track jacks on a flat spot of desert a hundred meters or so away from the road. I wonder if Greg knew I still needed time when he asked me to set up the LZ. My stomach probably showed on my face.

At some point I used an MP Humvee radio to call the battalion TOC. I reported our position and requested immediate Medevac. After the failed initial effort to free the trapped soldiers, Vanderwerker retreated to the MP Humvee on the other side of the road, squatted, and began to bawl. Dock went over and sat with him, and thirty minutes later Vanderwerker returned to attack the cab with a vengeance. A small man, he eventually wormed himself inside the cab on the driver's side to cut metal away and apply pressure to the driver's wounds. I later learned from Dock that Vanderwerker had sidelined himself after taking a blow from his past: A car accident had decapitated his prom date; he put her in the body bag.

When the Medevac first landed, I spoke with the dismounted chief medic. Procedure did not allow the helicopter to shut down because it would have taken too long to fire back up once the patients were on board. Nor could it sit on the ground with blades spinning and dust spewing into its engine. It took flight and spent the time until we freed the soldiers circling and sporadically touching down to check on our progress. Like a buzzard, I thought.

With Vanderwerker on the driver's side, Brunner wedged himself into the passenger's side to help the other soldier, who happened to be a young woman. Brunner stabilized her head and tried to talk her out of her impending shock.

I played crowd control, helped dump sand and water on the spilled fuel, then directed parking to keep the Medevac LZ and its route to the truck free of Arab civilian cars whose drivers had pulled off the road to help, or simply watch.

Greg Jackson described the wails of the trapped driver as sounding like the turbine whine of the Medevac Blackhawk standing by.

After several hours we freed the two soldiers. After the war, back at Fort Stewart, I learned that they had suffered no permanent injuries.

I dwelt on the accident for the remainder of the day and much of the next. I thought about needless pain, suffering, and death. I considered the nature of my job: the willful infliction and risking of pain, suffering, and death. Our first military science class at West Point, "Introduction to the Military Profession," had tagged us officers-in-training as future professional "managers of violence." Accidents cause enough tragedy. We didn't need to be in the business of creating more. I thought again of going to the chaplain and quitting. Again, I deferred.

Brunner and Vanderwerker received their medals upon our return to Georgia.

■ The bright spot on Rob Holmes's crew was his nineteen-year-old driver. "Pfc. Chris Bell was a high school state champion wrestler still in peak physical condition. His boyish face was topped with already-thinning blond hair. He shared my hometown of Atlanta and had been on my tank since my arrival at Fort Stewart. Bell absolutely loved being on the platoon leader's crew. I used to overhear him bragging to the other privates about 'hanging out with the lieutenant.' Bell was consistently in a good mood, a team player who worked hard and never bitched. In Georgia he always started conversations by asking if I had seen the Braves game the night before. I usually had, so that gave him at least five minutes of face time with the platoon leader. I'll talk Braves baseball all day long.

"Bell loved getting mail probably more than anyone else in my platoon. His new bride and former high school sweetheart wrote him almost every day. Bell liked everybody else's mail also. When a package arrived, he would rifle through it before even the recipient had a chance. Nobody cared. Bell was the most innocent, good-natured person in Saudi.

"One night in early November, the battalion chaplain woke me where I slept on a cot in my tent. Capt. Tim Bedsole was a soft-spoken Southern Baptist from Dothan, Alabama, who never missed an opportunity to be with the troops, to pray, or to sing. We were good friends, but I knew that night wasn't a social call.

"Bell had a younger sister back in Atlanta. The two of them had been adopted together by an Atlanta couple and were very close. The preacher softly told me that she had been killed in a car accident earlier that day. I could hardly believe it. I felt sick inside. Tim asked me if I wanted to tell Bell. On mental autopilot, I muttered *yes*.

"Tim and I walked over to my tank. Bell could sleep through anything, and like most M1 drivers, he slept in his driver's compartment. He would recline the seat, close his hatch, and enjoy more comfort and privacy than any of us. He sat there when writing letters back home — pictures of his nineteen-year-old wife were taped to his control panel. In his driver's compartment he escaped from Saudi. That night he was fast asleep inside.

"I drew my .45 pistol, dropped the magazine out of its well, and pounded with it on his hatch to wake him. He opened the hatch, smiled, and asked if I needed anything. I couldn't recall any class at West Point on how to tell a soldier his sister was dead. She was the only one in the world who shared his blood, and I had to tell him she was gone.

"'Bell, your sister was killed in a car accident earlier today.'

"Bell lost his smile. 'Yes, sir.'

"'Bell, I'm sorry.' I had no idea what I was doing.

"'I know you are, sir.' His eyes watered a little, and he shook my hand. He sunk back down into his compartment and closed his eyes tightly.

"The chaplain addressed my driver by his first name, Chris, and said a brief prayer. I told Bell we would send him home immediately. He opened his eyes and climbed out of his hatch. I helped him gather his belongings, neither of us saying another word. He picked up his gear and walked down the sand dune with Chaplain Bedsole to a waiting Humvee.

"I thought I would never see him again. It was easy for people who went home to finagle a way not to come back. I was the highest ranking man in the platoon, and Bell was the lowest, but we had developed a strong friendship in the desert. If I had to go to war, I wanted my crew to include Bell. But for his sake, I hoped he didn't return. After the months in this wasteland and losing his sister, Bell had suffered enough.

"A week later, another Humvee pulled up. To my surprise, Bell jumped out, smiled, and saluted me. In the field, soldiers are never supposed to salute officers so as not to tip off a sniper. Bell always forgot this, and I think he enjoyed saluting anyway.

"'How are you, Bell?' I asked.

"'Fine, sir.' He walked to our fighting position and began checking over his tank.

"I learned in the desert that the trust between an officer and his soldiers was more important than any other quality. I would have done anything for Bell, and I knew he would do the same for me. I was grateful to have him back."

■ For my own morale and comfort, I turned to my friends. The other lieutenants in Bravo Tank — Greg Jackson, Bob McCann, and Matt Hoagland — kept me sane, kept me laughing. Neal, Rob, and Dave felt the same way about the lieutenants in their companies.

Once, under Greg Jackson's inspiration, the four lieutenants in Bravo Tank took mess detail from the NCOs, donned paper chef hats, and served chow to the company. The soldiers loved it. One day in November, after Bob McCann licked the bottom of a plastic pudding container clean, he told me we had to do something to keep our tongues in shape. Unlike officers of the same rank, soldiers never addressed one another by first name, and they teased us for it. "Hey sir, *Matt* is looking for you. I think he wants to know if you can go out and play with him and *Bob*." Bob quipped that the legendary buffoonery of second lieutenants was part of our job, a morale boost for the soldiers.

As much as I leaned on the other lieutenants, when they faltered, so did I. The XO especially; Greg Jackson's influence on me was enormous. One of the catalysts for his down days — he suffered severe mood swings that lasted days — was his brother's letters foretelling the apocalypse. The Jacksons were devout Baptists. According to the brother, the events in the Gulf conflict matched the signs in the Book of Revelations. *Dear Greg: the End is near, the End is here, and you're smack in the middle of it.* Greg didn't subscribe, yet the letters still got under his skin.

Greg and I discussed God privately several times. One night in my tent, Greg told me he prayed for my soul every night because I didn't share his faith. He loved me, he said, and wanted me in Heaven with him where I deserved to be. He cried for me because I didn't believe what he believed, because I wouldn't be with him in Heaven; I was bound for the other place.

I sympathize with commanders and specialty platoon leaders, like Greg Downey, who did not have such a local support group. I experienced a little of this at my platoon position when attached to 2-4 Cav: no one to discuss training and personnel issues, no one to share thoughts and feelings with. Everyone around you a subordinate with a line betwixt — a necessary, difficult line.

Leaders and Leadership

The platoon leader is responsible to the commander for the discipline and training of his platoon, the maintenance of its equipment, and its success in combat. He must be proficient in the tactical employment of his section and of the platoon in concert with a company team or troop. He must have a solid understanding of troop-leading procedures and develop his ability to apply them quickly and efficiently on the battlefield.

The platoon leader must know the capabilities and limitations of the platoon's personnel and equipment; at the same time, he must be well versed in enemy organizations, doctrine, and equipment. He must serve as an effective tank commander (TC). Most important of all, the platoon leader must be flexible, using sound judgment to make correct decisions quickly and at the right times based on his commander's intent and the tactical situation.

Platoon leaders must know and understand the task force mission and the task force commander's intent. They must be prepared to assume the duties of company commander in accordance with the succession of command.
— FM 17-15, *Tank Platoon* manual

For Lt. Nathaniel Tripp, being an infantry platoon leader in Vietnam became a form of fatherhood. He took care of his soldiers, and they depended on him, he came to feel, as a father and his sons. I heard the former lieutenant Tripp read from his recently published memoir, *Father, Soldier, Son*, at Pentagon City Border's bookstore over Memorial Day weekend, 1997. He looked more like a professor than a soldier. He wore a slightly-too-small jacket over a casual shirt and jeans; his hair and eyebrows were anything but dressed and covered; his wide mouth was pulled back in a perpetual grin. And his familial analogy was wrong.

No, not wrong. Just not true. Not true to my experiences as the youngest of three sons.

With my soldiers I felt brotherly, felt that they looked up to me more as younger brothers look up to the eldest than as sons to their father. We were in it together, after all, living in the same tank and tent. We had a father figure also, our company commander, whom they called — as soldiers do their commanders — the "old man." And while listening to tales of the young Lt. Tripp, it finally dawned on me why the mantle of leadership had sat so awkwardly and uncomfortably on my shoulders: As the youngest brother, I was the one doing the looking up to, the one doing the following. That was the natural order of things. My natural order, anyway. Being looked up to as a platoon leader turned my world upside down.

After he finished reading, when it was my turn to hand him my copy of his book for a signature, I let him know that I had been a platoon leader in the Persian Gulf War. Then I asked him if he were an only child.

Yes, in fact, he was. What made me ask?

I drove away from the bookstore thinking the Greeks had it right when they made Apollo the bright and shining god of war and his younger brother Hermes the mischievous, artful god of letters. The medieval nobles too, who sent the oldest son to the army, the youngest to the clergy.

Rob is the oldest of two boys. Greg is a middle son, with younger brothers looking up to him — the first to graduate from college, after all. Neal, with two older sisters and no brothers, is the only son and namesake of a general officer. Dave, the only one of the five of us to stay in the army and command a company, is a middle son with an older brother and a younger sister. Fine. I've at least helped explain things for me.

At twenty-three, I was one of the younger members of my platoon and the youngest man on my tank. S.Sgt. Rivera, my usurped platoon sergeant, was in his thirties and had three children. Sfc. Freight, the inept usurper, was in his late forties. Just as older cadets at West Point — cadets with perspective shaped by more than high school — fared better in leadership roles and rankings, older second lieutenants generally fared better as platoon leaders. Junior officers with prior enlisted experience brought with them professional knowledge we green butterbars still had to acquire, but I attribute their leadership edge more to their maturity than to their more-practiced military skills. Leading a platoon demands the physical rigor of a young man and the maturity and experience of a much older person. I often compared myself with 2d Lt. Matt Hoagland. Our company's Third Platoon platoon leader, Matt had become an officer through OCS after having worked several years on the family farm; if I remember correctly, he was a year older than Captain Swisher. He handled himself and his soldiers with a detachment, style, good humor, reason, and also strictness I admired.

The platoon leader stands in the liminal position between the officer corps and the enlisted soldiers. To his soldiers, he represents the entire chain of command. To his chain of command, he voices the needs of his soldiers. Slipping back and forth between those roles dizzies. It is tempting and easy to carry out your superiors' orders while letting your soldiers know you disagree with those orders; you echo your boss with a wink and a smirk. And fail him in your lack of support. It is equally difficult sometimes to properly and aggressively express the needs of your soldiers to your commander, as well to solve problems yourself without getting the commander involved.

Difficult too to discern when to be sympathetic, when to try to accommodate a soldier's complaints, or when to tell him to buck up and deal with the situation. It took me several rounds of playing musical crews over several months before I realized that I could never achieve a perfectly harmonious arrangement, before I flatly refused all future requests from soldiers to change tanks because of a personality conflict.

And what do you do when a good young private returns from a detail at the division's logistics base at the port with supplies he snitched from the boxes he hauled and sorted for several days? When your platoon needs what he has brought back, when by all accounts he has taken a nickel compared to the bank-vault robberies of other soldiers? When you hadn't been getting supplies because filching all along the route from the U.S. to us, the last stop, left the boxes empty? When one of the icons of American film culture is the scrounging sergeant or corporal whose scrounging saves the day, wins the battles, the war? You smile, say nothing, and take nothing for yourself. You don't even consider reporting the event, other than to raise to your commander the general issue of what you had suspected and now know happens to supplies. Because after your soldier's resourceful actions at the port, you still have several others with holes in their boots.

In every encounter between subordinate and leader, a challenge taunts. A test. Of what the soldier can obtain, of how he can sway his LT, of what the LT will permit and what he will insist upon. Of the line between them. Every encounter shifts the line. Sometimes you submit to your urge to draw and enforce the line of authority — not because of your indubitable correctness as the superior, but for the sake of the line. So that the next time, or the time after that — the time it matters — the precedent will favor you.

"Living together without normal distractions turned my life as a leader into what Gen. George S. Patton once called a parade," writes Dave Trybula. "My soldiers were always watching me, trying to understand what made me tick, trying to discover my weaknesses. When I was strong, they would be strong. We leaders quickly learned to act naturally. Our soldiers knew our routine. My platoon could tell you not only when I shaved but how many strokes it took me. My platoon sergeant and I talked continuously to make sure we were doing the right things. However, the time I spent talking with my fellow platoon leaders was the most productive in developing leadership techniques."

Before Hussein invaded Kuwait, Rob Holmes had learned a leadership lesson from his first two company commanders. "When I first reported for duty in Delta Company in December 1989, my commander was a Captain Green. It was soon all too evident that the unit had horrible morale and severe discipline problems because of his lack of leadership.

"For example, physical fitness is a big deal to soldiers. Put simply, the men don't want their officers to be wimps. Captain Green rarely ran with the company during morning training. When he did, he couldn't finish a slow, two-mile jog. He would drop out of formation and walk alongside as his soldiers ran by and laughed at him. I would rather have busted my spleen and collapsed in the gutter than have my men laugh at me. Once, when the scale in the company orderly room showed him over the army's weight standard, he declared it out of calibration and adjusted everybody's weight enough to make himself fall within the standard.

"Worse than being a wimp in the soldiers' eyes, however, is being an elitist. Before I joined Delta Tank, the battalion had gone to the field for training, but not the company commander. At night Captain Green would drive back to post to sleep in a warm bed with his wife. He would leave sixty men sleeping with the mosquitoes and water moccasins of the Fort Stewart swamps while he spent the night cozy and dry. He would arrive the next morning with a fresh uniform and clean shave. To top it off, Captain Green was a blatant bigot. He divided the company along racial lines. No, I could hardly have found a worse command environment.

"Dave Hubner took command in May 1990. He was modest, intelligent, and had a 'damn the torpedoes' wild side to him I found refreshing. Even as a large man, he was fit and could run and play basketball with the very best of the soldiers. He had also just returned from duty on the German border. Dave Hubner was a field soldier, and the men knew it. The company's morale improved immediately. I had yet to maneuver my platoon in the field, I still had a great deal to learn about attacking and defending, but my first two company commanders had already taught me a lot about leadership. If I didn't lead by example and genuinely care for my soldiers I would never be respected. This wasn't news, but now I had two real-world case studies of how not to be and how to be when leading men.

"A company commander and a battalion commander are the two loneliest positions in the field. I could walk five hundred meters in any direction and find another lieutenant. They did not have the luxury of an accessible peer support group. Lieutenant Colonel Gordon had taken command of our battalion only a month before we deployed to Saudi. I first met him during the alert; when he asked why we hadn't met before, I told him I'd been on leave taking courses at the London School of Economics. The conversation quickly deteriorated.

"A Virginia Military Institute graduate, not tall but built like a linebacker, 'Flash' Gordon never looked as comfortable indoors as he did in the field. In the desert he was always sandy, wore a bandanna neckerchief, and carried everywhere the brand new Beretta 9-mm pistol he had annexed from a newly arrived lieutenant. He walked around like a cowboy in desert fatigues. He had spent a career preparing for the Soviet invasion. It never came, but he was ready. Nobody loved being on a tank or commanding in the field more than Flash. We joked about how he was on God's green earth to command a tank battalion in combat. He was tough as nails and incredibly demanding on leaders. Unlike his predecessor, a jovial politician who led by patting officers on the back, Gordon preferred to kick people in the butt. I liked him very much, but some didn't. We all agreed, however, he was someone we wanted on our side in combat. I didn't need a pat on my back. I wanted someone who could destroy the enemy and bring me home.

"By November, I had lived in the desert with my platoon for three months, and we had come a long way toward becoming a cohesive team. Though by no means a veteran, I was no longer the green butterbar I had been when leaving Fort Stewart. I felt I had grown and learned and was a far more competent platoon leader than when I arrived in August. Unfortunately, my maturation got me in a bind, sort of. Looking back, I guess it was a good bind.

"One day in November, I looked down across Graceland from my tank's position and saw Captain Hubner lumbering through the soft sand. Dave took great big strides and seemed to have two huge pistons as thighs as he pumped his way up to my tank. The sand was so soft in this area of Saudi that walking fifty meters was a workout. Dave arrived a bit out of breath and nodded to my tank crew with a pleasant, 'Fellas.' I was relaxing under the camouflage net with Underberg, who was kicked back with his Walkman and a new *Playboy* while I read *The Economist* and peeked over his shoulder. A normal Saudi day.

"Dave and I walked over the dune. When we were well out of earshot, Dave got down to business: 'Flash wants to make you his support platoon leader. You should be flattered.'

"The fact that he added the flattered part told me that he knew this was going to be a tough sell. An armor battalion has three specialty platoons for first lieutenants: scouts, mortars, and support. Operating behind the battalion, the support platoon provides its lifeline in terms of fuel, ammo, food, water, and supplies. Without it, tanks don't go very far.

"'You've got to be kidding,' I responded as respectfully as I could. I was not flattered.

"'Just think about it for a second, Rob.' Dave had planned this pitch. 'I don't want to lose you, but the colonel needs a strong lieutenant in the job, and he thinks you can do it. It would be the first promotion for one of the line platoon leaders, and he chose you. That's a compliment.'

"'Sir, you know there is only one job I want after this one: the scouts. Greg is too new in the job to change, but by the time he's ready, that's the one I want.'

"'Rob, I'm not sure how much choice you have in this one. The colonel thinks very highly of you. You ought to be excited.' Flash hardly knew me. What he knew, he knew from Dave. Although he did not want to lose me, Captain Hubner had been looking out for my best interest by putting in good words for me with the colonel.

"'Sir, do you think I could talk to him about this?'

"Hubner set up the meeting for the next day. I really hadn't come up with a logical pitch as to why I should have much say in the matter, nor why I shouldn't take the job. I cleared a sand berm and found myself at the opening of the commander's tent. There stood Flash in his usual desert glory: sandy fatigues, olive drab bandanna around his neck, with a scruffy day's growth and wavy hair. While most of the officers and men cut their hair very short for the sake of ease, Flash and I probably had the longest hair in the battalion. Both of us were within regulation, but I guess we both wanted to look good. At least not like a marine.

"'Rob Holmes,' Flash began, as if he were announcing me to an audience rather than greeting me. I was surprised that he used my first name. 'Let's get in the shade.' I followed him into his tent. He had two cots, one for him and one for his executive officer. He had a .50-cal ammo box full of books which all appeared to be war novels. He had rolled maps all over the place and a flashlight hanging from the tent's support poles. He had a picture of his young, attractive wife, Debbie, and a box of cookies. This was kind of cool — I was inside Flash's lair. I was also a tad nervous.

"He began talking as soon as I sat down. He was steady and measured, and sort of rumbled in his Virginia drawl. He outlined the support platoon job, his expectations, why he wanted me — and though I appreciated his comments, it sounded like he was reading from a card prepared by Hubner. He told me that understanding logistics was critical to one day being a successful commander and this would be a great job for my career. He folded his arms. 'But Captain Hubner tells me that you don't want it.' He paused before firing: 'Why not?'

"'Sir, I really appreciate your offer, but I want to be the next scout platoon leader.'

"'Downey has another year.'

"'I'll wait, sir.'

"'I can't wait, lieutenant.' I'm not sure how I thought this was going to go, but it didn't seem to be going too well. Then Flash gave me a small opening. 'Why would you make a better scout platoon leader than support platoon leader?'

"I was only twenty-three years old, but I had a pretty good handle on my talents, or at the very least what I liked to do, and logistics wasn't it. I tried to articulate this in the most positive spin. Flash sat and listened as I rambled. It boiled down to the fact that I didn't want to be a quasi-REMF while my friends engaged the enemy. If anyone could understand this, this guy on his cot across from me would. I finally blurted out like an unhappy little kid, 'Sir, there is no way Rob Holmes is going to go to war in a supply truck. It's just not right.'

"He laughed. He unfolded his arms, stood up, walked out of the tent, and after I had followed, shook my hand and said that he would think about it. I smiled sheepishly and set out over the dunes back to Graceland. Whatever my chances, at least he had given me a fair shot.

"The next morning Hubner told me the colonel had decided to keep the current support platoon leader and me where we were. I probably had been more scared about being stuck with that job than anything else in the desert. I could not imagine delivering beans from a truck instead of sabot rounds from my tank's main gun. That would have been embarrassing as hell."

Rob writes more sympathetically about Lieutenant Colonel Gordon than a number of officers and soldiers might about our battalion commander. Compared to the last commander's basset hound eyes and hand-on-shoulder leadership style, Flash Gordon ate rocks and breathed fire. A fair portion of the officers had not taken the change of command well. Gordon knew it, we suspected, and resented the lingering loyalty to the man he had replaced. Desert Shield happened so soon after his assumption of command he had not had time to establish his presence, to be fully accepted. "Flash" was perhaps the kindest nickname we gave to him. "The Prince of Darkness" more accurately reflected some of his subordinates' feelings. To his credit, in recent years he has on occasion signed emails with this latter name, and at least all his names indicated respect — another task force commander in the division was stuck by his subordinates with "Weasel Six."

Greg Downey corroborates the idea that Flash had issues with those officers selected by the last commander:

"I didn't always agree with Lieutenant Colonel Gordon's model of operation and didn't hesitate to deviate from his thinking. Gordon had not chosen me to lead the scout platoon; his predecessor had. I often sensed some resentment in Gordon about that. Still, he was an excellent tactician with an uncanny ability to read terrain, to see every tactical advantage and disadvantage the ground offered.

He would survey an engagement area for hours, looking for every fold in the terrain, visualizing how the enemy would maneuver in response to direct and indirect fires. He would conduct entire battles in his head, commit them to memory, and return to his TOC to think. As his scout platoon leader I spent more time with him than any other lieutenant in the battalion, and I learned a great deal. Gordon had been a career cavalry officer, so he knew his scout tactics. He would grill me for hours on concepts of scout maneuver. He was also a very demanding leader who did not accept defects. He and I collided on several issues, but I can honestly say that he taught me more than any leader or school I encountered in the army."

As for my own encounters with Gordon, one happened at the field hospital when a mess of us were down with food poisoning, and he congratulated another lieutenant instead of me for "a great job with the Cav." When the other corrected him — "That was Lieutenant Vernon, sir" — he didn't then bother to find me. Another was the one visit he made to my company after giving us to Task Force 3-15. He sat with Bravo Tank's five officers for half an hour. He instructed us to imagine with him what combat would be like. To imagine the gore and the screams of pain. The chaos and the death. That's the leader's job, he said. To keep the horrific images of combat at the fore of the mind, to ensure everything we do readies us and our soldiers for it. I was ill. He left without speaking to any of the enlisted soldiers. *Dispirited* doesn't do justice to how the lieutenants felt after Flash mounted his Humvee and drove into the sunset. We were depressed.

As much as I fought Gordon, I also let a little of his warrior spirit inside. A few weeks after his morbid and depressing visit, I started a similar conversation with the other two platoon leaders. My hypothetical: You are leading an assault on an objective; your loader is hit and falls to the turret floor. Blood is spurting. What do you do? My answer: Let your gunner leave his position and perform first aid; notify the medics you will need them on the objective; and drive on. Let your other three tanks do all the firing and do your best to ignore the screaming loader. Because if you stop the company may stop, lose its momentum, and even more soldiers risk being wounded and killed. Having thought through the scenario, if it did happen, I would not panic. I would know what to do.

Postwar Rob Holmes dubbed Flash the "smash-the-glass" commander, the man everyone hates during peace and who during peace ought to be stored behind glass like a fire extinguisher. When war breaks, you smash the glass and put him in charge. Since the war, since leaving the army, my admiration for Gordon has increased. He had taken over the battalion weeks before the alert, sure that Iraq would annex Kuwait and we would deploy. The battalion was on block leave the day he took command — block leave being a nontraining period when a unit encourages its soldiers to go on vacation. Over half his soldiers were on leave.

Neal was humping at Ranger School. I was playing at the beach with Maria, Rob was studying economics in London, and Flash was, *we were*, facing war. We didn't have a clue; but he knew. He found himself in an awkward situation: "I could not get comfortable and though it was not in my nature to make such a drastic splash in a unit, I felt I had to press the unit into action and build more depth in the unit's techniques and procedures. . . . All I ever wanted was to embed enough discipline into the junior leaders so that they had the competence and confidence to take the initiative. Instead they simply feared me."

I have learned sympathy for him and his position. I have also gained an immense respect for his competence. But in the desert I hated him. I hated him because he was a warrior. I hated him because he personified what I resisted becoming. Flash Gordon was my antithesis. Where I focused on self-distraction, he focused on fighting. Where I pained to make my soldiers like me, Flash, not caring what his subordinates thought of him, pained us so we would be ready. If any of us had to go to war again, and had our choice of commanders, we would without pause smash that glass and reach for Randy Gordon.

■ For our senior leadership, from 2d Brigade's commander Colonel Paul Kern up to the commander in chief, President George Bush — and including the country's past military and civilian leaders responsible for rebuilding the force in the twenty years since Vietnam — I only have immense gratitude. Our success in Desert Storm evinces the strength of their leadership.

The one grudge I still carry for my several company and battalion commanders is my moral outrage over their refusal to relieve my boob of a platoon sergeant. Unquestionably the largest event of the war for me was Sfc. Thomas Freight. And Freight was an event for me, the thing I could not, have not, will never, get over.

Freight had been in the army twenty-four years; he admitted to me that he was waiting for one more promotion before retiring. He came to me after acting as a basic training drill instructor, having not been on a tank in five years and never on an M1. By my second week in the desert I began complaining about him in letters home and in person to Captain Baillergeon. Freight knew very little and displayed no desire to learn. The discipline in his tank section had already deteriorated: Its soldiers were always late, perpetually out of uniform. They slept late. They declined to monitor the radio during night guard. They said "fuck it" a lot. Freight's crew hated him; the platoon ridiculed him.

I recall three specific events involving Freight in September, when the platoon with Delta Mech was with the Cav on Tapline Road. The first happened during training I had scheduled on the Vinson, the electronic scrambling and unscrambling device by which we secured our radio transmissions from eavesdroppers. Freight expressed excitement when I told about it: "I've never used a Vinson before." But during the class, he stood outside the tank smoking and joking — he didn't listen to word one. I said nothing at the time because I did not want to undermine his authority and competence in front of the entire platoon; when I confronted him later, he assured me he had wanted the privates to get a good view, and would have his gunner teach him. Sure he would.

The second event occurred over morning PT. Someone on my tank crew had fallen asleep during his guard shift, so I was not woken for my shift and consequently I could not wake the platoon. Freight had been awake that morning but saw me asleep and assumed I had canceled PT in order to sleep in. This was his way — presuming whatever allowed him to escape the effort of work or thought.

And finally: Before taking my tank to the squadron TOC to display it for Secretary Stone's visit, I had instructed Freight to have one man awake on each tank at all times, and to have one tank pulled up to the ridge to scan the road. With my tank gone and another at the UMCP, the remaining two crews did not have sufficient manpower to man the OP and the tanks. I returned the next morning to find that he had instead pulled both tanks to the ridge and had one man awake for both tanks. My intent had been high security with low exposure; he chose high exposure and low security. He initiated the same plan with my crew for the next night before I knew what was going on — that was in fact how I discovered his failure to follow my orders. Everyone was naturally excited for the extra sleep.

Freight's incompetence continued when the platoon rejoined Bravo Tank in October. Only now I seriously began to question his basic mental capacities. He had trouble understanding the simplest instructions. He could not plan training by himself; he could not even take notes at a meeting and relay the information to the platoon. Once when I was training with Delta Mech, Freight attended a Bravo Tank platoon leader meeting in my stead with Captain Swisher. I returned, checked in with the other lieutenants, and then asked Freight about the meeting. "Well, you know, sir, I'm glad you spoke with the other lieutenants 'cause Captain Swisher he just talks a way I can't follow. He's not near as clear as you." I learned to garner basic information communicated by the first sergeant to the platoon sergeants from the other platoon leaders, who told me what their platoon sergeants had told them. Greg Jackson, who as the executive officer sometimes worked with the platoon sergeants on logistical issues, told me Freight had trouble comprehending him and doing simple math.

On 15 October, Freight signed and submitted his request for retirement in December. The same army Stop-Loss policy that had saved Mary Creighton's career after Major General McCaffrey asked her to resign in order to stay behind with her baby daughter Katherine precluded Freight's retirement.

I began counseling Freight. On a rock perch, with a pen and yellow legal pad, I would draft a several-page counseling statement detailing all his failures to understand instructions, follow orders, and tell the truth; write a more legible final copy, and sit with him to review it. At the end of each session we would both sign the document. I did this three or four times. His performance never improved. I finally handed the documents over to Swisher to present them to whichever lieutenant colonel might be inclined to fire Freight. They were eventually lost.

My troubles with Freight peaked at the December platoon gunnery. Before our first platoon mission, the captain from brigade staff assigned to evaluate us assembled the platoon and had select soldiers perform a weapons check with their .45s. Because of the sand and grime, some could not cock the barrel back; none knew the proper steps. Not even a couple of the NCOs. Although everything in the platoon was my responsibility, maintaining equipment and individual skills was Freight's job. I have never been so professionally embarrassed. When the captain reviewed my platoon with me at the end of the evaluation period, he called Freight "brain dead" and agreed to bend Swisher's ear about firing him. "In the meantime, you need to figure out how to get him to do his job, or how you and your other NCOs can pull his slack."

After the platoon fired its day gunnery, I ordered Freight to ensure that each crew cleaned its gun tube. I then sat on my tank watching the platoon work, and watching my tank crew not clean ours. Freight shortly reported that all the tubes had been cleaned. "What about mine?" I asked.

"Let me see, sir. Hey Dock, you clean your tube?"

"Yes, sergeant," my gunner answered from the front slope, knowing I was listening, knowing I knew he had not.

"Yes, sir," Freight relayed to me.

"Sergeant Freight, Dock hasn't cleaned his tube, and you know it. Why are you lying to me?"

"Well I know, sir, but Dock lied to me. What am I supposed to do about it?"

After we fired gunnery that night, Swisher burst over the radio. "White Three" — Freight's wingman — "this is Black Six. Get in uniform now! White One" — me — "meet me on the ground." Swisher had spotted White Three's gunner clambering out of the turret with nothing over his torso but his T-shirt. He buzzed over to my tank in his Humvee, hollered at me while jabbing at me with an index finger. "Discipline in your platoon sucks, lieutenant, and I don't want to hear your excuse of having a bad platoon sergeant anymore. You are responsible. You're in command. Fix your platoon now."

I wanted to scream back in his face, *If I'm in command, then let me fix my platoon my way! Let me fire Freight!* Instead I yielded to his command: "Yes, sir." I knew I was responsible. But Swisher and I also knew that a decent platoon sergeant, not to mention a stellar one like Staff Sergeant Rivera, would never have let such a mess of discipline happen, nor let such a mess, once discovered, go uncorrected.

I contemplated resigning as platoon leader several times throughout Desert Shield, once to Captain Baillergeon with 2-4 Cav, mostly to Captain Swisher. The usual motivation was my constant faith in my incompetence. Once my frustration with Sergeant Freight nearly drove me to resign, the closest I actually came to doing so. It happened right after the turbulent December gunnery. The day before going to Swisher, I confided my design to the company's second in command and my emotional anchor, Greg Jackson. I planned to deliver an ultimatum to Swisher: either Freight or me. Because if Freight wasn't the platoon's leadership problem, it must have been me. Or the problem was Freight, in which case I did not want to work for a commander who did not support me, who tells me I am in command and am responsible to fix my problems but does not allow me to resolve them my way, by firing Freight. Greg attempted to dissuade me, though when I entered the captain's tent the next day, I fully intended to quit.

Swisher, Top, and I talked for ninety minutes. Despite my evidence, neither of them believed Freight had "crossed the line of incompetence." I told them that neither of them saw Freight in action, that Freight's sending of a few soldiers for some menial detail to Top when asked was hardly evidence of combat leadership competence. Swisher tasked me to train Freight — to train a senior NCO, who had been in the army over twenty years, who had himself been a drill instructor. *When is it too late to teach an old dog?* I wanted to cry. *When is it time to put him to sleep?* Top cautioned me that my counseling statements on Freight sounded like I was "after him." No kidding, first sergeant. For all that, I could not muster the fortitude, the spine, the whatever, to tell Swisher I wanted out. I left the tent enraged at them and at myself.

Captain Baillergeon had fired a first sergeant. In his time as a platoon leader, Delta Mech's Lt. Brian Luke had three platoon sergeants fired. Bob McCann also rid himself of a bad platoon sergeant. How could the chain of command help these officers and deny me? What had I done to lose my commanders' implicit trust in my judgment and my abilities to perform my office? In trying to fire Freight, what missteps did I make? What else could I have done?

I didn't know it, but I wasn't alone in my struggles with an incompetent platoon sergeant. In October, Greg Downey "realized that I was not getting the required support from my scout platoon sergeant, Sfc. Smith. This was something that had been evident to me when I took over the scout platoon, but I had hoped he would come around. During Desert Shield, Smith continued to be uninvolved in all aspects of training, maintaining, and taking care of soldiers. It was clear to me that he was concerned with one thing: self-preservation. I knew I could not count on him in peace, let alone combat. I asked Lieutenant Colonel Gordon to relieve him and appoint S.Sgt. Lester Deem as my platoon sergeant, which unknown to me was exactly what Sfc. Smith wanted.

"Staff Sergeant Deem was 100 percent soldier, as coarse and gritty as the sand we lived on. Tough, mean and feisty, he reminded me of my dad. He even looked, acted, and talked like him. He was extremely competent, tactically and technically. The idea of combat did not excite him, but he knew it was his job. We talked about it at great length. We both knew there was no glory in what we might have to do. A few months before deployment, Deem had come off recruiter duty. He had been hungry to soldier again. But like me, he was frustrated by this platoon and its lack of competent NCO leadership. He kept his section tight but felt limited to it — he was not in a position to discipline the rest of the platoon. That belonged to Sergeant Smith. I wanted to turn the platoon over to Deem, let him take over as platoon sergeant to fix our problems. But I couldn't do it without the support of the battalion commander.

"Gordon relieved Smith for one day. I still do not know why he was sent back to be the platoon sergeant. I decided to work around him and use Deem as my platoon sergeant, which worked well for everyone involved. Deem accepted the responsibility, and missions were accomplished. Smith continued to avoid every opportunity for providing leadership to the platoon."

Perhaps what a friend has since postulated about my situation holds true for Greg as well: that maybe our commanders believed in us so much that they did not doubt our abilities to overcome the dead weight of a Freight or Smith, that our commanders chose to leave them in our capable hands because it would be far better than saddling less-able leaders with them; that our commanders' only mistake was not admitting to us their faith in us.

Because I had good moments in the desert, moments touched by encouragement. Moments I actually felt confident. That time after Thanksgiving when one of another lieutenant's soldiers, during a platoon training maneuver away from camp, waited for his crew to turn its back to eat their MREs and walked away, off into the desert, having quit. (He was eventually found. I was grateful that none of my soldiers had walked off.) The time I received a letter from my father, who had just gotten off the phone with Becky Ulsaker. Becky's husband Jon was a platoon leader in Delta Tank with Rob. She had called to let my father know that I had a reputation as a competent lieutenant who cared about his soldiers. The time Greg Jackson told me he had spoken with some soldiers, and the general consensus in the company was that folks wanted to be in my Second Platoon because they had confidence in me. Times when it occurred to me that I might know more about what I was doing than I normally imagined.

M1A1 Transition

So perhaps a Good War is not a matter of morality after all; perhaps it's only a matter of space, and freedom, and the right machine.
— Samuel Hynes, *The Soldiers' Tale*

In the last days of December 1990 and first days of January 1991, the 24th replaced its old M1IP (Improved Product) tanks with new M1A1 Heavy Armor models, or M1A1 "heavies." The A1 incorporated four major enhancements over the IP: an upgrade of the 105-mm rifled main gun to a 120-mm smooth bore cannon and consequently a decreased basic load from fifty-five to forty rounds; an NBC overpressure system that actively blew air out through the cracks to prevent contamination from slipping in, increasing survivability as well as operability, as crews no longer had to fight in protective masks; mine plows and rollers as add-ons, essential for assaulting heavily prepared defensive positions; and improved armor. The heavy version of the A1 included an additional slab of armor on the tank's front. But the primary motivation for the transition was concern over the condition of the division's M1IPs; as of 24 November, the division had replaced over sixty engines and anticipated replacing another fifty in the next couple of months.[6]

Before upgrading to the A1s, my platoon's operational readiness rate with the IPs we had brought from Fort Stewart swung faithfully between 50 and 75 percent, one or two of my four tanks not fully mission capable at any given time. According to a "Maintenance Snapshot" of 24 December 1990, immediately prior to our transition to the A1, the division had made 386 significant repairs to its fleet of 232 tanks since 12 September, while boasting a 97 percent operational readiness rate.[7] I remember civilian technicians from the Abrams's manufacturer visiting our desert living area to help us fix our more troublesome tanks. To know that though the decision had not been made by 24 November — "We can go either way," a note from Major General McCaffrey of that date reads — and that we received training on the new tanks in mid-December and received our new tanks from their storage in Germany by the first week of January, amazes me. We apparently had priority over other units: The 3d ACR did not complete its exchange of M1A1s for M1A1 heavies until 23 February, the day before the ground war.[8]

Transition training occurred in the weeks prior to the actual swap, beginning with a several-day excursion back to the Ad Dammam port. Greg Downey and his scout platoon were left behind. "I must admit, the scouts did feel left out when the tankers got new tanks. We had devoted endless hours of work to our vehicles but would have eagerly accepted new, upgraded Bradleys. But no. We would have to fight with what we had." That the 24th's old Bradleys brought from

Fort Stewart, beat through years of rigorous training and field exercises, kept up with the new M1A1s during the war is a testament to the Bradley's design, the division and the theater's logistical support system (built from scratch), and the company-level mechanics, grunts, and scouts whose technical expertise and hard work paid off.

I would qualify my experience at the port for M1A1 transition training as ambiguous. For some, the port transition training marked personal transitions from questioning our combatant status future to accepting its certainty. Neal stood in the tanks' fenced holding area on the pier with one of 1-64's company commanders, Capt. Steve Winkler, gazing on the rows of tanks, dressed right and covered down, still decked in their German forest greens. "Sure as shit," the captain told Neal, "we're going to war." Still, we spent more time at the port not preparing for the transition but relaxing and touring. I chose to wallow in the sweetness of the escape. It was easier than acknowledging my fear of the new tanks, of that enormous black breach and the combustible rounds that had killed soldiers in the turret before, and the overpressure chemical defense system and the mine roller and plow attachments and the reality it all signified. The precision of it all.

Bravo Tank arrived on at the port 14 December, a day after returning from gunnery. We lived on rows of cots in walled bays, similar to the unwalled bays that housed us our first night. Hot-water showers, catered buffets for breakfast and dinner. Lovely, temperate coastal weather. We also saw some of the apartment buildings where soldiers stationed at the port lived, scorning them, pitying ourselves, with pride.

The next day I ran into Rob Holmes. We sat on my cot for a couple of hours talking and catching up. He gave me an article from *Rolling Stone* magazine, in which P. J. O'Rourke described the Middle East as "a quarrel with borders." I cackled. It was only the second time during Desert Shield I had seen Rob. The first time had been at a demonstration for all brigade officers on the MLRS artillery rocket system. At that time we had talked about a pair of brothers in the brigade, two captains. The older one, after graduating from the University of Kansas and Ranger School, had been a tank company commander much admired for winning training battles both at Fort Stewart and the NTC. But he was now riding in a Humvee in charge of a headquarters unit. His younger brother, full of respectful sibling rivalry, had gone to West Point, then Ranger School, and now commanded a tank company. Rob and I knew the older brother hated not being in a tank at the front of a company, and we wished he were there, too. We complained that the army was committing a disservice to its soldiers by not ensuring its aces led the way.

The afternoon of the sixteenth was our field trip. Our first stop: the King Fahd Military City mosque. A Muslim professor showed the grounds to us, beginning with the ablution chamber and concluding inside the mosque. In my single semester art history elective at West Point, I had studied Islamic art and architecture somewhat and so appreciated seeing a "live" mosque and reacquainting myself with some of the motifs and terms: *mihrab*, the designs on the prayer rug that indicate the direction of Mecca; and infinite patterning, the term used for the noniconographic, geometric treatment of walls, floors, and the like. In the ablution chamber, the bespectacled professor explained the requirements and methods of ablution, Islam's ritual bathing. In the mosque he recited and translated, line by line, the call to prayer and again described the reasons for and methods of praying. The mosque was a perfect square, with three sets of three windows per side, except for the side facing Mecca, which had in its center an alcove I believe the professor called a *kaaba*. A podium for the prayer leader stood in front of the kaaba. The mosque had plain walls and a green carpet with white bands, which the Muslims used to form rows for praying.

We ended in the mosque room with a question and answer session. Some of the questions posed by American soldiers:

"Is there premarital sex?"

"Do kids have any choice, or are they forced into Islam?"

"Can you criticize it?"

"Why is there so much strife between Arabs and Jews?"

Astounding.

After the mosque we went to the ARAMCO museum, where we saw a film on the history of this joint Arab-American Company oil venture, walked through, and left for the mall. The mall felt like a square cement box crammed with cheesy jewelry and electronic shops from the streets of New York City. Europeans and Asians everywhere. The women dressed in Western clothes, only a few in the traditional abha robe. I ran into Jeannie Novak, the lieutenant from Hunter Army Airfield. She and another American woman, a captain I think, were both in civilian clothes. Their unit had packed civies when they deployed, which their women were told to wear — pants and long sleeves — whenever they would be in urban settings and around Arabs to avoid offending Islamic principles against exposed female skin and working women. I capped my trip to the mall with Swensen's ice cream.

The first training the company received consisted of a couple of briefings in rooms at the north end of the bay, on 17 December. We watched films on the potential for turret fires with the combustible casing for the A1's main gun rounds — the rounds from our old IPs used copper casing ejected from the breech like the shells spit out of rifles and pistols, whereas the A1's casings were incinerated in the gun tube upon firing. We spent the eighteenth training on the new tanks, each crew on a tank with an instructor, in the original motor pool where we had parked vehicles as they came off the ships in August. From atop the tank we could see Tent City, where we had spent our first days in country. The tents that we had helped throw up were now dressed right in proper rows and columns, with exact intervals. Two gigantic white tents crowned the tent city to the north, and the motor pool had trailer-home offices along the fence by the eastern gate.

Dropping myself through the loader's hatch and seeing the 120-mm breech for the first time wigged me. Compared to the IP's 105-mm breech, this 120-mm breech filled the turret. It was also much more square, with sharper angles, than the softly rounded 105 breech. Sharp angles, black, smooth, cold: I marveled at the mastery of its engineering and, thinking on its purpose, quaked a little inside at its cold beauty. It was undeniably beautiful, a perfect marriage of form and function. A horrible beauty.

Before we boarded the busses late that afternoon for our return to the desert, our 1-64 commander, Lieutenant Colonel Gordon, gathered his unit around him. Because half of us had been task organized to Task Force 3-15, Flash had not had so many of his men assembled since we deployed. His speech at the port was as grim as the one he made on his sole visit to Bravo Tank's officers. He was, I know, preparing us for war, helping us screw our heads on right. The result, though, turned many against him. A soldier shouldn't be depressed after a commander gives words. Motivation doesn't work that way. *What a dickhead* was the consensus among those I spoke with.

Bravo Tank signed our M1IPs over on the last day of 1990 to a National Guard lieutenant who, growing up in Indiana, had played "Dungeons & Dragons" with Bravo's Third Platoon leader. Rob Holmes's Delta Tank was one day ahead of us on the transition schedule; as I was turning in my tank in on New Year's Eve, Rob received his new one. "The battalion had set up a gunnery range for us to test-fire our new rides that night. I loved shooting an M1 tank. I loved anything competitive for that matter, and everybody's ego got involved in gunnery practice: who was fastest, who was most accurate, who was the most lethal weapon in the company. To my relief, my braggart of a gunner lived up to his proclaimed greatness.

"As my tank rolled off the range just after midnight, our commander met us as he did every tank in Delta that night, with a bottle of champagne. We called firing our tanks 'popping caps' — who would have thought we'd be popping champagne corks that night? I don't know where Captain Hubner got them, but even that nonalcoholic brand made it not such a bad New Year's Eve. My crew guzzled away on the drive back to Graceland. I remember feeling pretty happy. I had a new tank, my gunner was lightning, and I had a bottle of champagne. Granted, we had no women to kiss, but life wasn't so bad just then. Either that or it was really awful, and I didn't realize it anymore."

Happy New Year: My own company received A1s on New Year's Day. We spent the first full night of 1991 on the tanks all night, under generator-powered lights, inspecting the tanks, drawing equipment, doing thorough maintenance to catch any problems before we owned them, painting our bumper numbers and unit symbols on them, and finally uploading them with our gear. The following day we took the tanks to the gunnery range, where we spent two days verifying their fire-control systems. I huddled in my tank for most of the day on the second, its hatches closed, to stay out of the weather. It rained off and on the entire day, more on than off, hard rain, and the wind blew. Cold. Bitter.

When my tank's turn to fire came, we had a misfire on our second round. Dock had pulled the trigger, and nothing happened. In his loader's position Brunner started to open the breech. Dock and I saw wisps of smoke emerging from it. We were both thinking about the films we had been shown back at the port when Dock hollered "Breech fire!" into the intercom, and we scrambled out of the tank and onto the ground in an instant. Dock jumped onto the front slope to help Vanderwerker out of the driver's hole. We jogged off the line, and Captain Swisher radioed the other two tanks on the firing line to back away. From Swisher's Humvee we watched the tank for ten minutes. Nothing happened. After a short while Sergeant Sebastio, the company's master gunner, went to the tank. When he came back, he reported that the smoke had been left from the first round. The second round was fine. I expected the incident to inspire much chuckling at our expense, but no one chuckled, and I think most people forgot about it in a few days. It seems I wasn't the only one intimidated by the new gun.

My crew was mulling now over the possibility of war. "Sergeant Boss talks about war and all of us getting killed," said Vanderwerker, "but I think we'll find some lame excuse to avoid war and I won't get my combat patch."

"I don't know what's going to happen," Brunner replied. "I just want to go home."

Preparing for War

I told [my commanders] before this thing started, that basically Americans are natural fighters. We've always sort of hated to say that, because we don't want to sound like we're warlike. But I've always believed that. . . . When the shooting starts, they will move toward the sound of the guns. Indeed the problem is trying to restrain them and make sure that they run the combined arms operation. They are very alert, they're thinking, they're aggressive, they're team players, they have a sense of discipline that comes from high school football teams rather than from the lash. They don't do things because you can punish them; they do things because they want to be part of a winning team. And all that makes for rifle platoons that are aggressive, and that's been my experience having been a platoon leader in combat, and in company actions, etc. . . . They don't wait around to get told to do something and they are not all that impressed by position. . . . Americans are really good at [combat]. They were in every war we ever fought.

— Maj. Gen. Barry McCaffrey, Oral History Interview, Euphrates River Valley, 28 February 1991

While the tankers spent New Year's Eve and New Year's Day with our new tanks, Greg Downey spent it at his scout platoon assembly area in Hinesville. "The thirty-first of December arrived. What was it really going to be the eve of? Disaster? Defeat? Victory? Peace? Tomorrow the math would be easy: just count down to January 15, the UN's deadline for Iraq to withdraw from Kuwait.

"I took a short walk at midnight. I knew the Iraqi army would not withdraw in the next fourteen days. I gazed at the stars, so beautiful in the desert; bright, magical, unmolested. That night the stars took me back to Nebraska, to my family. I felt close to them, closer than I had since arriving in Saudi Arabia. I knew they were looking at the same stars, standing under the same moon, wondering the same things. It comforted.

"At such times you begin to reconcile with yourself. You think through every thought, search your mind, question everything. One question weighed heavily — Had I done everything possible to prepare myself and my soldiers for combat? I realized at that moment how lonely I had been throughout the deployment. I truly missed the camaraderie of my fellow platoon leaders. When I was in my old tank company, I used the other tank platoon leaders as sanity checks and sounding boards. In the upcoming battle I would have to make decisions that would affect an entire armored task force, over seven hundred lives hinging on the decisions my scout platoon would make. I had never thought about it in that context before.

"The days continued to tick away. A last ditch effort at diplomacy raised the hopes of everyone. A meeting was scheduled for 9 January between Secretary of State James Baker and Iraqi foreign minister Tariq Aziz. Every half hour my platoon gathered around the little Sony radio that provided our only link with the world, with breaths held. The news of the Iraqi withdrawal did not come that day.

"The next morning the bottom fell out of the sky. The rain reminded me of the late afternoon showers of Fort Stewart's coastal Georgia, only this rain didn't end when evening came.

"'The angels are crying, sir,' came a voice from the driver's hatch. I was standing in front of the Bradley.

"'Say again, West?' focusing my attention on the soldier peering through the small crack in his partially closed hatch.

"'It's the angels, they're crying,'

"'You think they're trying to tell us something, West?'

"'I think that they know a lot of people are going to die for nothing, sir.'

"'Well, West, I guess as long as they aren't crying for us we'll be okay,' I answered.

"'I miss my wife, sir.'

"'I know you do, West. She misses you, too.'"

■ The rain was still coming down the next day, 10 January 1991. It alternated between constant dribbles and coldly slicing sheets. I huddled up on my cot in the corner of the platoon tent for one of the last times and wrote Maria.

We are, it seems, bound for war. Greg says he is "resolute." Bob at least can smile. Matt has not changed. I am terrified.

I had three letters from Mom, all from Christmas time. I read them, in my tent, and started crying. I left the tent and ran into Lt. Novak, who had come to visit. I chased her off, "too busy packing."

I am terrified. We are packing our gear. Most stuff the army will take from us in the next few days; it leaves us with our "go to war" gear. All the latrines in the company but one, and all the showers and heaters but one, disappeared today. Tomorrow we begin wearing our chemical suits, flak vests, and steel pots as our regular uniform.

I cannot handle this. I am not cut out for it. All I want to do is cry. Nothing makes sense. I think I wrote earlier that knowing the plan set me somewhat at ease, because I knew something. Well I was wrong. Now I see that I know nothing of the future. Nothing. It is the most terrifying vision, this black hole of a future. It's sucking me close, and I cannot see through it, or behind it. I see pure blackness; that is my future.

I know I am not supposed to write letters like this. I apologize for upsetting you. When you get this, we may already be fighting. I am sorry you must suffer also. This is not right, not fair, not just. That humans allow themselves to suffer so, that they bring suffering and misery upon themselves, is wrong.

I love you and miss you, always,

Alex

P.S. Sent poem to DESERT SHIELD creative writing contest today. Doesn't appear I'll have the leisure to do short story or essay. Fuck this world — no decency, no civilization. Tell my parents, and my brothers, that I love them.

Wasn't I a peach?

Over the course of the next few rain-filled days, Bravo Tank decamped Assembly Area Hinesville. My two duffel bags of personal gear were loaded on a truck with everyone else's, leaving me with rucksack, CVC bag, and tanker's roll. The space in the bustle racks occupied by the crew's duffel bags would soon house small arms ammunition, light antitank weapons, claymore mines, extra track blocks and cans of engine oil, and whatever else we might need and could secure to our tanks. Even with all my "leader" gear, I had packed the lightest in my platoon. When the truck came and took our bags away, I felt it physically, a punch to the stomach. Umph.

Small arms ammunition was issued on the eleventh. People spent the day cleaning weapons. Our full uniform now included our MOPP chemical gear over our NOMAX tanker's suit, which did not make sense. We wore the NOMAX to prevent flashes from the breech catching us on fire; covering those suits with charcoal-lined MOPP suits struck most of us as fairly stupid. We were told this was a "temporary posture" — someone up high expected Hussein to do something. Our commander's update for the day included a rumor that Hussein had announced a "present to the world" planned for delivery on the thirteenth. I also heard a rumor that President Bush might grant an extension of the deadline. A grace period.

We also spent the day digging pits outside our tents as protection from artillery and missile strikes. In the rain.

January 12, the task force had orders to prepare to move to a staging position some twenty kilometers northeast. I remember two reasons being briefed to me: to confuse Iraq about our intentions, and to dodge any preplotted retaliatory Iraqi artillery, SCUD missiles, or air strikes against our position — the move was scheduled for the day before the UN's deadline for Hussein's withdrawal from Kuwait. We would move under the cover of night on the fourteenth. The move to the staging area would also prepare the units logistically, forcing them to dump their excesses, pack for combat, and cut any too-tight ties to support organizations and As Sarrar, thus reestablishing their relative independence as mobile fighting bodies. It was time for the team members to redo their shoelaces, stand up from the bench, down the last swigs of Gatorade and drop the cups on the sidelines, and stretch their legs. As the units prepared logistically, soldiers prepared psychologically: We were physically, literally, *finally*, going north.

We spent the twelfth finishing the razing of the assembly area. Our last shower and latrine, and our tents, went away. Our tanks again became our homes. It drizzled all day; it had not let up for three days. I ate my last meal of foodstuffs from home: White Premium canned chicken and strawberry preserves, both on crackers. Then I grabbed a trash bag and walked around my platoon area cleaning up the desert, as if cleaning an apartment for the landlord's out-inspection. We filled one of the artillery protection pits we had dug the day before with trash, food from home, and gear we couldn't take with us, and burned the mess of it. Four other such fires burned in the company area, and over the ridge I saw the smoke from fires from other units. In Alpha Tank one of Neal Creighton's sergeants had doused the platoon's burn pit in mo-gas. Neal was walking to Third Platoon to coordinate with its lieutenant when one of his young enlisted soldiers, thinking the pit had been juiced with diesel fuel, bent down and touched his cigarette lighter to the trash. All the sergeant heard was the click of the soldier's lighter; everybody in Alpha heard the explosion. As Neal turned around, he "imagined the whole platoon had blown up, it was that loud. I raced back. The sergeant had been blown in the air and landed several meters away, unhurt. The soldier's face was burned badly enough that he was taken to a field hospital, though he returned before the ground war started."

Rob Holmes remembers one night in Graceland as the moment he came to terms with his now-almost-certain path back to Georgia, by way of the Euphrates River Valley. It may have been when he first learned about the attack plan; it may have been when we first received word to start breaking camp; it may have been when we received word to prepare to displace to the staging area twenty kilometers north. What Rob does recall, vividly, are his actions afterward. He remembers them so well because he "was one of the naïve fools that thought this was never going to happen. When it became evident that it most certainly was going to happen, I immediately put on my game face and prepared for war. I never doubted again that we really were going north.

"I began the return walk to my tank's fighting position. A crisp January breeze blew across the desert. The six months of working, waiting, and wondering had ended. Desert Shield had been tremendously maturing. The pressure of holding together sixteen men had made for a fast twenty-third year of my life. No air-conditioned computer simulator at Fort Stewart could teach this.

"Jeff White had been walking with me. Neither of us said a word. His platoon would be on my right flank as we attacked. Even after six months of thinking about it, how do you tell men whose lives depend on you that they are really going to war? With a nod, Jeff peeled off and headed toward his platoon. I was almost to my M1.

"As I arrived Bell jumped up, beaming. 'You got a package from Kelli. Can I open it, sir?'

"'Go ahead, but I want to at least see everything before y'all divvy it up.' I walked over to the 'desk' I had built with MRE boxes for writing orders and letters. Around it I had used pieces of camouflage netting and a couple of tarps to form a little tent. It protected me against the sun and sand, and worked pretty well as an office. I had hung flashlights from the top with shoe laces so I could work at night. Bell had filled sandbags to make a seat for me. An empty .50-caliber ammo box kept my reading and writing material dry. That place was where I escaped from Saudi.

"Underberg, my brash Californian surfer, cruised in directly. 'Okay sir, what was your meeting all about? Are we going home?' Underberg always claimed to have the latest scoop on rumors about going home. The eternal optimist, he was certain we were going to be relieved by another unit soon, before anything went down. He stood there convinced of the accuracy of his intelligence.

"'Yeah, Underberg. We're going home. Not quite yet, though.' I yanked on one of the tarps that made up my makeshift office, and the fiberglass support poles came clanging down.

"'What's up, sir?'

"I didn't answer, and Underberg knew when to shut up. He stood and watched as I folded the tarp. I was not deliberately ignoring his questions; I didn't know what to say. I unplugged the phone line that Underberg had run into my office, connecting it to my fighting position, to my other three tanks, and to Captain Hubner's tank. Underberg had set me up so that I didn't have to leave my sandbag couch to answer the phone.

"I loosened the ties on the sandbags and dumped out the sand. I had become reasonably comfortable, and in some respects I had become soft. That made me mad, to think how I had let myself become very nearly as soft and naïve as my predeployment, stateside self had been, as much as the desert permitted softness, that is. I looked at all the crazy amenities my crew and I had rigged and collected: sandbag couch, hanging flashlights, business magazines scattered around. The time for that was over. The nights of staying up late reading or writing letters had passed. The days of relaxing on my couch as we shared a new package from home were gone. I rolled up the phone line and walked it over to the tank. Sergeant Downing sat on the front of the M1's hull, his back against the turret. He had been watching me tear down the office over the beeps of his Nintendo Gameboy.

"'What's my lieutenant doing now?' You know you are doing something right when your sergeants refer to you as *my* instead of *the* lieutenant. 'Where are you going to read your fancy magazines, sir?' Downing burst into his wild laugh. He would always be his own greatest fan.

"I dug a hole and started throwing trash in it. My three crew members watched as I tossed into the pit nearly all the letters I had received. We were ordered to burn correspondence from the States because of the concern that an Arab could get a return address and use it against us. In that crazy world, who knew? I saved a few special ones. I lit the pit on fire.

"Underberg tossed his contribution into the fire. Bell, who had been buried in my package from Kelli, was intently watching me now. He walked over and asked softly, 'How was your meeting, sir?' Downing and Underberg were all ears, too.

"'We've got a lot of work to do, Bell. Will you get the tank ready to move?' I hadn't even finished the sentence before he was moving toward his tools. Sergeant Downing jumped off the tank and ordered Underberg and Bell to bore-sight the tank's main gun. I unpacked my rucksack and dumped all my belongings. I pitched all but a few army T-shirts and socks and a couple of uniforms. If I did not use an item several times a week, I burned it.

"My office was gone. The wind blew the sand and gently erased any evidence of my Graceland existence.

"After repacking my bags, I stripped down naked and dumped a canteen over me, lathered up with soap, and dumped a second canteen to rinse off. I put on a fresh uniform and got the maps which would lead us from the Saudi border to Basra, 475 kilometers inside Iraq. My crew hadn't even known I had them. I began to acetate the mapsheets to protect them from the weather and to enable me to write on them with alcohol pens; Bell and Underberg quickly relieved me. I was never much good with acetate, and they were excellent. They gasped hard at the sight of the maps but went to work. My burning trash pit was dying down as our worldly possessions turned to ashes and were quietly scattered by the blowing sand.

"With the sun setting behind me, I looked out from Graceland east across the desert floor toward As Sarrar. It was beautiful. It was also time to go to war. Fifteen lives depended on me. Not including my own. My world had become very simple: destroy everything in my path and bring these guys home. The sun set. Desert Shield was over."

■ Assembly Area Hinesville, where I had lived with Bravo Tank for nearly four months, had become a mud bowl. Muddy, filthy, overcast, windy, wet, gloomy. Airplanes in the sky, day and night. At night their lights blinked, so many fireflies among the stars.

Over the days of our decampment, Freight continued to challenge all notions of competence. The XO reported that Freight had an awful time understanding the amount of each ammunition type he was required to draw and even more difficulty drawing the correct amount. Then he defied a direct order from the commander. When we were packing our gear in duffels to be taken away, Captain Swisher had ordered that we pack away all electronic gadgets, namely games, cassette players, and radios. The commander believed they would distract soldiers from their mission. "Tell them if any officer or NCO finds one, we will crush it under a tank track."

I disagreed about the radios. They had been and promised to be our only source of current news. When I issued the order to the platoon, I had no intention of actively enforcing it, not with the radios anyway. But Freight would have none of it, and after I issued the order he announced his intention to disobey. "The commander will have to deal with me before I make you get rid of your radios," he declared. "I'll tell him how it is."

All eyes in the platoon fell on me. I repeated the commander's order, louder this time. Freight and I had a stare-off. I stared him down; he turned and walked away, muttering.

Shortly before we moved out on the evening of the fourteenth, something, I have forgotten what, prompted Freight to threaten to beat the first sergeant to death. He told this to me in his huffy, boastfully empty way: "I'm dead serious, sir." I seized the opportunity and reported it to Top. Top said he would deal with Freight later. I don't believe the subject ever came up again.

When Greg Downey headed out with 1–64 that night, he "took one last look at what had been our home for the past few months. The rocks where we had sat and talked, the sand where we had drawn pictures with our feet, the hills we had climbed to escape from it all. I felt like I was saying good-bye to an old friend. One that had offered everything it had had to offer, knowing it could never be enough. Someday, I will return. I imagine it will be waiting, like an old friend, to say hello, and ask me how I've been."

Dave Trybula drove through the start point on time, exactly at midnight. As Dave pulled into the staging area, he heard on the radio that Delta Tank had flipped a tank during the road march. "The company XO had gone forward in a Humvee to quarter the new position, and the rest of his crew had fallen asleep while bringing the tank up. It had driven off the trail and rolled into a quarry-like pit, where it came to a stop upside-down. The crew was scared and embarrassed, but uninjured."

I led the company column on the night road march following Neal Creighton and Alpha Tank. At the end of the short trip, the task force's infantry and armor companies formed a circle around the task force TOC. This was not a defensive position. The battalion was packed closely together, no more than ten or fifteen meters between tanks within a platoon.

My tank gained a name either on our first day at our new position or in the last days at Assembly Area Hinesville. The crew first wanted to name it *Bald Beaver Bound,* which I rejected under the directive of my chain of command: black paint, three-inch stenciled letters, on the bore evacuator, and nothing crude (alliteration with the company name was unanimously assumed). Their second choice: *Balls to the Wall.* Not as crude, but still too crude I knew for Captain Swisher. Third choice: *Blaze of Glory,* after the Bon Jovi rock song lyrics, "going down in a blaze of glory." I rejected that one for its dooming implications. I suggested *Blitzkrieg*, defining it for them as German for "balls to the wall." I briefed them on World War II history, and they loved the idea. Sergeant Dock, who manned the paintbrush and stencils, spelled it with a hyphen. Greg Jackson, a J. R. R. Tolkein fan, christened his tank *Balrog*. Another crew in Bravo Tank chose the more obvious *Baghdad Bound*. Freight, meanwhile, named his tank *Bart's Battle Buddy*, after the animated television show character Bart Simpson, a notorious and proud underachiever. It was a weirdly ironic moment of unconscious self-revelation for him. Or one of willful spite for me? No: Freight wasn't that clever.

Several weeks before, Neal Creighton's crew had named his tank *Wild Thing* as a joke after the pitcher in the movie *Major League*, who was fast but could never hit the strike zone. At the time tank names were unauthorized; Neal had to fight off the pressure to have it removed. His crew was proud to have the only tank in all fifty-eight of the battalions with a name.

On the sixteenth the platoon received a mine plow. I chose to mount it on Sergeant Rivera's tank, since as my wingman he was always in the lead section. The plow weighed four tons. Two enormous, ugly steel claws hovered, one in front of each track. If we encountered a minefield, a control in the driver's hatch allowed him to lower the plows so they could push the mines aside and clear a lane. A chain draped between the claws was supposed to set off tilt-rod mines — mines with rods sticking out of the ground to catch the front of a passing vehicle and at a certain angle detonate the mine under the vehicles' vulnerable belly — before the tank straddled it. Rivera would go first, with the plow; I would follow immediately behind him, to lead the company in the assault on the other side of the mine belt.

I asked Swisher again to present my case for firing Freight to Lieutenant Colonel Gordon. He said he would reconsider. Greg Jackson promised to help me with my cause; he felt "morally obliged."

I had recently switched my driver, Spc. Vanderwerker, for Rivera's Pfc. Reynolds, an older soldier who often boasted about his pre-army career as a professional dirtbike racer in Texas, a career his wife made him quit because of the danger. So he joined the army. Reynolds called to my attention that people more and more were talking and singing to themselves.

3

Desert Storm: The Air War
17 January through 23 February 1991

Iraq will take a terrible pounding during the air campaign. Will absorb more
bombs in the first 24 hours of the war than was dropped on North Vietnam.
— Maj. Jason K. Kamiya, "Memo for Record Regarding Main Points
  Discussed During CINCCENT [General Schwarzkopf] Visit to DMAIN on 14
  Jan 91," 15 January 1991

17 January–21 February 1991

According to the Eighteenth Airborne Corps chronology, OPLAN
Desert Storm was put into effect at 0152 hours on 17 January with the launching
of one hundred Tomahawk cruise missiles from U.S. Navy ships in the Gulf.

Hundreds of miles away, in Task Force 3-15's temporary staging position, I was
curled asleep in my customary position on the blow-out panels behind my
hatch. Months before I had figured out how to sleep on the three rectangular
panels by wedging my hipbone in the crevice between the center panel and one
of the others, and my shoulder and outstretched arm in the other crevice. At
0300 Sergeant Dock was on guard, and he had turned on his contraband radio
when he saw an unusual amount of traffic in the sky. He woke me and set the radio by my head. "Sir, it's started. Listen to this."

I heard Marlin Fitzwater, the White House spokesman, make the announce-
ment. "The liberation of Kuwait has begun." This may have been the first time I
learned the operation's name: Desert Storm. Before hitting the sack the previous
evening I had received the latest installment of articles from the journal
Parabola, sent to me by my oldest brother, Walt. The theme of the issue from
which these articles came was "Liberation."

Neal calls Orion the Warrior "God's eternal monument to soldiers." The poet
and mythologist Robert Graves — also a veteran of the war to end all wars —
calls him the Hunter. But to me he is the Liberator: For a beautiful woman's

hand, Orion liberated her father's island kingdom of the monstrous creatures that had overrun it. Orion then boasted he would liberate the world of all its monstrous creatures, and his constellation preserves his fatal combat with one of those, a giant, carapace-armored desert scorpion.

I lay awake watching the sky. Watching the blinking lights of warplanes.

S.Sgt. Lester Deem woke Greg Downey at 0400. "Sir, I think the shit's about to hit the fan." Greg looked up: "The dark sky was filled with an armada of blinking lights, and the desert night was roaring. The reality of combat is both frightening and exhilarating. I sat in awe watching the coalition air power operate above. I could not take my eyes off the dozens of fighter aircraft flying over us, circling in the air behind the larger KC-135 refueling planes, topping off their fuel tanks for another run. I felt I was in a dream, knowing that history was unfolding before my eyes and that everyone around me would be playing a part."

Rob Holmes too was asleep on his usual turret-top position. He had gone to bed at midnight, knowing "that something had to happen soon. My men were beat up from the conditions and worn out from the stress of our six-month sentence in Saudi. We were ready to go home regardless of what we had to do to get there. Tensions ran high." His company commander's gunner, Sgt. Tom Wannamaker, climbed aboard the tank, woke him, and whispered, "Sir, I've got a message from the commander. Desert Storm has been executed." Wannamaker paused. "Do you know what that means?"

Rob pulled out a beat-up old radio he had gotten in a trade to an Arab for a case of chem lights: "Hell, yes, I knew what that meant. The BBC commentators were chattering away, detailing the Americans' start of the air war. Desert Shield was over. Desert Storm had begun. I lay back down and listened to the BBC as I watched the planes overhead. Every so often the horizon would light up, and thunder would roll across the desert a few seconds later. We were really bombing Iraq. At some point it would be the army's turn. I didn't sleep the rest of the night, but I was relaxed and calm as I watched the planes fly above, about like I had spent countless nights in the desert watching shooting stars. Even doing the play-by-play for a war, the unflappable British accent on the radio I found rather soothing.

"Most of my soldiers were awake, watching and listening. We had all heard exploding ammunition before. This sounded different. A gunnery range is a hodgepodge of distractions, frustrations, of *hurry up and wait,* the rounds firing fitfully. But this was almost like a concert, a symphony, its rhythm pulsing across the desert.

"I knew we would be going home soon, but our path would be through Iraq. No one bothered me the rest of the night. I just lay there listening to the rumble and watching the flashes on the horizon. It was an awesome night."

Neal Creighton was sleeping on the back deck of *Wild Thing* when Spc. Gullet woke him. "Sir, the commander wants to see you."

"All right," Neal replied. He crawled out of his sleeping bag, pulled on his desert parka, and groggily dismounted the tank. As he approached Captain Schwartz at his Humvee, he could hear the AM radio.

"Neal, we are bombing Iraq. I just wanted to let you know it has started."

But Neal didn't need to be told: "I knew. We were quiet for awhile. Eventually I found something to say. 'I guess we weren't kidding about the UN's deadline.' I went back to my tank and as the sun rose, I could see planes heading north.

"That morning, I told the platoon we were at war. We listened for the early damage reports on the Voice of America and the BBC. The news was good. As we were listening, one of my sergeants asked me the same old question: 'When do you think we are going to get home, LT?'

"'You know how I usually answer that question, Sergeant Davis — I don't have a clue. I'll tell you what. I'll take a wild-ass guess and say we will stomp the Iraqis and be home by March twentieth.'

"The sergeant pulled out his calendar and wrote a cluster of stars in the box for the twentieth of March. 'See these stars, LT? These are the stars you are going to see if we don't get home by March twentieth. If we do get home by then, I owe you a case of beer.'

"'It's a deal.' I laughed. Then I turned from him to search for pen and paper. The reality had finally hit me. We were going to war, and my platoon was in the front. If the enemy was as good as we were, my chance of survival was not high. I began to write a letter to my daughter:

Dear Katherine,

When you get this letter, you will be learning how to walk and it will be years before you understand what I have written. I am writing at a moment when our country is at war. Right now your father feels tired, but my morale remains high.

I do not know if I will survive this conflict. I want you to know in my own words who I am and how much I will always love you. During my short life, I have had both setbacks and victories, but I always tried to do my very best. I was born into a military family. My father was a career officer, but despite his busy life, he always made time for his children. I think I was my mother's favorite just like you will always be mine.

During my school years, I lived all over the world and made many friends and saw many places. I was a good athlete and participated in football, wrestling, and tennis throughout high school. After high school, I enlisted in the army and later received an appointment to West Point. I went through

Airborne, Ranger, and SERE courses. Ranger School caused a lot of strife in my life, but I'm proud to say that I wear the Ranger Tab.

Right now, I am the lead platoon leader for a 750-soldier task force. We may soon fight, and your father will be in front. Everyone knows fear, and I am afraid that I may not come back. I know my platoon will do well, and I hope very much to return home soon.

Take care of your pretty mother. She has made a lot of sacrifices for our family and she loves you very much. You are the joy in my heart. I will always love you.

Dad

Reading Neal's letter, I can't help but recall that early fall day in 1989 at Fort Knox when I learned of Mary's pregnancy, when I learned how truly surprising it was to them, because they had been told they could not have children.

■ With the sunrise on the seventeenth came a SCUD missile warning. Gas masks were donned, then doffed some twenty minutes later. Otherwise, a surprising mood of jubilation carried the soldiers. People smiled and joked at breakfast. From the relief I supposed. It was finally happening. From the relief, and the knowledge that the beginning of the war took us one step closer to home. I had felt it twice before: first when we arrived at Hunter Army Airfield to wait on our flight, finally putting to rest the initial tension and questions of the deployment, and played Frisbee and paddleball; then when we landed in Saudi Arabia, stepping out of the plane past the crying stewardesses.

For Greg Downey, "it all seemed so sterile at first. Our air power ruled the skies, and we were not being subjected to the same bombardment that the Iraqi army was receiving. Our mood was high. Everyone wanted to get into the fight. The harsh reality of combat did not hit me until I saw one of the first casualties of the air war. One of the coalition planes screamed one hundred feet overhead, the pilot doing his best to nurse a severely damaged fighter jet back to an airfield farther south. I wondered if he'd make it back. I still do."

On the eighteenth, the hair clippers sang and danced again. Some of my guys shaved their heads except for a one-inch Mohawk strip. They ran about laughing and taking pictures. It reminded me of the surfer hitting the waves after a battle in *Apocalypse Now*. The clowning ended, and the Mohawks came off.

Sfc. Freight continued to be a problem for me. I asked Swisher to ask Lieutenant Colonel Gordon if I could gain an audience with him to plead my case. I asked Captain Baillergeon to ask the same of Lieutenant Colonel Barrett. And I told Greg Jackson that I was about to fire my platoon sergeant myself, without endorsement from my chain of command. Order him off his tank and out of the platoon, order him to report to the first sergeant, order him publicly and loudly so the entire company sitting in our tight line would hear. Order Rivera to become the platoon sergeant again. Dare Swisher to countermand me, or fire me, publicly and loudly, so the entire company sitting in our tight line would hear. Greg again attempted to dissuade me. He implied that I could get myself in serious trouble — neither of us thought Swisher would court-martial me, but he could have, and in either case I was jeopardizing my career. And how would it stand the platoon if I were fired and did not lead them into battle?

Once again I did not have the audacity, the whatever, to act my conscience. I wonder how intent I was, how much of my plan was less plan than outburst of frustration and indignation.

The big event on the twenty-second was Lieutenant Colonel Barrett's briefing of the concept of the ground war plan. I had already learned something about it the first week of January; my letters first refer to it anyway on the fourth: "Greg [Jackson] and I avoided Swisher today together for a half hour and talked about things, our situation and our feelings. We have a good idea of our role (as a division) in an offensive. We have no idea when. Greg mentioned something about Baker and Aziz meeting in Geneva." This was right after we had drawn the new tanks, just before the task force obstacle breach when I would dream about Maria being pregnant, and see the sheep giving birth and the breast-feeding Badawiyah. Swisher must have sketched the plan for his lieutenants, though I don't believe he had been allowed to know at that point either. Flash Gordon has since informed me that he and his fellow battalion and task force commanders "were not allowed to brief the plan until near execution date. I did not agree, but that was the guidance. I did brief the company commanders early because we needed their planning input." I presume either Barrett had similarly briefed Swisher and his other company commanders, or Swisher learned from Gordon.

For Barrett's official unveiling of the plan on the twenty-second, all of Task Force 3-15's officers and first sergeants crowded into a GP Small tent. Armed guards outside the tent checked our IDs while Captain Swisher verified our identity for them. The guards collected our personal weapons; the infantry lieutenants carrying M-16s had to stack arms, leaning their rifles against one another in teepee clusters, so that the several stacks outside the GP Small looked like a diorama of a Native American campground. We were prohibited from writing home about the plan and ordered not to reveal it to our soldiers, so as to prevent the possibility of an intelligence leak. We were also not allowed to take notes during the briefing.

Our Eighteenth Airborne Corps would over the upcoming weeks make an enormous tactical displacement nearly five hundred kilometers northwest to attack positions along the Saudi Arabia–Iraq border. From those positions, we would launch our attack deep into Iraq and around Kuwait. The French Sixth Light Armored Division would be on the corps's left flank; the U.S. 3d ACR would be on the right. Our mission was to sever the routes and communication lines into and out of Kuwait, encircling, enveloping, and trapping Hussein's occupying army between us and Seventh Corps. The U.S. Seventh Corps (still arriving in Saudi Arabia from Germany),[1] the marines, and all coalition forces except the French would attack into Kuwait. As Greg describes the plan, "Seventh Corps would be the hammer and we would be the anvil." If I remember correctly, at the time of this initial concept briefing, the plan called for the 24th to spearhead the attack hours, perhaps an entire day, before all other units. This running start would ensure we had time to cover the distance and be in position north of Kuwait to block retreating or reinforcing Iraqi forces. If noticed by Iraq, our movement might also startle them enough to the advantage of the allied forces attacking into the heavily fortified and expectant Iraqi positions in Kuwait. Any Iraqi attention shifted our way, any adjustment or movement to deal with us, could only upset its main Kuwait defensive plans. And it appears that my memory is not far off the mark: The division's Desert Storm Operations Plan of 15 January indicates that the 24th was to attack with the rest of the Eighteenth Airborne Corps on G-Day, H-Hour, about twenty-four hours prior to the Seventh Corps's main attack."

We would fight during the day. This afforded enormous advantages. Imagine the impossibility, in the case that we received artillery with or without chemical agents, of maneuvering at night buttoned-up, peering into the darkness through the periscoping vision blocks that surrounded the tank commander's cupola, each vision block all of about one inch tall and four inches wide. I don't think our night vision goggles would have done much good through the vision blocks. Those difficulties aside, Iraq most likely expected us to hit them at night. From whenever our senior leadership had made the decision, the media coverage of our night-fighting capabilities did not abate. A day attack would be a surprise. And finally, night maneuvers increased tremendously the danger we presented to ourselves. So many armored vehicles, of different makes and silhouettes, feeling their way through the featureless and unfamiliar desert in the dark, and gunners inside with fingers on triggers, gunners who have never been in combat, waiting to meet the enemy, to shoot him before he shoots you. Slight deviations in routes or pacing could place friendly units in one another's path. Unit identification symbols would not be visible, nor would the bright orange VS-17 floppy nylon panels we tied to the top of our tanks so the air force jets providing close air support could discern us from the other sand-colored moving blurbs on the ground[2] (after the war I heard that Lieutenant Colonel Gordon had decided not

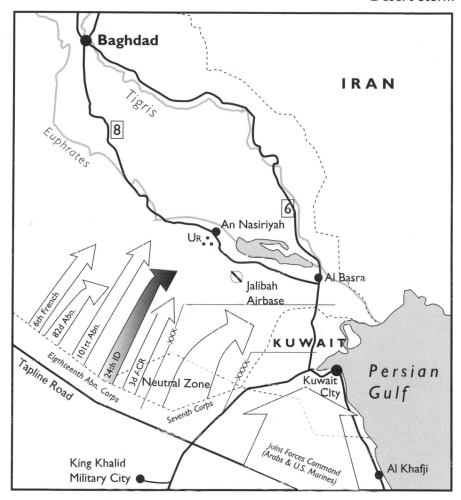

Ground Attack, Operation Desert Storm 24–28 February 1991

to use close air support at all during combat to avoid the possibility of air-to-ground fratricide).

To close the briefing, Lieutenant Colonel Barrett repeated his stock heroic phrases: "high adventure," "a night to remember," "Lawrence of Arabia stuff." I could hardly wait.

I didn't know until researching for this book that the division's planning for the offensive to liberate Kuwait from Iraq had begun the last days of August 1990, while well over half of 24th Infantry was still deploying to the Dammam port. Major General McCaffrey initiated this planning effort less than four days in country, as described by his division chief of plans, Maj. David R. Apt: "We were sitting at the port and had about half a dozen tanks on the ground. . . . We went up into a warehouse in an air-conditioned room because it was 120 degrees. We sat down and [McCaffrey] gave us his intent and [we] started planning from there."[3]

At the battalion level, Lieutenant Colonel Gordon and his staff by late October independently "had the attack plan figured out, but did not anticipate the Seventh Corps deployment. That was my only real surprise. Mostly because I could not see why we needed them." Nor did McCaffrey: "I thought in September or October the initial force could have recaptured Kuwait. I thought there was a degree of risk involved with it at the time, but I felt strong."[4]

The one-corps plan devised by Schwarzkopf's own planning team had not satisfied him, Gen. Colin Powell, Secretary of Defense Richard Cheney, or President Bush. Even with a two-week air prep, the one-corps option risked an unacceptable number of American casualties. It would surely succeed, only at too large a cost. By 15 October, Schwarzkopf directed his team to plan for a two-corps attack. On 8 November, the president announced the deployment of the Seventh Corps.[5]

The issue of an additional corps notwithstanding, our division leadership had foresight in spades. And I for one am thankful those other soldiers joined us.

The same day Task Force 3-15's leadership received the briefing, Task Force 1-64's operations officer, Maj. Jim Diehl, presented the plan at that task force's staging area to the assembled commanders, platoon leaders, and first sergeants. Rob Holmes remembers maps posted all around the tent. As the leaders filed in, Diehl stood commanding the center of the tent, hands on hip, war face on, "in no joking mood."

Rob relives his train of thought: "Second Brigade would lead the division. Wonderful. Task Force 1-64 would lead the brigade. Great. Delta Tank would lead the task force. Terrific. Second Platoon would lead the company. All eyes in the tent fell on me. My platoon had just been tapped to blaze the trail for the entire division.

"The news needed to be digested. The clichés raced through my head: No big deal. I'll do the best I can. I'm just proud to help the team and serve my country. *Why the hell me?* also tore through my head. Being chosen was a compliment; though it could also mean that I was expendable. No. Captain Hubner and Lieutenant Colonel Gordon trusted me. Our country invests a lot of money and confidence in West Point officers. They don't do it so that when we go to war, Academy graduates are two hundred kilometers south counting MREs and sorting mail. My new mission to lead the task force was what should be expected of me and those like me.

"I took a deep breath and, for the rest of the time I was in that crazy world, put on my game face. My responsibilities were never more clear."

Greg Downey felt no small amount of relief that day in the briefing tent: "I had spent months watching our task force intelligence section plot the Iraqi army's complex obstacle network on the southern border of Kuwait — three successive belts of mines, wire, and tank ditches. Some had speculated that the ditches were filled with gas to be ignited when we tried to cross. I had assumed we would attack through this nightmarish barrier into the jaws of the Iraqi army. Thankfully, we weren't going near it.

"In my fledgling army career, I had grown accustomed to grandiose operations orders and graphics, with task force OPORDs reaching forty pages. Such tomes provided information about everything from where to be on the battlefield at a certain time to where to pick up logistics at what times. The Desert Storm OPORD was instead a seven-page list of Grid Index Reference System points. A GIRS point was nothing more than a map coordinate with an associated name, like 'V25,' which we would plot on our maps. With GIRS we could control unit maneuver and fire, quickly changing our plans and reorienting the force as new situations presented themselves.

"The simplicity of the OPORD attack plan made it easy to grasp at all levels. The mission statement from Lieutenant Colonel Gordon was as basic as possible: Task Force 1-64 Armor will conduct a movement to contact using the battalion diamond formation and conduct battle drills to defeat the enemy when encountered. Technology may have taken huge bounds from earlier wars, yet the human dimension of war fighting still thrived on simplicity. The soldiers may be smarter, but the simple plan is always the best plan when it is time to execute.

"The only question left was *when*.

"Walking back to the scout platoon after receiving the attack plan, I met Capt. Steve Winkler, my company commander.

" 'Hey Scout, I've got a new body for you. Meet S.Sgt. Hightower, fresh from Fort Benning. Been in Saudi for three days.'

"This was not what I wanted to hear. Since this guy was a staff sergeant, I would have to assign him as a Bradley commander and move one of my other BCs to a gunner's seat. I had spent the last five months training my BCs, all of us coming together as a team, knowing how one another thinks. I rearranged my platoon to make room for Hightower, and had no sooner finished my first crash-tutoring session of my new BC when Winkler returned with four more soldiers.

" 'Jesus Christ, sir, why now?' I fumed.

" 'These are combat engineers sent down from brigade to give us some engineer expertise in the scout platoon.'

"My scout platoon was rapidly growing at the worst time. I was not only concerned about getting unfamiliar soldiers into the platoon, but I was also trying to figure out how to fit their bodies and gear into the cramped vehicles, already overloaded from extra ammunition, extra scouts, and extra rations. I assigned one engineer to each of my three scout sections. I told my Bradley commanders to stow the new guys' gear wherever they could. 'Teach them the vehicle, how to fire the twenty-five mike-mike [25 mm], and as much about how we do things as possible. Then introduce these new guys to the rest of the platoon.'

"The battalion chaplain, Capt. Tim Bedsole, had been standing behind me when I used the Lord's name in vain talking to Winkler. He always made me feel guilty about using foul language.

"'Chaplain, I need a miracle,' I stated.

"'Maybe if you would pray to Jesus Christ instead of condemning Him for your struggles, He would answer,' Chaplain Bedsole preached, in his slow, Southern Baptist drawl.

"'Hell, Chaplain, I do pray . . . every goddamned day,'" I said, echoing my favorite line from the movie *Patton*.

"Bedsole laughed and asked if he could do anything for the platoon.

"'I need you to help me with two things, Chaplain. One you can handle yourself, the other you'll need the Big Guy's help with. First, I'd like you to bless the scout platoon and the vehicles. We'll need all the help we can get to survive this thing. We can't do it on our own.

"'The other thing is out of your hands, but I would appreciate it if you spent some prayer time on it. I want you to pray for guidance on the battlefield for my Bradley commanders, so they don't get lost.' I knew the chaplain didn't understand my concerns about navigating in the featureless desert. He never had to deal with it.

"'Lord,' he began his blessing, 'we stand here today facing the unknown, thinking about what our fate might be, what Your plan for us is. We ask that You provide protection for these young warriors, for they are being asked to give up their lives so that others may live, just as You had Your only Son give His life so we could live.'

"I looked into the eyes of my soldiers, seeing tears well up in many of them, feeling my throat tighten as I listened to the chaplain pray for us with every ounce of faith in his soul.

"'And Lord, we ask that You guide these vehicles. Even though they are weapons of war, use them as instruments of peace, that they will bring this conflict to a quick end with as little destruction and death as possible. Look over these scouts, for they are the angels of the battalion, providing protection for over seven hundred other warriors. In Your name, we pray. Amen.'

"I tried to dry my eyes before looking up. The chaplain had finished the last precombat check I had on my list. I was thanking him for his prayers when I heard the voice that struck fear in most of the task force's officers.

"'Scout, Merry fucking Christmas,' Lieutenant Colonel Gordon announced. He had a box under each arm. He looked at the chaplain. If Flash Gordon believed in God, he'd never let on.

"'Now you don't have an excuse about being lost. I hope you know how to use them,' he said. He always laced his conversation with sarcasm.

I opened up the one of the boxes. Inside was a Trimpack GPS navigational device. The GPS calculates its position on the ground by signals received from orbiting satellites. Truly a gift from Heaven, and the answer to my prayers. Well, to somebody's prayers.

"'Damn, you work fast, Chaplain,' I said.

"'The Lord works in mysterious ways, scout,' preached Chaplain Bedsole, grinning beneath his slight mustache."

The next day, Rob Holmes happened to be at Task Force 1 64's TOC when a contingency of replacement soldiers arrived, among them a group of officers. "I remember when the Humvee dropped them off — three second lieutenants and a captain. The captain, as friendly as he could be, shook my hand. One of the lieutenants asked if there was a chance for them to get a platoon. 'Yeah,' I said, 'if one of us dies.' Their faces dropped. I don't think it was from disappointment because they weren't going to walk into a platoon. They realized we could die."

Rob was right, of course. The new junior officers were there in case anything happened to any among the current set. Platoon leaders historically suffer more casualties than other soldiers since they lead the way. To position his replacement platoon leaders as near as possible to the platoons they might "get," Gordon assigned two of the lieutenants as track commanders in the Tactical Assault Command, the handful of task force command vehicles that traveled in formation with the line companies. The third rode in a fuel truck with the support platoon. And he asked the new captain to volunteer to be the loader on his own tank, where he was as close as he could be to any company he might be called on to command.

I didn't meet any of these men until after the war. I wasn't even aware of their arrival, much less the purpose of their presence. Knowing my imagination, it was probably best that way.

■ The week between the start of the air campaign and the western displacement to our attack position along the Saudi-Iraqi border was, except for the initial concept briefing, fairly uneventful for our two task forces. The war taking shape around us touched us only indirectly. In our daily updates, passed from commander to commanders to platoon leaders to soldiers, we received word of some of the events happening elsewhere in theater, mostly SCUD missiles fired at Dhahran, Riyadh, King Khalid Military City, and Israel; and limited ground action. One report from the Eighteenth Airborne chronology reads familiar, reads like I might have heard it before. It is the oddity of it: "Two unidentified individuals in SCUBA equipment are observed in the water near Warehouse #20 in the Port of Dammam; they disappear after being engaged by military police."

Bravo Tank loaded its vehicles onto American HETs the afternoon of the twenty-fifth; as I vaguely recollect, we were one of the last companies in the brigade to make the move. The night before my company moved to the HET upload site, queues formed for the last sit-down latrines we would experience for an unknown period of time.

The loading area was a patch of desert off Tapline Road. The HET National Guard transportation unit hailed from my home state of Kansas. Their platoon leader, a woman lieutenant, found me after one of my soldiers told her I was from Kansas as well. I remember spying peripherally some of my guys, above and behind her on the tanks, making goo-goo eyes and obscene gestures while she and I made small talk. I remember finding her far too excited about the whole venture. More than likely she had not been living on her Humvee in the desert for the past five months; more than likely she would not soon be attacking Iraq. Maybe her giddiness was simple delight in meeting another Kansan halfway around the world. What were the odds?

Just as we had covered our vehicles' identification markings before loading them on the ships (to hamper enemy intelligence) we covered the bumper numbers again for the move west.

We left at 1730. Near-freezing temperatures and rain for much of the night. We rode in the tanks on top of the HETs. I remember we had been briefed on the threat from enemy air: all those defenseless tanks arranged in rows for easy picking. So we had to ride in the tanks on top of the HETs, ready for the HETs to pull off the road and the tanks to come down. The two machine guns on top of the turret were locked and loaded, and one soldier per tank, an air guard, had to stay awake at any given time. When I wasn't air guard, I passed the hours shifting around in my seat in a daze between sleep and consciousness. Before sinking into my daze, I chuckled to myself listening to the National Guard lieutenant on the radio. She was obviously a newcomer to the army radio net. She sounded like all of us did our first time in the field, articulating everything, not using voice recognition after the initial identification, not using radio shorthand, keeping the conversation going much longer than necessary. Such protractions fill the airspace and give the enemy the opportunity to track the signal.

We arrived at our download site at 0900 on the twenty-sixth. I was fortunate to have traveled for only fifteen and a half hours; Neal Creighton's journey lasted nearly twenty-four. Back at the upload site, Dave Trybula's company was just getting under way. Dave's HET trip took a little longer than most: "My HET made it approximately halfway before too many of its tires gave out. We had to off-load the tank somewhere along Tapline Road. The HET went back for repairs, promising to send another to pick us up. So my crew and I sat. Out of radio range, we couldn't inform the commander of our situation. We didn't know where the company was, much less when we would meet back up with it. Late in the afternoon on the twenty-seventh, an Arab civilian stopped and asked if we were going to be there for another hour. I told him I expected so. He left and returned an hour later with a gigantic platter of chicken and rice. He said that this was his way of showing appreciation. My crew thanked him between gobbles of the steaming hot food. Late that night another HET finally picked us up, delivering us to the company's laager early on the twenty-eighth. That morning was our first desert frost. The weather had indeed changed."

The terrain at our download site, roughly 480 kilometers inland in the vicinity of the town of Nisab, stretched much more flatly than had our more coastal desert. The wind swept unimpeded; the weather was *much* colder. According to Greg Downey, we were some forty kilometers shy of the Iraqi border.

It rained incessantly the day my company arrived and throughout the night.

The next morning I spent huddled behind Greg Jackson's tank against the cold, asserting to him that large, armored battles between armies belonged in history books. They had no place in the present.

The company spent the rest of the day bearing the wet cold, waiting to move.

As soon as his Bradley Cavalry Fighting Vehicles backed down off the HETs, Greg Downey's scout platoon was ordered north to conduct a relief-in-place mission with a unit from the 3d Armored Cavalry Regiment screening the Iraqi–Saudi Arabia border. He had received reports that the 3d ACR had had sporadic direct fire contact with the Iraqis, most likely the platoon-on-platoon firefight the evening of the twenty-second recorded in the Eighteenth Airborne chronology, in which two or three 3d ACR soldiers were wounded and six Iraqis captured.

"I knew my FM radios would not be able to transmit back to the task force TOC, which would be over thirty-five kilometers away. Battalion told me to move out anyway, knowing that I could not both carry out my screening mission and keep the TOC informed. Battalion leadership fully understood the situation, yet failed to provide me any additional support.

"Once again I found myself caught in the army's *just-get-it-done* mentality, which ignores the difficulties of the assigned task for the sake of getting started.

I was just as often guilty of it myself, not wanting to hear *why* my intent couldn't be done, instead just wanting to know *when* it was done. It feels worse when you're on the receiving end of it.

"The scout platoon moved north until we arrived at the designated screen line. I was very confident in the navigation skills of each scout section now, as my section leaders had learned how to use the newly acquired GPSs. We occupied our screen during daylight, allowing us to find good observation locations that provided defensible terrain. I attempted to make contact with battalion throughout the night, but as predicted my radio transmissions could not reach the TOC. I even moved my vehicle south to reestablish communications, finally opting to abandon the idea and return to the screen line with my scouts where I belonged.

"At about 0300 hours, two Humvees arrived at my location. For the next fifteen minutes, I was on the receiving end of a one-way conversation with Major Diehl. We both knew the cause of the communications problem, but I did not want to argue and he did not want to listen.

"The battalion moved north the next day and joined us on the border. The task force staff developed a defensive plan for the slight chance that the Iraqi army would attack into our area. We would spend the next weeks conducting rehearsals, precombat inspections, and maintenance."

■ Late in the afternoon on the twenty-seventh we moved north to occupy our attack position. The brigade sat just south of the western edge of the neutral zone. Task Force 3-15 occupied the brigade's and the division's eastern flank, tying in with the westernmost unit of the 3d ACR, and formed a conventional horseshoe task force defensive position around an engagement area. Three kilometers north of Delta Mech's position was the edge of the neutral zone. Eight kilometers farther, a long, manmade berm stretched along the actual "de facto" boundary between Saudi Arabia and Iraq.

The days seemed to be growing longer. Days of the week meant nothing. Dates meant little as well. Our sense of time stretched in both directions from H-Hour on G-Day, the time and date the ground attack would commence. Days leading up to G-Day became, say, G minus 3 (G-3), and subsequent days became, say, G plus 2 (G+2). Not that we knew the scheduled G-Day date.

The evening of the twenty-seventh, I drew a sand table on the ground beside my tank and briefed the larger plan as I knew it to my soldiers. This was, as far as I knew, a violation of orders. They were not yet allowed to know.[6] I felt I could not withhold any longer. The ground offensive loomed more likely with each passing hour, and they deserved to know the plan on which their lives depended. The knowledge appeared to comfort them.

We did not discuss the chemical or fratricide threats. The one didn't need to be mentioned as it had been festering in everyone's minds for the past six months, and the other, despite some training snafus, remained fairly inconceivable. That a friendly could shoot us meant that any of us could shoot a friendly, meant that we and our technology were fallible, and that we were far more vulnerable than we cared to admit.

The next afternoon, the platoon mounted up for our short trip to link with Delta Mech. As I led the platoon away from Bravo Tank, I radioed back to the XO. When you enter a unit's assigned radio frequency, you must request permission. When you leave, you announce the fact.

"Black Five, White One." Then Greg Jackson in that soothing, parade-announcing voice:

"White One, Black Five."

"This is White One, leaving this net, over."

"This is Black Five, roger, out."

My stomach dropped. I flipped the radio switch to Delta Mech's frequency and adjusted myself to my new call sign. Gold Six. The radio dials whirred into position, the antenna clacked to its proper, new setting.

Dave Trybula retells a story originally told to him by his commander, a story about our growing paranoia: "Division had discovered a series of fifty-five-gallon drums on a north-south trail right at the Saudi-Iraqi border, and suspecting that the Iraqis might have filled them with nerve agents or foo gas, sent a team to check them out. Dressed in MOPP IV — chemical suits, masks, and black rubber boots and gloves — the team sent one man to the nearest drum while the others watched. He kicked the first drum and ran back to the others. He made his way back and kicked a second drum; then a third. A Saudi border patrol had been watching them and drove up. The team from division tried to wave the approaching Saudis away, to protect them from the danger. The Saudis didn't understand. They pulled up to the team. When a member of the team explained the situation and asked the border patrol to remove themselves to a safe distance, the border patrol laughed. Saudi Arabia had set up the drums years ago to stop people from inadvertently crossing the international border. The drums were full of sand."

According to my letters, I finished Henry James's *The Americans* the afternoon of 29 January. Of the several books I read in the desert, *The Americans* is one of the most discussed in my letters. It is also the only book I had entirely forgotten having read until I reread my letters for the first time since the war, writing this book. As for my present memory of the novel, of plot, of characters: nothing. After finishing it, I dropped the novel into the bury pit beside my tank.

I did not feel the boredom as severely as my soldiers did. In addition to my escapist reading and letter writing, I had leadership duties. I met at least daily with Captain Baillergeon and the other lieutenants. I also had maps to assemble. So many maps. Whereas at the NTC in the California desert, where we conducted our most expansive maneuver training, we dealt with at most four mapsheets for our run across the Arabian peninsula we had over thirty sheets to manage.[7] Connecting eight of these three-foot-square mapsheets as required would have made a six-by-twelve-foot monstrosity. I instead grouped my maps only one sheet high, enabling easy accordion unfolding and refolding. The entire bunch, once assembled and marked with operational graphics, I stuffed in marching order in my map satchel, which rode in the sponson box beside my hatch. As we attacked I would swap the map group in my hand with the next one in the satchel. In addition to the thirty-some 1:50,000 maps, we also carried a set of 1:250,000 maps showing the entire division maneuver plan. At the battalion and lower levels, we were accustomed to the 1:50,000 and the even more detailed 1:25,000 scale. The world of the small unit leader is the world of individual draws, spurs, wadis, berms, creeks, powerlines, and the subtlest of elevation changes. The more details, the better. But even on a 1:50,000 map, a blank expanse could be a mess of berms, gradients, and depressions, difficult to navigate and easy hiding for the enemy.[8]

The map satchel bulged with its cargo. The roll of some 250 remaining map sheets I stored in a tank main gun round shipping tube tied outside the bustle rack on the turret rear. We would need these maps in case our battle plans changed.

The sound of firing artillery rounds interrupted my map making on 30 January. Rounds leaving tubes: a dull hollow sound, the successive distant thuds forming a single rumble. It must have been the first ground war action I experienced. I am remembering the sound came from behind us, possibly from 3d ACR; I do not know.

To my west, in 1-64's tactical assembly area, Dave Trybula was penning a letter to his girlfriend Jill: "I have been keeping very busy trying to make sure we're ready for anything. This is the only thing that scares me — that I will send men to their death because of a mistake I will make or because I forgot to train them in some way. This is something that will always remain in the back of my mind."

Before the arty salvo, I watched a butterfly alight upon the ground between me and a showering Sergeant Dock. After the artillery another gorgeous sunset capped my day. The sun left vibrant peach-pink airbrushed clouds in its wake.

That evening's intelligence update dashed the calm. The night before, Iraq had conducted preemptive ground incursions out of Kuwait into Saudi, in the Marine Corps sector on the coast. One part of the attack involved a tank battalion; one (it may have been the tanks) penetrated the border and seized a Saudi coastal town, Ra's al Khafji, located about ten kilometers from Kuwait, before being repelled. I noticed more air sorties than usual that night. We received a warning order for an on-order mission to displace south one kilometer, to allow an MLRS unit to move forward to fire its missiles deep into Iraq. The move would remove us from the MLRS danger area.

The on-order displacement mission did not come.

Intelligence update about the assault on Khafji came the next day: American A-10s and B-52s had hit a seventeen-kilometer-long Iraqi column moving south, destroying two hundred tanks. We would not learn until 10 February that during the fight for Khafji, a U.S. Air Force air-to-ground missile may have destroyed a Marine Light Armored Vehicle, killing seven.[9]

The soldiers can take the unrelieved tension and the unrelieved boredom only so much. Then they outburst. On 3 February, it was my driver, Pfc. Reynolds. He clambered out of and off the tank, where he had been hiding from the wind, and onto a small pile of rocks, where he shouted "Bullshit!" at the top of his lungs. He returned tankside, under the bustle rack, out of the wind and sun, and sat next to me on a grease can. "Waiting is bullshit."

I tried to explain my position, how waiting increased our chance of living.

"Waiting is bullshit, sir. We should have attacked back in October. Gotten it over with. Surprised him."

I explained that in October, we had had one mechanized division on the ground. Ours. I reminded him of the state of our old M1IP tanks we had brought from Stewart, of our operational readiness, in October. Attacking, I felt, would have amounted to suicide.

"So? We'd be home one way or another by now."

"Doesn't it matter that you go home alive?" I asked.

"As long as I go home."

"Then if you're tired of waiting, and if life means nothing to you," I challenged, "why don't you just put your .45 to your head and blow it off?"

Just then Sergeant Dock emerged from the tank. With blue ink he had scrawled "FUCK" on his forehead and "IT" on his chin. He paraded himself around to the other tanks, giggling to himself. Sergeant Dock, my gunner, the NCO in charge of my tank, for that instant no icon of small-unit leadership but a living monument of the soldiers' frustration.

I suspect my soldiers sensed my fears about battle. Maybe my evident terror was counterbalanced by my continued presence, my willingness, and my surface equanimity, the whole effect serving to mollify their own fears. A case of unintended leadership by example: *Look at the lieutenant, he's scared too, and he's okay.* Maybe not.

Pvt. Doug Powers caused one of my most troubling moments during the final weeks preceding the ground war. He came to me one day because he was scared. Powers loaded for Sfc. Freight. He didn't trust Freight. "Sir, he doesn't know what he's doing. Sergeant Wingate does half Freight's job for him, and Wingate is frustrated because he's been a tank commander before, he knows he's better than Freight, yet he can't command the tank from his gunner's chair, and I know he worries that Freight will get us killed." The respectful private would not explicitly label his platoon sergeant a moron or idiot; he approached me with his own problems, not Freight's. He was the most professional nineteen year old I've ever met. A few days earlier he had restored the morale of Sergeant Boss, a pissed and despondent NCO who had refused to leave his gunner's position for three days, not speaking to a soul. I left him alone, in the hope that his hibernation was gestating an improved psyche. Boss emerged when Private Powers asked for help writing a letter. In the "To Any Soldier" letter lottery, Powers had won. He corresponded with several pretty girls, one gorgeously cute Texas blonde, the twenty-year-old Miss Melissa, who promised to take him to dinner when he got home. Powers was from Texas, too. From his first letter to these girls, Powers had entreated Boss's assistance, which the latter confidently provided. As I write, I wonder if Powers really needed Boss for a letter that day, or if the young man knew better than I did what Boss needed: a gesture of respect from a subordinate, an invitation for Boss to assert himself in both a manly and sensitive way. After the letter, the sergeant was his old self.

I did my best to assure Powers that his life hardly depended on Sfc. Freight. He had three other tanks in the platoon looking after his, and ten other Bradleys in the company. His tank would never be alone against the Iraqis; his tank would never be without the rest of Second Platoon. I don't know how much comfort I afforded Powers. I liked and respected him — he was the most able, mature, and amiable of my enlisted men. Facing him then deluged me with feelings of sympathy and helplessness and fear and outrage, and left me numb.

My personal campaign to relieve Freight persisted until G-Day, if my efforts had waned for want of response. On one of those final February countdown days, Freight boasted to me about the gang rape of a young woman soldier he had orchestrated in the backwoods of Fort Knox. I think he said she was the training battalion colonel's Humvee driver, with whom she had been having an affair. "She was a real tease, sir, to the rest of us; she deserved what she got. I had her drive me out to where the road ends in the middle of nowhere one night, told her to put out or get out. Had her drop her pants, bend over and lean up against the vehicle, and took her that-a-way. From behind, know what I mean? Meanwhile, what she didn't know, I had me a bunch of my buddies follow us, and as soon as I finished with her they had their turn. Learned that girl a lesson, and she liked it, too. Yes sir, she sure did like it."

I did not believe him for a second. Freight lied to impress. During our month with the Cav, my tank crew and I overheard him telling Delta Mech's 1st Sergeant Burns that, like Burns, he had been in Vietnam. Freight had never mentioned this to anyone before. Nor did he wear a combat patch on his right shoulder for the unit in which he claimed to have fought. Burns asked him his Vietnam unit. Freight scratched his head. He'd forgotten. Burns asked for the nearest village to Freight's unit's base camp. Freight stroked his chin. He'd forgotten that as well. As if a combat veteran still in possession of his mind could ever forget his wartime unit or the ground he'd fought over. I have never seen a person's mouth as wide open in disbelief and hilarity as Pfc. Vanderwerker's as we eavesdropped. McBryde sat on the turret top giggling through his Cheshire grin. Between his own suppressed outbursts, Sergeant Dock called Freight a "stupid fuck." All three watched me as they listened and held back, quietly ferreting my response.

Four months later, newly armed with a rape confession, I reported to Captain Baillergeon. "The UCMJ statute of limitations for a felony is five years, right, sir? I'd like to court-martial him." I did not expect Baillergeon to take me seriously. It gave him and the other officers a good laugh while giving me the opportunity to broach the tired subject again. Baillergeon agreed to mention it to Lieutenant Colonel Barrett once more. I had no reason to be hopeful.

■ My letters of late January and February talk more and more of my homecoming. One to my Philadelphia belle lists my repatriation plans in ironic imitation of our offensive operations order: Repatriation Day (R-Day), fly to Kansas City. Buy convertible; drink with friends. On R+5, the fifth day after repatriation, Maria flies to Kansas City. R+7, drive with Maria to Philadelphia. Et cetera. Another chats on the new clothes I would need to buy those first days back. I wrote about graduate school. *I drool for school.* I spent more time thinking about my homecoming and postwar life than I did about the war. *I still find myself fighting my position and circumstances,* I wrote on 27 January. *I do not want to lead men into battle. I want nothing to do with the things leaders do. I must change my state. I must plan, and assemble maps, and consider.*

Letter of 12 February: *We hear and feel the bombing occurring fifteen miles to our northeast, in another unit's sector. At night we see the flashes.*

At least once a day a pair of helicopters buzzed overhead on their way north.

Always in the back of my mind were the news articles and radio stories, and letters from home about articles and radio and TV stories, in which "our pundits" predicted that the upcoming ground war "will be the bloodiest battle since Normandy, . . . akin to the battle of Verdun, fighting through the fire trenches, on and on." That's how Major General McCaffrey summarized them.[10] He and others may have known better, but we did not. We could not. Any reassurance our leadership might have given us — I remember nothing specific — would have felt like exactly that: mere reassurance from our leaders. A pep talk about a plan we weren't supposed to know.

Rob Holmes and his fellow Delta Tank platoon leader, Jeff White, paid me a surprise visit the next day. They drove their commander's Humvee, having just come from visiting Neal Creighton in Alpha Tank. Rob made that trek, he writes, because he "had recently learned about leading the task force, and to be completely candid, I was a little nervous. To this day I maintain that I never once thought I would leave the Middle East with so much as a scratch on me. I don't say that with bravado. My father was raised Southern Baptist, my mother Lutheran, and I went to an Episcopalian elementary school and a Catholic high school, and as a Presbyterian I believe in a sense of purpose and destiny. This all can't be an accident. Whatever my purpose is, it wasn't to die in that damn desert. I was, however, absolutely terrified of getting one of my guys hurt. I couldn't bear the thought. I guess that's why I was a little bit nervous before we attacked, so I wanted to see Al and Neal. I didn't know if they were nervous also, but I figured it would help me if I could shake their hands before we launched, and maybe it would help them as well. It wouldn't have been in my character to have told them at the time why I came calling, but that's the reason. Confidence is contagious, and there is strength in numbers. I knew they were on my flank, and that made me feel better; I guess I just wanted to make sure by actually seeing them before we attacked."

BBC report on the radio, 16 February: Hussein offered to follow UN proscriptions, and Bush restated his position to continue bombing until Hussein begins to withdraw or unconditionally surrenders. Two days later, Tariq Aziz (ironically enough a Christian), given Hussein's calls for a jihad against the largely non-Muslim forces gathering against him,[11] met with Mikhail Gorbachev, the latter trying to convince Iraq to quit the field. We heard about the meeting at a commander's update the following day. Aziz and Gorbachev met several more times until the start of the ground war, teasing me, stringing me along. I don't remember when I resigned myself to the war's inexorability.

Some time during or just before the air war, I heard that a group of American citizens threatened to form a human shield between Kuwait and Saudi Arabia to try to stop the war. Our commanders' response: The desert is a big place; we'll try not to run anybody over.

Prior to the air war, Dave Trybula had received two reports that bolstered his confidence and his soldiers' morale.

"First, we were told that the Iraqi front-line tanks carried the same basic load of ammunition as they had at the end of the Iran-Iraq war. This meant that most of their tank rounds were antipersonnel and not antitank, since the Iranians had few tanks and had relied heavily upon human assault waves. In other words, these battle-proven warriors with these awesome tanks were handicapping themselves by basing their ammunition loads on their experience against Iranian infantry rather than on intelligence of our armor. Second, we were informed that while Iraq bought their tanks from the Soviet bloc, they made their own ammunition to save money, and tests done on it showed it to be so substandard that it would require an extremely close shot, and a lot of luck, to damage our tanks. It didn't seem to matter anymore that their tanks outnumbered ours two or three to one. This great news increased everyone's desire to get across the border and finish the job we had come here to do."

Two different pieces of information assuaged my own fatalistic mood those final days before the ground attack. Captain Baillergeon shared classified information with me, assuring me of the Abrams's superiority over the T-72, Iraq's most modern tank. "You don't have anything to worry about." He had the information firsthand — that was all he could tell me. And a BBC report estimated 30 percent of Iraqi tanks and 40 percent of Iraqi artillery had been destroyed during the allied air campaign. I swore I'd buy a drink for every air force pilot I ever met.

We were briefed once, at our final assault position in front of the berm, on possible enemy locations along our route. At Task Force 3-15's TOC, the task force leaders walked through our actions on meeting the enemy at each of these locations on a sand table. Lieutenant Colonel Gordon conducted a similar session over in Task Force 1-64. According to Greg Downey, this "battle-drill rehearsal ensured everyone in the task force knew, in detail, how he fit into a battle. All vehicle commanders, both tracked and wheeled, and gunners, drivers, and battalion staff participated. The terrain board was the largest I had ever seen, covering one full square kilometer. With each vehicle's crew walking the terrain board, every formation was rehearsed, every battle drill executed, every contingency exercised. The battle drill, the most basic and essential form of fighting, was validated in the minds of every soldier there." After 3-15's sand table walkthrough, the air force air liaison officer (ALO) assigned to the task force passed out copies of leaflets being dropped on the Iraqis. After dropping a five hundredpound bomb inside a crate floating down on a parachute, we dropped an identical crate-parachute configuration, which upon bursting rained leaflets down on the shocked, cowering troops. (An army guy joshed the ALO: "M113s don't have ejection seats, captain." A mild titter went a long way in the desert.)

In that final week, Captain Baillergeon distributed to his platoon leaders a number of photocopied sketches. Most of these consisted of task force positioning at various objectives along the route. One of them depicted our entire route, the known Iraqi units to our east, their estimated strengths, and the approximate time it would take them to reach us. The closest, the 26th Division, had all of thirty-five T-55 tanks, the oldest brand in Iraq's - - in anybody's — inventory.

Task Force 3–15 alone had twenty-eight M1A1s. Most of the sketched units fell into Seventh Corps's avenue of advance. I was more concerned with our destination north of Kuwait, when we would find ourselves sandwiched between Iraqi forces in Kuwait, both those in defensive reserve and those retreating, and Iraqi reserve forces in Iraq. Hussein held his elite divisions, his Republican Guard, as his reserve force. Rob Holmes shared my concerns, as did I imagine nearly every soldier in the 24th: "If we did not make it to the Euphrates River before the Iraqi army, we could wind up chasing the Republican Guard to Baghdad. And if the American and coalition forces to our east were not effective pushing the Iraqis out of Kuwait, we would be deep in enemy territory, tethered to a long and vulnerable supply line."

Task Force 3-15 practiced crossing the border the evening of the eighteenth. We did this by literally rotating the graphics one hundred eighty degrees on our maps in order to execute the practice mission to our rear in the south. All the Bradleys and tanks, and a representative portion of the battalion train vehicles, participated. The mission took place at night and was a fiasco. It ended after the task force failed to regroup on the other side of the make-believe berm and when, cruising through a flat tract of desert with half the task force behind me, I lifted my PVS-7 night vision goggles and an American attack helicopter filled my view. I hollered at my driver to make a hard right; we dodged the thing, then we stopped. I look around with the PVS-7s — we were surrounded by attack helicopters. I did not want any of our tanks or Bradleys to smash an Apache days before the ground war. Captain Baillergeon agreed. We abandoned the mission. It was 0200.

The next morning, winding our way out of the area, we passed a support unit. They had themselves a regular camp: vans, tents, showers. All the luxuries we had left behind, and here they were just kilometers south of our position. The support soldiers, dressed in T-shirts and baseball caps, waved to us. Not a weapon, helmet, or flak jacket in sight. I cursed them to my crew over the intercom: "You should see these fucking REMFs."

Greg Downey could feel the tension mounting in his scouts as the days ticked down to war. "Everyone had been 'leaning forward in the saddle' for an extended period of time, waiting for the big moment. A person can only take so much before lashing out. Perhaps it had more to do with impatience of getting this over and going home than anything else, but I began to truly and deeply hate the enemy. We had been in Saudi Arabia over six months, enduring the austere conditions, waiting for something to happen to justify our presence. Seeing pictures of the Iraqi soldiers demonstrating, and burning American flags, really fueled my fire. If Iraq withdrew from Kuwait now, it would be a bittersweet victory."

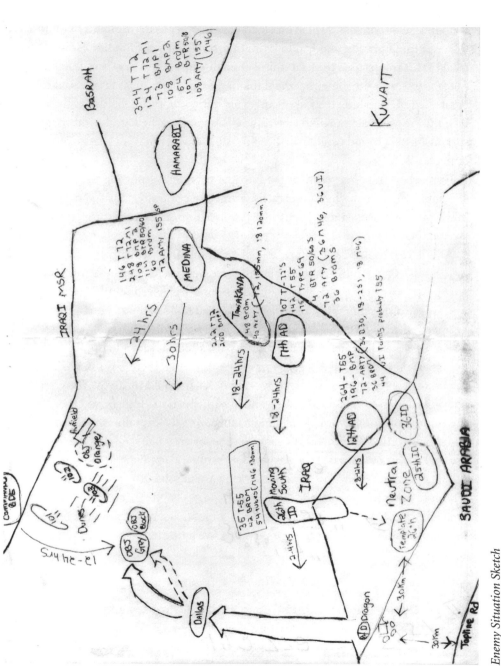

Enemy Situation Sketch

It rained fiercely over the night of the nineteenth. I initially mistook the thunder for artillery. We slept in fetal curls inside the tank. When we emerged the next morning, we found our tank sitting in a small lake. Brian Luke, Delta Mech's first Platoon Leader, who had slept in his customary manner underneath his Bradley, woke spitting up water and had to swim out from under his Bradley. He and I talked as his troops used the heat from our engine exhaust to dry their gear. Despite the wet, we were somewhat thankful for the rain. Rain sucks for the soldier, but it also refreshes him. It always changes his spirits; afterward, he always smiles broadly. We were also thankful because G-Day approached, and a thorough soaking of the ground would help keep the dust down, out of our faces, out of our gun sights.

Gorbachev and Aziz resumed talks on the twentieth. Knowing the ground war imminent, Gorbachev desperately wanted a cease-fire. Bush and Italy's president urged Russia and Iraq to hasten their process. Ground forces were awaiting Bush's order.

The next day Rob, Jeff White, and their company's artillery fire support officer, Mike Francombe, visited again. All three were excited by the Gorbachev-Aziz peace prospects. Flash, they claimed, no longer believed we were going to war. Was he disappointed? So many girls had called Rob's parents about him that his mother had to take notes to keep track of them all. Rob had written me a letter on the eleventh, which I did not receive until after this second visit. If we did not attack until March or April, he reported in his letter, there was some talk of my becoming his company's executive officer. That would make me the company's second in command, over Rob and the other platoon leaders, and the acting company commander if something happened to the captain. He also wrote about how we might be out of the army in time for graduate school in the fall of 1992, which meant we'd have to start taking exams and applying in the summer of 1991. "That's as soon as we get home! We'll have to sober up pretty quickly after our homecoming because we have work to do. . . . Well, Al, it looks like we're going to war. God be with you. . . . When it comes down to it, West Point exists to produce young men to lead such missions. We'll be fine. See: II Timothy 1:7, Romans 8:29–38. Take Care. Rob."[12]

Cross-Border Operations: 21–24 February 1991

CBS had a segment on about the nucleus of our war machine. In case you have had the impression that none of us know what you are going through, the network special was about you. They talked about the 23-year-old M1A1 commander and the necessity for the effort of that young man, and his ability to think quickly and correctly. They called you the "most vital link" in the weapons system. Must give you an awesome sense of power to know that you are that important.

— Bryant Jensen, letter to his nephew, Alex Vernon, 24 February 1991

On 21 January, the Eighteenth Airborne Corps directed its major subordinate commanders to plan deep operations in preparation for the ground offensive. The 24th Infantry Division's plans for these cross-border operations — what *The Victory Book* calls "intrusive reconnaissance operations" — command an entire section of the *Historical Reference Book's* five sections. It is easy to forget that the ground forces were at war prior to G-Day on the twenty-fourth. *Forget* is not the right word. Those of us on the ground lived largely unaware of the action taking place on the ground around us and elsewhere in the theater. Though the Eighteenth Airborne Corps's chronology has significant omissions, it nonetheless portrays a busier and more dangerous pre-G-Day period for coalition ground forces than I had believed. This action intensified on 15 February, when the corps commenced its cross-border operations: attack helicopter raids, air assault raids, A-10 air strikes, psychological operations, artillery missions, Special Forces and LRSD insertions, and mounted armored incursions, all to gain intelligence and to eliminate any resistance on the other side of the border that might slow our attack.

Neal Creighton participated in an artillery mission against a border post in the first hours of 21 February. Neal's fire support officer targeted the building for a single 155-mm copperhead round. "I will always remember how accurately the copperhead struck the building. Dead center." A dismounted patrol from Neal's company cleared the site. "All that was found in the rubble," reports Neal, "was a pair of scorched boots."[13]

Around 2000 that evening, Captain Baillergeon called the company to REDCON 2; our scouts had spotted enemy vehicles and possible artillery pieces in our sector. We put our sleeping gear away and moved to our crew positions. A little later, Baillergeon reported that four SCUD missiles had impacted to our east. At 2400 we returned to REDCON 3. The sleeping bags came back out. As I went to bed I heard a series of four bomb rumblings.

Meanwhile, Greg Downey was on the first of his two cross-border operations. "The three scout platoons in 2d Brigade would conduct zone recons from the Line of Departure to Phase Line Opus, about twenty kilometers north of the border. The purpose of this zone recon was to identify any enemy positions and gather information on the terrain. First we conducted a dismounted recon of the berm along the border to determine a suitable crossing site. Just after darkness fell, we crossed into Iraq.

"As my CFV drove over the berm, my driver Specialist West reported over the intercom that the engine was running hot. A few seconds later flames shot out of the engine access panels and for a split-second engulfed West. After stopping to extinguish the oil fire with handheld fire extinguishers, we determined the fan tower had seized up. I transferred over to my wingman's vehicle, moving its commander to the gunner's seat. I sent my own Bradley back over the berm. My first combat mission was getting off to a rough start.

"The zone recon was very controlled. The brigade headquarters coordinated the movement of all three battalion scout platoons to ensure we stayed on line as we moved north. Because the whole task force was listening to our radio transmissions, we tried to give a good picture of the terrain and any other intelligence we could gather.

"Even though we had been at the border for weeks and not seen any enemy activity, I had an eerie feeling running through my body. We were on the bad guy's turf now, waiting for him to see us, waiting for him to start a fight. The terrain took on a life of its own: Rocks looked to be moving, vehicle tracks looked recently drawn, dust clouds seemed to be fresh. My eyes strained as I peered into the darkness, looking for any indication of movement. Every muscle in my body was flexing, anticipating a sudden encounter with the enemy.

"'Sir, I've got a moving target . . . range two thousand meters,' Staff Sergeant Hightower called from his gunner's seat.

"My stomach moved into my throat. As I crouched down into the turret to look through my thermal sight, I radioed my platoon to take cover behind available terrain and occupy a hasty defensive position. I then called the report to Lieutenant Colonel Gordon. The vehicle put off a heat signature like a BMP-1, a very common vehicle in the Iraqi army. Every gunner in the platoon had his finger on the trigger. Since I wasn't sure if it was friendly or enemy, I instructed the platoon that only my vehicle would fire. I received 'affirmatives' from Red and Blue section leaders.

"The lone vehicle was traveling straight south at a high rate of speed. We soon clearly identified it as an M3 Scout Bradley. The thermal sights in the M1 tank and M3 Bradleys convert heat from the source into a visual image with amazing details. The closer you are to the source, the more vivid the image. I alerted brigade, who reported that all friendly scout vehicles were accounted for. I knew better. This CFV was heading directly through my zone and threatened to cause an engagement between two friendly forces. I had my platoon back down into hide positions, totally masking their vehicles behind terrain, and let the vehicle drive by. The lost Bradley CFV sped right past my vehicle and a near disaster had been avoided. Thirty minutes later it crossed back into Saudi Arabia in my task force's zone. I later learned that when the Bradley's commander realized he had been separated from his own scout platoon, he shot an azimuth straight south and raced back to the border.

"We continued to Phase Line Opus and set our screen. The scouts were pumped. Without a word from me the platoon established local security, wired hot loop communication between section vehicles, and checked vehicle maintenance. We screened until 0430 hours, then returned south before the sun rose. After debriefing the brigade staff, we returned to the border."

■ Sergeant Dock and I were warming ourselves behind the tank just after stand-to on the twenty-second when we heard thuds to our north and east — very close, closer than anything previously, anyway. Then we saw to our front the flashes of rounds landing, maybe ten miles north. But this was difficult to know given how sound and light travel across the desert. The barrage continued about forty minutes, thuds on the right and up front, the quick successive thuds of intense bombing. And the light — at first single flashes, then flickering as if we were watching a fire through a screen. This all in conjunction with the rising sun. The thuds petered out in pairs.

Sometime during the course of morning I learned the date set for G-Day: 24 February. In two days. I presumably also knew by this time that the plan had changed, and the division was not scheduled to LD until the following day, G+1, on the twenty-fifth. Rivera reported the news of widespread disease and misery among Iraqi citizens and soldiers — he had his news from his contraband radio. Hussein had agreed to Gorbachev's withdrawal plan and terms, and though these did not include all twelve conditions in the UN Resolution, Iraq would return all POWs immediately. The decision fell to President Bush.

That night my company, Delta Mech, executed a cross-border operation mech pure — without my tank platoon, that is. Bradleys only. My tanks were attached to Bravo Mech, in an overwatch position, platoons on line, in sight of the berm that demarcated the border, in case Delta Mech needed us.

Shortly after Delta Mech crossed the berm I saw Bradley 25-mm tracers zip across and ricochet off the struck object into the air. A second burst followed, and then nothing. I hooted, beat my hands on the tank. The adrenaline flooded me. I wanted to get the call, I wanted to fire up my tanks and charge through the breach. The way a humid summer day swells and swells and swells until at last it breaks, and the rain pours — that was how I felt, after the months of Desert Shield, the swelling pressure, and then to finally fire on the enemy.

Mixed reports followed. The firing gunners swear they saw troops in a truck and had actually waited to fire so that one of them could finish urinating and return to the truck. Others on the mission saw nothing. No evidence of enemy vehicles in the area was found.

I didn't know that other units were also operating across the border that night. Greg Downey's scout platoon was conducting another zone recon to

Phase Line Opus to set up a screen for the night while Alpha Mech established a hasty defensive position three kilometers to his south. According to Greg, "the brigade's other two battalions, Task Force 3-69 Armor on our left and Task Force 3-15 Infantry on our right, would also be sending units to Phase Line Opus; only 3-15 was sending an M2 Bradley infantry company without its scout platoon.

"My scouts crossed the border at 2000 hours. My CFV had been repaired that day, so I had my crew back. We had moved about two kilometers into Iraq when Red Section, my right flank scout section, came under direct fire. I saw the rounds before Staff Sergeant Deem, my Red Section leader, contacted me. The fires were coming from the right rear of the section. I saw the familiar red tracer rounds impacting as I had seen on so many gunnery ranges. We were being engaged by friendly units. The Iraqis used green tracers.

"Deem stayed pretty calm as he maneuvered for cover. Wiggins, Deem's wingman, panicked. 'Black One, this is Red Three . . . I'm pinned! I'm pinned!' He was terrified. I was already on task force command frequency telling the TOC to tell 3-15 to stop shooting us up.

"'Jesus Christ, sir, we're taking fire!' screamed my driver, already trying to pull down into the low ground. I had just completed the transmission when my own section started receiving fire. Rounds were impacting around my CFV, kicking up dust and flying above my turret. I wanted to move forward to low ground, but a 25-mm round skipped off the front deck of my vehicle, making a zinging noise and sending sparks jumping into the air.

"'Get us down low,' I told West.

"'I can't see over this ditch — it looks like it's deep,' West spat back.

"'I don't give a shit how deep it is, get down into it!' I yelled, ducking my head low into the turret.

"My vehicle felt like it fell off the face of the earth as it poured over the edge. It crashed to a sudden halt when it reached the bottom of the ravine. Not a very graceful landing, but a safer place compared to where we had been. Once my CFV stopped, I tried to piece everything together. I got Lieutenant Colonel Gordon back on the net. He confirmed that a 3-15 infantry Bradley platoon had acquired and pinned two-thirds of my platoon down. It took five minutes before 3-15 got the Bradley platoon under control.

"I was more angry than scared. My biggest fear had always been not being killed by the enemy but being killed by our own people. It's probably the biggest concern for all scouts, knowing that the likelihood of being shot from behind by a friendly unit is better than being engaged from the front by the opponent.

"Task Force 3–15 was claiming that their infantry platoon had fired on a truck, but the only thing at that location was my scout CFVs. A big contributor to this near-fratricide was the fact that 3-15's scout platoon sat out the mission, so that a combat unit had been allowed across the border with no recon assets. Evidently, some nervous gunner or Bradley commander saw us moving and was not clear about the missions of flank units.

"Wiggins regained his composure. I was still fuming about the whole incident but pressed on with the mission. Alpha Mech had been crossing the border when my platoon had been engaged. It took a few minutes to get everyone focused again before we moved north to PL Opus.

"We returned south and back across the border early in the morning on 23 February. Once again, we debriefed the brigade staff. Col. Paul Kern, the brigade commander, was not happy about the friendly fire incident. He made himself very clear: It would not happen again."

The first time I read Greg's account, my stomach turned over, and my skin turned cold. What I had been so ecstatically cheering could have been his death.

■ President Bush had given Hussein until Saturday the twenty-third to pull his army out of Kuwait. I wrote only a brief note to Maria that day. Believing that we would not LD until the twenty-fifth, at G+1, I concluded: *Like the rest of the world, we go to work early Monday morning.* But Greg still had one more cross-border mission, this one with Rob Holmes's Delta Tank.

"Lieutenant Colonel Gordon visited me a few hours before the next mission. I was dumbfounded by his behavior. He was very complimentary, almost friendly, showing a side of himself that I had never seen or knew he was capable of.

"'This is the best scout platoon I've ever worked with. Your maneuver and control is great. Keep up the good work.'

"I was speechless. I think he was finally at peace with himself, knowing that he would be going into battle.

"I went over the details of the 23 February mission with Capt. Dave Hubner. Since his Delta Tank would be the most forward company in the task force formation during the attack, I had worked closely with him throughout Desert Shield. Hubner intrigued me. On the outside he looked like a big lug, the guy you see at a party carrying the beer keg on his shoulders and drinking straight from the tap. But he proved sharp as a tack, extremely intelligent, and quite knowledgeable.

"I was starting to feel the lack of sleep from the past three days. Little rest goes hand in hand with being a scout, but anything less than four hours a day over an extended period of time invites trouble. Captain Hubner's tank company was very well trained, making me more confident that no mistakes would occur. The mission was the same, a zone recon to Phase Line Opus, where we would establish a screen. But this time we would not return south. We would occupy Opus until the rest of the task force joined us on the twenty-fifth for the attack.

"The zone recon to Opus was uneventful. No surprises. Though after getting shot at the night before, I kept thinking about the tankers behind us seeing my scout vehicles in their thermal sights. A very uncomfortable feeling I had better get used to.

"As the sun started to rise over the horizon, I looked out across the desert. This was the first time I had seen this area in the sunlight, even though I had spent the last three nights here. It didn't look as dangerous or eerie as it did in the dark."

Rob Holmes led Delta Tank's move across the berm. Delta Tank had an infantry platoon from one of the Mech companies attached to it for the night. It was 1900 hours when he received the call from Captain Hubner. Rob replied in kind:

"'Black Six, this is White One. Sabers ready, over.' My voice broke the silent night as I radioed Hubner to let him know my platoon was ready to roll.

"'This is Black Six, roger. Execute.'

"With this brief transmission, my M1 moved forward from our attack position and approached the berm. Tanks don't like crossing over hills because it exposes the soft underbelly, so our engineers had blown a hole in the berm that we could pass through. My other three tanks followed and formed a wedge behind me. Captain Hubner followed my platoon, and the rest of the company trailed him. Radios were silent. I searched for the military police escort that was to lead us through the friendly reconnaissance units in front of us and to the breach in the berm. This drill is called a *passage of lines* and was particularly dangerous because as we passed through friendly units everyone was trigger-happy and tense. Coordination and communication had to be perfect. Before mounting up, I had tried to joke a bit with my tank commanders to loosen them up. Now that we had to be quiet on the radio, there wasn't a whole lot I could say to keep people calm. I had to rely on our training to give my men the confidence to do their jobs.

"I looked forward to crossing the berm if for no other reason than because once we were on the other side, anything that turned up 'hot' in our sights was enemy.

"A blue flashlight flashed twice at my two o'clock about two hundred meters away. Recognizing the MP escort's signal, I gave a quick flash from my own. As we got closer, the MP Humvee pulled alongside my tank to lead us to the berm. We traveled north for about five minutes, and then our escort again flashed his blue flashlight and peeled off. We were on our own.

"My gunner was traversing the turret smoothly from left to right and back again as he searched for the green chem lights marking the breach in the berm, the same lights truckers use when parked on highways. Break them, shake them, and they glow all night. The Arab kids around As Sarrar loved them. The only English they knew was 'chem light' and 'Victory' — the motto of the 24th

Infantry Division. The kids would run up to the tanks giving the Churchill victory sign and screaming 'chem lights!' until we threw them a box.

"My turret stopped scanning; Sergeant Downing whispered into the intercom, 'Got it, sir.' He had locked the sights on the chem light. My driver Bell only had to follow the tank's main gun tube to the passage point.

"'White One, this is Black Six . . . contact?'

"Captain Hubner had seen my turret swing and steady-on the target. Like many officers, the world could be crashing down, but as long as he knew what was happening he was fine. Uncertainty and absence of communication drove him crazy. Our battalion commander was the same way, and I knew Hubner was asking me what his boss had just asked him.

"'Follow me,' I whispered over the radio back to him.

"My platoon formed two staggered columns on cue without my issuing a command as we approached the breach. We had spent days rolling across the desert practicing formations and movements just as I had drilled for parades at West Point. My four M1s knew when to change direction, formation, speed, and distance from one other, based upon the situation, with one or two words over the radio from me.

"My tank glided through the breach in the Iraq border at 1910 hours. The platoon rolled through after me, reconstituted the wedge formation, and headed north. The desert looked the same as it had on the Saudi side, but it sure felt different."

Desert Storm: The Ground War
24 February through 8 March 1991

Man is but a handful of dust,
And life is a violent storm.
— Arabic adage

24 February 1991 (G-Day)

By the final Desert Storm plan, H-Hour had been set for 0400 hours. While off-coast marines feint an amphibious landing, another marine unit and part of the Arab Joint Force attack into Kuwait up the coast in conjunction with the Arab Joint Forces's major inland attack into Kuwait. The light component of the Eighteenth Airborne Corps, farthest west, also launches its attack at G-Day, H-Hour. Twenty-six hours later, on G+1 at 0600, Seventh Corps begins the main attack into Iraq and then hooks east into Kuwait to strike the Iraqi's rear defenses from the flank, with the Eighteenth's 24th Infantry and the 3d ACR attacking at the same time on its western flank with the mission of bypassing Kuwait entirely and blocking the Iraqi routes into and out of Kuwait from the north. The division's operational plan characterized corps operations as having "a rapid operational tempo that employs complementary heavy and light corps forces supported by massed fires. We accept risk in the depth of Corps operations to surprise the enemy and gain positioning advantage and flexibility for our forces."[1]

The three maneuver brigades of the 24th Infantry Division were to cross the Saudi-Iraqi border abreast. About thirty-five kilometers into the attack, at Phase Line Colt, the division would collapse into two columns: our 2d Brigade leading on the right as the division's main effort, with 1st Brigade following us; and the 197th on the left.

The brigade's three battalions would maneuver in an inverse triangle. Task Force 3-69, at the triangle's point, trailed the other two in the reserve position.

Task Force 3-15 Infantry led on the right, with Neal Creighton as its lead platoon leader and myself leading a company-team to Neal's rear right in our task force diamond. And Task Force 1-64 Armor led on the left, with Greg Downey as the scout platoon leader out front, Rob Holmes as the lead platoon leader in their "Rogue Diamond" formation, and Dave Trybula leading the battalion's reserve tank company at the opposite point on the diamond.

With Rob at the head of 1-64, Greg scouting to the front of 1–64, and Neal at the head of 3-15, I could not have chosen three more able lieutenants to lead the brigade into battle.

ALEX VERNON (Delta Mech, Task Force 3–15 Infantry)

That day Captain Baillergeon gave to each platoon leader in Delta Mech a message from Major General McCaffrey to read to our soldiers. Elsewhere the ground war had already commenced, at 0400 in the morning, though our division was not scheduled to attack until 0600 on the twenty-fifth. I read the letter at Sfc. Freight's tank. Titled "General Order to Attack," and dated 15 February, it read:

> Soldiers of the Victory Division, we now begin a great battle to destroy an aggressor Army and free two million Kuwaiti people. We will fight under the American flag and with the authority of the United Nations. By force-of-arms we will make the Iraqi war machine surrender the country they hold prisoner.
>
> The 26,000 soldiers of the reinforced 24th Infantry Division will be the First to Fight. Our mission is to attack 300 kilometers deep into Iraq to block the Euphrates River Valley. Our objective is to close the escape route for 500,000 enemy soldiers in Kuwait.
>
> On D-Day, 24th ID (M) will be the point of the spear for a general offensive by 700,000 Coalition Allied soldiers. The Victory Division attack has the central purpose to smash into the enemy rear and destroy their will to fight. The shock action and violence of the 24th Infantry Division assault will save thousands of American lives from the bloody work of fighting through the fire trenches of Kuwait.
>
> There will be no turning back when we attack into battle. One hundred thousand American and French soldiers of the XVIII Airborne Corps will fight on our flanks. We have the weapons and the military training equal to the task. We pray that our courage and our skill will bring this war to a speedy close.
>
> In WWII, in Korea, in Saudi Arabia . . . the soldiers of the Victory Division have never failed America. We shall do our duty.[2]

I can't remember what else I may have said. I do remember, while walking from tank to tank checking on morale and equipment readiness, seeing Freight

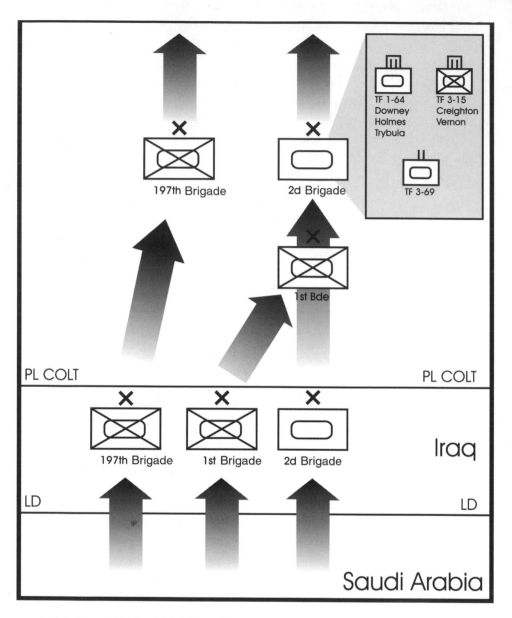

24th Infantry Division Initial Formations

on the top of his tank battling the wind trying to put his maps together. He had the only other set in the platoon. He had not marked the necessary graphics on any of them. What had taken me several days over the course of a couple of weeks, he tried to do the afternoon before the attack. Perhaps I should have supervised him more closely, to ensure those maps were assembled; but he'd never

1st Lt. Greg
Downey

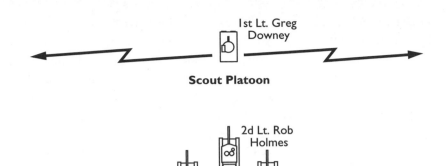

Scout Platoon

2d Lt. Rob
Holmes

Delta Tank

Alpha Mech

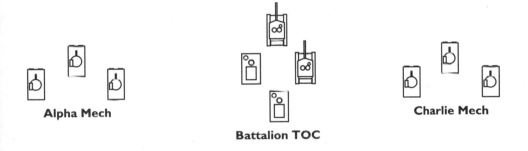

Battalion TOC

Charlie Mech

2d Lt. Dave
Trybula

Charlie Tank

Task Force 1-64 in "Rogue Diamond" Formation

Note: vehicle icons in company formations represent platoons.

be able to read the maps anyway. It was like the load plan. We were supposed to load our tanks so that no gear strapped on the side of the turret jutted above the top of the turret. This would ensure that, if we had to button-up during combat, our fields of view through the vision blocks at the base of the commander's hatch would not be obscured by a duffel bag or MRE box. Some platoons required all four tanks to have identical load plans in case crew members had to switch tanks. I only required my tanks to keep the vision blocks clear. Three of my four tanks complied with my order the day I issued it — the tank commanders were grateful they could organize their gear to suit them, as long as they met the basic requirement. But Sfc. Freight, the platoon sergeant, the example NCO, did not. Nor did he the next day. Nor the next. I repeated the order every day. Perhaps I should have stood there while he put his tank in order. I did not. I had given up on Freight long ago. His tank would roll across the border looking like the Beverly Hillbillies' family wagon.

Early in the afternoon Captain Baillergeon called us to REDCON 2 — ready to move with fifteen minutes notice. We were going to take advantage of the daylight to cross the berm that marked the border and reassemble in task force formation on the other side. We were also instructed to begin taking the pyridostigmine bromide pills we had been issued a few weeks before. The PB pills were a preventive measure against certain chemical agents, and we were to take them on a schedule, I think every eight hours. My crew hesitated before popping the first pill; we looked at one another, swallowed, and checked out watches. The company led the task force column through the berm — the battalion command sergeant major had positioned his Humvee on the Saudi side of the berm, where he flew both the battalion colors and the American flag. On the other side the task force linked with Alpha Tank, which had spent the night securing the far side of the berm.[3] Fuel HETs drove through each company, to each vehicle, topping us off.

Crossing the berm early also meant moving the LD. The LD, or line of departure, is a graphic control measure used on maps to coordinate the attack of different units. The LD had been the berm; now Phase Line Opus, about ten kilometers farther north and where our forward units had spent the night, became the LD.

Just before 1500 hours, Baillergeon called again to put us in REDCON 1. The D-Day H-Hour fixing attack into Kuwait by the marine and coalition forces in the eastern part of the theater was progressing more rapidly than anticipated. And in our Eighteenth Airborne Corps's western zone, the lead elements of the 6th French Light, and the American 82d and 101st Airborne Divisions, were meeting effectively no resistance. We were fifteen hours ahead of schedule. It was time.[4]

GREG DOWNEY (Scouts, Task Force 1-64 Armor)

February twenty-fourth started as a clear day, with a slight wind and blue skies. About 1000 hours, the remainder of the task force moved north to join us at Phase Line Opus. The desert wind began to pick up, and visibility was getting worse. I had Specialist Lowther monitor the radio while I walked around checking vehicle maintenance.

"Hey, sir, Rogue Six wants to talk to you," Lowther said, out of breath from running to get me. Rogue Six did not like to wait for you on the radio. I jogged back to my track, Lowther behind me, my gas mask bouncing off my hip, my arms swinging wide around my flak vest.

"Rogue Six, Scout Six, over."

"Scout, this Rogue, go to REDCON 4, acknowledge, over."

REDCON 4: ready to move in two hours. I didn't have to ask why. The clock was ticking. The task force bumbled a little as all the units scrambled to get into their formation positions.

"Rogue Six, this is Darklord Six, over." That was Captain Hubner, Delta Tank's company commander. Delta would lead the task force's Rogue Diamond formation.

"Rogue Six, Darklord needs Class III now, over." I sensed the urgency in Hubner's voice. Delta Team had to be low on fuel after last night's mission. They had come with me across the border last night and had not taken on fuel since. Not good. Hope they get it quick.

"Scout Six, go to REDCON 1 minus, over," ordered Lieutenant Colonel Gordon. Often he didn't bother with his own call sign. He didn't need to. We all knew when the Prince of Darkness was speaking.

"This is Scout Six, wilco," I responded. The call meant I had to be ready to move immediately. It had not even been an hour since the REDCON 4 order.

Well, here we go. This is it. I felt very detached from what was happening. I heard and saw what was going on around, but it didn't feel like I was a part of it, like I was there. Except for the changing weather, that is. The sand was starting to sting a little harder, decreasing our visibility by the minute.

"Scout Six, LD time now," came the call from Rogue Six.

LD time now. The most destructive force I had ever witnessed had just been put into motion.

ROB HOLMES (Delta Tank, Task Force 1-64 Armor)

My report broke the radio silence. "Lima Delta, continuing mission." I had called the LD to Captain Hubner countless times in training. That night, it had new meaning.[5]

Hubner's M1 followed directly behind mine, about two hundred meters behind my platoon's wedge. First Platoon was behind me to my left and Third Platoon behind me to my right. I headed north at fifteen degrees for eight kilometers toward checkpoint Romeo 54, our first stop on the long march to Basra. I looked over my shoulder as the task force spread out in the diamond formation across the desert. I noticed that another tank had pulled behind me next to Captain Hubner. This would normally be the company executive officer, or second in command, who maneuvered as Hubner's wingman. But experience leading the task force told me the tank beside Hubner wasn't our company XO.

"White One, this is Black Six," Hubner radioed. "Rogue Six says your wingman is too close."

Rogue Six was Flash, the battalion commander. Hubner didn't need him as an excuse to give me an order. It was his way of apologizing for micromanaging my platoon, because Lieutenant Colonel Gordon was micromanaging his company. Hubner and I had learned to deal with Flash. Tactically, we both knew that Flash probably knew best anyway.

The task force traveled in a diamond formation due to the 360-degree nature of the desert battlefield. Delta Tank led, putting the firepower of our fourteen tanks up front. The two mechanized infantry companies held the flank positions. This gave the task force the flexibility to dismount grunts and provide fire support from either direction. As the task force reserve, Charlie Tank held the rear point of the diamond, to serve as a counterattack or maneuver element in any direction, once one of the other companies had engaged the enemy. The symmetrical shape gave us security on all sides, and the ability to react in any direction with either tanks or infantry, as the threat demanded. To use a boxing metaphor, Delta Tank jabbed, then Charlie Tank would swing around from a flank, like a hook. The two mech infantry companies could hold the enemy from each side like a bear hug.

There wasn't supposed to be anything at Romeo 54; it was just a spot on the map Major Diehl thought would make a good rally point for a refuel. Enemy contact was possible, but most likely we would use this stop simply to refuel. The M1's turbine engine really guzzled fuel. As we marched north into Iraq, we would have to replenish our tanks about every one hundred kilometers. Another problem with the turbine engine: As it "breathed" air in, it also sucked in sand. In order to keep our filters clear so that the engine wouldn't suffocate, we had to periodically blow its filters clean with an air hose attached to another tank's turbine. During Desert Shield we had practiced refueling and blowing out our air filters to ensure that in battle we didn't sit still too long.

We hit Romeo 54 at about 2030 and stopped with the three platoons in columns abreast, and Hubner, the XO, and Flash in a fourth column. The fuel trucks moved through us, refueling two tanks at a time. Each tank crew went to action, as synchronized as a stock car pit crew: One soldier prepared the tank to take on fuel; one checked the tracks for loose connectors, broken shoes, and bad tension; the third, in conjunction with a soldier from a neighbor tank, blew out the air filters. Meanwhile the tank commanders met me on the ground, a routine we did so I could learn any concerns of theirs and update them with any new information or orders. This time I also wanted to check everybody's nerves and settle them down. We spoke briefly. I joked about the sand being nicer in Iraq, and we broke after the tank commanders gave logistics reports to Sfc. Sikes.

I walked to Hubner's tank where I linked up with the other two platoon leaders, Jon Ulsaker and Jeff White. Red One and Blue One from here on out. I was White One.

No news from Black Six, Captain Hubner.

We returned to our platoons. The company mounted up, and my platoon led the battalion north. Our next destination was Objective Gray.

NEAL CREIGHTON (Alpha Tank, Task Force 3-15 Infantry)
At 1500 hours on February 24, 1991, Task Force 3-15 was ordered to attack. We were in the midst of receiving fuel when a sandstorm hit. I couldn't see more than two hundred meters in any direction. Captain Schwartz tightened our company formation as we moved forward.

I had marked every leg of the attack on my map with distance and azimuth and written them on index cards. My driver Forbes had a duplicate set of cards and his mission was, once again, to keep track of the distance and tell me when to change azimuth. Our technique worked despite the sandstorm. To verify our location, every ten kilometers I would get a GPS reading over the radio from 2d Lt. Jimmy Kim, the company's fire support officer.

We sped unmolested for over 150 kilometers into Iraq that night. All the task force maneuver training was paying off. We halted short of our first march objective, Objective Gray, in the early morning hours. After stopping, I looked up at Orion. He seemed to shine brighter than ever.[6]

DAVE TRYBULA (Charlie Tank, Task Force 1-64 Armor)
The main body of Task Force 1-64 had just crossed the Iraqi border in the neutral zone as a sandstorm was beginning to build. The storm was easily the worst I had seen in my six months of desert life. Visibility was a quarter mile at best, and this was reduced even more by the large number of vehicles moving in the same area. While the weather hid our attack, it also hid the enemy. I worried that the Iraqis had picked up our movement and were repositioning one of their available divisions. I feared they would attack our flank as we attacked toward their rear.

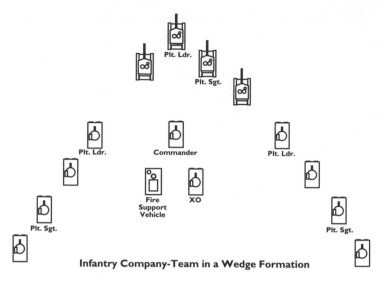

Infantry Company-Team in a Wedge Formation

Note: The two flanking Bradley platoons are shown here in "echelon" formation; they can be in column, staggered column, or wedge formation as mission, terrain, and proximity to other units dictates.

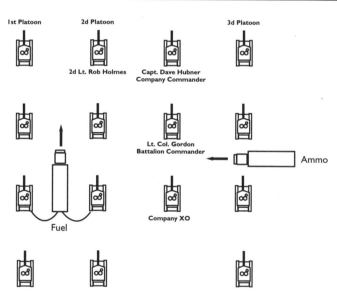

Delta Tank Hasty Resupply

About twelve hours into Iraq, my XO called down that the brigade was by-passing an enemy light infantry regiment. The enemy had to know we had attacked into their homeland, yet they showed no sign. My concern grew as the storm worsened and as we progressed deeper into Iraq. Every major American newspaper and news magazine had published a frightfully close version of the attack plan — could the Iraqis really not know where we were? To ensure my platoon would be ready for an Iraqi ambush or counterattack, I put my crews on a rotational sleep plan, drivers with loaders and tank commanders with gunners, ensuring that each tank had two soldiers alert and ready to fight.

We continued to move deeper into Iraq. At about 0200, roughly 260 miles into Iraq, Captain Hadjis spoke over the radio. "Just got an intelligence update from higher. The State Department announced a short while ago that the attack into Kuwait is going ahead of schedule with minimal loss of life, and that the United States would not violate the territorial integrity of Iraq." If we weren't violating Iraqi territory, I wondered exactly what we were doing.

My crew let out a cheer. A huge weight had been lifted off our shoulders. No longer was I concerned about the Iraqis counterattacking into our flank. I was sure that they had no idea where we were. We were about to close the door on their retreat from Kuwait. The synergy of the raised morale made crews more alert, calmed fears, and focused everyone's attention on the battle ahead.

We pushed through the blinding sandstorm.

GREG DOWNEY (Scouts, Task Force 1-64 Armor)

The terrain was unforgiving as the scout platoon moved deeper into Iraq. The rocky desert ground was extremely rough, and sheer cliffs were everywhere. Drivers had to feel their way through the terrain. Their passive night sights only amplified existing illumination. They were almost totally ineffective due to the blinding sandstorm.

"Sir, I can't see," was West's refrain, all night long.

"That makes two of us, West," I would reply before climbing down off my CFV to check the black hole of terrain in front of us. Incredible. As if what we were doing wasn't hard enough, without the extra crap of the sandstorm. My gunner was having an equally hard time seeing through his thermal sight.

"How far can you see, Lowther?" I asked him.

"About five hundred meters, if I'm lucky," he responded. If we made contact with the Iraqi army, it would be a close-range engagement.

The divisional cavalry moved ahead of us initially, but we passed through it the night of the twenty-fourth. Now everything forward of my scout platoon was enemy. That made my job much easier. We received orders over the radio to continue to Attack Position Dallas, about one hundred kilometers into Iraq. My scout platoon conducted a recon of the area at Dallas to be occupied by Task Force 1-64, clearing it at 0400 hours on 25 February. For the next few hours we screened forward of the task force. Aside from updating some map graphics and getting some intelligence summaries from the task force intelligence officer, all was quiet.

ALEX VERNON (Delta Mech, Task Force 3–15 Infantry)

The sun did not linger. My impressionistic account of that first night consists of rain and sand and cold, of sounds of radio chatter and track movement and the hum and clanging echoes from inside my turret. With a low ceiling of clouds blocking light from the moon, with falling rain and blowing sand, and still more sand kicked up by the tracks of dozens of armored vehicles, we were blind. Once Baillergeon and I disagreed about the company-team's position in the battalion formation. I knew he could not see as well as I could, since he had his driver literally follow in my tracks, my dust in his face. But Baillergeon would not give; he ordered me to take a sharp left and gun it. A minute later the dust and rain cleared enough for me to see the right skirts of a tank, presumably one of Alpha Tank's, not five meters to my front. I screamed into the intercom for my driver to make a hard right. We missed colliding with that other tank by inches.

Occasionally one of my tanks would slowly drop behind, and I'd call that tank commander over the radio to wake him to wake his driver. My own driver fell asleep fairly often as well. To keep the soldiers rested, all my tank crews had their loaders take turns driving. Some gunners and tank commanders also switched, though I did not, since I led the company.

Sometime during the blur of the night a loud *snap!* cracked over my left shoulder and the tank jerked left. It continued to pull left while slowing to a stop. I clambered down — the snap and pulling were familiar. As I had figured, the tank had broken track. I would have to jump track, to switch to Sergeant Rivera's tank, and he would take over my broken tank. The company-team meanwhile had stopped behind their crippled lead vehicle, though the task force was driving ahead. Jumping track was always a scramble because I had to grab my maps and battleboards and disconnect and take with me both my ten-channel radio and the auxiliary speaker to swap with Rivera's single-channel in order to monitor both platoon and company nets. If it took too long, we'd lose the rest of the battalion. I thrust the radio and aux to McBryde, the wing tank's loader, and climbed up over the back deck and to the turret. I hollered at McBryde to tell the driver to move as I was lowering myself into the hatch. McBryde and I would have to mount the radio on the move while I tried to relocate the battalion. We accelerated past my broke-dick tank; Rivera and my crew already had the track jacks out and were going to work. It didn't take long to catch the battalion. Maybe twenty minutes later Sergeant Rivera called me on the radio: "Gold Six, Gold Two, I got you, over." I turned around in the hatch and lifted my PVS-7s from around my neck to my eyes. In the green light of my night vision device, I saw my tank passing the lead Bradley in the platoon following me on the left and moving into place as my wingman in the platoon wedge. Rivera, Dock, and Brunner had fixed the track in the dark, with the wind and sand and rain, with other vehicles flying past them, and found us in amazing time. At the soonest opportunity Rivera and I returned to our proper tanks.

I was glad Rivera had convinced me to keep him as my wingman. A few days before the ground war, I had considered balancing the platoon by swapping him with Sfc. Freight's wingman, putting the more experienced wing tank commander with the less-able section leader. Rivera advised me against it. The platoon leader's wingman ran twice the risk of being left behind to fend for himself, since if either his tank or my tank went down, he would stay with the broken tank. And Rivera was the best man for the job. If he hadn't been able to fix the tank, he would have sat stranded, to be policed up by whatever support unit happened to stumble upon him, or to fight whatever enemy stumbled upon him and his disabled tank.[7]

Once we passed a cluster of stationary M113s. I saw a number of figures and small light sources. Somehow I have the idea that this was 2-4 Cav's TOC. I also remember passing a stationary self-propelled 155 artillery battery. I'll never forget the eerie vision of those boxy tracked howitzers stopped in a semicircle, seen through the green filter of my handheld night vision device and the blowing sand. I did not understand how the unit had gotten ahead of us, as our 2d Brigade was supposed to be leading the way. We refueled once: Alpha Tank set a hasty defensive position to the north of the fuel trucks while the task force rolled through, two tanks per fuel truck. When Bravo and Delta Mech had finished and had assumed defensive positions, Alpha withdrew to refuel.[8]

Despite our blindness that night, in our seventy-ton Abrams tanks and thirty-ton Bradleys we flew. Those soldiers stuffed deep inside the vehicles, the tank gunners and the infantrymen and scouts in the back of the Bradleys, who were more blind than those of us with our heads poked out of the turrets straining to see, must have felt like human cannonballs jettisoned headlong and powerless.

We hit rough terrain in the first hours of the twenty-fifth, about Phase Line Yaz. The task force came to a stop until someone found a route through, and we proceeded single file. The natural obstacle turned out to be an extremely deep wadi with nearly vertical walls. As I approached the passage point, trailing Alpha's last tank, I watched the vehicle enter the wadi. I had never seen anything like it. One moment the green glow of the night vision device was filled with the tank's taillights and its hot exhaust, then the bottom of its tread, and then nothing but green darkness until after a few moments more the turret top appeared perpendicular to the ground as the tank climbed the far side; then, again, the taillights and hot exhaust. When we started down, my body told my head that my tank was going to flip over, head first. Had I not witnessed the tank in front of me clear the chasm, I would never have dared it.

On the other side of the wadi the task force clustered together, more or less companies in staggered columns. Vehicles were so close you could in some cases take a long step from the top of one onto another. It was about 0400; we would move again at 0600. The battalion commander must have had complete confidence in the lack of an enemy threat to allow his task force to sit so vulnerable. One artillery round or air bomb could have destroyed several vehicles, and one infantryman's automatic weapon could have sprayed at least a platoon's worth of men.

The storm had stopped.

I had my platoon pull 50 percent security, two men per tank at the ready, the other two asleep. This gave each soldier an hour. I slept on the first shift, as I was the only one in the platoon who had not been able to catch any shut-eye during the night. I also wanted to be awake during daylight, and during wake-up, to ensure everyone woke and was ready to roll. After my nap I ate an MRE, brushed my teeth, and ran an electric razor over my face (you need to be clean-shaven for your gas mask to seal properly). The fuel trucks came by about 0530. The soldiers who slept the second shift were shorted; if the fuel truck didn't wake them at 0530, I woke them at 0545.

25 February 1991 (G+1)

ALEX VERNON (Delta Mech, Task Force 3-15 Infantry)
We moved again at 0600. Again we fell into a task force column, as the day's journey began with the climbing of a steep escarpment to our front by a serpentine trail up the side to gain the plateau above.

The task force paused on its way to our first objective during the artillery preparation. Just as my tank pulled to a stop, we felt the familiar snap of the tank track. While my crew set to work, I had the rest of the platoon pull a quick maintenance check on their tanks. Staff Sergeant Rivera discovered several missing end-connectors, center guides, and track shoes on his tread — he would have to break one track side to properly fix it. If he didn't, he risked throwing track and being left behind, or worse, throwing track and becoming a sitting duck during a fight.

Before G-Day I had preset one of my main radio's ten frequencies to the one assigned to Bravo Tank in case I ever needed immediate communication with

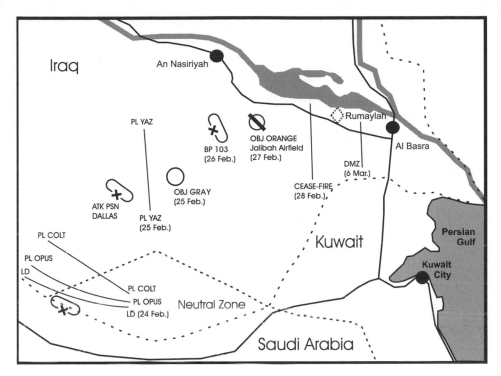

Desert Storm Select Operational Graphics.

my tank company. I flipped the switch and called Greg Jackson. After fixing my track the first night, and two tracks now, my platoon was starting to run low on track elements. Greg jumped in the company's maintenance M113 PC and ran to me what parts he could spare. Sometimes I suspect I did not need those parts, but I took the opportunity to hear Greg's voice on the radio and possibly see him in person.

When the task force moved again, my track was up, but Rivera's was still a few minutes away. Since he was my wingman, I decided to stay with him. The task force's XO drove up in his Humvee and screamed at me to leave Rivera. We were closing in on the objective. I took off and rejoined Delta Mech. Rivera caught us six minutes later.

GREG DOWNEY (Scouts, Task Force 1-64 Armor)

At 0845 hours, we continued the attack. It was the fastest zone recon ever done. Division headquarters was pushing us hard, and we stepped up the tempo. The visibility was improving, observation now about two kilometers. The brigade was headed to Objective Gray, an area that was supposed to have been cleared by the 24th ID's Long Range Surveillance Detachment. The LRSD ("lurs-dee") is usually inserted prior to an operation in order to provide accurate enemy situation reports of particular areas. Negative contact was reported up to Phase Line Meadow, about ten kilometers short of Objective Gray. As the task force stopped for a resupply on the move, the scout platoon pushed forward.

"Contact! Contact!" It was Staff Sergeant Deem, over the radio. A few seconds later he reported seeing tents and antennas, an early warning radar site. No soldiers or vehicles were observed, but brigade wanted to drop indirect fire on it. It was time to see if our artillery units were as good as they boasted.

The self-dubbed "King of Battle," artillery batteries usually travel five to ten kilometers behind the armor and infantry units, coordinating their movements to ensure they can support the most forward unit, normally the scout platoon. The pace of this attack would not allow for any delay in their movement. The artillery units could receive a fire mission when on the move and perform a "hip shoot" by conducting a short halt, quickly lining up the guns, getting the target data, and firing its first volley.

There were three different sites across my front, so we requested 155-mm howitzer rounds on one site, eight-inch howitzer rounds on the center, and MLRS rockets at the remaining targets. The destruction from the howitzers was immediate — I did not have to call in an adjustment for a second volley. But the MLRS rockets impacted one kilometer over and one kilometer to the left of the target. Initially, I thought I had sent bad target data, but after checking my coordinates, I concluded that the rockets should have hit the radar site dead on. After determining nothing was at the site anyway, we pressed on.

Twenty kilometers later, we met the enemy. My gunner reported targets. We moved closer, discovering the Iraqi soldiers to be young boys and old men. They were a sad sight, with absolutely no fight left in them. Their leaders had cut their Achilles' tendons so they couldn't run away and then left them. What weapons they had were in bad repair and little ammunition was on hand. They were hungry, cold, and scared. The hate I had for any Iraqi dissipated. These people had no business being on a battlefield. The humanity and restraint of my scouts was commendable, above professional standards. We gave rations to them from our own supplies, and my medic administered first aid. We passed the forty-five Iraqi prisoners of war off to Alpha Mech.

As we moved forward to screen Engagement Area V20, we continued encountering Iraqi soldiers, only these were better equipped and in better shape. I told my scout platoon to shoot warning rounds over their heads and give them a chance to surrender. This worked well until we occupied our screen line that night.

Setting a screen line in total darkness was difficult. This was compounded further by the still-raging sandstorm. At 2030 hours, all three scout sections reported they were set. At 2035, I observed green tracer rounds and a rocket-propelled grenade impact near Red Section.

"Black One, this is Red Two — Contact! Contact!" It was Staff Sergeant Deem again, followed seconds later by the thump-thump-thump of his 25-mm chain gun answering the enemy's fire. During times like this, I had learned to let my leaders fight their battle and not bother them with unnecessary radio traffic. Deem had his hands full enough without my bothering him. I reported to battalion that we were in contact. They wanted to know details I could not give them at the time.

As the fight continued in Red Section's sector, my gunner reported targets moving across my front. I had him fire warning shots over their heads first to see what they would do. After ten rounds of 25 mm, the Iraqis hit the ground. One by one, they stood up, arms extended as high as they could reach. Major Diehl called for a situation report. I told him Red Section had its fight under control. No friendly losses.

Iraqi soldiers were emerging out of holes all around us. My scouts had evidently occupied a screen line in the middle of their defense. The task force was about twelve kilometers behind us, set in a hasty defense, so they did not receive any contact.

Staff Sergeant Deem updated me on what had happened. As far as he could tell, Red Section had killed six to eight Iraqis — the 25-mm high explosive rounds did not leave much left of whatever they hit. I didn't think a body count was really necessary, but battalion was pushing me for one. We counted feet and boots that had feet in them. The platoon took a total of sixty-five Iraqis prisoner that night. Throughout the night, whenever we received sporadic enemy fire, we responded by firing our chain guns in the general direction of the enemy.

ROB HOLMES (Delta Tank, Task Force 1-64 Armor)

The sun was rising as the battalion rolled on. I could now look around and see over fifty armored vehicles in our diamond formation. Captain Hubner and Lieutenant Colonel Gordon were still right behind me. Hubner was in his hatch reading his map and eating an MRE. I don't think the colonel needed a map. He'd been studying the route for months. Hubner and I, on the other hand, each had navigation devices called Lorans. They were designed for boating and fixed your position by triangulating off ground-based transmitting stations positioned around the world. Dave Hubner was really good at using his. I think he wanted to master it for his shrimping trips off Savannah.

I got my Loran only a week before attacking. It came with two AA batteries, and Hubner told me that I was on my own for replacements. I quickly sent a letter home to my mother and requested two hundred batteries. Believe it or not, she was usually faster than the army. In the interim, Sfc. Sikes confiscated every AA battery in our platoon. Soldiers lost the use of their Walkman radios, flashlights, Nintendo Gameboys, and anything else that used them. My platoon sergeant said he didn't have time to wait on my mother. Underberg meanwhile had rigged a metal clip from an ammo box to hang the Loran inside the tank next to my seat. Then he ran a wire into the light inside the turret so that the Loran ran off the M1's main battery. Now it didn't need AA batteries unless we dismounted. For his services, Underberg negotiated to get his Walkman back from Sikes. The Beach Boys were back.

I looked down at my map. We were close to where the scout choppers had spotted infantry.

The sun was fully visible to my right now. Sergeant Downing was scanning the horizon for contact.

"Sir, I think I see a building and a water trailer."

M1 gunners can usually see about three thousand meters and clearly identify targets as far as twenty-five hundred. I could see something on the horizon from my hatch without my binoculars, which I never used much when we were moving. I didn't like anything draped around me that I didn't absolutely need, so the binos stayed in their box.

I sent a spot report to Captain Hubner. "Black Six, this is White One; one building, direct front, twenty-five hundred meters, continuing mission, over."

"Fire!" Hubner immediately called back.

"Fire!" he yelled again across the radio.

"Sir, I'm not sure what's out there!" Downing protested to me through his intercom. He was so well trained in peacetime that he instinctively hesitated to fire at an unidentified target.

I dropped down to my seat in the turret and looked through the .50-caliber machine gun sight. The weapon had been in the army inventory for decades and was still loved by soldiers. Back at Fort Stewart, I trained with the .50 cal in the computer simulators. It was about the most fun I had back then, better than any arcade game. I had gotten to the point where I could hit anything, moving or stationary.

The .50 was designed to operate in the defense while stationary. We were approaching at fifteen miles per hour what was in fact a small building and a water trailer about fifteen hundred meters away. I figured why not — this is combat — and pulled down on the red elevation handle, which was connected by wire to the weapon's butterfly trigger, sending a burst of bullets flying high over the targets. I spun the handle to adjust my elevation and fired a second burst, also wildly missing as my driver Bell bounced our tank across the desert. Later, I took much grief from Captain Hubner for even using the weapon while moving, let alone missing way high. Nonetheless, I figured that it was time to quit screwing around.

"Downing, pump a sabot through that building," I ordered through the intercom.

We had battle-carried sabot — had loaded a sabot main gun round in the breach based on the anticipated threat, the Iraqi tanks. An M1A1's sabot round is a 120-mm depleted uranium kinetic energy antitank round that explodes from the tank's main gun at about eighteen hundred meters per second, so fast the main gun doesn't need rifling to keep the round flying straight. Nothing stops it. As a sabot round penetrates a tank turret it fragments the inside turret wall, and these pieces — called *spalling* — join the sabot's high-speed ricocheting inside, shredding the crew and sometimes exploding any rounds waiting to be fired. (Tanker lore also claims that a sabot can enter one side of a crew area and exit the other, the resultant vacuum sucking the occupants out the small exit hole.) A building really called for firing a high explosive HEAT round instead of wasting a tank-killing sabot, but we were closing fast and I was too impatient to order Underberg to reload.

"On the way!" Downing yelled as he squeezed the trigger.

The explosion shook the tank as the turret filled with that distinctive smell of cordite and gunpowder. The sabot round rocketed from the gun tube like a thunderbolt and flew through the building, caving in the wall. Immediately dozens of Iraqi infantry appeared and scattered about six hundred meters in front of us like honeybees from a knocked-over hive.

This time, without even having to think about it, I gave a fire command to my whole platoon. "Dismounts! Direct front! Fire!"

We cut loose with machine guns from all of our tanks at the Iraqi infantry in front of us. The platoon's drivers accelerated to close in on the enemy as the gunners fired several quick bursts. One of the least appreciated aspects of the tank is its shock effect. The weapon systems and optical sights are so sophisticated that we tend to focus on the tank as a long-distance killer and forget the tank's awesome capability in taking ground and crushing obstacles and enemy in its path.

The enemy dismounts threw up their hands as we barreled toward them. My platoon ceased firing, rolled past them and over a dune on the far side of the building.

"Underberg, fire up that building," I ordered. I wanted to ensure we roused anything left after Downing's sabot.

Underberg loved firing his loader's machine gun. He jumped up in his hatch, swung it around, and put one hundred rounds through the target in a few seconds. The building caught fire. A few Iraqis ran out a door. Underberg cut them down, riddling them with machine gun bullets.

As the platoon rounded the far side of the building, we found another fifty dismounts just sitting on the sand in a big group. Arabs never ceased to amaze me. In the last two minutes, about twenty-five .50 cal rounds, a sabot round, and hundreds of machine gun bullets had flown all around these guys, torching their building and killing or wounding who knows how many. It hadn't seemed to bother these folks at all.

At least they mustered the energy to raise their hands to surrender. Had Underberg not been reloading, he probably would have already wasted the whole lot. My platoon rolled a couple hundred meters past the building and set up in overwatch as the other two platoons encircled the enemy dismounts. We dispersed each tank about 150 meters apart and scanned the horizon.

Our new prisoners barely qualified as soldiers. They were poorly clothed and hardly equipped. They looked gaunt and undisciplined. They were very old and very young. They looked pathetic. Quite a contrast with us. Sure, we looked pretty beat up after seven months of living in the desert, but still, every American had a complete uniform, including a bullet protective vest and Kevlar helmet, a functioning weapon, and plenty of food and water.

Tanks are great for closing with and destroying the enemy, but they aren't worth much in capturing and processing prisoners. I hated sitting still. Let tankers roll across the open battlefield shooting and crushing stuff in our path, and we are happy as clams.

Captain Hubner radioed Flash to request grunts from one of the infantry companies from 3-15 attached to Task Force 1-64. Soon after, a platoon of four Bradleys appeared. Out jumped their dismounts, led by 2d Lt. Mark Jennings. Mark had been my class's first captain our senior year at West Point, the highest ranking cadet in the corps. His predecessors have names like Lee and MacArthur. Mark loved being an infantryman. He looked the part: tall, lean, strapping, handsome. And after six months under the Saudi sun, tan.

I kept one eye on our horizon and the other on Mark's platoon as they processed the captured Iraqis using their five Ss checklist: *seize* the prisoners, *secure* their weapons, *silence* them, *separate* the officers from enlisted men, and *search* them for maps or other information.

Have fun, Mark. The rest of us needed to get moving again.[9]

Hubner gave us the word, and we headed north. We rolled on, firing up dismounts, herding prisoners, and always moving. We encountered similar skirmishes more frequently as we penetrated further into Iraq. As we approached the Euphrates River, however, the quality of enemy soldier improved. Better equipped and considerably more tenacious — at least these guys shot back at us in a somewhat organized manner. We had yet to face a credible threat to a tank battalion, but the danger was noticeably increasing.

The desert changed as well as we traveled north toward the Euphrates: more vegetation, flatter terrain, and even running water. Underberg kept feeding me mapsheets as we left one and moved to the next. We were both surprised at how quickly we were advancing.

A little later that day, during a refuel on the move (ROM) in the middle of a pretty bad sandstorm, the company first sergeant was trying to bring the fuel trucks to us and got lost. No one knew what to do. We didn't have a clue where he was, and he didn't have a Loran or GPS or anything. I was listening on the company net. Hubner was almost in pain — I could hear it in his voice — trying to talk First Sergeant Walker back to the company. Somehow Sfc. Sikes figured out where Top was. It was amazing. Sikes took off in his tank into the sandstorm, found Top, and brought him and the fuelers to the company. Previously there had been a lot of bad blood between Sikes and Top, due in no small measure to the fact that Sikes had seniority over Walker but the latter was the company's first sergeant. The company listened to Sikes and Top over the radio, very much aware of the animosity between them. But none of that mattered. They had risen above their old feelings and got along fine after that night. The more I think about it, the more I think Sikes damn near saved Walker's hide, or at least kept him in the game, at the risk of getting himself lost or killed. His actions were comparable to diving into the water to rescue a man overboard.

DAVE TRYBULA (Charlie Tank, Task Force 1-64 Armor)
Later on the twenty-fifth, Captain Hadjis spoke over the radio, "Execute desert laager, REDCON 2, leaders my fix in ten." During the resupply, the commander wanted me at his tank.

I relayed the order to my platoon. "Desert laager, REDCON 2, I'll be at the CO's tank. Take a good look at your vehicles while we have the chance and clean the air filters."

My platoon came to a halt in a column with approximately fifty feet between tanks. I had climbed out of my hatch and was putting on my gear when my loader yelled, "One-Two's on fire!" I looked up and saw flames shooting fifty feet skyward from the back of my wingman's tank. I yelled to my gunner, "Sergeant Godfrey get me the fire extinguisher!" It seemed to take him an eternity. Blood rushed through my head and my mind raced. There had been no explosion so I was pretty sure the fire had not been caused by the incoming Iraqi fire. But the flames and smoke were a sure sign of our presence to anyone within twenty or thirty miles. Godfrey finally unfastened the fire extinguisher and threw it out of the hatch to me. I caught it and began to run, forgetting I was still on top of my turret. Somehow I vaulted the nine feet to the ground in stride and continued to run toward the burning tank, arriving at the front of C12 as the driver pulled his lever to activate the tank's halon fire extinguisher system. I moved to the tank's rear, shouting for everyone to move back as well.

The tank's commander, S.Sgt. Bill Brackett, had gotten his handheld fire extinguisher from his gunner, and the two of us stood side by side, discharging our fire extinguishers at the increasingly dangerous flame. The fire was close to igniting the five hundred gallons of jet fuel and the tank's entire basic load of ammunition. I was sure our two five-pound fire extinguishers were futile against the raging inferno.

By the grace of God, we somehow extinguished the flame. I didn't know how. I gave Sergeant Brackett several more fire extinguishers in case the fire reignited, then checked on the rest of my platoon.

When I returned, I spoke to Sergeant Brackett. "Okay, I think we've got this under control. Let's keep a couple of people on it with fire extinguishers just in case, and call maintenance to check out your tank."

Sergeant Godfrey came running up, interrupted, and blurted, "Sir, Black Six wants you on the radio now! He said to grab you and get you talking to him ASAP!"

Not knowing what the CO wanted and concerned that the fire had indeed been seen by an Iraqi unit, I instructed Brackett to check out the vehicle and determine how much damage was done. I ran back to my tank and spoke with the commander. He told me a movement order would be issued soon.

My heart was still pounding. The fire reinforced in me the need to check equipment for serviceability. We would have lost one tank, and possibly several soldiers to injury, if the fire extinguishers had been empty or not accessible. The whole incident made me extremely proud of my platoon and more confident that we had prepared sufficiently to react to emergencies.

The maintenance team arrived, assessed the vehicle, and fixed it within minutes. Almost as soon as it was ready, we began moving again.

NEAL CREIGHTON (Alpha Tank, Task Force 3-15 Infantry)
We had stopped for a short while. First Sergeant Foote came over to my tank and got out of his Humvee to say something to me. I got out of my hatch and was standing on top of the turret. I don't remember what he told me. When he left I turned back around and stepped into the open loader's hatch. My loader Carroll caught me as I fell on top of him, grabbed my feet, and shoved me back toward the hatch, which was in its upright, open position. My glasses fell off, and I hit the hatch right beneath my eye. I was out, laying on top of the turret.

For a good thirty seconds I didn't know where I was. I got off the tank and headed for the medic; my gunner asked me where I was going, and all I said was "Band Aid." As soon as I got back Captain Schwartz was on the radio telling me to move out "now." I started navigating again, although I still didn't quite know where I was. For the first two or three minutes leading the task force, I was out of it.

ALEX VERNON (Delta Mech, Task Force 3-15 Infantry)

We hit Objective Gray about 1600; it was an empty sand bowl. The battalion's combat companies formed a circle around the bowl. We refueled and pushed on.

I don't remember much else of this day. At some point we passed another artillery group traveling three or four columns abreast, which held up in a wadi to our south to let us pass to their front. The task force halted again when, driving by a dry creek with greenery, someone spied Iraqi soldiers in the creek. Either the task force scouts or a platoon from Delta Mech were sent to clear the creek. We sat and watched from a distance, Sergeant Dock looking through his sights to give the crew a blow-by-blow account. We recovered a number of weapons and captured several Iraqis. My brief letter of the twenty-eighth, the first I had a chance to write, gives the entire day only two sentences. The second records that on the way to our objective, which we hit about 1600 hours, "our scouts captured about ten POWs." I don't now know if these are the same soldiers as those captured at the creek.

As we watched the infantry investigate the dry creek, the weather turned, dark blue clouds encroaching. By the time we stopped for the night the cold and dark had returned.

When we stopped, Captain Baillergeon called the platoon leaders to his track. An Iraqi Republican Guard division was headed toward us. I believe the unit was retreating through our area, not knowing we were there, instead of counter-attacking us. Baillergeon sketched in the sand the different company positions and the engagement area, where all the battalion's fires would be concentrated. He assigned each platoon a portion of the company's part of the engagement area and ordered our platoons into defensive positions covering assigned areas.

The terrain, however, did not accommodate the plan. We sat in an unwaveringly flat piece of desert. No cover or concealment of any sort. The engagement area also had no identifiable features by which we could distinguish it, much less sectors of responsibility to assign each of my tanks within it. So I set my platoon as I had my first night in the desert with 2–4 Cav: I spaced them far enough apart so that no two tanks could be ranged by a single incoming indirect fire round, and far enough apart so that an enemy vehicle could not acquire two tanks in his sights at once, but near enough that we could communicate orally. I did not bother trying to hide us behind any military horizon because the terrain was simply too flat. I arranged the platoon so that if each tank scanned from fender to fender, we would ensure overlapping sectors of fire within the platoon and also with the flanking infantry platoons. Two soldiers awake per tank, and two tanks scanning the engagement area throughout the night.

Early in the evening several Bradleys, Humvees, and medic M113 PCs flew by from the task force combat supply trains behind us toward Alpha Tank's position to our right front. I would later learn from Baillergeon what happened, what Neal Creighton was about to discover.

When my tank wasn't scanning I slept on the back deck. It drizzled all night. I pulled my poncho liner over me and got two or three hours of sleep.

No Iraqi units appeared.

NEAL CREIGHTON (Alpha Tank, Task Force 3-15 Infantry)

Around noon on the twenty-fifth, we attacked Objective Gray. Captain Schwartz gave the word to hit the gas, and we went full throttle. First Platoon moved up on line with my platoon and the Bradley platoons swung in behind us, covering the gaps in the formation.

Looking to the west, I saw a group of Iraqi soldiers sitting huddled together. They waved a white cloth as we stormed past. We continued to push forward while the gunners scanned for enemy combat vehicles. The company came to a halt on Gray and then moved quickly into hasty defensive positions. Sergeant Davis spotted more enemy soldiers to the north through his gunner's sights, and I reported their location to Captain Schwartz. He ordered a section from my platoon forward with a section from one of the Bradley platoons.

I took my tank north and sent Sergeant Jones northeast. Jones immediately spotted a group of Iraqis and moved toward them with his tank and a Bradley. I saw nothing in my sector and radioed the supporting Bradley to move back to the company. As our driver turned the tank around, we almost ran over twenty Iraqis hiding in a shallow wadi.

"Stop!" I yelled into the mike.

"I got 'em, sir." Sergeant Davis had trained the coaxial machine gun on them.

I stared for about half a minute at these fierce soldiers whom we had heard so much about. They were in mixed, dirty uniforms. They looked helpless and desperate. My trance was broken by Pfc. Carrol as he screamed at them in Arabic to lay down. Fear spread across their faces.

"Sergeant Davis, I'm jumping down, so don't shoot or move the turret. Carrol, cover me." Carrol manned the loader's 7.62. I jumped down and walked toward the group. "Carrol, yell out 'friend' in Arabic," I said. Carrol did, and several of the Iraqis rushed up and bear-hugged me.

The nerves on both sides faded. Carrol jumped down to help me frisk the prisoners. Some of the Iraqis began to frisk one another, as if they thought this was some type of American greeting.

Lt. Alex Vernon in the loader's hatch in the battalion motor pool,
Fort Stewart, Georgia, spring 1990.
Courtesy of Alex Vernon.

Lt. Neal Creighton at Ranger School graduation
at Fort Benning, Georgia, August 1990.
Courtesy of Neal Creighton.

24th Infantry Division soldiers saying good-bye to friends and family through the fence at Hunter Army Airfield, Savannah, Georgia, 24 August 1990. *Courtesy of Alex Vernon.*

Lt. Alex Vernon's tank position on the cavalry screen line watching over Tapline Road in eastern Saudi Arabia, September 1990.
Courtesy of Alex Vernon.

Marty Klugg (*left*) and Greg Downey (*center*) being promoted to first
lieutenant by Lt. Col. Randy Gordon (*right*) at AA Augusta, southwest of
Dharhan, Saudi Arabia, 1 September 1990. An M1 decoy is in the background.
Courtesy of Greg Downey.

Lt. Dave Trybula in MOPP1 chemical protection and flak jacket at AA Hinesville, vicinity As Sarrar, Saudi Arabia, October 1990.
Courtesy of Dave Trybula.

opposite
Lt. Rob Holmes in AA Hinesville, vicinity As Sarrar, Saudi Arabia, October 1990.
Courtesy of Rob Holmes.

Gen. Colin Powell (*at left*) shakes hands with Lt. Neal Creighton during
General Powell's first visit to Saudi Arabia during Desert Shield, October 1990.
Courtesy of Neal Creighton.

Lt. Neal Creighton (*at left*) and crew (*left to right*): Sgt. Barry Davis, Spc. Forbes Watkins, and Pfc. Peter Frank Carrol. The photo was taken by a *Time* magazine photographer during General Powell's October 1990 visit.
Courtesy of Neal Creighton.

Bravo Tank's encampment at AA Hinesville, vicinity As Sarrar, Saudi Arabia, October 1990.
Courtesy of Bob McCann.

Lt. Dave Trybula at AA Cobra Rock, October 1990.
Courtesy of Dave Trybula.

Lt. Col. Randy Gordon posing with local Saudi Arabian officials in front of an M1 tank during Operation Desert Shield, vicinity As Sarrar, Saudi Arabia. *Courtesy of Randy Gordon.*

Lt. Greg Downey at AA Hinesville, vicinity As Sarrar, Saudi Arabia,
November 1990.
Courtesy of Greg Downey.

A Bradley Fighting Vehicle on maneuvers in Operation Desert Shield, Saudi Arabia, September 1990.
From *The Victory Book.*

Using the "trim vane" from a pair of side-by-side Bradleys for a stage, comedian
Jay Leno performs for Task Force 3-15 Infantry at AA Hinesville, vicinity
As Sarrar, Saudi Arabia, 24 November 1990.
From *The Victory Book*.

On 31 December 1990 Delta Tank received new M1A1 tanks—and a familiar visitor.

Courtesy of Rob Holmes.

American soldiers loading an M1 tank onto an HET during Operation
Desert Shield.

From *The Victory Book.*

Delta Tanks during ROM: *(top)* refueling and *(bottom)* cleaning the V-Pac air filters. This photo was taken on the first day of the ground campaign, 24 February 1991, in southern Iraq.
Courtesy of Rob Holmes.

Iraqis surrender to Lt. Rob Holmes's platoon, 25 February 1991, southern Iraq.
Courtesy of Rob Holmes.

An Iraqi T-55 tank is destroyed by an 8-inch artillery round requested by Lt. Greg
Downey, 26 February 1991, southwest of Objective Orange (Jalibah Airfield),
southern Iraq.
Courtesy of Greg Downey.

opposite
Col. Paul Kern (*left*), commander of the 2d Brigade, consults with Maj. Gen.
Barry McCaffrey, division commander, in southern Iraq during Operation Desert
Storm, 24–28 February 1991.
From *The Victory Book.*

Iraqi soldiers posing on a T-72 tank prior to the ground campaign. This photograph was developed from a roll of film discovered on an abandoned T-72 by Bravo Tank soldiers during the 24th Infantry Division's occupation of the DMZ in southern Iraq in early March 1991.
Courtesy of Bob McCann.

A destroyed Iraqi BMP with its turret blown off, southern Iraq, 27 February 1991. *Courtesy of Greg Downey.*

Lts. Rob Holmes (*left*) and Alex Vernon on their first night home, 20 March 1991, Fort Stewart, Georgia.

Courtesy of Rob Holmes.

We ran over their weapons with our tank and loaded the prisoners on top of our vehicle. As I hopped back on the tank, I heard an explosion and saw a dust cloud rising over the company location. We headed slowly back to the company with the Iraqis clinging on to the top of the turret and hull of our tank.

As we neared the commander's tank, I saw my first dead soldiers. Unfortunately, they were Americans. Two fine young men lay in the sand. They were from the Bradley that had supported my move forward only ten minutes earlier. The soldiers were victims of a terrible mistake. Their platoon leader had instructed them to wear grenades on their LBEs for the several-hundred-kilometer ride in the back of their Bradleys. The vibrations and limited space of the Bradley caused the safety clip to fall off the pin from one of the soldier's grenades. When the Bradley stopped on Objective Gray, the infantrymen exited from the cramped rear door instead of exiting by the dropped Bradley ramp. As the soldier's equipment rubbed the side of the steel doorway, the pin was yanked from the grenade. The explosion killed the soldier and the man behind him. A third soldier was wounded.

The soldiers did not need to wear their grenades for the duration of the movement. They would have had more than enough time to uncrate the grenades when needed. I attributed the mistake to our lack of combat experience. A lesson was learned from the sacrifice of two Americans.

First Sergeant Foote covered the bodies and removed the unexploded grenades from the dead soldiers' belts. He tied strings to the safety pins, placed the grenades outside of our perimeter, and detonated them remotely by yanking on the string. My tank was the closest to the grenades, and I didn't know he was doing this until after the explosion startled me.

I moved our tank into a hasty defensive position and put out a net call to my platoon. "All white elements, we will remain here tonight and resume movement tomorrow. Begin preparing hasty defensive positions and start priority of work, out." I looked out over the desert and began to wonder if death would find more of us tomorrow.[10]

26 February 1991 (G+2)

NEAL CREIGHTON (Alpha Tank, Task Force 3-15 Infantry)

We moved out again early in the morning. The fog was so thick I couldn't see fifty meters in any direction. The company tightened the formation and took the lead as the task force advance guard.

As we moved, intelligence reports came over the command net about the enemy on our next objective, Objective Orange. This time we would fight a Republican Guard unit on Jalibah Airfield. We had briefly planned the attack on the airfield, though we had not updated the order given the most current information on enemy locations and dispositions. I really never thought we would make it so far so quickly. I relayed the intelligence reports to the platoon over our internal radio net.

Late that night we stopped just short of Jalibah. As darkness fell, the artillery lit up the sky with a constant barrage on the airfield. We would attack very soon. I fell asleep.

ALEX VERNON (Delta Mech, Task Force 3-15 Infantry)

We moved at 0300 hours.[11] The weather was worse than the first night: rain and zero illumination. With my PVS-7s, I could only see the taillights on other vehicles that were yards away. Distinguishing tanks from Bradleys, then one unit from the next, was nearly impossible. The "bud lights" we strapped to our taillights — small, infrared light-emitting diodes visible through our night vision devices, and powered by common rectangular twelve-volt batteries — were invisible. Over the radio we directed each other to flash brake lights, wave flashlights or chem lights, spin a turret, or move a gun tube up and down, to identify one another. The task force took over an hour to form, a task that in good conditions takes minutes.

The day eventually cleared, and again as we traveled we encountered surrendering Iraqis. There were too many this time for the scouts to handle, so Lieutenant Colonel Barrett tasked my company to police one group. Initially my tanks sat in overwatch while the infantry searched the POWs, removing weapons and papers, and binding their hands. I joined the First Platoon leader, Lt. Brian Luke, on the ground to survey the situation. The Iraqis were in rows, most on their knees, some supine. They were dirty and ragged, and a number did not have shoes. Some had light wounds. Across the road, on the other side of a low mound of sand, Brian and I saw three or four wild dogs, their heads bent, busy, bobbing on the ground; when we approached, we realized they were feeding on Iraqi corpses. Brian chased the dogs off. They hung on the periphery, knowing we'd have to leave eventually, when they could resume their meal.

Brian and I had to move the POWs several kilometers to the task force's collection point. From there, either battalion trucks would transport them to some collection site further back, or they would wait under guard for a collection unit coming forward to gather them. My platoon started walking the POWs, the group sandwiched between my two tank sections; Sergeant Freight's section was leading, their turrets swung to the rear, machine guns ready, my section trailing. Several grunts from Brian's platoon walked on the outside of the Iraqis. Not two hundred meters into this march, we knew it would take too long to walk them to the collection point. I decided to load the Iraqis on the tanks and drive them. Freight's section would carry them, my section would follow, our machine guns locked and loaded.

Because the POWs' hands were bound behind them, Sergeants Boss and Dock hauled them onto the back decks of Freight's two tanks. From the ground Dock would get a POW halfway up, the POW's foot on the tank track and Dock underneath him, and from the back deck Boss pulled the man the rest of the way, often by the man's belt. We squeezed about fifteen Iraqis on the back of each tank — those without shoes hung their feet off the sides, away from the blazing hot engine. I ordered the crews of both those tanks to unload the turret-mounted machine guns and button-up inside the turret, hatches closed and locked. This got them out of harm's way, either from an Iraqi or from the machine guns from my section's two tanks, trailing the two tanks carrying the prisoners and now free to shoot without risk to our own.

We delivered the POWs without incident a short time later. The battalion captured roughly one hundred POWs that day.

Later in the afternoon the terrain changed. The dusty, rocky flats gave way to a maze of wadis, berms, and dunes. The dunes particularly were precarious because the sand slid under the vehicles. Twice my tank drove over the tapering end of a dune and slid down the side several meters. A vehicle that crossed too high on a dune could have easily flipped. After passing over the edge of one dune, I looked back to watch my wingman go over, and saw a Bedouin family clustered against it, the parents and two children, hidden from the view of oncoming vehicles. They had been smart to pick a dune, since we couldn't cross straight overtop. Still, they weren't entirely out of danger. I warned my platoon and then the company to stay clear.

The company alternately traveled in staggered-column and single-column formation through the mess of wadis. For much of this leg of the day's attack I could not see Alpha Tank, the battalion's lead company, on which I guided my movement. I caught glimpses, guessed, and sometimes asked Captain Baillergeon to guess for me. Each fork in the wadi, each berm or dune, we had to dodge, presented a choice that could separate us from the task force. Each fork we took, each berm or dune we dodged, also contorted my sense of direction. I did not have a GPS, I did not know to what GIRS we were headed or where we were in relation to that GIRS. The map gave no details of the terrain that Baillergeon and I might have been able to use to steer the company. He and I navigated by glimpses and hunches, and somehow we came out the other side in formation.

GREG DOWNEY (Scouts, Task Force 1-64 Armor)

At 0430 hours my scout platoon continued the zone recon. It had been a sleepless night for all my scouts. The pace exacted a toll on us. I could tell by the voices on my platoon radio frequency that we were getting tired. During the last five days, I had slept a total of no more than ten hours. Easy mental tasks were becoming increasingly difficult. My drivers were getting some rest, but the gunners were probably in the worst shape. Lowther had a permanent bruise across his brow from the padded headrest over his gunner's sight. His eyes were fried, shot through with red, from the constant peering through the sight. Yet he never complained. Once in a while I'd nudge him when I thought he'd drifted asleep, when the turret stopped tracking the horizon. He would resume scanning.

We were moving toward Objective Orange, Jalibah Airfield, deep inside Iraq, almost directly north of Kuwait. I had seen satellite imagery a few weeks before that showed Iraqi tanks and BMPs — the Iraqi version of the Bradley — dug-in around Jalibah. A fight was waiting for us.

En route to Battle Position 103, a position west of Objective Orange, two OH-58D helicopters and an AH-1 Cobra from the divisional air cavalry flew over my section. They landed before I could look up their radio frequency and talk to them on the radio. I dismounted to speak with them. The pilot was pretty shaken up. They had just been engaged by direct fire east of our location. He didn't have much else to tell me. Something was up ahead.

I called back the report to the battalion TOC and pushed to the east. We recon'd through BP 103 and cleared the task force's area. Lieutenant Colonel Gordon had been keeping my scout platoon anywhere from ten to eighteen kilometers forward of the task force. We pushed east of 103 to screen the zone. First Brigade was passing through our zone behind my screen.

ROB HOLMES (Delta Tank, Task Force 1-64 Armor)

Sometime during the sandstorm, we knew there were targets in front of us. We didn't know what they were at first. No one could really see what was going on, but we knew there was something out there. They turned out to be Iraqi scout trucks. I gave my gunner the order to fire. Sergeant Downing hesitated.

I started to drop down in my seat to grab the override and do it myself when he fired the gun. He shot way over. And he did it on purpose. I know he did. This was the man who claimed to be the best gunner in the army, and who might very well have been. After Downing missed, my wingman blasted the Iraqi truck from my right flank, igniting a huge explosion.

When things settled down, Downing and I got off the tank and proceeded to yell and scream at one another. He was in tears. I didn't know what to do. We're in the middle of Iraq, and I've got a gunner who hesitated pulling the trigger. To be honest I don't remember how I dealt with him. We mounted back up and kept going. Needless to say the incident stuck in my mind the rest of the time we were in Iraq.

Sergeant Downing was very devout, very evangelical, and during Desert Shield had been really opposed to our attacking. He was never vocal about it, and he maintained his professionalism, but he made it very clear that he did not want to go to war. Hell, none of us did, but we all sure wanted to go home alive. Here's an NCO who has been in the army eleven years, and it wasn't like any of us wanted to go to war, yet his attitude seemed to be, "I can't believe you're asking me to do this."

I'd like to think that I never had any bloodlust. When I gave an order to fire it was with as much prudence as I could have. For the rest of the war I couldn't shake it: He had missed on purpose. I almost looked forward to our next engagement with the enemy, so Downing could destroy a target and restore my confidence.

GREG DOWNEY (Scouts, Task Force 1-64 Armor)

"Jesus Christ, what was that!" screamed Lowther, as dust bellowed in the turret from the concussion.

"West, get us moving!" I yelled over the intercom.

"Blue Six, get your vehicle moving!" I ordered over the radio to S.Sergeant Hightower, my wingman.

The sound of incoming artillery broke up the hum of my vehicle. Hightower and his crew had escaped death by inches. An Iraqi forward observer had eyes on us as we occupied the screen. The artillery was not very heavy but pretty accurate. My section was the only one under fire, so I tried to reposition just myself and Blue Six. We received artillery each time we moved. The impacts produced severe concussions inside my vehicle, and the scouts in the crew compartment in back were feeling every round.

"Blue Six, this is Black One, over," I called again.

"Goddamn-it, West, keep us moving, try to find some cover," I said. It was an impossible task in the incredibly flat piece of desert.

I kept waiting for Hightower to move his vehicle or to answer my call on the radio. Neither was happening. The artillery continued to fall around his vehicle, rocking the twenty-six-ton Bradley from side to side. Incoming artillery plays with you. You never know where the next round will fall. I had terrible feelings of paranoia, like somebody was looking at me through a pair of binoculars, carefully plotting my location, and calling for the next barrage. Which is exactly what was happening.

"Answer the goddamned radio, Hightower!" I yelled inside my own turret. "West, come in from behind Blue Six's vehicle; it looks like there's some low ground. I can't reach him on the radio, so get me close enough that I can run over to talk to him."

West positioned our Bradley behind Hightower's. As I was dismounting, an artillery round impacted off to my right, blowing me off the front slope of my vehicle. Sergeant Hightower was only fifty meters from my vehicle, but in that short gap rounds were sporadically falling. I could not see him looking out his hatch. The vehicle did not look as if it had been hit. I climbed up on his vehicle and looked down at him through the hatch. He was frantically trying to call me on the radio, not knowing I was only a short distance away. His radio was working fine; he was talking to Sergeants Deem and Smith. Looking back at my vehicle, I noticed one of my radio antennas was missing.

I had made it to his vehicle with no problem, so I figured the chances of making it back to mine were good. I had been a sprinter in college. I always liked the one hundred-meter dash — mad and short and over in ten seconds, barely enough running to make me breathe hard. Even though the distance I had to cover back to my vehicle was less than fifty meters, it looked much farther. And now my competition was artillery rounds.

Racing back in a dead sprint, I heard it coming at the last second, like a superfast lawn sprinkler, the type that rotates, spraying a stream of water, rattling. I remember seeing sky, ground, sky, then ground, then my face shoved into the sand. I landed on my head, dazed and startled. I didn't feel any pain at first. Then my right side started to throb. Everything was still attached, but my chemical suit was torn on the right side and I couldn't hear out of my right ear.

Still in shock, I pushed my body up with my arms and got up. I saw something on the ground, something silver. A chain. A medal. My Saint Christopher's medal. Ironic — the last time I had lost it I almost lost my life. I grabbed it, put it in my pocket, and kept running. I didn't bother to check for any blood until I made it back to my vehicle. My hip was numb, but otherwise I felt all right. I replaced the damaged antenna with a new one, regained communications with the platoon, and moved out of the impact area.

I could soon tell from where the enemy was firing the artillery. I was now looking down on its defensive position. I called the battalion fire support officer for some artillery support, but before I could finish the transmission, division artillery was already firing on the Iraqi artillery. Division radar can detect artillery immediately after it is launched and determine its origin within seconds. Then it targets the firing enemy unit for a counterbattery strike. American artillerymen brag that they can get rounds in the air before the initial enemy rounds hit their target.

Once the Iraqi guns were silenced, I went to work on the defenses below me.

The FSO relayed to me that the artillery units were ready to fire. I had already made polar plots on the target. A polar plot is the most accurate means of calling for indirect fire. You use your own known location and a distance and a direction to the target. The Trimpack GPS provided my ten-digit grid location, the lensatic compass gave the direction to target, and my GVS-5 handheld laser range finder gave me the distance to the target within five meters.

Before high technology made its appearance on the battlefield, survey crews would have to come out to the point on the ground where the polar plot would be called in from. They would survey the site, recording the grid location for the artillery observer. The compass has been around for decades, always providing direction for the observer. Distance was determined with a graduated scale superimposed in the lens of the binoculars. Place your target in the scale, do a little battlefield arithmetic, and cross your fingers. As the first rounds hit, you called back adjustments. This method was very time consuming and required firing many more artillery rounds to hit the target.

The first artillery rounds fired were from an eight-inch howitzer. A battalion's worth of artillery impacting all at once is a terrifying sight. I could observe Iraqi infantry moving to the west side of their defensive positions. I was a safe two kilometers away and could easily observe them. Rockets from MLRS came next. I gave different firing data to the FSO because of my previous experience with MLRS rounds landing one kilometer over and one kilometer to the left. This time the rounds were on the mark. We pounded the target area for forty-five minutes. Darkness had fallen and the firing eventually stopped.

My scout platoon continued to screen Task Force 1-64's portion of BP 103 until the task force arrived into position. Iraqi soldiers started moving toward my section at about 2000 hours. As we watched them come to us, some of them fell down, too injured to walk farther, or dying. I dispatched a dismounted patrol, along with my medic, to gather them up and guide them to my location. The medic, Specialist Burton, administered first aid to those who had a chance. Some were not going to last another hour. An Iraqi captain was one of the survivors. To my amazement, he spoke fluent English. I spoke with him for a few minutes to see what he knew while Burton put a tourniquet on a soldier missing his hand.

The Iraqi captain told me he was in the Republican Guard 26th Commando Brigade and that there had been 650 men in the brigade. When I asked him how many more men were alive, he said, "This is all . . . this is all." He started weeping. Only forty-nine Iraqi soldiers remained, all standing before me with horrified looks on their faces. They had just glimpsed hell.

I had called the artillery that erased the lives of over six hundred human beings. In forty-five minutes, I had killed more people than what lived in my hometown of Merna, Nebraska. Combat is a series of contradictions. One moment you're trying your best to kill the enemy, the next moment you're doing your best to save him. I looked at the shock in the Iraqis' eyes. For the first time during the ground attack, I felt guilt and sorrow.

We handed the POWs off to an infantry platoon from Charlie Mech. I told the platoon leader not to let any others die. There had been enough dying for the night.

The scout platoon moved back to the task force's location to be resupplied. We were low on fuel, food, and water. We had plenty of ammunition, but the medic had used up all of the morphine and most of his first aid supplies on the Iraqis. This was the first time I had seen the battalion in two days. Despite our lack of sleep, we could feel the momentum racing throughout the battalion.

My vehicle radiator had developed a leak, probably from the artillery, so we used some silicone to patch it up. It worked a little, but most of the thirty-five gallons of water we carried for drinking was drained into the radiator. It would be a constant battle to keep the vehicle engine cooling properly.

ROB HOLMES (Delta Tank, Task Force 1-64 Armor)
Late in the afternoon my loader Underberg handed me a special map-sheet. This one had my notes all over it and had been subject of much discussion back at Graceland. I had spent many nights wondering what would happen to us when we arrived at Objective Orange.

Flash had briefed us all about it back in Saudi. The Iraqi Republican Guard used Jalibah Airfield as a key logistical site for fuel, ammunition, and supplies. They defended it accordingly: two tank companies, artillery and mortars, and about one thousand infantry. Jalibah was critical. It sat in the path between Baghdad and Basra. Once we captured it, we closed the door on the Republican Guard's escape from Kuwait. If we could meet the Republican Guard in the flat, open Euphrates River Valley with the main allied force pushing the enemy from behind and the air force ravaging them from above, we would obliterate the enemy.

The sun was setting with Jalibah only about thirty kilometers away when Captain Hubner radioed that we would attack at midnight.

I was not thrilled. The conventional wisdom was that we always want to fight at night because we have better vision. Our thermal sights see three thousand meters while Soviet-made tanks see only about fifteen hundred meters. That's fine if you're getting twenty-five hundred meter shots and the enemy can't touch you, but who cares if you are caught up in an airfield complex and are engaging at three hundred meters? Furthermore, we were still very inexperienced combat soldiers. Regardless of the night sights, command and control suffers at night. Leaders have to spend much more time on navigation, coordination, and most importantly, distributing firepower. I was specifically worried about friendly fire.

My platoon led the task force to an attack position eight kilometers southwest of Jalibah. We parked, lined up, and did our pit crew drill as the fuelers replenished our tanks. Gunners updated their sights; loaders checked their ammo racks; drivers inspected their tracks. Everyone knew the test waiting for us ahead. I walked around my tanks and gave a quick greeting to each of my soldiers. They were all busy refueling and blowing air filters, so I was brief with a handshake or quip. They were all good men. In peacetime I could easily rank my soldiers based on discipline, competence, and intelligence. Some were terrific; some were a nightmare. At this point though, all I could think about was what good men these guys were. They knew the significance of Jalibah and its heavy defenses, but they all went about their jobs and returned my smile and handshake as I walked by.

Crazy as this sounds, I wasn't nervous. I wasn't even scared. I have always been someone who tries to visualize the future and pray for it. I didn't know what was planned for my future, but I never once thought that I would leave Iraq with even a scratch. Now was no different. The thought of one of my guys getting wounded or killed, however, was absolutely intolerable. I was directly responsible for the men in my platoon. I had seen all the old movies about the officer writing the letter home to the family of a soldier who had been killed. I thought of my parents and brother and my soldiers' families. I couldn't bear even to consider not bringing one home.

As I walked around while we refueled, I had on my game face like never before. I didn't jump around like at a pep rally, didn't want to go "kick their ass" or anything like that. I just felt intense and focused. My world was very simple. We were about to attack a heavily defended objective that threatened the lives of my men. Get in my way, and I will kill you.

Before we could pull any triggers that night, however, Hubner radioed after having just talked to Flash. Evidently, someone higher had decided to wait until dawn and attack Jalibah with the whole brigade instead of just Task Force 1-64. In addition, two artillery battalions would move up to pound the airfield prior to our assault. I love artillery.

I mounted my tank and realized that we had a couple hours of waiting before we attacked: *Sleep!* The cliché about combat being a continuous series of emotional swings is really true. I went from being a loaded, cocked, lethal weapon to a sleeping baby in a matter of minutes. Sergeant Downing set a schedule for my crew so that three could sleep while one listened to the radio. In four hours we would attack a heavily defended objective, but right now I could crash and make up for the last forty-eight hours of fighting and moving three hundred kilometers through Iraq. I grabbed a blanket, jumped onto the back deck of the M1, and I was out like a light.[12]

ALEX VERNON (Delta Mech, Task Force 3-15 Infantry)

We stopped about 2200 in our assault position for the next morning's attack on Objective Orange. Captain Baillergeon disappeared to the battalion TOC for his orders. On his return trip, he radioed ahead so that the platoon leaders would be waiting at his Bradley. This was about midnight. He briefed us; we returned and briefed our platoons. Fifty percent security again for the remaining hours of the night. I remember lying awake, watching the lights of aircraft overhead, and hearing the distant rumble of bombs.

The plan as I remember: The task force would travel to the airfield to our direct east in a box formation: Bravo and Alpha Tanks the front left and right corners (respectively), and Bravo and my Delta Mech the rear left and right corners.[13] As we neared the airfield my company would move forward, on line with and on the right of Alpha Tank to prepare to assault the runway, while the left side of the box would peel off to the northern edge of the compound to occupy a hasty defense guarding our flank. Meanwhile Task Force 1-64 Armor, to our south, would also hit the airfield with two companies, and leave two companies watching its flank on the southern edge of the compound. As 3-15's rightmost unit, my company team was to link with 1-64's leftmost unit at the west side of the airfield for our synchronized run across it, four companies with all platoons abreast. I remember Delta Tank, Rob Holmes's company, as 1-64's leftmost unit in the assault plan, the unit with which I was to ride side by side down the center runway.

Splitting the assault force between the two task forces did not make much sense to me. I regretted already that the only way I could talk with the company beside me was by calling up the chain from company to battalion to the brigade net, where the task forces talked, and then back down Rob's chain to his company. Not the sort of immediate communication you need with the fellow beside you in a battle. It did not occur to me at the time to set one of my programmable frequency switch settings to Delta Tank's net so I could talk to Rob during the assault, much less call his unit to attempt some sort of pre-attack coordination. I was tired, I guess, and not used to thinking beyond my express orders. Battle drills don't leave much room for creative initiative — for much of the war I felt very much just along for the ride. I did not look forward to the battle; nonetheless, I did look forward to seeing Rob, my Fort Stewart roommate and one of my closest friends, on my right flank. One of our cadet company mates, a man from small-town Mississippi, had once described Rob as having been born with a horseshoe up his butt. Short of my being in Delta Tank or his being in Delta Mech, I could not have been any closer to that horseshoe.

DAVE TRYBULA (Charlie Tank, Task Force 1-64 Armor)

Just prior to dusk on 26 February, the company commander returned from a quick orders brief at the tactical operations center and called all the platoon leaders and the company's fire support officer over to his tank. He spoke in a quiet voice:

"We're going to stay in our hasty defense tonight until around 0300. Then we will move as task force reserve in the rear of the diamond while the brigade conducts a deliberate attack to seize Jalibah Airfield. Task Force 3-15 will attack in the north. Okay, let's look at the map. An on-order boundary has been established between us and 3-69 along this road south of Jalibah," he said, pointing to the road on his map. "We anticipate setting a base of fire with the mechanized infantry companies along this position and conducting a western envelopment with Delta Tank and us. The runway is our on-order boundary with 3-15 for the assault. We will use company Vee formation, which means that Dave, you'll lead the company's envelopment. Remember to make a bold movement to the flank prior to turning back toward the assault position. Rogue Six said he would work a smoke mission to mark your turn. Any questions? Good, go back to your platoons, make sure they know what is going on. We will pull out of the hasty defense and form up not later than 0300. Anticipate receiving an intelligence update from battalion prior to movement. Keep your sleep plan going. Your people need to be fresh in the morning."[14]

27 February 1991 (G+3):
The Assault on Jalibah Airfield

GREG DOWNEY (Scouts, Task Force 1-64 Armor)

After the resupply, the scout platoon moved out at 0200 hours. The task force was right behind us. Lieutenant Colonel Gordon was gambling that we would not hit any resistance as we approached BP Bed, our attack position for Objective Orange. It was a very secure feeling. An armored task force that could defeat anything the enemy had to offer surrounded me. I was accustomed to having only my wingman, with my other two sections two and a half kilometers away on each flank. I realized it wasn't me against the whole Iraqi army, though at times it had certainly felt that way.

We closed on BP Bed at 0300 hours. Rogue Six's voice came up on the net. Flash Gordon sounded like an old man, the weariness of battle having begun to take its toll on the tough warrior. The words were drawn from the bottom of his exhausted lungs. Despite his fatigue, he knew exactly how the battle would be fought. He had visualized this fight in his mind for several weeks, analyzing the

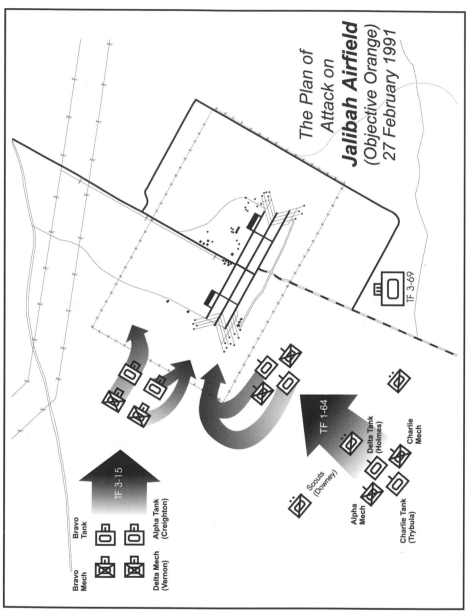

The Plan of Attack on Jalibah Airfield (Objective Orange), 27 February 1991.

enemy's actions and reactions, developing counteractions for the task force to respond with, and picturing himself and his armored task force destroying the enemy in a very detailed manner. In Gordon's mind, the battle had already been fought and won.

The scout platoon was to run coordination points between the flanks. Red Section would tie into Task Force 3-15 Infantry, the battalion on our left. Blue Section would tie into Task Force 3-69 Armor, the battalion on our right. My section would go forward of the task force, providing a security blanket for Delta Tank. Blue Section was successful with their link-up with the left flank company of Task Force 3-69, but Red Section could not establish link-up with 3-15. I had my Red Section return to my location after receiving approval from Lieutenant Colonel Gordon.

We moved east to observe the objective. We had not traveled far when I could see the huge hangars through my thermal sight, the heat of the concrete-constructed hangars illuminated through my optics. At 0500, the artillery preparation started. Once again, the devastation was unbelievable. I watched Iraqi soldiers running across the airfield to the west side. The enemy knew our approach direction because of where the artillery was coming from. What they did not know was that an armored brigade of 116 M1A1 tanks and over sixty M2A1 Bradley Fighting Vehicles would descend upon them within the hour.

"Lowther, what do you think is going through their minds right now?" I asked, squinting my eye against my thermal sight, observing the chaos on the airfield.

"I don't know, sir, but in about an hour, their asses will be going through it," said Lowther, laughing as he traversed the turret to another part of the airfield.

At 0600 hours, the brigade started its move.[15] Red Section was driving along the left boundary of the task force, and I pulled my own section over to its location. I wanted to get out of the way before the task force rolled up to the airfield.

"Black One, this is Red Two," S.Sergeant Deem called over the radio, "I've got a missile coming." Deem's report immediately sent my eyes into a frantic search. Deem had observed a white puff of smoke rising from the corner of the airfield, the signature of an antitank missile. I focused my eyes on the area and could see the wire-guided missile flying our way. The missile moved more slowly than I thought it would, giving us time to react. Before the war I had skeptically received training, and skeptically trained my platoons, on the *sagger dance* battle drill, named after the popular Soviet-manufactured version of this infantry weapon, the cousin of our own TOW. I thought we'd never have time to dodge an incoming missile, but they didn't travel nearly as fast as the tank's sabot rounds, and we watched this one coming. It was tracking Deem's vehicle.

"This is Red Two, I'm popping smoke, then doin' a hard left." Deem was telling his wingman what the signal would be to start his evasive maneuver. The smoke would also help throw the missile off course, as it would cloud the view of the Iraqi soldier tracking Deem's Bradley in his sights to guide his missile, through the wire, to its target.

"This is Red Three, roger, what about me?" came Wiggins's response, a few octaves higher out of nervousness.

"This is Red Two, take a hard right, and do it fast!" Deem yelled.

He launched his on-board smoke grenades to provide a smokescreen and did a hard left turn. The missile hit right where he turned from, throwing debris back into his wingman's vehicle. A near miss, but enough to let us know they had some fight left in them.

A white phosphorous artillery round hit directly on top of the position where the enemy missile had been fired from. No more missiles were launched from that location.

"Contact, contact . . . choppers! Engaging one HIND!" came S.Sergeant Deem's voice again, mixed with the distinctive *thump-thump-thump* of his chain gun. Deem was quickly becoming an enemy magnet, engaging an MI-24 HIND-D helicopter on the north side of the airfield. The blades were moving, and the crew was desperately trying to get it off the ground.

"Black One, this is Red Two . . . I've lost my turret, no power . . . I can't fire!" he screamed over the net an instant later, his fury transmitting over the radio. He had squeezed off twenty rounds at the helicopter before his turret lost all power, shutting down his weapon systems. The helicopter exploded, the fuel and ammunition igniting from the 25-mm rounds. Deem was finally rattled, the first time I had ever seen him lose control of his emotions. Within one minute, he had dodged a near miss from an antitank missile, destroyed an attack helicopter, and lost his weapon system.

"Black One, this is Red Three, target . . . target destroyed!" Sergeant Wiggins announced over the radio, finishing the job that Red Two had started.

"This is Black One, roger, get Red Section over here behind this hill," I said, trying to get them under control. I brought them back to my location, where we were pulled up behind a small hill. I looked at Deem's face as he pulled his vehicle over to my location. It was the face of combat; dirty, greasy, dark circles under tired eyes, stress lines chiseled in his forehead. He gave me a look that said he'd had enough.

"Lowther, go over to Red Two and see if you can get his turret running again," I said, sending my gunner to work his magic with his self-taught mechanical skills. "And don't come back until it's fixed."

"Back in two, sir," Lowther bragged, smiling as he slid up through the small hatch on top of the turret.

I looked out across my front. The dust clouds rose from the battlefield. Task Forces 1-64 Armor and 3-15 Infantry were beginning the main attack on the airfield. For once it was time for my scouts to sit back and watch.

NEAL CREIGHTON (Alpha Tank, Task Force 3-15 Infantry)

The radio broke my half-conscious daze. "White Six, report to my tank, over." I had slept for only an hour the past day and the commander's voice seemed as if out of a dream. The MLRS battery had pummeled the airfield all night long, and the spectacle and my nerves kept me awake.

"Lieutenant Creighton, did you hear the CO call?" asked Sergeant Davis from the gunner's position.

"Yeah." I keyed the radio, "Black Six, this is White Six, I'm en route to your position." I turned to Davis, "Tell the platoon to get ready to move and that I went to the commander's tank to receive the attack order." I crawled out of my tank commander's position, grabbed my map and compass, and jumped off the tank.

As I arrived at Captain Schwartz's tank, he took roll call of all four platoon leaders, the XO, the fire support officer, and the first sergeant. "We don't have much time and the attack is going to be simple," the captain said as he pointed to his sand-covered map. "Neal, the airfield is that way about five kilometers at a ninety-degree azimuth. Due east. You get us there and to the right hasty defensive position. When Neal's Second Platoon busts onto the airfield, First Platoon will bring its tanks on line with Neal's, and the Bradley platoons will fall behind the tanks, on line, covering the gaps. We still think that a battalion of T-55 tanks is protecting the airfield." Before the captain could start another sentence, the battalion commander broke over the command net.

"Wild Bunch Six, move now."

Without even looking at the commander, I raced toward my tank and mounted the side. I was in the hatch within twenty seconds. This was not how I had pictured combat. Our first major objective and I had not thoroughly updated my platoon. Now that we were past Objective Gray, we were just reacting to fragmentary orders. The brigade staff probably had time to update this attack order, but by the time the plan was finalized and had gone through the battalion, the company had no time to change anything.

For anything unexpected we now had to rely on all the training and battle drills developed during Operation Desert Shield. Any last minute update was a formality and only a confidence builder. It was better that the platoon had received some rest instead of doing rehearsals all night. Desert Shield had been our rehearsal.

I put on my helmet and keyed the mike. "All white elements, enemy airfield five kilometers at ninety degrees. Possible T-55 battalion in defense. Follow my move in wedge and at the airfield come on line, out."

Without further communication, my platoon moved forward at fifteen miles per hour. I looked behind to see fifty-four other combat vehicles behind us in the task force formation. My position was the tip of the task force spear. Eventually, the entire force would move into a box formation with the two tank company-teams on line and the two mechanized company-teams following, on line and in reserve. All this would happen when my tank hit the airfield.

In the distance, I saw a great plume of smoke rising over the airfield, probably caused by a fire started during the night's artillery strike. Then I spotted a Bedouin family squatting in a wadi to our direct front. "All white elements, Bedouins direct front. Don't run them over, out." The family had camped right on the task force route and now clearly feared for their lives. The women and children were lying down headfirst while an older male stood erect waving a white flag to protect them from us. I could not help but admire the courage of this Bedouin who was facing such a strange and terrible sight. He stood firm. The task force stormed past his family without injuring them.

The perimeter of the airfield came into view. We closed quickly on a chain-link fence that was supported by large cinder-block posts. I saw Task Force 1-64 Armor moving across the southern sector of the field as we approached.

"Sir, should I run over the fence?" asked Forbes.

He thinks this is training. "Center on a cinder block, and Sergeant Davis, move the gun tube over the side so it won't get smashed." We exploded through the fence. The First Platoon moved on line with mine, and the Bradleys moved into our gaps. Bravo Tank maneuvered up on line with our company, and the attack speed dropped to around eight miles an hour. I heard a loud boom and ducked down in my hatch as the enemy fired their mortars.

ROB HOLMES (Delta Tank, Task Force 1-64 Armor)

I must have jumped three feet, drawn my .45, and landed inside the turret all in one motion. I woke to what sounded like the end of the world. Ten kilometers south of us, two artillery battalions had begun the most awesome display of firepower that I had ever seen. The sky was ablaze as rockets flew over us headed toward Jalibah. I was eight kilometers away from the airfield, asleep on a seventy-ton tank, and I felt the concussion like I was in an earthquake. My nap was over.

All of us woke and watched the sky and horizon on fire. As far as I was concerned, the artillery could do this for days. I knew, however, as always, it would soon be our turn to actually take the objective.

At dawn my platoon moved forward in a wedge formation with Delta Tank and the rest of the task force behind us. We rolled north at fifteen miles per hour headed to Jalibah. I didn't need a map. We were only eight clicks away, traveling almost straight north, and besides, I could navigate based on the explosions of the artillery barrage that I could see and hear. Bell wasn't accelerating, but as we got closer to Jalibah I felt we were moving faster, as if we were being drawn to it. The sand was rolling and firm with sparse vegetation. Tank country. To the east the sky was a brilliant blue and orange; to the west a silent darkness lingered.

Artillery was flying over us and raining down on Jalibah. I looked right and left as First and Third Platoon came abreast of mine in attack formation. We were now only about four kilometers away from the objective. Charlie's tanks did the same on our right. The task force's two mechanized infantry companies followed behind our tanks with their Bradleys on line.

We crested a dune and rolled gently into a huge basin. There it was.

Don't picture LaGuardia. There were two paved runways with several hangars on both the north and south sides. A chain-link wire fence surrounded the complex. We accelerated to twenty miles per hour and led the battalion into the valley. Artillery was landing all over the objective as Task Force 1-64 rolled into the basin. I saw Flash over my shoulder, bandanna blowing and sunglasses on, as he barked orders into his radio demanding more artillery.

"I got something hot!" Sergeant Downing screamed into the intercom.

"Fire and adjust!" I answered.

My command gave the gunner control over the fire system so he could engage without approval from me. This allowed him to acquire and engage targets at will while I maneuvered the platoon. There were no friendlies on Jalibah, so anything that came up hot Downing was free to blast. I had matured a lot since my first skirmish with dismounts only forty-eight hours earlier. I wasn't screwing around anymore with my .50-caliber machine gun.

Downing didn't waste time. The turret exploded as he fired the main gun. Underberg reloaded the breech, and my gunner engaged another target in a bunker adjacent to a hangar — my confidence in Sergeant Downing was back.

I had told my platoon to fire first and fast the night before, and they listened. As we rolled onward toward the airfield, my gunners were blasting main gun rounds as fast as the loaders could heave them into the breech. I scanned the airfield for targets and talked Downing onto those he didn't see.

Task Force 1-64 was an awesome display, thirty M1s shooting on the move as we assaulted the objective. We rolled into the valley closer to the airfield as artillery continued to pour down.

Then I felt like I was hit by a freight train.

Next thing I knew I was crumpled in a heap inside the turret. My head was spinning and my helmet was on crooked. I tried to pick myself up, not really sure what had just happened. I was dizzy but could stand. I looked around inside the turret: Everybody seemed okay. Bell was driving. Underberg was loading, and Downing kept engaging targets. What the hell just hit me?

I stood back up in my hatch and looked around as we rolled toward the airfield. Violent clouds of sand and smoke were exploding all around us. The Iraqis were mounting a defense, launching mortars at us as our tanks rolled closer. One must have splashed next to us, barely missing my tank and knocking me over with its concussion.

My platoon crashed through the chain-link fence around the complex and led Delta Tank into the hangar complex. Iraqi infantry immediately surrounded us. Arabs have a weird way of appearing out of nowhere. This was not good. Tanks hate urban terrain that restricts maneuver. We were boxed in because of the fence and hangars, and these guys weren't surrendering. Iraqi grunts were everywhere. I couldn't believe anyone was still alive after our arty barrage. My platoon's gunners switched from their main guns to machine guns, and our tank turrets spun around spraying bullets in every direction and rumbling in a constant purr.

DAVE TRYBULA (Charlie Tank, Task Force 1-64 Armor)
At 0245 I began pulling my platoon out of its hasty defensive fighting positions and headed back toward the company commander's tank to take the lead in the company's formation. The foggy darkness made our night vision devices range to only fifty feet. The only means of seeing was through the gunner's thermals. To see in a particular direction, we had to point the main gun that way. I didn't like pointing my gun at things we didn't intended to shoot. By 0300 hours, my platoon was in formation and we waited for the word.

While we waited like thoroughbreds before the Kentucky Derby, the battalion gave an intelligence update with the exact location of two enemy light infantry battalions and two tank companies in the vicinity of Jalibah Airfield. I plotted these locations on the map, and I ensured all my tank commanders had the same information. I also told them to switch to sabot after firing their first HEAT round.

The attack began with my company trailing as the task force reserve, and it stayed that way until the lead company was in range to set up a support-by-fire position near the airfield. As Delta Tank, the lead company, set the base and oriented north-northeast, Alpha Mech and Charlie Mech moved to reinforce them.[16] A platoon and the executive officer from Alpha Mech broke west to provide flank security. The task force was to leave a kilometer gap for my company to move through in order to assault the enemy's flank.

As Delta set the base, the task force commander ordered my company to "punch left." We began a bold movement to the west to gain an assault position on the enemy's flank. The two mechanized infantry companies relieved Delta Tank, which joined us in the assault position. This created an L-shaped brigade formation as Task Force 3-15 stampeded the enemy directly to the north.

When the commander ordered the envelopment, I quickly turned west to push through the gap that Alpha Mech was supposed to create on our flank. The company was racing behind me. As I approached Alpha Mech, I could clearly see them firing toward the airfield. Knowing the gap was to the west, I angled more to the left and rapidly found the point of penetration. Instead of being one kilometer wide, the gap was closer to five hundred meters, and our forces were firing directly across it. Realizing the danger of crossing there, I started moving west and reported the situation to my commander. "Black Six, the flank platoon of Alpha Mech is split only a little but is oriented back toward the airfield and is firing at this time. I am executing movement to the west of the entire unit and will not shoot the gap."

"Roger, Red One, execute. Rogue Six has called in a smoke mission where you are to execute your turn."

As I closed on Alpha Mech's flank platoon, I made sure that they saw me and understood my company's intention not to pass through the gap but to move around it. Maneuvering past them, I was now in the lead. There was no one in front of me to guide off and no visible security. There was just open desert and the sounds of firing tanks, Bradleys, and artillery thundering across the battlefield. The white phosphorus round hit just in the distance, showing me where to turn east. When my platoon started to receive mortar fire, we closed our loaders' hatches, leaving only the tank commanders exposed so we could better maintain command and control and prevent fratricide. As we neared the smoking remains of the white phosphorus shell, we turned and headed for the main runway. The remainder of the company moved on line and continued rolling toward the assault position. I could now see the fence around the outer edge of the airfield. The fence was made of simple chain-link, seven or eight feet in height, attached to cinder-block pillars. Each pillar was four inches by four inches. As we approached, I told my driver to center on one of the pillars in order to concentrate the whole force of the tank at a single impact point. We crushed the pillar like papier-mâché.

The fence clung to the mine plow mounted on my tank's front slope and was dragging alongside my vehicle. There was a real possibility of the fence becoming entangled in the track and disabling my tank. Before I had time to figure out a solution, my wingman accelerated his tank forward on my right side and stopped on the fence. As my tank moved forward, his halted tank created enough tension to snap the fence. He repeated the same procedure on my left side. With the fence now gone, we reached the main runway and stopped to establish an assault position. We waited for Delta to arrive on our right. I saw Task Force 3-15 continuing the attack in the north.

ALEX VERNON (Delta Mech, Task Force 3-15 Infantry)

The shaking tank, shaken by the ground reverberating from the artillery barrage against the airfield several kilometers away, woke me. It was still dark. Behind me, to the west, the horizon flashed white when our artillery fired — the white streaks from the MLRS missiles like laser beams streaming overhead, so close they seemed that I felt an urge to reach up and touch them — then before me, to the east, the horizon flashed orange when the rounds impacted. I remember retreating behind the tank against the morning chill with my gunner, talking with Sergeant Dock about the devastating amount of ordnance falling on the enemy while we basked comfortably in the warmth of the tank's turbine exhaust. The next thing I remember, the task force is in formation rolling toward the objective. Ahead of us the ground peaked into a military horizon; once we rolled over that rise, we would be able to see the airfield.

A tank main gun fired. It had come from Bravo Tank, my armor company, on the battalion box's upper left front. Captain Baillergeon reported that an Iraqi truck had been spotted and fired upon. Later I learned that the firing tank did not have time to call for permission, as the truck had almost crossed the military horizon and gone out of sight. It had to be destroyed before it could get word to the airfield's defenders of our attack. We peaked shortly thereafter and saw the airfield several kilometers below us.

About halfway to the airfield I made my move, breaking right and increasing speed to come on line on Alpha Tank's right. I was the task force's rightmost unit; once we hit the airfield I was to link with Task Force 1-64's leftmost unit and assault down the runways. As we approached the fence I saw the leftmost 1-64 unit, which I presumed to be Delta Tank — I may have seen the identifying sideways triangle markings on their track skirts — to my right. Our two companies were angled toward one another, toward the same space. Behind my platoon and Delta's lead platoon the companies were already cramming together with no room to pull up into a line formation and much more vulnerable to indirect fires. I veered left to make room.

Just before we struck the fence, Private Brunner, my loader, pointed to the gun, and I yanked back the commander's override joystick control for the main gun, putting the gun tube in the air so it would clear the top of the fence — otherwise the gun would have struck the fence before the tank, which at the very least would have thrown the MRS boresight. On the tip of the gun, the muzzle reference system is set during boresighting so that if combat throws off a gun's boresight, a gunner can quickly do an MRS update to restore some measure of accuracy by "reminding" the gun where to point. Like any memory system, this one wasn't perfect, but we didn't need to worsen matters by ramming it head-first into a fence post.

Past the fence a lone concrete building and a few underground bunkers, only their sandbag tops visible, lay between my platoon and the airfield. Sergeant Dock asked to fire on the building; I issued the command: "Fire and adjust." In a billow of smoke the front wall disappeared. We rolled past. I didn't see the sandbag-covered bunker directly in the tank's path until we were too close to fire it up with a HEAT round, and the coax machine gun would have been in-effective against such a deep and fortified position. I could try to dodge it, po-tentially screwing the formation behind us and allowing Iraqi infantry to pop out of the bunker after we passed, with easy shots at our rear; I could attempt to straddle the bunker, exposing the tank's thin underbelly to whoever inhabited the bunker; or I could order my driver to aim one tread at the bunker and squash it. "Hit the bunker, Reynolds. Crush it." We hardly noticed the bump.

NEAL CREIGHTON (Alpha Tank, Task Force 3-15 Infantry)

We weren't firing and there were targets everywhere. "Sergeant Davis, we have MIGs and choppers. Fire the sabot in the tube at that bunker. Carrol, load HEAT until I tell you different."

Sergeant Davis fired the main gun, and a 120-mm armor-piercing sabot round sped across the field and slammed into a bunker and out the other side, the concussion probably killing anyone inside. Carrol loaded HEAT as my pla-toon erupted in a volley of fire. "Sir, I got a chopper," Davis screamed.

"Let me see." I moved down and checked through the sight. "Okay, it's a HIND, fire!" The round hit squarely on the chopper, and it disintegrated into a ball of flame.

I moved back up to look out. "All white elements, this is White Six, I want all tank commanders up unless you're clearing fires — otherwise we will shoot each other, our formation is too tight!" Fear had caused a number of vehicle commanders to stay down within the protection of their turret armor. In that position, they were unable to see adjacent vehicles and were hitting each other with their coaxial machine guns and near-missing each other with main gun rounds. My tank commanders followed instructions and popped back out of their hatches.

My wingman, Sergeant Jones, was deadly. He shot two helicopters and a MIG before my own tank could get a round off at them. The company hit the center of the field and bypassed a T-55 hidden in a berm complex. The enemy tank opened fire at our rear. Within two hundred meters of the enemy tank, Sergeant Harris traversed his main gun over the rear and fired. The T-55 exploded and we moved on. At that range it had probably filled his entire sight picture. No need to lase for distance.

Enemy infantry tried to hide in shallow bunkers and some tried to surrender. Most that moved were quickly cut down under a swath of machine gun fire. The burning helicopters, jets, and dead soldiers seemed almost unreal. Task Force 3-15 rammed through the fence on the northeastern side and left the airfield perimeter. To our rear we left behind the burning wreck of Jalibah Airfield. My soldiers were alive. It was the happiest moment of my life.

ROB HOLMES (Delta Tank, Task Force 1-64 Armor)
This was wild. Iraqis were everywhere. While Sergeant Downing sprayed rounds at the enemy dismounts, I searched for heavy targets like tanks that could do real damage.

I shouldn't have dismissed the immediate threat. Underberg jumped into the turret and pulled me down from inside after him. He screamed and pointed out the hatch. I looked up and heard bullets flying overhead. Some enemy dismounts had gotten behind our tank. Not good. Antitank weapons work best when fired at the tank's rear, where the armor is thinner. A tank's design is a balance of three variables: firepower, maneuverability, and survivability. The more armor, the more survivable, but the less maneuverable. The armor is thinnest at the least likely target areas: the bottom of the hull, the top of the turret, and the rear. Dismounted enemy, therefore, try to get in behind a tank to fire missiles at its rear.

Underberg jumped up into the whistling bullets, swung his machine gun to the rear, and let loose a burst of his own. Underberg wasn't even thinking; he was just fighting. To this day I marvel at the bravery of my men. When he ran out of ammo, he dropped back down into the turret. Another batch of enemy bullets flew over our hatches.

Sergeant Downing meanwhile was engaging targets to our front and searching for Iraqi tanks that could have wrecked our day with one shot. I still needed to deal with this punk rag to my rear. Captain Hubner had bailed me out of varying degrees of trouble ever since he'd taken command of Delta Tank, and I needed another favor.

"Black Six, this is White One; I got a dismount behind me. Can you get him?" Hubner replied from behind us by opening up with his coax machine gun. It was only a quick burst. After a pause, I heard his main gun fire.

"I got him." Hubner radioed calmly. I later learned his gunner's coax had jammed, so he had switched to his main gun and pumped a 120-mm sabot round through the Iraqi grunt. He got him all right. *Vaporized* is Dave Hubner's word for what he saw — one instant there was a man in front of his tank, and the next instant nothing.

Flash ordered the battalion to sweep to the left around the hangars and charge down the runways. This was classic Gordon: bold maneuver and attack, attack, attack. No one hated being caught up in the hangars with enemy grunts crawling all over us more than Flash. I led my tanks around the hangar complex. One hundred meters to my left, my platoon sergeant was crushing bunkers and anti-tank weapons beneath his tread. His turret was traversing smoothly right and left, discharging main gun rounds about every ten seconds.

He looked over at me and smiled. Sfc. Randy Sikes was one cool customer. All hell was breaking loose around him, but he could still find a way to give a nod of comfort to his young lieutenant. While I took a half a second to remember how lucky I was to have him in my platoon, he pulled out a camera and took a picture of me! After that, I wouldn't have been surprised if he got out a thermos of coffee and taken a little break while his gunner took out more targets.

"Choppers!" My wingman, Sergeant Garback, shouted across the radio. He had rounded a corner and found four helicopters lined up on the runway. Garback was from Lexington, Kentucky, and usually had a wad of tobacco in his mouth. Now was no different. As I looked over, his tank fired at the nearest chopper, and the target exploded. From his commander's hatch, Garback discharged a stream of spit. Then Third Platoon, like a shark feeding frenzy, unloaded on the remaining three. Jeff White in his Alabama drawl calmly sent his report to Captain Hubner: "Black Six, this is Blue One; three choppers destroyed, 0730, continuing mission, over."

"Save some for us, Bambi!" my loader radioed anonymously to Jeff. Anonymously, yet unmistakably Underberg.

Sergeant Downing continued engaging targets at will. Underberg had reloaded his 7.62 mm, and when he wasn't slamming the next round in the tube for Downing, he was at his weapon spraying dismounts. Bell just kept driving. Before any maneuver, I always would go over the mission with my driver and let him get a good look at the map. Bell had a high IQ and was a very quick study. He always knew what we were trying to do and could generally be counted on to drive without a whole lot of supervision.

My platoon rolled down the runways. I looked over, and parallel to us was my roommate, Al Vernon, and his four M1s. I had seen him only twice since August. We made eye contact, and he gave a little wave. We kept rolling and firing. Seven months ago, our lives had revolved around beer and girls, and wondering if we would ever get any field time. Well that had certainly changed.

My platoon reached the end of the runway, having blasted everything in our path. Flash ordered Delta Tank to set up defensive positions and let the infantry root through all that we had shot up. I love grunts. They are great to have around for stuff like this. I saw my classmate, Mark Jennings, dashing around with his platoon, herding prisoners and clearing bunkers.

After a wild-as-hell forty-five minutes, a calm settled over the battlefield. I pulled myself up out of my hatch, sat on my turret, and drank a canteen of water. Underberg popped open a Mountain Dew. Bell jumped out of his hatch to take a leak and quickly check the track on his tank. Downing was already asleep inside the turret. The last hour had been pretty crazy. I looked over at my other tanks. The crews were stretching, walking around, and shaking off the fury. Some were shaking their heads; others were reenacting the battle with hand gestures; Howard was yelling at someone. Thank God. Everyone seemed to be okay.

DAVE TRYBULA (Charlie Tank, Task Force 1-64 Armor)
I set my tank on the center runway and began to scan for targets. We rapidly spotted several enemy aircraft sitting on the tarmac. My platoon sergeant called me and requested permission to fire. I told him to open fire, then reported to the commander that we were in contact with the enemy. An enemy HIND-D attack helicopter was hit with a HEAT round and vanished in flames. My gunner next identified a MIG-23 aircraft and was ready to engage. I dropped down and looked through my sight. As I told him to fire, I saw a sabot round go through it. We were too late — someone else had hit the bull's eye. My platoon erupted in a volley of fire, hitting enemy targets at will. Then we were told to move forward. The entire airfield was on fire. The action so far had seemed to take fewer than fifteen minutes.

As Task Force 3-15 finished its violent charge in the north, my commander issued another order: "Execute assault, keep it slow and deliberate, make sure you are on line with the guy on your left and right." As we started rolling forward, someone started humming "The Battle Hymn of the Republic" over the radio. The music gave me chills as we finished off the enemy at close range.

I made sure I could see all of my tank commanders out of their hatches as we started to engage Iraqi tanks to our front. The tanks were so well dug into the ground it was almost impossible to identify them until we were right on top of them. Fortunately, their positions were pointed south, and we were assaulting from the west. I saw an enemy tank emerging from the ground: "Enemy tank direct front." I grabbed the override and slewed the gun onto the tank. "Do you see it?"

My gunner responded, "Identified, I got it sir!" Letting go of the override, I yelled "Fire!" Sergeant Godfrey pulled the trigger. I watched our sabot round hit the enemy vehicle. The tank exploded. The sabot round had caused a catastrophic kill.

We were straddling the runway and devastating the enemy. Within minutes my platoon had shot fifteen tanks, two MIGs, and one helicopter. This was significant work for my four tanks. Most important, all my soldiers were alive.

As we continued to push forward, my platoon was on line with Task Force 3-15 to the north and Third Platoon from my company and Delta Tank to the south. Second Platoon and the headquarters tanks from my company were behind us because there just was not enough space on the airfield to fit them on line with us. This was extremely dangerous because the trailing tanks were shooting between the tanks in front of them. Mostly the tank commanders stayed up, out of their hatches, so they could maintain awareness, but in at least one case the tank commander sat in his seat inside his turret to look through his sights with his gunner when he gave the command to fire, without having ensured they were clear of friendly personnel. I know this because that sabot round whistled by so close to me that its wake picked me up off of the tank commander's seat that I was standing on. I had to catch myself on the vision blocks around the hatch to stop from falling to the turret floor on my way back down. I called that tank commander on the radio and told him to get control of his tank.

As the battle finished, I updated my commander on what had happened. We were sitting on the east side of the airfield. Out of the blue, a master sergeant came over to my tank carrying a tape recorder and a notepad. He told me that he was an army historian. I thought he had lost his marbles. There was no way a historian would be here so soon. I made a radio call in order to verify the historian's identity and then we sat down on top of my tank and talked [17] The brigade was waiting while 1st Brigade moved north across our front heading for the Tallil Airfield. During this time we called the support platoon forward to top us off with fuel and ammunition. We expected the worst was yet to come and wanted every bullet possible when the big fight with the Republican Guard Divisions came.

ALEX VERNON (Delta Mech, Task Force 3-15 Infantry)

Rounds of some sort ricocheted off the right side of my turret. I felt fairly safe. I had ordered my tank commanders to ride open-protected for the attack, though I think that most other tank commanders assaulting the airfield rode with their hatch fully open. The tank commander's hatch has three positions: open, open-protected, and closed (buttoned-up). In the open position, the hatch is swung open and locked vertically behind the commander, covering his back and allowing him to stand on his seat and out of the hatch from the waist up. With the hatch closed, the commander must sit in his seat and use periscopes that peer out at the base of the cupola to see. The open-protected position is the compromise between the vision of the open position and the safety of the closed. The hatch locks horizontally several inches above the commander's head. He stands on the bottom of the commander's platform, with overhead cover and about six inches between the top of the cupola and the bottom of the hatch by which he can see the battlefield. Given the speed of our attack, a bullet or piece of shrapnel had only a very slight window of opportunity on any of my commanders. From the time we crashed through fence, my platoon's loaders had been down in the turret, doing their job, heaving rounds into the breech, and unexposed to rounds and shrapnel. Occasionally one of them might pop out of his hatch to help the tank commander scan for targets and threats wherever the gunner wasn't looking, wherever the main gun wasn't pointed.

I also saw rounds striking the ground beside my tank, "walking" in the direction of the attack. I called Baillergeon and told him to call off any Bradleys firing — they were at this point still behind my tanks and had no business shooting through my platoon. I don't know if what I saw striking the ground had come from friendly Bradleys, and I have a hard time imagining them shooting the ground fifty meters to their front. It could have been shrapnel from Iraqi mortar rounds (which I didn't know were fired at us until reading these other accounts while writing this book), though once I called Baillergeon, the problem stopped. After the battle, Staff Sergeant Rivera bragged about his "window shot," which at first I didn't understand. He apparently had not only shot out of his sector but also *between* my and Sfc. Freight's tanks. From his place in the platoon wedge to my left rear, Rivera's round had flown behind me and in front of Freight, who trailed me on my right. What I saw divoting the desert to my right could have been the shoes from his sabot round. A sabot round is a dart of depleted uranium with a diameter much smaller than the 120-mm gun that shoots it. It has a pair of "shoes" that fit around either side of the dart, giving it the proper 120-mm diameter while the projectile shoots down the tube. Once the round leaves the gun the shoes fall away, like the space shuttle's booster rockets. I told Rivera to never do that again.

When I had veered left at the fence, to make room for the converging companies, I must have veered too far. My platoon, with my company behind me, never linked up with Task Force 1-64, and never found the runway.[18] We crept slowly along what must have been the north side of the complex. A series of buildings stood to our immediate right, and between these I saw open space with some Abrams in the distance, what could have been the airfield proper, where I was supposed to be. The Bradleys of Bravo Mech — or maybe the Bravo Mech Bradleys attached to Alpha Tank, the unit that was supposed to be on my immediate left — fired their 25-mm chain guns on anything and everything that wasn't a good guy, once on a rust-red cylindrical storage tank on stilts not twenty meters from me. The storage tank smoked but did not explode; it had probably stored water instead of fuel — not that the trigger-happy Bradley gunner could have known it. We drove beyond the buildings and into an open space — this too may have been the airfield, though again I never saw any tarmac. We rolled east, Task Force 1-64 somewhere in the south to my right, and Bravo Mech (as I recall thinking) on my immediate left (though if we at all managed to maneuver according to the plan, Alpha Tank — with a platoon from Bravo Mech — was the unit on my left). You could still see the fence marking the northern edge of the airfield several kilometers away. The tops of antiaircraft guns poked out of the ground. Dug-in positions, protected by sandbags, also pitted the area. Sergeant Dock fired his second main gun round at one of the antiaircraft guns and joined the rest of the platoon in spraying the dug-in positions with coax machine gun rounds. Brunner may have fired some 7.62 from his loader's position as well. I never bothered to fire my M2 .50 caliber; it was too unwieldy for such close quarters, there were no valid targets for it which the tank's two 7.62 machine guns couldn't handle, and I had a formation to control and a company to lead.

I don't remember the two Bradley platoons of my company-team ever coming fully on line for the course of the battle. We kept more or less in our company wedge formation. The battle was over by 1000 hours, according to a letter I wrote several days later. I did not see a single enemy soldier.

On the eastern side of the airfield we halted in formation. Fuel trucks came forward. Sergeant Freight gathered ammunition expenditure information over the platoon net, added the numbers, and relayed it to First Sergeant Binion over the company net. My crew heard what he reported and knew he had added wrong. I radioed Freight on the platoon net and told him to try again. Again, he reported a bad total count to Top. "Jesus Christ, sir," muttered Dock. At my tank was Vanderwerker, my old driver, who busted a gut laughing at Freight. Said Freight needed to enroll in a remedial math class. I didn't respond to Vanderwerker. With the eyes of the crew on me, I called Freight on the platoon net and told him the correct numbers to give to the first sergeant. My four tanks had fired a total of eight main gun rounds. If we had fired more rounds than Freight had fingers to count them, I might have felt more forgiving.

We listened to some small arms fire from the airfield behind us; a number of Iraqis had hid in their bunkers and hangars and emerged after we had swept by. Friendly infantry — either some of ours sent back or from a following unit — were clearing the objective while we ate lunch, cleaned our weapons, and took on ammunition.

GREG DOWNEY (Scouts, Task Force 1-64 Armor)

I watched as Task Forces 1-64 and 3-15 rumbled across the far side of the airfield. I felt like I was sitting on the bench at a basketball game. I wanted to be up there with them — until a radio transmission brought me back to reality.

"Rogue Six, this is Hammer Six," came a distress call over the task force radio frequency. This was the Charlie Mech commander, Capt. Bob Hamowitz. He sounded pretty shaken up. "Rogue Six, Rogue Six, this is Hammer Six, I'm taking casualties! Receiving fire! Receiving fire!"

"This is Rogue Six, settle down or you're going to lose more soldiers." Gordon was trying to bring Captain Hamowitz to his senses. Three M2 Bradleys had taken direct hits from behind.

ROB HOLMES (Delta Tank, Task Force 1-64 Armor)

I didn't have a scratch, but I was exhausted. The fuelers and ammo trucks quickly arrived and replenished the tanks. I jumped off my M1 and walked over to Sfc. Sikes. He was sitting on the turret with his coffee thermos. He looked like he had just finished a run at a gunnery range for the thousandth time. Sikes made a pretty weird sight, sitting on his tank drinking coffee while the airfield burned behind him and choppers flew above. He told me he would get me a copy of the picture he had taken when we got home. He also added that he would get the logistics reports from the platoon after he finished his coffee.

I walked over to Captain Hubner's tank. He was devouring an MRE while still in his hatch. He needed a shave, a new uniform, and about a month of sleep. He looked like the rest of us.

"How are you, Robert?" Hubner had been under a lot of stress from the weight of command and the expectations from Flash. Now, however, he was smiling and eating as we rehashed the battle.

In a cloud of dust, Rogue Six rode onto the scene. Hubner looked at me as he stuffed an entire chocolate bar into his mouth. "Back to work," he mumbled.

Flash jumped out of his hatch and stood on top of the turret, surveying the destruction. He then dismounted and walked over to us, cracking a smile at me and nodding with a gruff "Lieutenant Holmes" as he looked up at Hubner.

"It's over, Dave." Flash proclaimed. Perhaps he forgot we were still deep inside Iraq. He looked at me and announced, "We beat 'em to the river. We can turn east and crush them head on."

He was right. The 24th Infantry Division had won the race to the Euphrates and could now meet and destroy the Republican Guard as they fled Kuwait. Saddam's forces couldn't hide in the desert, and now they couldn't run either.

I left Hubner and Flash and walked back over to my tank. Along the way I saw a West Point classmate, John Ford, being escorted to one of the medic choppers. He had taken an AK-47 round while we were mired in the hangars. He was walking fine and his arm was already bandaged up, though he had a pretty bad grimace on his face. We made eye contact, and he managed a slight nod as he climbed aboard the chopper. His father had won a Purple Heart in Vietnam; now John has one, too.

A calmness settled over the battlefield. Buildings were burning, choppers were buzzing above us and grunts hustling around us, but it was better than the past hour. Regrettably, the calm didn't last.

"Cease fire! Cease fire! Cease fire!" Captain Hubner screamed into the radio.

No one in Delta Tank was shooting. No one was even moving. First and Third Platoons were relaxing outside their tanks just as we were. It was very unusual for Hubner to sound this frantic on the radio. Dave could certainly get excited, but we had all grown used to his calmness and politeness. He ordered his platoon leaders to switch to the battalion frequency immediately.

A sickening feeling settled in on the task force. As 1-64 and 3-15 assaulted the airfield, the brigade commander had held Task Force 3-69 Armor in reserve, in a support-by-fire position south of the airfield. After our tanks had raced down the runways, a platoon of our infantry Bradleys pulled into the hangar complex to kill or capture anything we had missed. Tanks from 3-69, from about twenty-five hundred meters south of Jalibah, misidentified the Brads as enemy vehicles still in action. In about ten seconds, friendly sabot rounds obliterated three of the four Bradleys. Americans had been killed by Americans.

Fratricide is an awful subject. Better communication, coordination, and rehearsals can reduce it, but the fact remains: Warriors have suffered from friendly fire accidents since the days of bows and arrows. Later, I heard many versions of what happened, but I really don't think any of us even cared who did it. We all hated that it happened.

I watched from atop my turret as the choppers flew in to evacuate the wounded. I saw the horrible sight of full body bags for the first time. About a dozen men were wounded and six were killed. It was an awful feeling. Until now, we had always moved on before anyone had time to process the casualties, who had always been dead Iraqis anyway.

As if this wasn't enough, Delta Tank's first sergeant, Randy Walker, walked up with a horrible look of disgust. Having just processed a group of prisoners, he was shaking his head as he told me these Iraqis had been captured barefoot with bloody feet, some with cut Achilles' tendons. They had no choice but to fight; they could hardly walk.

I looked over at a pathetic assembly of prisoners crying out as our medics tended to them. The Middle East is another world. I just wanted to finish this job and get back to Georgia.

GREG DOWNEY (Scouts, Task Force 1-64 Armor)

Our first fratricide incident had just occurred. As we discovered later, a company from Task Force 3-69 Armor had engaged what they thought were enemy vehicles; instead, they were friendly ones from my task force. Two soldiers died, several were injured. A terrible waste of lives at the hands of our own people.[19]

Objective Orange was secured at 0730 hours. Isolated pockets of resistance were still present on the airfield, but every enemy tank or BMP was destroyed. My scout platoon moved forward to screen east of the task force.

ALEX VERNON (Delta Mech, Task Force 3-15 Infantry)

According to the division's postwar *Victory Book,* some two thousand Iraqi soldiers, eighty antiaircraft guns, twenty aircraft, several helicopters, and a tank battalion were "knocked out of action" during the fight for Jalibah. Another source cites Colonel Kern, our brigade commander, in its claim that about one thousand Iraqis defended Jalibah: Approximately 150 were killed, the rest captured, and twenty-four T-55 tanks were destroyed.[20]

While Delta Mech refitted, Captain Baillergeon vanished to the task force TOC for orders, and when he returned he called his platoon leaders to his track. We were going to continue east on a movement to contact mission; our objective was not a piece of ground, in other words, but any Iraqi units we happened across. Division expected us to encounter a Republican Guard Division.[21] The RG were touted as Iraq's best. Furthermore, battalion only carried with it one full replacement set of M-1 main gun rounds, and that was now substantially diminished without guarantee that the battalion stores would be able to restock from the division's support battalions before our next fight. When I briefed the order to the platoon's tank commanders, I instructed them that all fires had to receive my permission, except in the case of immediate danger. I wanted tight control over my ammunition. I did not want to waste rounds and then run out in the middle of a tank battle.

By noon or so Task Force 3-15 continued mission. South of us, to our right, Task Force 1-64 paralleled our move.[22]

27 February 1991 (G+3): After Jalibah

ALEX VERNON (Delta Mech, Task Force 3-15 Infantry)

Just east of Jalibah sat a large storage site surrounded by a fence. Partially underground storage areas were visible as rows of humps. As we approached the site, Captain Baillergeon ordered me to pull alongside the company to my front left — Bravo Mech, I think, or maybe Alpha Tank. I refused. A number of the Bradley turrets of the platoon I was to pull beside were pointed ninety degrees off their right side, where Baillergeon wanted me to go. I was remembering the Bradleys' wild shooting at nothing at Jalibah and refused to move until those turrets spun forward. It took several minutes, and several repetitions of my request, before all the Bradley guns faced forward and I moved up.

A main gun blast from my right surprised me. I looked over to see the smoke dissipating around Sfc. Freight's gun tube. Out of the blue, he had fired at a truck clearly out of range. I chastised him over the platoon net for engaging without my permission. I reminded the platoon of the ammunition shortage. We were expecting to hit the Republican Guard units, armed with T-72s, the best tanks in the Iraqi inventory. My gunner also spotted two trucks on the horizon, in the storage area, retreating from our advance. Dock wanted to shoot. But the range demanded a main gun round over machine gun, the trucks were in fact on the edge of the main gun's range, we needed to conserve our main gun rounds, and the trucks presented no threat to us. They were fleeing the battle. I did not let him shoot.

We passed on the north side of the storage site and pushed east following an unbelievably high powerline strung along gigantic steel beam towers. The terrain was as flat as any we had seen in the Middle East. We stopped once, when the scouts identified several occupied enemy bunkers. Lieutenant Colonel Barrett chose to deploy the battalion mortars against them, even though the scouts were danger-close. I am thinking now that some of the mortar rounds did indeed fall dangerously close to the scouts. I believe the bunkers were eventually taken out by TOW missiles from either the scouts or one of the infantry companies' Bradleys.

GREG DOWNEY (Scouts, Task Force 1-64 Armor)
Operational graphics were now issued over the radio. We had very few graphic control measures beyond Objective Orange. The GIRS points we plotted on our maps before the ground attack became critical. We drew lines from one point to the next, much like a connect-the-dots puzzle. As the lines were drawn on the map, I could see we were headed toward Basra, Iraq, located at the tip of the Persian Gulf.

Maj. Ken Boyd, the task force executive officer, issued a fragmentary order to me. Objective Storage was an unplanned mission. We would conduct an area recon of it and report back to battalion. We arrived at Objective Storage at 1300 hours. I could see enemy soldiers running around the area. Objective Storage was an ammunition depot that covered a square kilometer. A huge powder keg.

"Sir, I've got infantry running for cover," Lowther reported over the intercom. My gunner was not as nervous and jittery as he was when the ground attack first started.

"West, slow down, I don't want to get too close. Pull around to the right of that high ground. Stay low, slow down!" I said to my driver, trying to keep some terrain between my vehicle and the Iraqi soldiers who had already spotted me.

"Blue Five, follow me," I called to Staff Sergeant Hightower, my wingman, who was covering my movement from a few hundred meters away.

I ordered the platoon sergeant's Blue Section to get a closer look while I maneuvered my section around the south side. As I worked my way around the area, I started receiving direct fire from an S-60 antiaircraft gun.

"Damn, sir, that's awful close," West offered from the driver's seat.

"West, get us moving! Go, go, go!" I hollered back, trying to steer the vehicle over the intercom.

Sand was flying into the vehicle as the incoming rounds impacted nearby. I moved to the first piece of low ground I could find. The gunner on the S-60 lost sight of my section, but I had backed myself into a corner. We had no way out without being seen. I radioed Sfc. Smith, the platoon sergeant, and instructed him to get some artillery firing on the target. I received no response. He had not been very dependable prior to the ground attack, and I knew he was not going to help me out now.

"Lowther, watch the radios. Tell Rogue Six what's going on up here. I'll be right back." I climbed out the hatch.

"Where the hell you going, sir?" Lowther asked, trying to figure out what had just happened.

I dismounted my vehicle, low-crawled up to the higher ground with a pair of binoculars and compass, and tried to observe the target. The S-60 was only about four hundred meters away. The enemy had heard us coming and waited for me to come around a berm before engaging. Luckily for us, the S-60 is an antiaircraft weapon, not designed for ground battles. It is slow, and the gunner does not have much protection.

I radioed my polar plot to the task force FSO. It took only about three or four minutes for the eight-inch rounds to land on the target. I made sure the FSO knew my section was danger-close, and he relayed the message to the artillery battalion. The first volley destroyed everything. Secondary explosions went off inside the ammunition depot. I contacted the FSO for more artillery and made adjustments that would destroy the entire area.

I watched as Iraqi soldiers ran from bunker to bunker, wagering their lives on where they thought the next artillery barrage would land. Looking through my binoculars, I could see their faces and sense their fear. It was strange being within shouting distance of these guys but experiencing nothing close to what they were going through. I felt like I was watching a movie, totally detached from the agony and suffering.

Lieutenant Colonel Gordon wanted the battalion mortar platoon to fire some missions for me. I called a polar plot to the mortar platoon leader, and the mortars fired a few missions. They had just pulled out of their firing points when artillery impacted right on top of them. I saw and heard the rounds impact behind my position, not knowing the mortar platoon was the target. The FSO found out that our division artillery counterbattery radar had picked up the mortar rounds' trajectory signature, assumed they were Iraqi, and called a mission on them. Fortunately, we did not sustain any losses, but our artillery units learned a valuable lesson. I later discovered that during Desert Shield a memorandum had been passed down to artillery and mortar units, cautioning them about friendly mortars being identified as enemy artillery.

ROB HOLMES (Delta Tank, Task Force 1-64 Armor)

Division Intelligence detected an enemy position to our front. Flash ordered Delta Tank to stop and await fuel while he moved the battalion's mortar platoon out in front of the diamond formation. He ordered them to launch a volley at the objective to soften them up before we hit them with the tanks. Fine with me. We needed fuel, and I needed sleep. It would take the mortars probably thirty minutes to execute the movement and fire, so I had some time. I sank down into my hatch, leaned against my .50-cal sight, and was asleep immediately.

I woke to an exploding horizon and rounds landing one hundred meters in front of my platoon. I was beginning to wonder if I would ever sleep again. Waking up was hell. I jumped up and saw flame, smoke, and sand, and the mortar platoon racing past us to the rear.

Bell already had the engine started, but before moving he asked excitedly, "Sir, can I back up?" Tank drivers never reverse without permission because they can't see anything to their rear. In this case, however, Bell's courtesy was really annoying.

"Get us out of here, Bell!" I ordered my platoon back and radioed Black Six.

Captain Hubner responded nonchalantly, "Rogue Six says not to worry — that's friendly artillery."

I didn't give a hoot in hell about the origin of the artillery. Its destination, on the other hand, was damn relevant. My platoon stopped about five hundred meters back and watched the rounds fall smack dab where the mortars had been and just in front of where I had taken my little siesta. Thank God our arty was slow because they were definitely accurate. Had the counterbattery strike come just a couple minutes earlier, they would have been successful.

DAVE TRYBULA (Charlie Tank, Task Force 1-64 Armor)

Leaving Jalibah on our way east toward Basra, the task force identified an enormous ammunition stockpile, something like twenty-two acres of ammunition, and called artillery fire upon it. Unfortunately, the artillery rounds would not start the ammunition on fire, so the mortar platoon was called to the flank of the task force to do a quick hip shoot with white phosphorous rounds to ignite the ammo. The mortars rapidly positioned themselves, hung two rounds each, and departed the area. No sooner had the mortars cleared the area than an incredible mass of artillery rounds came crashing down on the area. The mortars were out of the area just in time to avoid injury from our division's counterbattery fire.

GREG DOWNEY (Scouts, Task Force 1-64 Armor)

My scout platoon moved around Objective Storage, now ablaze from secondary explosions within the ammo dump. The task force had closed in on us, closer than I preferred. We were encountering numerous bunker complexes, therefore slowing my movement as we recon'd the zone.

"What was that?" West mumbled.

"Goddamnit, somebody is shooting at us!" I said, knowing it wasn't enemy.

The tracer of a tank round caught my eye as it blazed across the front of my vehicle, just under the barrel of my 25-mm chain gun. Glowing bright red as it flew away, it impacted down range from me.

I yelled over the battalion radio frequency to cease fire. Lieutenant Colonel Gordon asked who had fired the round. Captain Hubner, Delta Tank's commander, admitted it had been one of his tankers. One of his gunners had caught a glimpse of my turret as we worked our way through the bunkers and fired before correctly identifying the target. I wiped the sweat off my forehead. The incident was much too close for me. We had survived too much and too long to die from friendly fire. Rogue Six slowed the battalion so I could get the scouts farther forward of the task force.

We continued our zone recon up to BP 1-64. Encountering light resistance, we avoided bogging ourselves down with POWs and kept moving east. By 1800 hours, the task force intelligence officer reported that twenty-one Iraqi divisions had already been significantly destroyed. It seemed the war would be ending soon.

The scout platoon screened five kilometers forward of BP 1–64. We were overlooking a highway that initially did not have traffic on it. As the night passed, I started observing vehicles moving north on the road. Red Section was reporting artillery fire on its location, so I pulled them back. Gordon sent Charlie Mech forward to give me more direct firepower.

As the columns of vehicles approached, I gave my polar plots to the FSO over the radio. Calling for fire at night made determining the direction a little more challenging. I had devised a technique to determine target azimuth by placing a strip of luminous tape on the end of my vehicle's 25-mm gun barrel. My gunner would aim the main gun at the target, and from the top of my vehicle I would shoot an azimuth in the direction that the gun barrel pointed. I lined up my compass parallel to the glowing tape. My azimuth was always accurate. All I had to do then was estimate the distance to the target by using the reticle in the Bradley's thermal sight.

We waited to make sure that the targets were the enemy before we engaged them. The columns consisted of wheeled and tracked vehicles. As soon as my gunner identified a BMP, we requested artillery. The M2 Bradleys from Charlie opened up and dished havoc on the column. After about thirty minutes of direct and indirect fires, the enemy quit using the route. We had caught part of the Iraqi army by surprise during its withdrawal north.

The operational graphics were passed out over the radio net for our next mission. Staff Sergeant Deem came over to my vehicle to chat. We looked at the map graphics and the reports of heavy enemy armor in our zone. The Republican Guard was somewhere ahead.

"Deem, if we survive this battle tomorrow it will be a miracle," I soberly remarked. It probably was not the most professional thing to say to one of your soldiers, but we both knew it to be true. After being fired on by both enemy and friendly units, I felt our luck was about to run out. Deem evidently agreed.

"Shit, sir, this is longer than I thought we would live." He said it matter-of-factly, then rubbed his tired eyes with his dirty hands.

I stood there, trying to focus on the map, my eyes and my mind long past the threshold of effectiveness, totally fatigued by the last few days of nonstop activity. I was too exhausted, mentally and physically, to be afraid. Fear takes energy, and I simply didn't have any to spare. The darkness of the desert night hid the destruction going on around us. You could hear it though, artillery rounds landing in the distance, tanks firing, and fighter aircraft flying above.

ALEX VERNON (Delta Mech, Task Force 3-15 Infantry)

Our direction of attack took us through Iraqi farmland. MLRS missiles continued to streak overhead. Large berms and ditches, segregating the land into squares for irrigation purposes, made the area difficult to maneuver through. The battalion moved through these in two columns, both steering through the fields as best they could, occasionally colliding, occasionally almost losing sight of one another. We could not go around the farmland because we did not know its extent — it was not on any maps — and we did not want to deviate from our assigned axis, and risk moving into another unit's sector, or creating a detour that would take too much time to recover. We did our best to avoid mangling the farmland, steering around the perimeter of each square from one break in a berm to the next. Iraqi farmers — *fellaheen* — waved and clapped as we rolled through. One bearded, turbaned man with bright eyes and a huge smile tossed tomatoes up to us, which my loader Brunner and my gunner Dock ate like apples. Was he thanking us for so obviously sparing his farmland? For ending the war? For taking on Hussein? Maybe he was simply reaching out to us, tired man to tired men. I can't claim to really remember what those tomatoes looked like, but in my mind's eye they were large, plump, red, vine ripe, and blemish free. Their juice and seeds oozed down Brunner's face, which he wiped with the sleeve of his MOPP suit.

We stopped for the night at what must have been the eastern edge of the farmland. In the dark the battalion formed into a horseshoe-shaped hasty defense around a common engagement area. Captain Baillergeon sent a Bradley to drive the engagement area, a common procedure in preparing a defense, if one has the time. The vehicle driving around in the engagement area helps the rest of the company judge ranges, keys them to rises and dips in the terrain that the enemy might use for cover, allows platoons and sections to coordinate who can see and engage what areas of the battlefield, and reveals to the commander where he needs to preplot indirect fire (wherever his direct fire weapons can't target). It also identifies sectors of responsibility, and some vehicle commanders use it to practice crew gunning drills. We could also boresight our guns on the vehicle if it stood stationary long enough. That night this preparation drill was cut short when a Bradley in its defensive position reported two Iraqi BMP fighting vehicles in the engagement area. The Bradley driving the area saw nothing but sped back to its position. The company never acquired a clear fix on either BMP other than a few Loch Ness glimpses of what might have been something.

We were to move again at 0600 hours the next morning, maybe earlier, for an attack to our final objectives. On the way we expected to meet and do battle with the Hammurabi Armored Division, the only Republican Guard unit still combat-effective, estimated at 60-percent strength, and equipped with Iraq's best tanks, the T-72.[23]

I once again hit the back deck for my allotted sleep time. I was not there long when the ground shook with falling artillery, much closer than anything I had yet felt. It had to be Iraqi. I moved toward my hatch to listen to the radio. The next explosions rocked my tank — I jumped into my tank commander's position, bringing down the hatch and locking it behind me, faster than I ever had before. While Brunner closed his loader's hatch, I called "incoming" across the platoon net and heard myself echoed on the company net. Artillery terrifies tanks. Not only does it carry the threat of chemical and biological agents, it also comes from above, and the turret top has some of our thinnest armor. A few moments later the shelling lulled; I donned Kevlar and flak vest, ordered my crew to stay buttoned-up inside, and headed on foot to the commander's and the XO's Bradleys. We weren't using our radios unless we absolutely had to, so as not to give our position away, and I wanted to know what was going on. During my fast walk the shelling picked up again, though a little farther away. At the headquarters' section, I found the artillery officer assigned to the company, 2d Lt. Bill Lockard, on the radio and in a huff. I learned that the second round of shelling, the close call that had rocked my tank, had been our friendly response to the shelling begun by the Iraqis. Bill had heard an officer on the battalion's artillery fire support team call the mission to the artillery unit, and as the artillery fell on our position he realized that the coordinates he heard that officer or NCO give were the coordinates Bill had earlier reported to the battalion fire support team as our Delta Mech company-team's position. It took him several minutes to have the mission aborted. I still remember his fuming: "That idiot should lose his job over this. He ought to be relieved right now. Fucking moron. He ought to be court-martialed."

DAVE TRYBULA (Charlie Tank, Task Force 1-64 Armor)

As we closed on the city of Basra we halted short and moved all of the artillery forward in preparation of the attack toward the city. We reduced security to 50 percent so we could get some sleep before we started rolling again at 0500 the following morning. But all night long artillery and rockets shot from all directions around us toward Basra. We had a hard time sleeping. The time to depart came and went and we did not move; I was not sure what was going on, but the artillery had finally stopped shooting. As I looked to the sound of an MLRS launcher shooting its rockets, I noticed that the rockets did not have their normal trajectory. They looked like an Apollo moon shot and were actually ATACMs missiles being fired at great distances.

ROB HOLMES (Delta Tank, Task Force 1-64 Armor)

The sun was setting as we pulled into a hasty battle position and waited on more fuel and ammo. Captain Hubner summoned his three platoon leaders to his tank and told us that Saddam was trapped. Allied forces had pushed the Iraqis out of Kuwait and forced them smack into us. He also reported that a Republican Guard regiment was bottled up to our front, bounded by the Euphrates to the north and the allies to the south. He figured that this would be the final battle, but it could get pretty bloody.

Planes filled the sky and artillery shook the ground that night. Saddam's forces were getting pummeled. I settled in my hatch and waited for Hubner's call to attack. We had been baptized at Jalibah, but I could tell people were stressed about this next trial. We all sensed that things had gone well so far. My dad always joked about how the closer you got to a war, the less you knew what was going on. Nevertheless, we all knew where we were on the map and what that meant. It really was almost over. I just hoped no one started getting too cautious.

"All elements, this is Black Six," Hubner's voice broke the radio's silence. "As of 0600, fire only if fired upon. Repeat — fire only if fired upon."

What? I jumped off my tank and ran over to Hubner's. This was quite a change in the rules of engagement, and I didn't like it. I worried we were getting timid after the fratricide at Jalibah. I hated the friendly fire, but three hundred kilometers inside Iraq was no time to start tying our hands.

"What's up, sir?" I asked. Hubner was slouched on his turret eating an MRE.

"I think it's over. President Bush is speaking at midnight," he announced with a smile.

I yelled over to Underberg to get my beat-up old radio from my bags. Hubner and I trotted back over to my tank, arriving just in time to hear the distinctive *bing* preceding the commentator's classic opening, "2400 hours Greenwich Mean Time, this is the BBC World News." My tank commanders gathered around. The president's address was short and sweet: total surrender by the Iraqi forces in theater.

I couldn't believe it. I thought Desert Storm would last a month, two weeks at least. I never figured we could do it in four days! In one hundred hours, we had dismantled the fourth-largest army in the world. The 24th Infantry Division had traveled farther and faster than any division in military history, and Task Force 1-64 had led the way. Happy as we were, congratulations could wait. I was ready to get the hell out of Dodge and catch the first plane back to Georgia.

ALEX VERNON (Delta Mech, Task Force 3-15 Infantry)

At 0400 on 28 February, the task force began to assemble, fully expecting to hit an Iraqi division head-on that day. The artillery preparation for the morning attack had already begun. By 0430, Baillergeon relayed to the company that as of 0500, we were to cease fire on order of President Bush. The war was over. I felt some relief. But I had heard enough stories of the skirmishes still going on across the DMZ in Korea to stay wary. We were still deep in Iraq, between retreating Iraqi units and Baghdad. We were not yet home. My weapons remained locked and loaded.[24]

The Cease-Fire: 28 February–8 March 1991

Before this had come the news of the battle of Cambrai. There for the first time the Tanks had fought as we had always wished, across good ground, without a preliminary bombardment, and in large numbers — over 400. With their help General Byng had won what up to that time was the greatest victory of the war, the greatest in the territory gain and prisoners captured, and the greatest in its economy both of lives and ammunition.

— Lt. Col. Sir Albert G. Stern, Tanks *1914–1918: The Log-Book of a Pioneer*

ALEX VERNON (Delta Mech, Task Force 3-15 Infantry)

Our artillery barrage continued until exactly 0500;[25] later in the morning, rumors of approaching enemy armor started the shelling again.[26] We spent the morning in the same location we had spent the night. Delta Mech's infantry patrolled the immediate area and discovered a bunker complex, where they captured nine soldiers, including two colonels and one general. Some soldiers had not wanted to surrender because they had heard we would torture them before executing them — I remember talk of an Iraqi soldier either committing or threatening to commit suicide rather than be caught by us. Some of the Iraqi privates' identification cards revealed that they were all of fourteen years old. The complex proved a souvenir cornucopia: Our infantry found brand new 9-mm pistols still sealed in plastic, new boots, new jackets, wood-stocked AK-47s, folding AK-47s, money (the one bill with Hussein's picture), television monitors, typewriters, VCRs, and the general's oak desk. This apparently was a Republican Guard light infantry division command post. Captain Baillergeon made off with the general's rank insignia. After the war, I learned of an Iraqi officer found dead in a bunker, having been shot in the head at close range. The American officer who found him surmised that he'd been killed by an Iraqi soldier in his command.

My tankers pleaded to accompany the infantry on their next excursion to the bunker. I passed their request to Baillergeon, who summarily rejected it. Brian Luke, the First Platoon leader, kept us in mind and after his next trip brought some loot for us. Our first spoils. Brian gave me an Iraqi magazine and a Koran. He knew I liked books.

Baillergeon reported that in Bush's address to the nation on the cease-fire, the president described Hussein's confusion. Hussein didn't know the location or strength of his own units, and when he learned about the 24th sitting inside Iraq, he assumed we must be an airborne division. Other rumors I remember hearing around this time: The Iraqis at Jalibah thought our artillery preparation another air strike, some actually firing antiaircraft guns into the sky at nothing, and the rest leaving the safety of their bunkers when the arty prep stopped, thinking the air strike over, just in time to see us crash through the fence; and some Iraqi soldiers dubbed us the "Ghost Division" because we had materialized from the nowhere of the empty desert.

GREG DOWNEY (Scouts, Task Force 1-64 Armor)

For the first time since the start of the ground war, I reduced platoon security below 100 percent. I told my drivers, gunners, and track commanders to go to sleep. The rest of the crews manned the turrets and radios. Despite the excitement over the cease-fire, I immediately fell into a deep sleep.

Specialist Burton was standing over me when I woke. All I could understand was the order to move. I called the battalion TOC for details and was told to continue to recon east toward Basra. The cease-fire was in effect, but the scattered enemy may not have known that. I issued the rules of engagement that allowed us to engage any enemy that displayed hostile actions. Pretty broad criterion for ROE. We started out at about 1200 hours.

DAVE TRYBULA (Charlie Tank, Task Force 1-64 Armor)

Almost simultaneously with the order to cease offensive operations, we received the order to push east to occupy the outskirts of Basra. Cease offensive operations and move forward through enemy territory? I verified with Captain Hadjis that this did not restrict my ability to engage enemy targets encountered. The company's traveling formation spread out on line to cover the maximum width possible — we couldn't afford to bypass any pockets of resistance, equipment, or danger areas and leave them to surprise more vulnerable support units following us. We moved through abandoned bunker complexes and were heading east when Sgt. Steve Godfrey, my gunner, screamed for us to stop. He pointed out the half-uncovered mine directly to our front. I directed the platoon to drop its mine plows and clear lanes through the minefield. Before entering the minefield any farther, I backed up my tank to give our plow enough room to dig into the ground. I also reported the situation to the commander.

"Black Six, this is Red Six. Encountered minefield, dropped plows, making three lanes. Recommend White, Blue, and Black" — the other two tank platoons and the company headquarters' vehicles — "consolidate at my rear and follow through."

"Roger, Red. White and Blue, execute. Black Six out." With these two simple transmissions we were able to get the entire company through the minefield unharmed and continue toward Basra.

As I caught my breath and calmed from this brief excitement, I became irate at myself. I had known that the Iraqis emplaced minefields in front of their defensive positions, yet as I was coming through their positions from the backside

I had failed to apply this and had come close to injuring soldiers and damaging our tanks. I vowed to be more vigilant.

1 March 1991[27]

ALEX VERNON (Delta Mech, Task Force 3-15 Infantry)

We pushed east toward Basra. About twelve kilometers later, in the early afternoon, the company stopped at what we soon discovered was an abandoned medical complex. After an infantry platoon cleared it, Captain Baillergeon let my tankers explore the site. We found three modified American M113s and one 557 medic track. We also found a type 59 or type 63 Chinese command track, also modified into a medical vehicle. These were plush medical vehicles, with padded sides, padded seats and benches, and built-in supply cupboards. All were dug-in deeply, and all had Republican Guard markings. We also saw a dug-in black Chevy Beretta automobile in the center of the complex — one of those too-strange-not-to-be-true discoveries. Bob McCann, Bravo Tank's First Platoon leader, owned a black Beretta, and I regret not thinking to filch a hubcap from it to replace his missing one back home. (It has been speculated that the Iraqis placed junk in dug-in positions as decoys, that we might waste missiles, bombs, and artillery on them instead of on tanks and other combat track.)[28]

At first we were very careful about our search, as we feared the Iraqis might have rigged booby traps for us. It became quickly apparent, however, that the occupants had left in a hurry, and recently. Food was left on plates, pencils in notebooks on cots, clothes on the sand floor. They lived in bunkers, some dug deep with sand stairs and roofs; some not so deep, with draped canvas for walls and ceiling. The former were smaller and housed fewer people, probably officers. Most of the living spaces were not tall enough for any of us to stand upright. I scored a protective mask and a wood-handled bayonet for myself.

A Republican Guard division had occupied the entire area. Piles of ammunition littered the landscape — tank, artillery, and small arms rounds. This day, and for the next several days, we were accompanied in our traveling by the earth-jarring explosions of division engineers destroying these ammo heaps behind us.

Not long after the bunker, Sergeant Dock reported movement around a cluster of buildings a kilometer to our front. The company on our left noticed them as well. I plopped down in my seat and through the sight watched a handful of armed Iraqi soldiers dashing between buildings. A pair of vehicles in the area, not moving. Lieutenant Colonel Barrett gave the other company permission to attack. With a burst of Bradley 25-mm and Abrams main gun rounds, they closed on the area and secured it.

My company then ran into a truck sitting in the middle of the road we straddled. A running automobile sat stopped in front of it. Several Iraqis were leaning and reaching into the cab, doing something. Trying to start it? Recovering weapons? Booby trapping it? Baillergeon had a Bradley shoot warning rounds over the truck. The Iraqis scurried into the running car and sped away. Wanting to take no chances, Baillergeon chose to destroy it at a distance with a high explosive tank round. I asked my platoon if anyone had a HEAT battle-carry; Sergeant Miller assented. Baillergeon had his thinner-skinned Bradleys back off. I told Miller to lock on the truck, and for him and his gunner to speak their fire commands over the platoon net. I echoed every command over the company net.

"Ready."

"Ready."

"Fire."

"Fire."

"On the way."

"On the way."

I had expected a more dramatic explosion, as had the watching infantry. A small flash and puff of smoke, the sound of crunching metal and glass, and the truck jerked, then rocked back to stillness. Very anticlimactic, especially as it was the last round of any sort, large or small, Second Platoon, Bravo Company, 1–64 Armor, would fire.

Some minds might make something representative of the event, of the protracted, nervy anticipation, the lack of any backlash, the quick, almost anticlimactic end. The battle for Jalibah too feels slightly representative: the preparation by bombing; the overwhelming size of the attacking force, almost too big; the lack of fight in the defenders; and the greatest damage inflicted on ourselves we inflicted on ourselves.

We moved on.

NEAL CREIGHTON (Alpha Tank, Task Force 3-15 Infantry)

It was now two days after the battle of Jalibah. As I reached into my tank's bustle rack, I found an almost empty case of bottled water. Ever since eating the contaminated lettuce during Desert Shield, I was extremely careful about what I consumed. The thought of drinking the army's "purified" water did not sit well with me. Looking up, I saw Lieutenant Seal, one of the infantry platoon leaders attached to the company, walking toward my tank. "Hey Wayne, do you have any bottled water to spare?" I yelled.

"No, we're almost out, but I hear there's an enemy conex about two kilometers north of here loaded with bottled water. It's a Republican Guard supply point

that my guys saw while on patrol last night. Let's hit it! You ask the captain —
he'll let us out if you ask. You're his pet."

I grinned. "No, I think you're his pet. He keeps saying how he wants to put
you on a leash." Placing my CVC on my head and pressing the transmit key, I began to think about what I was going to say to the commander. "Black Six, this is
White Six, over."

"This is Black Six," he responded.

"This is White Six. We would like to replenish some Class 1. Can we talk at
your position, over?" I waited for his response wondering if he knew what the
hell I was talking about.

"This is Black Six, is this the mission Wayne wanted?"

Turning to Wayne I grinned again. "You already asked him, you bastard."

"Yeah, but he said 'no' to me," Wayne replied.

I hesitated and then grabbed the transmit key, "Roger, same mission, over."

"This is Black Six. Okay. I know where you are going, but be back in two
hours, out."

"You son of a bitch," Wayne yelled. "I told you you're his favorite!"

"Yeah, and I told you he wanted to keep you on a leash. I guess I'm taking you
for a walk." We discussed the mission briefly. Wayne decided to take his wingman
and his dismounts. I decided to take my wingman, Staff Sergeant Davis. After briefing the involved crews, we mounted up and headed north, Wayne's track in the lead.

As we moved through enemy territory, I was amazed. Everywhere lay abandoned vehicles, uniforms, weapons, and ammunition. It seemed most of the
Iraqi army had deserted wholesale. We halted temporarily as Wayne checked his
map. I dismounted with an M16 rifle and entered a bunker to the right of my
tank. Uniforms were scattered about the floor and food sat on an unlit butane
stove. Clearly, the last meal in this bunker had been interrupted. The most likely
explanation was that the U.S. Air Force had ruined these soldiers' dinner. Hard
to believe this was the same Republican Guard we were taught to fear. I moved
out of the bunker and remounted my tank.

We continued north. Eventually Wayne broke the radio silence. "White Six,
this Gray Six, I have the target in sight. Bring up the big guns, over."

"This is White Six, roger out." My two tanks moved forward until we had a
good view of the supply point. There were seven conexes — metal transportable
walk-in storage bins — surrounded by a bunker complex. No enemy movement.
After observing the area for several minutes, I radioed Wayne. "Gray Six, this is
White Six, negative movement. Let's move in."

Wayne's Bradleys moved in as my tanks covered them. "White Six, this is Gray
Six, we are in and it's the mother of all supply points, over."

"This is White Six, roger out." I brought my section forward to join Wayne. Once we had entered the supply point, I dismounted. "Damn, this place is stocked," I yelled to Staff Sergeant Davis. Most of the conexes were open, and bottled water was everywhere. I was again astonished at how quickly the Iraqis had abandoned things. I would have destroyed the water with main gun or machine gun rounds instead of allowing it to fall into enemy hands.

In one conex we found water with pictures of Saddam on the label and packets of Kraft cheese. I wondered if Kraft knew they were providing nourishment to the Republican Guard. Davis's crew began to load the turrets of both tanks with Iraqi water. Before we departed, Wayne took a picture of my watered-down tanks. We headed south, back toward the company area, with enough water to service the Alpha Tank *Wild Bunch* for at least three days.

2 March 1991[29]

ALEX VERNON (Delta Mech, Task Force 3-15 Infantry)
We followed a powerline east. In the late morning we stopped; tanks from Task Force 1-64, which had been moving parallel to us on our right, crossed in front of us barreling north. We were then about thirty miles north of Kuwait and about as far to the west of Basra, Iraq. I didn't understand. Why send the farther unit? Why have one unit cross in front of another? Captain Baillergeon ordered the company-team into a hasty defense in sector and called the task force for a situation report. The battalion gave him a nonanswer, which he relayed to me: "Never mind, just do your job."

I have since asked Dave Trybula what happened. He remembers that 1-64 "had just gone into a hasty defense and pushed our Mech companies forward when we got word of an Iraqi armor battalion approaching within five kilometers. Immediately we pushed the armor companies forward along with Greg's scouts. Fortunately, Greg correctly identified the battalion as our 4-64, the other armor battalion in the 2d Brigade, before we closed to do battle." Colonel Gordon recalls things somewhat differently: "Following 1st Brigade's engagement at Rumaylah Oil Fields, 1-64 was ordered into the complex and small town to secure it and block the road going east into Basra. To do that, we crossed in front of 3-15 at about 1500–1600 and occupied the positions. Your Task Force 3-15 remained to our south for the day."

As far as I knew, the cease-fire was nonexistent. I continued to hear rumors of Iraqi armored movement, and I continued to hear artillery and direct fire. I would later learn — much later, years later — that the other brigade's battle at Rumaylah resulted in the destruction of nearly one thousand Iraqi vehicles and unknown numbers of Iraqis trying to escape the area, some of whom were purportedly civilians (including women and children) fleeing Kuwait in this military convoy.

That day we found a group of abandoned artillery pieces, and with them some American equipment. Two M1A1 gunner's quadrants without serial numbers. A Texas Instruments calculator.

GREG DOWNEY (Scouts, Task Force 1-64 Armor)

Our zone went right through the Rumaylah Oil Field area, a congested, built-up area on the map. I anticipated a very slow rate of movement with us having to go block by block through urban areas.

As we worked our way through the oil refineries, we observed the devastating effect of our coalition air power. There was a large amount of unexploded cluster bomblets on the ground and numerous burnt-out hulks of former armored vehicles. My scout platoon moved very deliberately, bounding within sections, leap-frogging our way through the maze of buildings and huge oil storage tanks. There were so many places an Iraqi tank could be hidden. After moving across a wide-open desert for the last six months, I was becoming claustrophobic among the tight confines of this area.

I saw movement to my front left as we moved farther east. Looking through my binoculars, I could see the gun tube of a tank. After taking cover behind a berm, my gunner raised the TOW missile launcher. The tank had acquired us — we could see the end of his gun tube staring at us. The fire support office reported to me that all our artillery was out of range, so I requested permission to engage with the TOW. Although the enemy tank had not fired at me, he was tracking me and my wingman everywhere we moved. I could not maneuver any farther east with the tank there so I launched a TOW missile. My gunner tracked our missile to the target and destroyed the tank. We continued our movement east.

Red and Blue sections were not encountering any resistance. Abandoned tanks and BMPs cluttered the area, making it hard to move quickly. It was getting hard to determine which enemy vehicles were manned and which ones abandoned. As I moved over a berm, I came face-to-face with a BMP-1. It fired one 73-mm round at me, which hit in front of my vehicle. My gunner responded with a burst of 25-mm that hit the side of the BMP. My wingman was firing also.

Neither of us saw the red truck. Before we could stop firing, it had driven between us and the enemy. The BMP exploded first, then the truck burst into flames. I can't describe how it felt. Shock maybe. Panic. Seized. Overcome. We had inadvertently shot innocent victims.

I raced my section to the truck's location. What I saw sickened me. An old man, two women, and six children were jumping out of the burning truck. My soldiers poured out of our Bradleys, ran to them, and tried to administer first aid. They were in awful shape, especially the old man. He had taken a 25-mm armor piercing round through his chest. The majority of the children were injured from the high explosive rounds. One woman had lost her leg below the knee. I felt angry and helpless.

Why did they have to be in the wrong place at the wrong time? How could have this been avoided? I called for additional medical support. We were losing the old man. Specialist Burton was doing his best to keep him alive. The woman who had lost her leg was stabilized after Burton applied a tourniquet and gave her a shot of morphine. The kids were scared, but we patched them up. They would survive.

The battalion medical aid station arrived with the battalion surgeon. Lieutenant Colonel Gordon arrived with them. I felt horrible and expected Gordon to chew my ass out after he saw what had happened. Instead, he asked if everything was okay, then told me to continue with the recon.[30] My wingman's gunner, Corporal Saylor, was pretty shaken up. Along with my gunner, he had pulled the trigger.

"Saylor, you okay?" I asked, knowing he wasn't.

He couldn't answer; tears were coming out instead of words.

"Saylor, you have got to pull yourself together. Things like this are bound to happen, even when you don't want them to." I didn't know what else to say.

"Sir, let's give Saylor a break," Hightower offered.

"All right. A couple hours out of the gunner's seat, then you're going back to it," I said, remembering years before how my dad had forced me not to let my fears make decisions for me, and made me crawl back into the ditches after I had nearly died in one.

"Let's get going. We have work to do." I walked back to my Bradley, looking at the old Iraqi man lying on the ground, breathing his last breaths.

I couldn't take my eyes off of him. His face was blue from his lungs giving up. I tried to block it out, but the mental imprint it left would stay with me. He had been caught up in something out of his control, and it cost him his life as he tried to protect the lives of his family. This was the lowest, darkest side of combat. I wish that I had not experienced it. This incident continues to haunt me.

"West, get us out of here," I voiced over the intercom.

"Hey sir, the old man going to make it?" West asked.

"I don't think so, West . . . I don't think so," I replied, taking one last glance at him as the medics pulled out a body bag.

DAVE TRYBULA (Charlie Tank, Task Force 1-64 Armor)

We soon encountered the Rumaylah Oil Fields, or at least the main pipelines leading from the fields. Though not impossible to cross, the oil pipelines — about three feet in diameter and stretching aboveground — made for slow and difficult going. Next to each pipeline was a trench about six feet deep and eight feet across; evidently the Iraqis were preparing to bury the entire pipeline system under ground. Since we were heading perpendicular to the series of pipes, we had to drive the tanks gently over each pipe, which amazingly did not damage them, and then over the trench on the other side. We slowed to less than ten miles per hour.

When it seemed the series of pipelines would never end, we were through them and setting up a defensive perimeter at a power station just shy of Basra. After a quiet night we moved forward into the warehouse district of Basra and set up a perimeter inside a recently abandoned Republican Guard base camp. As the company cleared the camp, we opened an arms room and discovered brand new AK-47s and pistols still in cosmoline. We took these outside to provide Soviet weapons familiarization training on a life-sized picture of Hussein that was also in the camp. My gunner brought me the map that had been hanging on the brigadier general's wall. It was hand-drawn and showed his unit's entire defensive position, just west of the camp.

NEAL CREIGHTON (Alpha Tank, Task Force 3-15 Infantry)

In the morning I gazed through my commander's sight and saw fifteen Iraqi troop carriers moving through a four-lane intersection. I keyed the mike. "Black Six, this is White Six, observing fifteen trucks with troops moving northwest through an intersection two kilometers at ninety degrees, over."

"This is Black Six, roger, go forward and seal the intersection, out."

My platoon crept forward, bypassing numerous bunker complexes that seemed to cover almost every square kilometer of the Euphrates River Valley. The company followed one kilometer behind us. The other platoons stopped to drop thermite grenades down the hatches of abandoned T-72 tanks to destroy them. When we reached the intersection, the platoon formed a coil with each tank squarely facing down one of the approaching road sections. My tank pointed south, Sfc. Wilson's east, Sergeant Harris's north, and Staff Sergeant Jones's west.

"White Six, this is White Three, I have an enemy truck approaching," Harris shortly reported. I looked over and saw him peering through his binos.

"White Six, this is White Five, enemy truck my direction," radioed Sergeant Wilson as a transport approached him as well.

"All white elements, this is White Six. Do not shoot unless necessary. We are supposed to be at a cease-fire. Observe and report, out."

Harris waved at the enemy truck as it approached. The enemy driver hit the gas in an effort to run our roadblock. Now it was necessary to fire, since our mission was to prevent movement through the intersection. Sergeant Harris jumped down into the tank commander's position and let out a warning burst from his coaxial machine gun, the shots flying well over the truck. Iraqi soldiers jumped from the truck, searching for cover as they fired AK-47s at our position. Harris traversed his main gun and opened up with his machine gun, sending the Iraqi vehicle crashing into a ditch.

"White Six, this is White Five, I still have one approaching. Do you want me to hold fire, over?" I knew Wilson's gunner was adjusting his coax on the target.

"If he tries to challenge, open fire. If he stops, let him go, over." Then I spotted a truck coming down the road in my sector toward my tank. Damn. I didn't want to shoot any more of these guys. Why on earth were they challenging M1A1 tanks with AK-47 assault rifles? It was plain stupid. And didn't they know there was a cease-fire? I was angry at them for putting me in the position of potentially having to fire on them for no good purpose. The truck on my road looked like it was going to try to bull its way through our four, too. I instructed my gunner to fire a warning burst at the truck.

"Stoppage!" His gun had jammed. He was yanking the charging handle on the machine gun, wedged in the turret between himself and the main gun.

"Sir, can I fire from my position?" asked Pfc. Carrol in a low voice. He had never fired his loader's machine gun before, and this was a hell of a time to break it in.

"Okay, Carrol, but warning shots only."

"Yes, sir." He pointed and fired. The bullets sprayed wildly in the direction of the truck. The first burst hit the front grill. The truck flipped on its side and rolled into an embankment. "I didn't mean it, sir. It's just hard to fire!"

"One heck of a warning shot, Carrol. Good thing you didn't mean business." Enemy soldiers scrambled from the back of the damaged vehicle.

"Sir, we got troops coming out of the back with weapons, and I fixed the jam in the coax."

"All right, take them out."

I watched through the commander's sight extension as Davis placed the coax reticle on the lower part of the enemy soldiers' bodies and let go a one hundred-round burst, cutting most of the Iraqis down at the legs.

To my left rear, Sfc. Wilson was having a similar engagement with Iraqi dismounts, and Sergeant Harris had chased numerous enemies into bunkers with his fire.

"White Six, this is Black Six, continue to push northeast. The medic tracks are coming up to pick up the wounded. What's your status, over?" Captain Schwartz radioed.

"We have about twenty-five injured Iraqis up here and all other enemy movement has stopped. We need to be careful going by the bunker complexes. Some enemy took cover in them, over," I replied.

"This is Black Six, roger. Move now, out."

The medics arrived and began loading the injured Iraqis into their tracks. My platoon turned east in a wedge formation. To my right, one Iraqi lay dead and another lay dying. He looked up at me as we passed, raised his arm, and, looking straight into my eyes, made his last communication on this earth: a peace sign.

We headed toward Basra, not knowing we had fired our last shots of the war.

After the engagement at the crossroads, we sat twenty kilometers south of Basra for several days. The engineers began to blow up everything the Iraqi army had left behind. Every few minutes an explosion would send smoke clouds way into the air. At first I was startled by the force and concussion of each explosion. But, as time went on, I stopped noticing the blasts and even fell asleep to them. What amazed me was how the body became conditioned to the noise. Most sane people would be terrified after hearing one Iraqi ammunition dump explode. We no longer noticed.

3–8 March 1991[31]

ALEX VERNON (Delta Mech, Task Force 3-15 Infantry)

We stopped moving east on 3 March. In the evening, Reynolds and McBryde played catch with our football, Dock and Vanderwerker smoked orange spice tea bags, and I took a bitch bath, while two Iraqi artillery pieces burned about four hundred meters away. Around us the upward drifting black smoke of destroyed Iraqi equipment and munitions smeared the horizon. After my bath, my first in nearly two weeks, I burned my nasty undergarments.

About 2230 the following evening, Captain Baillergeon called me on the radio. "Have Reynolds prepare his gear; he leaves at 0530 with Bravo Tank's advance party to go back."

"How far back?" I asked.

"All the way over." Then Baillergeon called Lt. Brian Luke.

"Say again, Home Station, over?" asked an incredulous Brian.

"Roger."

"Wilco, out." *Wilco* is radio lingo for *will comply.*

What elation. People starting home. I jumped up and down on my seat in my hatch, banging the upright hatch behind me back and forth. I could hardly sleep that night.

The next day my platoon left Delta Mech and returned to Bravo Tank. Bob McCann, Bravo's First Platoon leader, had already departed with Brian, Reynolds, and the others in the advance party. I also learned that as the senior platoon leader I was originally to have gone home instead of Bob, but that would have left Sfc. Freight in command of my platoon — something Captain Swisher was not willing to do. Freight was good enough to take a platoon to war but not good enough to take it home. The day was cold, miserable, and wet. We spent most of the morning huddled in our vehicles out of the weather. We were to leave the next morning, 6 March, to pass through Kuwait and our Seventh Corps on our way to the port.

It didn't happen. I was told that Iraq had not released POWs on the fifth, as it was supposed to have done; also, our route out had not yet been established. We would instead establish positions on the Demilitarized Zone. Colonel Kern stopped down in his helicopter for a visit with the company. He told us the division would likely move on Monday the eleventh, straight through Kuwait, down the coast, to Dhahran.

After the brigade commander's Huey lifted away, the company moved down Highway 8 to its new position. Two platoons occupied forward positions along east-west roads at the edge of the DMZ to stop all military traffic — ours from wandering east, Iraqis from going west. The First Platoon, less Bob McCann, stayed at the company command post in reserve. Matt Hoagland's Third Platoon guarded a piece of the highway. They spent some of their time posing for pictures with a dead Iraqi soldier under an overpass and chasing off wild dogs with AK-47s. My platoon was assigned a dirt road parallel to and several kilometers south of the highway. I positioned Freight's section forward of mine about one hundred meters, facing east. My section sat back in reserve, and also to halt eastbound American traffic.

Iraqis came our way all day long from both directions. For those headed west that saw my platoon and tried to skirt around us to the south, I radioed the company, and the platoon in reserve was dispatched to run them down. The first group to pass through my position came on foot. Sixteen soldiers. We put them face down on the ground to search them. Sergeant Boss's rough handling surprised one man, who started to resist. Boss shoved him back to the ground. While Boss and several others frisked the Iraqis, Freight watched them from behind his .50 cal, and I covered them on the ground with an M-16. I remember how strange that felt, my standing over these men, my finger on the trigger, the safety off, ready. To kill. How unreal it all was. I felt very suddenly like a boy, a child out of place. Not like an officer in command. Not like a man prepared to kill. While the CVC worn in the tank fits snugly around the ears, the Kevlar helmet's sides jut away from the head, creating a hollow that catches air around the ears, an effect which at that moment amplified my self-conscious disjointedness.

After satisfying ourselves that the Iraqis had no weapons, we let them pass. I didn't know it, but while we had the Iraqis on the ground, Sergeant Miller had placed several dirty magazines open in the middle of the road. I saw them when the Iraqis saw them, as we walked toward the tanks. Most of the Iraqis laughed; others held their stern visage.

Captain Swisher had ordered that we give no food to the Iraqis. Despite my sympathy for these ragged scraps of men, I had enforced the order for the first several groups that had asked. But we had boxes of MREs to spare, and I finally stopped objecting to my soldiers giving MREs to any Iraqi who asked.

One group hung around us to hitch a ride from Iraqis who came through with vehicles. Once, when two Iraqi pickup trucks with room to spare refused to take on any others, the two groups cursed at one another before the trucks zoomed away. One of the Iraqis left behind turned to me and muttered, in perfect English, "Look — Arab dung."

When one crowded truck drove through, a passenger shouted "Chicago!" Another moment too strange not to be true.

The last group came from the direction of Basra. One spoke English and told us that Hussein had a unit of T-72 tanks assaulting the city. "Home, brothers, sister, no more." He asked which towns now had Americans, which Iraqis. I indicated the general location of the DMZ. He shook his head. "Saddam . . . finished . . . ," he said, crossing his arms at the wrists in front of his chest to express capture (I supposed) and drawing his finger across his neck. I didn't know just how close to Basra we were — I didn't have the 1:50,000 mapsheet with Al Basra on it, and didn't know that it was on the next mapsheet to the east of the one I had. We were on the outskirts; the main city was less than thirty kilometers away.[32]

The civil war being waged in Basra gave credence to many of the rumors and reports I had heard throughout Desert Shield and the air war of Hussein's adversarial leadership style: Some Iraqi soldiers occupying Kuwait, we had heard, provided weapons to the Kuwaiti resistance; others shot themselves (the Kuwaiti resistance managed to kill up to thirty Iraqi soldiers a day). By November there had been fifty-four Iraqi attempts on Hussein's life. One of Hussein's maltreated divisions had attacked one of his elite, well-fed, and well-equipped Republican Guard units. At a rally in Baghdad, Iraqi citizens chanted "we don't need Kuwait." Hussein executed his wife and some children. The starving Iraqi army occupying Kuwait resorted to eating animals from the Kuwait City zoo.

Part of my tasking that day on the DMZ involved occasionally sending out a section to patrol the general area. On one of its patrols, my section found an Iraqi military trailer. We pawed through it. The maps and plotting instruments led me to the conclusion that it had belonged to an artillery unit. I snatched a number of the maps for myself. I noticed one of them depicted the port at Dhahran, Saudi Arabia, where we had first stayed and where the ships transporting our equipment had berthed. Using the latitude and longitude of that map, I checked the others and verified that some of them were also maps of Saudi Arabia. At the time the discovery reinforced my belief that Hussein had had plans to move against us into Saudi those first weeks of Desert Shield.

We returned to the company for the evening. Another platoon relieved us.

That night a blast of light turned the sky orange. It woke me. The boom followed a minute later, shaking the tank. Smaller flashes and booms continued for several minutes. Wild dogs yelped.

One of the other Bravo Tank platoons reported stopping a truck with a box strapped atop the cab roof. When they asked the Iraqi soldier driving what was in the box, he answered, "My brother." Later the platoon stopped a bus of Kuwaitis returning home from wherever they had been held prisoner in Iraq. Some of their hands had been smashed flat with sledgehammers.

A number of us spent the next morning crawling all over a T-72 tank that First Platoon had recovered from the DMZ the evening before. Later, my platoon and the XO, Greg Jackson, recovered a T-55 with a mine plow from the DMZ. We hoped that the mine plow would make it compelling enough for the division to take home. It was not.

Both tanks were small, uncomfortable, poorly made, and dangerous. No comparison to our own. Our mechanics had tried to start the T-55, failed, and so towed it back to the company. I looked though its periscopes and sites. Terrible visibility. The tank had no radio or antennas indicating that it had once had a radio. The joint welding was crude. The turret interior was cramped and uncomfortable. These Soviet-made vehicles have a crew of three: the commander, the gunner, and the driver. An auto-loader replaced the human loader crew position. The rounds are thus stored in racks inside the crew compartment. The crew members surely bumped against the rounds as they worked, and any penetration of the turret becomes catastrophic. Crawling on these tanks, I understood why I had seen so many with their turrets popped off, and also why the Iraqis could never have conceived the distance of our attack, especially through the extreme terrain — the ravines, escarpments, dunes, wadi mazes, and soggy septkas — that they knew better than we did. And, as it happened, through that atrocious weather, and at that speed — "double the rate we had anticipated," reflected Major General McCaffrey, "and we had anticipated a rate of battle that was unheard of."[33] Those machines, and the Iraqi soldiers riding in those machines, could never have done what we had done. It would have been too much for them. Indeed Iraq's entire defenses were oriented south, toward Kuwait and the Saudi eastern provinces, and we had rolled in from the west.[34]

Greg Jackson's gunner found a roll of film in the T-72. Once home, he had it developed. A group of Iraqi soldiers, five or so, posing on the tank. Big smiles. A moment exactly like many of our own.

■ Captain Baillergeon, a few days into the cease-fire, had told his lieutenants that division staff was planning an on-order attack against Basra. Basra? Sir? The city was experiencing a civil war already. Our war was over. What was McCaffrey thinking? His trademark aggressiveness was about to go too far. So my self-preservation instinct protested, anyway. I didn't know that Basra had been a contingency objective all along. I didn't consider that McCaffrey was doing what good leaders do, what he had done at the port in August when an offensive was the last thing on everybody else's mind: planning for the most likely battle so that he and his unit would be ready in case the call came.

One hundred hours into Iraq, we stopped exactly when we should have. All other challenges of maintaining the coalition and continuing our attack aside — challenges of increasing the burden on a logistics system just beginning to really feel the strain;[35] of diplomacy, more restrictive terrain, additional casualties, collateral damage to the civilian population, the threat by the civilian population and a nation defending its home, a possible extended occupation force, and morale (both ours in the thick of it and the American public's) — the larger issues of mission and morality necessitated our ceasing violent operations. Once Hussein surrendered, we had lost our mandate. What could our mission have been? Removing Hussein either by force or as a condition of surrender would have only repeated Iraq's moral crime, the impingement on an independent nation's sovereignty (the latter solution of doubtful efficacy). It has been estimated that as much as one-third of the Iraqi army's armored force escaped our encirclement of the Kuwaiti theater back into Iraq.[36] But to prosecute the further destruction of the Iraqi army, of the disorganized, battered, retreating troops, would have been the moral equivalent (on a *much* larger scale) of shooting a mugger in the back after he's dropped his knife, turned, and fled. When you can no longer claim self-defense, the act becomes murder.

"Thank God we stopped when we did," Jeannie Novak, the lieutenant who had seen us off at Hunter Army Airfield and who had traveled with a support battalion attached to the division, has reflected to me. "We were too full of success. There had been too much winning."

We had succeeded in our purpose, the liberation of Kuwait and the restoration of its legitimate government, and it was time to go home. As my brother Eric wrote in a letter just prior to the ground war, "True heroes do what has to be done and no more."

5

After the Storm:
Redeployment and Reflections

Less than two hours from now, the first planeload of American soldiers will
lift off from Saudi Arabia headed for the U.S.A. That plane will carry men and
women of the 24th Mechanized Infantry Division bound for Fort Stewart,
Georgia. . . . Let their return remind us that all those who have gone before
are linked with us in the long line of freedom's march.
—President George Bush, Persian Gulf campaign victory speech, 7 March
    1991

Redeployment: Operation Desert Farewell

Dave Trybula had left Iraq with the division's advance party on 4 March.
He was the first of the five of us to leave for home.

"We had pulled back to our previous positions by the power station and stood
down to 25 percent security for the first time since entering Iraq. I had just slid
into my sleeping bag when Sergeant Godfrey, my gunner, asked me for my Social Security number. Why did he need this in the middle of the night? It turned
out I had been picked to lead the company's advance party leaving for Fort Stewart at 0500 the next morning. I was in shock. Was I really going home? How could
I leave my platoon in Iraq when clearly the situation was still dangerous? I
crawled out of my sack and found my platoon sergeant. Ron and I talked for several hours, and he finally convinced me that it was all right for me to go. I had
done my job by safely taking care of the platoon through its combat missions. I
let Ron go to bed, then spent the rest of the night going from tank to tank, talking to my crews to see if they wanted to send any words home with me, and to
ensure they would be fine after my departure.

"I left the company area in the morning in a company Humvee and at battalion transferred to a two-and-a-half-ton truck. From battalion we consolidated
at brigade and then headed for Jalibah Airfield, which we had taken only days

before. As we stopped outside the airfield in the early afternoon, it began to rain. The rain stopped the planes from coming, and naturally the trucks had no covers on them, so I spent my last night in Iraq in the back of a truck with my sleeping bag over my head as the rain poured down all night long.

"The following morning the planes arrived. My last memories in Iraq are of lining up five abreast on an airfield tarmac, marching into a C130 up the dropped rear ramp, and sitting on the cargo floor for the one-hour flight to Saudi Arabia.

"I arrived at Hunter Army Airfield in Savannah, Georgia, on the first flight returning from the Gulf just after midnight on 9 March 1991. I had anticipated a small reception. We were instead met by hundreds of cheering, screaming people and multiple television crews. I was overwhelmed. I had never experienced anything like it. Everyone treated us like heroes. Still, I had two concerns. The first was how the Vietnam War veterans were going to take the reception we were receiving, certainly unlike anything they had ever known. I hoped they would feel that the military had finally overcome its former misplaced image. I wanted them to be a part of this celebration of America's military.

"My other concern was when I'd see my girlfriend, Jill. She had actually seen me on CNN boarding a plane and started driving from Ohio so she could meet me. She picked me up the morning after my return, and we spent a couple of days together. But then I had to return to work, to prepare for the arrival of the rest of the battalion.

"While this was happening, I received news that four soldiers in my company had been wounded during a refueling operation on the way out of Iraq. I was not able to confirm anything more than their names and the fact that they were all alive. What followed was probably the most terrifying thing I had faced in my military career — I had to notify the families. I knew only who was injured, but not how seriously nor where they were. Fortunately, in each case, the families had spoken with their wounded loved one prior to my arrival, and they supplied me with the missing information."[1]

■ The brigade finally began its movement out of Iraq on 9 March. We were supposed to make a nonstop journey to Tapline Road, where we would meet the HETs and head back to the port for redeployment to Georgia.

I remember my amazement at the roads built by our engineers. As the combat units pushed the attack, the engineers followed behind us building the roads that would support our continued operations. The road we traveled that day was better than any other unpaved road I had seen in Iraq or Saudi. I also remember the day's aura: On ground level we had a normal, sunny day, yet the sky above had a deep, dark blue overcast, heavier to the east. Everything was cast in the oddest slight blue tint, and the air possessed a flavor — not a smell exactly, not a taste — that struck peculiar. Tainted. We knew that Hussein had ordered his retreating army to destroy Kuwait's oil fields, and I could only suppose that the aura was fallout from that massive destruction and pollution.

Once when we stopped for refueling, Swisher ordered everyone to stay on the tanks. In another unit soldiers had been injured, and I heard that one may have been killed, by stepping on unexploded cluster bombs littering the ground from either our air campaign or our artillery. It may have been the four soldiers in Dave Trybula's Charlie Tank or the private in the fire support vehicle whom Rob Holmes says "stepped on an unexploded shell and blew his foot off on our way back to Saudi. It was so unnecessary." If in different companies, all five soldiers may in fact have been injured in the same incident, the one the "Annotated Chronology" of the Eighteenth Airborne Corps documents on 10 March, in which five soldiers were wounded when a "soldier from 1st Battalion, 64th armor steps on submuntion at PU 068315 resulting in five wounded." Some types of artillery rounds and air-to-ground bombs burst at a certain altitude to pepper an area with a number of smaller bombs enclosed within its shell — the so-called cluster bombs and bomblets, or submuntions. Not every bomblet could be trusted to explode on impact, so Captain Swisher rode around in his Humvee hollering at soldiers hopping off the tanks to pull maintenance or relieve themselves. He was right to do this; still, the threat seemed so unreal to a gaggle of young men who had survived the mother of all battles unscathed and were now going home. I echoed Swisher's orders, though I did not watch for transgressors as closely as he did because the danger didn't feel real to me either.[2]

Having gone some nine hours and over 150 kilometers, with half the road march left, Task Force 3-15 halted and formed a hasty defense in sector, oriented east. We had been tasked as the division rear guard, to cover its withdrawal despite the complete lack of a threat. During this halt, the officers did the paperwork for awards. Each platoon leader had a certain number of Achievement and Commendation Medals to submit for members of his platoon. I think I had six total; I recommended an Achievement Medal to each of my four drivers since they arguably did most of the work, and Commendation Medals to Staff Sergeant Rivera, my displaced platoon sergeant, and to Private Doug Powers, the loader on Sfc. Freight's tank. I recommended Rivera because his official personnel file should read "platoon sergeant during combat," but it would not; because despite his reduced position he had been able to exert leadership and help keep platoon cohesion; because he had provided invaluable support and counsel to me, and to the rest of the platoon; because he deserved much more than I could award him. Powers was the soldier who, before the war, had pulled me aside and expressed his fear about being on Freight's tank. He had also during Desert Shield asked me if he could give his GI Bill money for college to his younger sister because he wanted to stay in the army. He was one of my youngest soldiers and one of the hardest workers in the company. He was intelligent and articulate. Watching him work with and relate to his peers and his superiors, watching him without complaint carry out orders with which I know he disagreed, I realized how mature and exceptional he was. Everyone liked him: He was genuine. And he had found a home in the army. *In about ten years a green lieutenant will have a Staff Sgt. Powers for a platoon sergeant,* I wrote Maria, *and I envy that lieutenant.* I recommended Powers because I wanted to encourage and further the career of a soldier who would serve the army better than most, and proudly.

I don't remember sitting in our covering force mission for three days, yet my letters record no other movement from the ninth to the twelfth, when we finally started out of Iraq.

While we manned the DMZ outside Basra, Greg Downey "had begun to question whether we should have stopped the attack when we did. I wondered if we were leaving unfinished business. I did not want to return to Iraq to fight another day, nor would I want any other American soldier refighting the war we had just won. I kept my thoughts to myself.

"Our movement south almost retraced our attack route north into Iraq. We had a 380-kilometer trip ahead of us, and with headlights on, we marched toward home. I had a lot of time to think on the way back to Saudi Arabia. The platoon was moving together and the task force followed closely behind. The radio net was silent and most of the crews were asleep. I never dreamed that returning from battle would be like this. It seemed like a drive through the countryside.

"My mind went back to when we first arrived in Saudi Arabia. So long ago. I peered down through my hatch at Specialist Lowther. He was sleeping in his gunner's seat, his forehead still showing the bruise caused by his head being pounded by the headrest above his gunner's sights. Was he the same person after all of this? Was any of us?

"I had experienced a glimpse of life that few people can claim to have seen. Although combat is a life experience, the focus is on death and destruction. Trade someone else's life for yours, the lives of the enemy to guarantee the lives of the friendly. What is it all for? A chunk of land, a religious vendetta, an attempt to gain natural resources, or an irrational leader who gets a thrill from projecting his military on an unsuspecting country?

"Who pays the price? The nineteen-year-old kid who joined the army for the college money, only to end up never seeing his twentieth birthday. The families who see the military officers coming up to their front door to announce the news they had hoped to never hear. The old man who died simply because he was at the wrong place at the wrong time, trying to get his family to safety. It all seemed so senseless.

"'Hey West, how you doing down there?' I mumbled over the intercom.

"'Fine, sir. I'm glad we're leaving,' he replied.

"'West, did you ever think this would be over?' I asked.

"'Sir, it will never be over, because nobody lives through something like this and forgets about it.'

"'You think you'll remember all of this fifty years down the road?' I inquired.

"'Sir, I may not be able to remember my name fifty years from now, but I'll sure as hell be able to tell stories about this.'

"He was right. I thought for a minute what events I could recall most vividly from my life. There were only a few that really jumped out at me. Those were the ones that left a permanent imprint on me, good or bad. This one would always be at the front of the list.

"'West, you're a good man, and there's someone at home who can't wait to see you,' I added, thinking about a place that occupied everyone's minds.

"'Sir, did we do okay? I mean, did we fight good?' West asked.

"'West, we all lived, right?'

"'Yes, sir, I guess that means we did okay,' he concluded.

"'Well, West, I'm sure your wife thinks you did just fine,' I said, remembering the day when West told me the angels were crying.

"As we approached the berm on the Saudi Arabian–Iraqi border, twenty-four hours after leaving Basra, I swelled with pride. History had been made and I had played a role. The scout platoon had proven itself in battle and would live to tell about it. Going home was just a few days away, when life would resume again."

■ We drove throughout the night of 12 March. I led the company, following Alpha Tank. For the first part of the night, we drove back through the farmland. This time, because visibility was poor and we moved fast, we drove straight through their fields, every hundred meters up and over another berm and ditch separating the square plots. We passed one farmer who was out waving us away from his mud home, having given up his efforts to keep us out of his fields. Once I also had to have Brunner slam a hard left to avoid colliding with an American attack helicopter — a Cobra I think — parked on the ground. I warned the company behind me and led it gingerly through the aviation company.

I spent the night fighting Captain Swisher on the radio. He wanted me to move slowly, each vehicle at a certain and short interval in the interest of keeping the company together. He rightly didn't want to lose anybody. But I was trying to keep up with Alpha Tank. Had I not pushed hard, I would have lost sight of the task force's lead company, with the majority of the task force following me. I had no GPS, no way to know where to go. So I would slow to appease Swisher, then accelerate to keep Alpha Tank in sight. When Swisher felt himself pulled faster, he would holler again. All night. Our constant push and pull kept the company together, in a tight formation, and with the battalion. Our fighting turned out to be a way of working together.

Toward morning we left the farmland behind us and traveled at a constant and manageable pace. The radio chatter vanished. On the last leg Neal Creighton's tank ran out of gas and stopped in its tracks. The task force XO pulled up and gave Neal all the spare fuel he was carrying in five-gallon cans on his Humvee. The XO sped ahead when Neal's tank began to move again. A kilometer later, just shy of Saudi Arabia, Neal passed the XO's Humvee. It had run out of gas.

About 0500 on the thirteenth we crossed the berm back into Saudi, I believe at the same place we had crossed nearly three weeks before. And again the task force command sergeant major greeted us with the battalion and national colors. By 0600 we stopped at Tapline Road. The other battalion, 1-64, loaded on HETs and left for the port. We were to leave the next day.

I showered between tanks, then donned fresh DCUs and brand new red plaid boxers sent by Maria. The company hooted seeing my skinny, white-bellied self naked but for overly large, bright-red boxers (most soldiers wore briefs). I had not worn the DCUs for two months; since transition to the A1s, we had trained in our green Nomax suits and fought in these with our green MOPP suits over them.

After my towel bath, I slept.

We woke at 0500 on the fourteenth. The HETs were to arrive at 0800. At 0830, they were to arrive at 1030. At 1400, they appeared. An Egyptian unit.

The Egyptians were larger and more handsome than the other Arabs we had seen. Olive skin, fuller bodies. Swarthy instead of scraggly. Clean, smooth, shaven faces. Their lieutenant, the tallest and thinnest of the bunch, made a fashion statement: With his khaki uniform small and tight, his tucked-in shirt unbuttoned several buttons and pressed open against his thin chest, he looked like he had had it tailored after American pop magazine photos from the 1970s.

When the lieutenant wasn't looking, his soldiers wanted to trade with us for, or buy, American stuff — mostly cameras, pocket knives, and skin magazines. "Fuck-a books," they called them. Later their lieutenant discovered the magazines and had his men burn them, much to the cartoonish wrath of some of my soldiers. One of the Egyptians also tried to steal my knife after I had laid it on the tank. Sergeant Dock and an Egyptian soldier spent some time trying to teach one another some choice words from their language. I only wrote down one, *zooba*, for penis. Trying to elicit the Egyptian word for *fuck*, Dock gestured with a finger going repeatedly in and out of a hole made by his other hand's thumb and forefinger, alternatively pointing back and forth between himself and the Egyptian. The Egyptian finally misunderstood. His eyes popped out — "Noooo! Nooooo!" — and he dashed away from the imagined proposition.

Two of the Egyptian HETs were broken, so Greg Jackson and I with our tanks and crews stayed behind when the company left. Two more HETs appeared that night to haul us off. On the journey he and I used my platoon frequency to play chess, each holding magnetic travel sets, and passing our moves over the airway: "pawn to queen four," that sort of thing. We moved on to trivia questions, and I had Greg stumped with the name of the French detective in Agatha Christie novels when the first sergeant's driver broke across the air with the answer. "Hercule Poirot!" We didn't know it, but we had caught up to the company, which had pulled over on the side of the road and had been listening to us for the last forty minutes.

In the morning on the fifteenth we passed an intersection with a few build-ings in the southwest corner and a hill behind it. I looked twice. It was the inter-section, the store, the hill, where my platoon had spent September on the cav-alry screen, where the ARAMCO civilians had grilled for us, where we had invented Silver Six, where Freight had lied about being in Vietnam, where one of my NCOs pulled a knife on the other, where I saw my first Arabian cloud, where one of my soldiers had word of the birth of his son, Sean Jr. I hadn't recognized it because I saw it from a new direction, and because it was green. Tall green grass covered the area that had been our first home. Spring had come to the desert. New life was coming for us, too. We were going home.

Vehicles crowded the last stretch of Tapline Road. We used both lanes for our one-way trip east. I remember some women soldiers who dismounted a bus stopped in the congestion and went over a hill to relieve themselves in private. When the columns started moving again, the bus took off without them. When we hit the coastal highway, we stopped briefly at a gas station for the HETs to re-fuel. We hit the john — it flushed! — and bought snacks. In the afternoon we arrived at a site for downloading our main gun ammunition, where 2d Lt. Paul Wynn waved my tank to the first download station. Paul had been in my cadet company a year behind me at the academy. Rob and I had recommended Fort Stewart to him because he was getting married and did not want a post with sub-stantial field time. He wanted time with his new bride. Sorry, Paul.

Somewhere near the ammunition download site I remember seeing Arabian horses trotting around in a white-fenced jumping area. That night we pulled the tanks into a line at the port for the wash racks and the customs inspectors. We had pulled abreast of several columns on our right; soon, another column began forming on our left. We slept on the tanks.

We spent the day of the sixteenth cleaning our equipment as best we could while still in line for the wash racks. Barrels for contraband souvenirs were placed every few hundred meters between the columns of vehicles. The division would not allow us to cart home firearms as souvenirs and so had placed these barrels into which soldiers could anonymously dump their loot. We spent that night on the wash racks, having been warned that the Saudi customs would not allow a single bit of Holy Land sand to leave. I guess I get the last blasphemous laugh: Working on this book, pulling out maps and letters and items I hadn't looked at since my return, I dumped two good handfuls of it on my North Carolina apartment floor.

At some point we moved to Khobar Towers, a vacant apartment complex built for settling the nomadic Bedouins. Its availability to us signifies the success of its original purpose. We slept en masse on the cold tile floor in empty apartments. Phone banks and hot meal areas had been established in underground squares between apartment buildings. I remember sleeping only one night on the floor at Khobar, which must have been the eighteenth; I don't know where we spent the previous night. A detail was left behind to load the vehicles onto the ships for the journey home. The *Mercury* was one of the first ships to be loaded with 24th ID vehicles, around the date we boarded the plane for the States. A Gemini, I like to think the *Mercury* carried my tank home.

(Mercury was most famously the messenger of the gods, but also god of travel, writing, and commerce, and was escort for the dead. A few months later, once again among the endless pines and the marshy coastal lowlands of Fort Stewart, Georgia — where at least once a week, as I drove the road through the Stewart's training area from Savannah to the main post, I saw the shell of an armadillo popped open by another soldier on his way to PT in the dark morning — I learned that a West Point classmate had killed herself during her stay at Khobar Towers. She was on her way home: a twenty-three-year-young woman, intelligent and not unattractive, a West Point graduate, the war behind her and her future before her. The explanatory rumors followed soon enough, but her death still confounds me. For those seven months of my life, survival was everything. I was headed into battle. The word *suicide* had passed out of our vocabulary; the idea of it had passed out of conceptual space.

The "Eighteenth Airborne Corps Annotated Chronology" records three other suicide attempts during the Persian Gulf War. Two occurred before the ground war. A soldier, sex unspecified, from a military intelligence unit; and a female lieutenant from a medical unit. Neither succeeded. The third soldier, an enlisted man, an infantryman, succeeded. Like my classmate's, his last act of will happened after the war, on his way home. I wonder how many others. I wonder when. I wonder about their success. I wonder about their sexes. I wonder about their units. I wonder why.)

I think we loaded busses outside the fence at Khobar on the late afternoon of the nineteenth. As we boarded, soldiers from division staff passed a letter to each of us from Major General McCaffrey. It was dated 12 March 1991, from the Basra Plain, Eastern Iraq. McCaffrey, it seems, was launching a preemptive strike on the history books:

On 24 February 1991, the 26,000 soldiers, 1,800 armored vehicles, and 6,800 wheeled vehicles of the 24th Infantry Division Combat Team and the attached 212th Field Artillery Brigade and 36th Engineer Group attacked into Iraq. Our primary purpose was to destroy an aggressor army and free the two million people of Kuwait. We have accomplished our mission.

In just 100 hours of battle, you attacked 370 kilometers deep into the enemy's flank and rear. We severed the Iraqi lines of communication through the Euphrates River Valley and systematically annihilated the 26th Commando Brigade, 47th and 49th Infantry Divisions, and four Republican Guard Divisions. You destroyed over 363 tanks and armored personnel carriers, 314 artillery guns and mortars, 207 anti-aircraft guns, 1,279 trucks, 19 FROG missiles, 22 MLRS, 25 enemy high-performance fighter aircraft and helicopters, and captured over 5,000 prisoners. The Victory Division also detonated over 1,300 ammunition bunkers with more than one hundred-thousand tons of munitions. The offensive capability of the Iraqi Armed Forces has been wrecked. Saudi Arabia and the Gulf States are now safe.

The 24th Infantry Division's attack spearheaded the ground offensive for the Allied Coalition Forces. Our advance moved farther and faster than any other mechanized force in military history. The speed, violence, and determination with which you fulfilled your mission completely destroyed the enemy's will to fight. Tactical victories such as Talill Air Base, Battle Position #102, Jalibah Air Base, Basrah Plain, and the Rumaylah Oil Field are now engraved in the history of the 24th Mechanized Infantry Division.

Each of you will return to families and to an American public filled with a great sense of pride and respect for your personal courage and sacrifices. Your accomplishments, together with thousands of other soldiers, sailors, airmen, and marines who took part in this battle, have rekindled a new spirit of patriotism throughout our great country. You have revitalized American's confidence in our Armed Forces. America is more safe and prouder because of your strength, discipline, and valor.

We must not forget our fallen comrades. Eight Victory Division soldiers were killed and thirty-six were wounded in this campaign. We will remember them with both dignity and honor. Their legacy is two million free Kuwaiti citizens and an enduring message to both free and oppressed people throughout the world . . . There is hope; freedom is never without cost; and Americans will fight and die for our principles.

The busses took us to the airfield at Dammam. Other American soldiers, not Arabs as expected, inspected our bags for contraband. They did not search our persons. I've heard it was easy to sneak out an Iraqi pistol by wearing it in your shoulder holster; the inspectors did not think to inspect a personal weapon. We hung around in a tent for hours waiting for our flight, which left at 0400 on the 20th.[3]

"Behind us," writes Greg Downey, "we left a part of our lives and a piece of our souls. We took with us memories that would last a lifetime. What awaited us at the end of our journey was exactly what we had fought so hard for: freedom, family, and the American way of life. This was the moment I had been obsessed with since leaving Georgia in late August 1990. But I was oblivious to all the celebrating going on around me. The reality of going home had still not sunk in."

■ *Man! What a knock-out!* thought Rob Holmes as he gazed at the first blonde woman he had seen in eight months alongside the other beautiful flight attendants who smiled as they welcomed him, and a few hundred others, aboard the Delta 1011. "We sat down quickly and watched in wonder as their slender arms and pretty faces went through the emergency procedures. Soldiers applauded their every move. Flotation devices and oxygen masks never elicited such ovation.

"We were headed home. I sat next to Jeff White just like I had on the way over. I'd have clung to the aircraft's wing if it meant leaving the Middle East. The pilot announced that he was a former naval aviator. Applause. We would be taking off momentarily. Applause. There was a surprise waiting for us in Frankfurt. Applause. The men's voices chattered happily as we taxied away from the terminal but rose thunderously as the plane rolled down the runway. The pilot pulled up, and the soldiers exploded into cheers and laughter as the wheels left the ground.

"As the plane climbed, the soldiers settled in to sleep and daydream the flight away. In eighteen hours we would be in Savannah. Dave Hubner was out like a light. I knew he would wake up for food once we landed in Germany. Flash was talking to his staff, probably planning the next three months of training. I was surrounded by lieutenants who were not nearly the goofballs we had been last August.

"The pilot announced we had left Saudi air space. Applause.

"We settled in for the flight to Europe. My back ached from the months of sleeping on my seventy-ton steel bed. My skin was baked and dry from sun and sand. The cushy seat of that plane was the softest thing that had touched my body in a long time.

"I woke up as the plane's wheels bounced down on the Frankfurt runway. Applause. We deplaned into damp, chilly Germany as the pilot reminded us of our surprise waiting on the ground. I could hear Underberg, who always claimed to be in the know, in the back of the plane predicting beer and women. Combat had not changed him one bit. We filed into a huge tent and there before us might as well have been gold bricks from Fort Knox. Still steaming in their little Styrofoam boxes were hundreds of McDonald's Big Macs. It was the greatest marketing ploy

I have ever seen. They were gone in a matter of seconds, devoured by the ravenous combat vets. Over the next several weeks, seven hundred thousand Desert Storm soldiers would forever be able to say that the first meal they ate after leaving Saudi was from the Golden Arches. It was the best burger I ever tasted.

"We were ordered to reboard the plane. Applause. At that point we would have stood on our heads if they told us to, if we thought it was part of the process of getting home. The wheels left the ground, and we settled in for the long trip across the Atlantic. Ten hours later, the pilot announced we had entered U.S. air space. Applause.

"We were in the queue to land at JFK, the pilot announced, and would have to circle for ten minutes. I looked out my window, and the first piece of America I saw was the Statue of Liberty. The men were very quiet now. We were really home. It was really over. We had been deployed in battle positions in the desert almost every day since August. No television, no Bob Hope, no beds or showers or bathrooms. Just sand and wind.

"The pilot came back on. Air traffic control, after learning who was onboard our plane, immediately moved us to first in line to land. Applause.

"Before leaving Saudi, the army had issued us new uniforms, with our division patch sewn on the right sleeve to signify our having been in combat with the 24th infantry, and had given us all haircuts. Thanks. We could have used new boots about three months ago. As always, I guess, and understandably, the army wanted us to look pretty in front of the great American public upon our return. Speaking of the folks back home, we really didn't know what to expect from the American people when we landed.

"We didn't have to wonder long. After docking at the terminal, the officers walked into the gate area in our new desert camouflage and were immediately swarmed by people in the airport. A woman with big hair gave me a hug. Little kids pawed all over us. An elderly gentleman stood saluting. We were mobbed by Americans saying thanks in every way. The support and gratitude was overwhelming. I was blown away; after all, this was New York City! I realized that instant that we had accomplished more than the liberation of Kuwait, which almost seemed secondary.

"An adorable little girl waved an American flag. Her younger brother stood with his mouth open looking up at the soldiers in camouflage. I wonder if he'll ever forget whatever he felt looking up at us. A woman asked if I knew her son. There were seven hundred thousand soldiers in theater scattered across hundreds of miles, but don't try to keep a mother from at least asking. A man introducing himself as a Vietnam veteran teared up as he said thank you. I really had no idea our reception would be like this. Thank you.

"We boarded our plane and headed for Savannah. Applause. We were laughing about the reception at JFK and joked about what was going to hit us once we got home to people who actually knew us. It got very quiet shortly after we took off. I think we were all praying that this was more than a dream from which we were about to cruelly awaken. After living in the desert for eight months, we had developed a healthy skepticism to protect us when things started going too well.

"When the wheels hit that Georgia runway I swore I'd never leave again. Unrealistic maybe, but that's how I felt. Pandemonium. High fives and hugs overruled rank. Even Flash Gordon smiled. We deplaned and jumped on a bus headed to Fort Stewart. All along the road were yellow ribbons and signs. Cars honked horns and flashed headlights. We pulled onto the parade field bounded by the bleachers full of families who had been waiting not so patiently for several hours. As it is the army's way to never miss a moment for pageantry, we assembled in a battalion formation and began to march across the field. But the army hadn't given drill and ceremony to the families in the stands.

"Wives and mothers with children in tow broke into a dead run and turned our parade into a mob scene. Sfc. Sikes's wife grabbed me by the shoulders demanding to know the whereabouts of her husband. As casual as always, he was just ambling along behind me in no big hurry. She found him, hugged him, and they were gone. Sergeant Downing had children hanging all over him and his wife bouncing up and down crying. Bell was off to my left making out with his young wife. Underberg was nowhere in sight. He had said his good-bye to me at the airfield and told me he had to 'blow this scene' as soon as we were dismissed. For a surfer dude, he was a total warrior who had played a major role in the platoon's success. Specialist Howard and his wife and three kids were all hugging in one huge mass of muscle.

"Flash Gordon was off to my right talking to a reporter from the Savannah newspaper. He had a big smile on his face, and his wife Debbie stood next to him just beaming. She was young and attractive and had married him just a few months before he took command and we deployed. While Flash had been responsible for five hundred men in Saudi, the twenty-eight-year-old Debbie had the unenviable job of caring for five hundred families back home. Welcome to the army, Mrs. Gordon. She looked glad this was over.

"I looked all around at my soldiers and their families and realized that for eight months, these women and children had been soldiers and heroes as well. A few soldiers didn't have anyone waiting. For them, the army was family.

"My mother appeared before me, and she hugged me. Because I hadn't known for sure when we would arrive exactly, my dad and brother hadn't been able to come to Savannah to meet me. My father had had minor surgery that week and wasn't supposed to move around, and my brother was caught at school. My mother, on the other hand, was standing by for my phone call from New York and at a moment's notice deployed from Atlanta to meet me as soon as I got off that bus. Desert Shield and Desert Storm had been rough on my parents. Mother's relief was visible.

"We had arrived much later than expected. It was almost 2230, so my mother asked me if I wanted to stay the night in a hotel and go to Atlanta the next day. By the time she had finished her question, I had her car started and was putting the transmission in drive. I bet that I set the land speed record from Fort Stewart to Atlanta. Interstate 16 was a blur of peach and pecan and pine trees as I sped home.

"That was probably the greatest night of my life. My mother and I talked the whole way back, but I was preoccupied, still remembering the scene of my soldiers hugging their families. To think that I played a role in that reunion will give me a sense of meaning forever. At that point, I didn't even care why we had even been in the Middle East. I did care that I led these guys in combat and brought them home in one piece. A platoon leader's life is very simple. We took every objective; we destroyed everything in our path; we all came home. Mission complete."

■ I sat next to Neal Creighton on the flight home; he had the right window seat. He and I did not talk much; we did not know each other well. The plane stopped over at an air base in Frankfurt, Germany. As we descended, the green, gentle hills and valleys reminded me very much of the green terrain boards on which we had studied fighting against the Soviet bloc in this part of Europe. A tent had been set up for us, with refreshments, televisions, nurses, and phones. I did not speak with Maria, but Greg Jackson spoke with his wife, who reported that Maria was on her way to Fort Stewart to meet me. The plane made one more stop, at La-Guardia. We landed on the runway that juts into the sound; we were allowed off the plane while it took on fuel. Ropes cordoned our waiting area from the rest of the airport.

My headphones worked this time for the in-flight movies: *Ghost,* with Japanese subtitles; *Pretty Woman* (again); and *Memphis Belle,* about the World War II bomber and its harrowing last flight. Flying terrifies me, yet I found it comforting to see that 1940s aircraft shot to pieces and still returning. That movie was also ironically prescient. It had been released in the States during Desert Shield, and my mom had watched an interview with the old woman who had been the pilot's belle, the plane's name's inspiration. After his return, he did not stay with her. She never married, and in the interview she was surrounded, like Dickens's Miss Havesham, by mementos of that love, including pictures of him and the plane that bore her name through the clouds. "Don't you dump on Maria, Alex,"

Mom had written about my Philadelphia belle. "Don't you break that sweet girl's heart." She's happily married now, but not to me; six months after my flight home, I wound up breaking that sweet girl's heart.

We landed at Hunter Army Airfield in the late evening. We boarded green army buses for the trip to Fort Stewart. Only one small group, just outside the south gate of Hunter, welcomed us home with cheers, yellow ribbons, and signs. For Greg Downey, "the forty-five-minute bus ride seemed like it would never end. My patience had run out after the seven months of waiting." To me the bus ride didn't seem too anything; it was what it was, a part of the experience we had been required to live. I think I enjoyed the time I had to stare out the bus window into the Georgia dark remembering the way home.

We unloaded the buses at Fort Stewart's track and assembled on one side. On the other side of the field, the bleachers were filled with family and friends. We began to march. At center field, in the middle of the march, we were given the order to "fall-out" — we broke for the bleachers, and the people in the bleachers broke toward us.

It was the homecoming Greg "had always envisioned. Chills ran up and down my spine, and tears swelled up in my eyes. My heart went out to the Vietnam veterans. They did not experience such an honorable welcome. A part of me felt guilty, thinking about the dishonor displayed toward them, having survived combat and hostilities in a foreign land only to face other hostilities at home. And my heart lingered on my men. None were the kids I had once considered them. All of us did some growing up over the last months. We had faced our fears, not letting them make decisions for us. We had been one another's family, lending a hand or ear when needed. We had listened to one another's dreams, problems, and concerns. Most of all, we had fought for one another, looking out for the welfare of everyone in the platoon. *Where do we go from here?* It was impossible to imagine what the next day or month would feel like. What was *normal*, and how would we return to it?"

Somewhere in the crowd I found Maria.

We stayed at a hotel that night. All my belongings were in storage. Greg Jackson lent me a set of clothes which fit fine but for the enormous shoes. The next day Maria and I went to the mall to buy me civilian clothes of my own. The mall felt weird to me, foreign; it was so loud, so colorful, so busy, so unreal. The din and buzz were constant and unsettling. So unlike the open desert where a single soft sound carried wide. In the mall, Maria tried a number of times to hold my hand, to touch me, but that too felt uncomfortable to me, and I brushed her off. I had forgotten how to be casually intimate. A few months later, when our relationship began to strain, I thought I remembered, when I first saw her, that my general emotions of being home were stronger than my particular emotions of seeing her. I shouldn't have dared parse my emotions at such a moment, much less allow those insane distinctions to influence my decision to remain or break with Maria. But life won't wait for veterans to readjust, and decisions must be made during the years our souls want only time, with all demands suspended, for restoration.

In the first weeks of our return, Sfc. Freight was removed from the platoon and Efrain Rivera, the "lowly" staff sergeant displaced by Freight in the days before deployment, the stalwart who went to war as my wingman (literally and figuratively), was restored as platoon sergeant. The battalion's command sergeant major needed a lackey for various beautification projects around the area, and my first sergeant offered up Freight. Good enough for a war bound platoon but not a platoon in peace. It was army-issue irony at its rawest grandeur, worthy of Joseph Heller's wry renderings. When I wrote the final evaluation in Freight's career, both Captain Swisher and the first sergeant counseled me against my candid remarks. "You just don't do this to an NCO," Top told me, dropping the *sir* as crusty old first sergeants sometimes do with lieutenants. Swisher added: "He's retiring. Why hurt his chances in the civilian world?" But, I responded, what justice do we do to the deserving, retired NCO applying for a civilian job at the same company that had hired Freight based on our recommendation? I mollified my evaluation enough to appease them while still saying what needed to be said about that man's incompetence. I did, in a consciously magnanimous act, put Freight in for a Meritorious Service Medal as his retirement award. The MSM is one notch higher than the Commendation Medal I would receive upon resignation, and he had after all served more than twenty years active duty to my two and a half. A few years later Rob Holmes, who stayed in the army long enough to witness Freight's retirement, told me about the award. "Can you believe they gave that dud an MSM?" This was about the time when I thought I saw Freight in the median of Highway 54 Bypass around Chapel Hill, North Carolina, saw him in an orange jumpsuit picking up trash. He was a native of Lumberton, North Carolina, about seventy miles away; maybe, I thought, he had gotten a job with the state. Road janitor.

In May, Dave Trybula was designated the Team Officer in Charge of the Victory Homecoming Team. Off and on over the next six months he spent traveling the eastern and northern states, doing static displays and parades with a team and vehicles in places like Detroit, Philadelphia, and Ferry Farm, Virginia. His team varied anywhere from 18 to 157 soldiers. The equipment was normally an M1A1 tank, a Bradley M3A1 Cavalry Fighting Vehicle, an M109A1 Self-Propelled 155-mm Howitzer, a Mine Clearing Lane Charge (MICLIC), and a Humvee with a TOW antitank missile launcher. "Everywhere I took the team, we were met with an incredible amount of enthusiasm and curiosity. People wanted to thank us for the job we did in the Gulf and find out what it was like."

Meanwhile, Major General McCaffrey continued leaning forward in the saddle. While we soldiers wanted to forget warfighting for a spell, training recommenced almost immediately, as did the organization and drilling of Immediate Reaction units. The intense training, combined with the captious investigations of soldiers who had legitimately lost equipment in combat by new commanders who had spent the war in Riyadh hotels, demoralized a number of us. McCaffrey also orchestrated a constant flow of VIP visits to the division. He was determined to ensure the division's survival of impending defense cuts and its properly prominent place in the historical record. He had his staff compile a three-volume set of texts on the war: the Desert Storm Operations Plan, the division's official history, and a miscellany of unclassified and declassified documents. According to Walt Meeks, the director of the Fort Stewart museum, the division printed only about one hundred of these three-volume sets, which McCaffrey presented to various VIP visitors and to members of such organizations as the Congressional Armed Services Committee. One set found its way to Duke University's Perkins Library in Durham, North Carolina, and thus into my hands. It proved invaluable for the compiling of this book.

I had often thought that if I ever were to write a book on the war, I would call it "Writing to the Wind." Because when I wrote home and read letters from home, I usually did it alone but for the ever present desert breeze, as if the very air that touched me and that I breathed came from and went back home. And because, as the song goes, the wind is called Maria. My last two letter entries to her, written on 16 and 20 March 1991, the latter on the plane trip home, I accidentally dated 1990 — as if trying literally, as I headed home, to recover the lost time. The final sentence of those letters evokes Julia Roberts's character in a scene from *Pretty Woman;* a more appropriate, more colorful ending here I cannot presently conceive: "Vivian wore a vibrant red dress."

Reflections

Indeed, just about everything in our world had become relative, subjective. . . . Your version of reality might not tally with the stats or the map or the after-action report, but it was the reality you lived in, that would live on in you through the years ahead, and become the story by which you remembered all that you had seen, and done, and been.
—Tobias Wolff, *In Pharaoh's Army*

NEAL CREIGHTON

(Bronze Star Medal with V-Device for valor in combat)

I left the army as a captain in 1994. Leaving the profession into which I was born was the most difficult decision of my life. After the Gulf War, the army began downsizing. The surviving units picked up extra missions, resulting in even more time spent away from the families and an overall lower quality of life. As a result, I decided that I was spending too much time away from my own family.

Also, after returning from Desert Storm, I felt unchallenged. Soon after my officer advanced course, I was offered a job as a company commander, but I had internally made the decision to leave the service. The prospect of a company command in a peacetime army struck me as bordering on boring. Maybe if my year group of officers had not experienced combat so early in our careers, things might have seemed more exciting.

My friends began to disappear from uniform as young officers left the service at an increasing rate. Out of the twelve tank platoons who fought with my battalion during Desert Storm, only one remains in the service. About a year after leaving the army, I was one of the speakers at a West Point alumni function in Chicago. A former commandant of cadets was the featured speaker. Before he spoke, I asked him privately what he thought about young officers leaving the army in such large numbers. "It is no real problem," he replied. "We're keeping all the good ones." I asked him to what study he was referring. His eyes broke contact with mine and he turned to speak with other West Pointers in his vicinity.

I do not blame the army for allowing so many fine officers to leave after the Gulf War. The army could not have prevented it. We just returned from the experience of a lifetime. We could have stayed in uniform another twenty years and not had an event to match.

Still, leaving the army caused a great void in my life, and I tried to fill it with Northwestern Law School. Life at law school felt mundane, and the egos of the professors were greater than any officer I knew in the service. I remember a law professor who at a party found out that I was a Desert Storm veteran. He came up to me and asked without shame, "Did you kill anybody?" His smile felt like someone poking fun at my soul.

"Yes, I have killed somebody," I answered. "Have you?"

The professor scoffed as if someone of his intellect would never be placed in such a loathsome situation. "No, I have not. How does it feel to kill?"

"It's incredible," I replied. The professor looked quizzical. "At first you feel raw power. This feeling is stronger than landing a big job, gaining tenure, having sex. The feeling is pure animalistic sensation that comes from the ability to snuff the very existence of life. You become the manifestation of strength and in an instant you can annihilate a family, end a genetic history, preclude future human life. You become God."

The professor's face contorted as if reading a case on which he disagreed with the court's holding. "You might want to consult a doctor, young man. You sound sick," he stated with a confident smile.

I felt even more disgusted. "I gave you an honest answer. You didn't ask me how it was to carry the guilt of the kill with me. After the initial rush, you realize that you are not God. You are a human who for one instant was either on the stronger side or had a cleaner shot. It's like your situation. You were lucky, lucky enough to be born with parents who had enough money to send you to the best schools, who provided you the means to excel. You are on the stronger side with a cleaner shot to the top. You could have been a bum, or a criminal, or even a soldier, if your environment had been different. Life is luck. The guilt of my luck is a heavy load. I think about it every day of my life."

The professor nodded in artificial agreement. "How is the guilt? How does it feel?"

I hesitated, "I don't discuss this openly. It's an invisible albatross carried around my neck. I wake up some nights after dreaming of a road junction where we killed several fathers, brothers, and husbands. The rush is gone . . . long gone. All that is left is the act, and I feel very sad. I would ask you how you would feel, but you would not know. You couldn't know. Your educational delay during Vietnam kind of stands in the way."

Mary and I spent long nights talking and worrying about our future. I had begun to question the decision I made to leave the army. During October of 1994, we went to West Point for my class's five-year reunion. It felt strange being around so many folks in uniform and not being saluted. Seeing the Academy was hard for me because it rekindled some of the excitement and spirit I had felt for the army most of my life. Four months later, I picked up the phone and called my former army branch manager hoping that I could talk him into letting me back in the service. I hung up before he could pick up. I did this a second time, then went into a back room in the Northwestern law library. As I looked out onto Lake Michigan, the tears began to flow, and I prayed that God would help me find a profession that could offer me the same sense of purpose the army once had. This was my catharsis. I dried my eyes, wiping away the guilt of leaving a profession that I loved and pledging to find one I could love as much.

At West Point for the reunion, I discussed the lessons learned from the Gulf War with many of my classmates and decided to organize a story about the Gulf War which would give soldiers of the next generation something valuable to read about modern warfare. Over the next two years I worked on the manuscript with three of the other officers you've read about in this book. I came to a point of frustration about getting it into publishable form when Al Vernon volunteered his talents. For that I will always be thankful. One thing the army teaches is teamwork based on maximizing the strengths of those within your unit and minimizing their weaknesses. That is how we finished this book — as a team.

It has been almost seven years since I returned from Desert Storm. I sat outside last night looking up at Orion and thinking about how my life has changed. I am eight weeks away from receiving my Juris Doctor and MBA from Northwestern. I work as a director in a startup company and invest more money a month than I made as a second lieutenant. Katherine is growing up, and Mary has developed a great career of her own. Yet I am still looking for the same things that I wanted when I came back from the desert. I am looking for a new challenge, for the feeling of purpose and excitement the army had initially given me and my family, for the destiny that must be out there for me somewhere.

After having the adventure of a lifetime, it is hard to find another to equal it. My experiences at West Point, Ranger School, and the Persian Gulf made me realize I could accomplish much more than I had thought possible, could push myself physically and emotionally beyond what I had ever imagined. I also learned that I was capable of bravery in very stressful situations. The army helped me learn who I am, and for this I am forever grateful.

Many of us who served are still searching for a challenge that will make us feel as alive as we did back then. I am truly experiencing life when I am challenged by a task beyond what I thought I could do, and when I overcome the challenge. I wonder how many people go through life without ever really living it; there are so many experiences people miss because they do not discover themselves by pushing themselves. Maybe that is why I have worked almost full-time while studying for two advanced degrees. Maybe that is why I often wonder what I might do next without thinking too much about where I have been. This book gave me one of the first opportunities to reflect on why I took certain paths in my life.

Looking back, I appreciate my family and friends so much more. Being the son of a general officer, it was hard to imagine life outside the army. To the surprise of many, my father and mother were the greatest factors in my successful transition to civilian life. Their support and understanding during a very difficult time taught me that parenting is a true gift. My father never questioned my decision, and he focused me on the future. They both helped me grow a new set of wings.

I knew when I left the army that it could no longer provide me with the experiences I needed. The most challenging thing for me was to start a new life in a world I knew nothing about. I was afraid I wouldn't make it. Today, I feel comfortable talking about law, business, economics, and technology with some very remarkable people. I have almost climbed to the top of another mountain in my life. Maybe I will look back at the last peak and see if it was bigger or just different from the one I will be standing on. Maybe I will look out and see another great peak and wonder if I can make it to the top.

The army gave me the courage and strength to truly live life. I am sure that it affected many young officers in the same way. Sometimes I close my eyes and see us all — our battalion marching across the parade field in desert fatigues as the band plays and the families wait on the other side. I hear screams of "welcome home" as the officers try to keep their men in formation. As we cross the center of the field, our emotions can no longer be contained. We break ranks and run to our families, not fully understanding how our lives have been changed forever.

ROB HOLMES
(Bronze Star Medal with V-Device for valor in combat)

Today, I am a civilian. I left the army one year after returning from the desert. I married my North Carolina pen pal, Kelli, earned my MBA, and currently am a shareholder and manager in two privately held companies in Dallas.

I don't often think about the desert these days, but it's still very much with me. At night, when I look up at the moon, I remember the brilliant Saudi sky and the shooting stars over the rolling white sand. I think about the seven months of nights lying on my tank, listening to my radio crackle with Major Diehl's and Captain Hubner's voices. I picture Sergeant Downing playing with his Nintendo Gameboy, Bell writing a letter home to his wife, and Underberg listening to his Walkman.

Sergeant Downing has been promoted back to staff sergeant and is at Fort Knox teaching new lieutenants how to shoot tanks. God knows how many young butterbars have heard how he was the fastest gunner in the Middle East. Many of them are better officers because of his instruction and skill, just like this one was.

Bell is divorced. I never understood why, except I guess because he and his wife had married so young. He left the army when his three-year enlistment expired, graduated from a junior college in Georgia, and is today a paramedic in Atlanta. He calls or writes me usually once a year and still begins the conversation with a question about the Braves. I love Bell.

My friend Underberg is dead. Two years ago he was diagnosed with a mysterious case of lung cancer. He had no history of heart disease or cancer and had never smoked a cigarette in his life. When he called me to tell me his news, he told me to get checked out because his doctor was suspicious of the uranium inside the sabot rounds and steel armor of our tank even though the M1's uranium has been "depleted" of radioactivity. Nevertheless, my surfer buddy, the man who pulled me down inside the turret as AK-47 rounds whistled over my hatch at Jalibah, died at age twenty-five.

These three men, these three heroes, so different, together were my security blanket. With all hell breaking loose outside my tank, they made me calm inside. I miss them.

When we returned from the desert, I was promoted to first lieutenant, decorated with the Bronze Star for Valor under enemy fire at Jalibah, and selected by Lieutenant Colonel Gordon to be his battalion scout platoon leader after Greg Downey moved on. It was the only job I ever wanted. I liked and respected Flash even more as we worked together. He was a warrior. What we were all supposed to be.

After the war Fort Stewart somehow unearthed plenty of training money. I lived in the field for most of the next twelve months, which was fine with me. The battalion received a batch of new officers who had not been in the desert to fill the jobs of those of us who had been promoted and taken other positions. In the field, Flash most often used my scout platoon to play enemy against his tank companies. We stayed out all night giving the new commanders and platoon leaders hell. I would sit in my Bradley hatch laughing, hidden in Savannah's swamps, listening to their frantic voices scream over the radio when my scouts raided their sleepy assembly areas. Though I enjoyed being Flash's scout, after a time these field events became too much of a game.

I remembered kicking myself many times in Saudi because I hadn't been tougher on my men and more demanding on my NCOs prior to deploying. I was a leader, responsible for my soldiers, and when we landed in the desert they were not ready to fight. That was my fault, and I never wanted it to happen again. Back at Fort Stewart, I had no patience for people who didn't want to do something the right way the first time. But instead of making us more serious and more focused on combat readiness during training, it seemed like Desert Storm made many soldiers lackadaisical. "Come on, sir," they'd say. "It's not like this is real." And their apathy became contagious. I was losing my edge in peacetime. I felt myself getting soft, and I began to consider leaving.

Dave Hubner discovered my inclinations in the worst possible way — the lieutenant grapevine. He confronted me immediately on a sidewalk and ordered me into his office. He was confused, angry, and hurt. I was disordered, embarrassed, and guilty. He could not understand why I wanted to leave the army. I was not prepared to discuss it with Dave, who had done everything in his power to further my career. It was a horrible, futile exchange for two people who would die for one another. The next week neither of us knew what to say when we passed. Then, just as he had when I had asked if I could attend summer school in London, he politely brought me into his office and genuinely wished me the very best. Neither of us are very expressive emotionally, but when he extended his hand I could each see a slight and uncharacteristic tearing in his eyes as I felt my own do the same. Captain Hubner had been much more than my company commander. He had been a mentor, a friend, and an unwavering champion of my progress. He would scold me, kid with me, and always believe in me. I don't have an older brother, but if I did, I picture Dave. I would go to war with him again in a minute.

Flash knew my plans. Dave had rushed to him for counsel after finding out about me. It had been a bad week for the battalion. My roommate, Al Vernon, had resigned that Monday, and by Wednesday four more lieutenants were making such plans. Gordon kept his distance. He waited for me to come to him. But first I called Atlanta. Colonel Holmes responded to my call at first with a glowing review of my military accomplishments. Then he exhaustingly detailed the changing world order and enumerated the limitless opportunities I would have as a civilian. He began to stammer and stumble, and his usual eloquence broke down into sobs. I held the phone tightly, bracing myself, not knowing what he would say next. He gathered himself and told me he could not bear the thought of his son going to war a second time. It was the first time I ever heard my father cry.

My mother was listening silently on another phone, characteristically solid as a rock, and when it was her turn to speak, she was very decisive. She wanted to know my plans. I wasn't sure, perhaps grad school. She wanted to know if I would return to Atlanta. I always did, Mother. She asked me if I would be happy out of the army: I was no longer happy in it. She told me that she loved me, and she told me to come home. I knew that after the sabers, sashes, and grandeur of West Point had come the most horrible nightmare of her life. She was calm that night on the phone, but she had had enough. She wanted her son home.

I went to Flash. Over the past week I had ordered my thoughts and mustered my courage to face him. One reason I think that he and I got along was that we were both direct, logical, and did only what made sense. I knew this meeting would be no different. He began by asking if my decision was made. It was. He asked why I was leaving. I wasn't challenged by a peacetime army. He snapped back, asking if I preferred being shot at. There was an uncomfortable silence as we looked at each other. As twisted as it would have been to answer *yes*, I missed the desert. I missed the challenge. The sense of mission. The constant focus on things that mattered. He did too. We agreed on a date for me to leave that was best for the battalion.

I am honored and thankful to have served under his command. Lt. Col. Randy Gordon was the most tactically and technically competent officer I ever met, a gladiator who understood his mission and calling: to lead men in combat. While some at his level said the right things and kissed the right asses, Randy Gordon prepared his soldiers to destroy the enemy and come home. God help anyone in that man's crosshairs.

I left the army 30 May 1992. I say today that the best decision I ever made was to go to West Point. The commercial is correct — the army is a great place to start. If a young man were to ask me if it was a good idea for him to join, I would say absolutely. I have no regrets. There is not a finer leadership opportunity on the planet. I accomplished a great deal in a short period of time. I had been a successful tank platoon leader, chosen to lead our company and task force for 450 kilometers into battle. I brought every one of my soldiers home to their families and was decorated for valor by the man I most respected, Dave Hubner. Afterward I was selected for the most coveted job in the battalion, the scout platoon leader, by the man whose opinion of soldiers I most valued, Randy Gordon. It was a good time to move on.

First, had I stayed in the army, I would have had a diverse career with various assignments around the world, but I would also have spent less and less time commanding soldiers in the field and more and more time in staff jobs. No thanks. Everyone who serves contributes in important ways in their capacities, but I couldn't imagine doing anything other than mounting a tank and leading men into the enemy.

Second, when I had a family, I wanted to provide for my kids at least as much opportunity as my parents gave me. I thank God for the opportunities my mother and father provided me. Not only did they give me love and counsel and my brother, they also gave me a terrific education and the opportunity to try anything I wanted after high school. That costs money, and ample income is not part of your government issue items in the army. It would have been tough if I had stayed in.

Third, the army is a huge organization. I had a real problem getting promoted to first lieutenant the same day as the rest of my Military Academy class. I certainly wasn't the best lieutenant in the army, but I have no problem saying I was better than some. The military's egalitarian mindset holds that "we are all in this together so be patient and you will get your turn." I am all for teamwork and unit cohesion, but egalitarianism did not build this country. This is just me: Whether I went to West Point and joined the military or went to college and worked for IBM, I would have suffocated in such enormous institutions.

Fourth and finally, today's army has a "zero defect mentality" that destroys many good officers. One mistake and your career is over. I do a lot of things well and plenty poorly. For sure, Rob Holmes makes things happen, and sometimes he makes big mistakes. Today's army won't tolerate that, and it's a shame. Especially when some of these mistakes have nothing to do with winning wars.

I don't think about these things anymore. I did when I was getting out of the army, but not now. I am happy, and I have many friends who stayed in who are happy. I am proud of them, and I pray for them in their service. I don't believe you must be a soldier to be a good citizen. Ultimately, we all must defend against enemies foreign and domestic whether we wear a uniform or not. I do think one should understand the sacrifices that soldiers must make. The military is a tough profession, and those who serve are heroes to me. We owe our security and our opportunities to them; the country should love them, and thank God for them.

Today, when I think of my service, I think of the desert. I dream of the beautiful nights and bitch about the blazing days. I tell stories of bathing out of canteens and eating MREs for eight months. I remember sandstorms and camels and Arabs. I think about church under the stars on Christmas Eve, listening to Tim Bedsole's sermon, Bell coming back to us after going home to his sister's funeral, and Underberg saving my life at Jalibah. I remember Sergeant Downing every time I see a little Nintendo Gameboy, and how much he loved his son, Kurt Jr. I laugh at the pearls of wisdom from my platoon sergeant, Randy Sikes, who was just taking care of his young platoon leader on his first field exercise (which happened to be combat). I marvel at the courage of my men and admire the love from their families when they returned. If I do nothing else in my life that glorious, bringing my platoon home makes me feel like I have not lived a life in vain.

What did I learn from Desert Storm? With faith, family, friends, and a little food and water, a man can survive anything.

The American soldier will withstand any hardship if he is treated fairly, loyally, and honestly. His bravery is unquestioned and his selflessness has no bounds. He has fought on battlefields around the globe and given millions of people who could not fight for themselves freedom, hope, and opportunity. There is no finer compliment in this world, no greater honor, than to be called an American fighting man.

The American people are the most gracious in the world. As long as the military has their support, no enemy can conquer us. As long as our leaders seek their support and commit their forces in a prudent way, they will respond wholeheartedly. Frittering away lives and money on insoluble or irrelevant problems will likewise result in their justified hostility. I pray that we always have leaders who understand that, and better yet leaders who understand what it is to be a young man in a far-away place getting shot at. Don't think that as a twenty-three year old rolling through Iraq I didn't appreciate how well President Bush understood what we were going through, given the afternoon he spent at age eighteen floating in the Pacific after a Japanese zero shot him down.

In addition, President Bush never could have put together the United Nations coalition that defeated Iraq had Ronald Reagan not already defeated the Soviet Union and won the Cold War. We drove Saddam out of Kuwait after only one hundred hours of fighting on the ground, but the war was truly won over the last decade as President Reagan built the most lethal military in history and cleared the map of the Soviet threat. It was his military that overwhelmed Saddam. Sure, outfitting us with the finest equipment in the world was expensive. Ask my mother if it was worth it. What could we have done without? The M1 Abrams that destroyed the enemy tank before he had a chance to shoot back? The Black-hawk helicopter that flew the wounded off the battlefield? Maybe the Kevlar vest or helmet that kept us out of the Medevac helicopter? When I pay my taxes now, I don't think twice about the amount of money spent ensuring our soldiers have the best chance possible of killing whoever gets in their way and coming home.

The United States is the only country in the world capable of doing what we did. We are one of the few nations on the planet that has the compassion, capability, and resolve to even try. When Gen. Norman Schwarzkopf returned home and addressed Congress he said, "We were the lightning and thunder of Desert Storm. We are the United States military, and we are damn proud of it."

I am a civilian now, but I am still an American fighting man, and I am damn proud of it and always will be. To those joining the military today, and to my friends who are still in, God bless you.

DAVE TRYBULA

(Army Commendation Medal with V-Device for valor in combat)

After the war I served as 1-64 Armor's Headquarters and Headquarters Company executive officer. Then I returned to Fort Knox for the Armor Officer Advanced Course, which all new captains are required to attend. Jill and I eloped on 21 June 1993 at Knox, right before the start of the Advanced Course. For the past couple of years we had tried planning six weddings, in Ohio, Georgia, New York, and Virginia. But my field time prevented us from ever finalizing plans. We were trying to set yet another date when the Creightons and another couple we had known at Fort Stewart convinced us to just do it. Neal, whose family had lived in the area with his mother's family during Neal Sr.'s tour in Vietnam, had recommended the Doe Inn, a historic inn that Abraham Lincoln's father had helped construct. Neal was my best man, and Mary the matron of honor. It rained pretty hard that day — the picturesque creek at the inn was large and full. With the men in their greens, and Jill and Mary in similar dresses, and a justice of the peace, Jill and I married around 1700.

We left Knox for Fort Hood, Texas, where I started as a battalion assistant operations officer before being given the privilege of commanding a company. I've since received an assignment to teach in the Department of Social Sciences at West Point and am studying for an M.S. in Economics at the University of Texas on my way to a Ph.D. Jill and I will move to West Point in June of 1999, where we plan to hold a church wedding.

And then there was one. Of the twelve tank platoon leaders that deployed with the Desert Rogues, only I remain on active duty. Only I have had the privilege and responsibility of command. Where have my fellow platoon leaders gone? I think of the army and our national defense: If we are not keeping the best, what state does that leave our defense in? As nice and comforting and tempting as it is to believe that I am the best of the twelve tank platoon leaders, I know it is not true. So is the reverse true? Are the junior and mid-level officer ranks depleted of the best? If so, why?

One possible explanation for the flight of officers is the impersonal, unforgiving, rarely rewarding, perfectionist "zero defect" nature of today's army. But why do some good officers stay? In my case the decision to stay is based on the belief that I can make a difference in the little piece of the army that I can touch and influence positively. Those I touch will go on to do the same. Maybe this is wishful thinking. Time will tell, by observing those who have worked with and for me.

Desert Shield gave us six full, uninterrupted months to focus on training to accomplish Desert Storm. Units were organized into task forces and combat teams to train as they would fight in the ensuing battle. Every soldier clearly understood the tasks at hand and spent much time and effort learning and training the tasks to be executed in Desert Storm. Now, however, as the army simultaneously downsizes and receives an increasing number of missions, we are losing the concept of training. As missions increase and money dwindles, training is the first to go. There is a common misperception now that we train through execution. But that isn't right: We were successful in Desert Storm not only because of Desert Shield but also because of the nearly twenty years of training and rebuilding the force after Vietnam. We fight the way we train. Training is best accomplished in steps — crawl, walk, run. The extent to which today's army does not train enough is evident in what a fellow commander told me shortly after he took command of his unit: "Dave, I don't know how to train; no one ever taught me. What am I going to do?"

With a smaller army it would seem imperative that incentives are instituted to develop and maintain combat-ready units. In my experience, however, commanders developing training plans receive very inconsistent signals. Combat readiness is not stressed; instead, statistics that supposedly convey combat readiness are. But which statistics matter? Tactical prowess should, proven by consistent victories on the simulated battlefield through massing combat power at the decisive moment against the enemy. These basic necessities to battlefield success do not, unfortunately, translate to a successful career for an officer in peace. I am well acquainted with a commander who routinely fought outnumbered six or seven to one through a year and a half of command and won every single action. Nor did a single of his subordinate units lose. Yet his consistent success became an afterthought on his officer evaluation report.

Critical to the success of the deployment to the Persian Gulf was the activation of family support groups, and this lesson is ingrained in the army from its lowest private up through all levels of command. The emphasis on ensuring the "chain of support" structure is in place and can be quickly activated has led to an increased role of families in the military. This has increased morale through improved understanding and availability of key personnel to concerned individuals.

The greatest lesson that the army has taken from Desert Storm and run with is the payoff of technical advantage coupled with soldiers who can use it. As a close observer of the army's endeavors to digitize and step into the twenty-first century, I am appreciative of the need to maintain our modernization edge and the premium that edge inherently places upon the individual soldier. As the army continues to modernize, I am confident that its focus on the training fundamentals will return and ensure our preparedness for any future conflicts. I will continue to strive to do what I can to make my piece of the army prepared and able to handle whatever the future holds in store. Being selected to command a divisional cavalry troop with 131 men, twenty-four combat vehicles, their support structure, and the families these soldiers support and look to for support was the greatest honor and privilege that could be bestowed upon me. I am also grateful for being respected as a soldier who has done his duty in all things. Whenever the multitude of missions and demands started to become overwhelming and disheartening, I was able to regain a positive perspective by simply looking at the hard work, dedication, and professionalism of the noncommissioned officers and soldiers around me. When Patton spoke of allowing soldiers to amaze you with their ingenuity, he succinctly paid tribute to the particular character of the American fighting man. The possibility of making a difference continues to inspire me.

GREG DOWNEY
(Bronze Star Medal with V-Device for valor in combat)

In June of 1993, I received my official orders for the Military Intelligence Officer's Advanced Course. During the long drive to Fort Huachuca, Arizona, I thought about how I would adjust to this combat support assignment. I had never imagined how much I would miss being a tanker and a scout, the extent to which being a tanker and scout had gotten into my blood.

Sitting in the Huachuca classrooms, I listened to instructors make remarks about how the "intelligence community wins the battle." I routinely scoffed at that declaration. I don't know if it was out of arrogance or disgust, but I could never accept their claim. My frustrations began to mount. I would never again climb onto an Abrams or a Bradley and fight at the front of the battlefield alongside my fellow combat arms soldiers. A war within myself was born at Fort Huachuca and followed me to Fort Riley, Kansas, where I began my new army career as the intelligence officer for, of all things, an armor battalion.

My friend Neal Creighton was an assistant operations officer in the same battalion. I looked forward to working with him again, but he was also dealing with an inner war. I remember going to the field and hearing the scout platoon and tank companies talking on the radio, fighting the OPFOR, while I sat in the battalion TOC writing down intelligence reports and sticking pushpins into a map. It was anticlimactic and unchallenging. I felt my skills and my spirits were going to waste. In the TOC I would look over at Neal and see his frustration. He was "gutting it out," doing his best to get through another day. I didn't see how either of us would reach our prime in those jobs, and I worried that neither of us would be happy any time soon.

After the armor battalion, I was assigned as an assistant operations officer for the division's military intelligence battalion with a future assignment to become a company commander in the battalion. But when the unit received orders for deactivation after the 1st Infantry Division was slotted for transfer to Germany, my future company command went with it. Someone was telling me to chuck the combat boots once and for all. An offer for a company command eventually came, but for a training company. I was disappointed, disgruntled, and disheartened. I couldn't imagine myself commanding an assembly line where new soldiers received some textbook training before moving on. I wanted more. I wanted to be next to my soldiers, getting dirty, bloody, fighting the enemy, and winning battles. I wanted to feel the rumble of the tracks of a tank or Bradley beneath my feet again, smell the fuel exhaust coming from the engine, feel the recoil of the weapon system after pulling the trigger. Most of all I wanted to be up front if we ever had to fight again. I felt I had been benched.

I declined the command and announced my intention to resign my commission and leave the army. I had mentally prepared myself for the reactions from my superiors, peers, and subordinates, drastically underestimating the amount of alienation I would undergo once the word hit the street. I felt as lonely as I when I had arrived at my first unit when I was a brand new butterbar.

Every day that I put on the uniform, I had a constant reminder of the importance of what I did for an occupation. Whether it be during a time of peace or war, my mere existence in the military ranks made a contribution. Anyone who has proudly served understands what I mean. You come to identify with the principles of Duty, Honor, and Country. I was no different. I transitioned to military intelligence after spending four years in armor. I gravely underestimated the significance of this transition away from being a tanker. Life would never be the same. I would never be the same either.

I left the army in March 1996 after nearly eight years of active duty service. I still ask myself if I made the right decision. Leaving something that has become a part of you is very difficult, much like losing an old friend or a spouse after a marriage. I felt a void in my life, an emptiness that could not be filled by anything civilian life had to offer. I struggled to determine where I fit in society. I guess they call it separation anxiety. Whatever it's called, I continually sought a replacement, not even aware of what I was looking for, of the elusive thing I found myself separated from.

With the years passing by, I have discovered that the void I have felt is the need to serve a higher cause, to contribute to a bigger purpose, to seek challenges that push me beyond the physical and mental thresholds that I set for myself. Any number of things in life can fill the void, such as being a loving parent to your children, a giving citizen in your community, a loving partner to your mate, or the restored hope in another person. All of these contribute, all help fill the void, although it will be difficult to completely replace the sense of fulfillment that came with freeing a nation from the chokehold of a ruthless foreign leader. I don't think anything will ever replace that feeling. But nothing has to. It will always be there; nothing can take it away. I only need other missions to sustain me as I move forward.

I don't think I could compose a list of the ways the Gulf War has changed me. I believe its impact continues to reveal itself on a daily basis. I know that my deep appreciation for life will never subside. Witnessing how fragile it is, how it can be taken away in a split second, has left me with an unforgettable mental imprint. Unfortunately, we often have to face dying to experience living. Ironic, but true.

The other mental imprint I will always carry is of the faces of the soldiers I served with during the Gulf War. I will remember them long after I forget the names. The different expressions I saw throughout Operations Desert Shield and Desert Storm tell the story. The looks of fatigue, fear, relief, joy, disappointment, anger, compassion, suffering, sorrow, and rage. The same expressions that have been flashing across the faces of warriors for centuries. As weaponry advances and tactics adapt, there remains one constant in the dynamics of combat: the soldier. Regardless of where and when the battle takes place, against whom and with what equipment, that human being pulling the trigger to extinguish the life of another while the other is trying to do the same will never change. They too will experience the fatigue, fear, relief, joy, disappointment, anger, compassion, suffering, sorrow, and rage.

Not a day passes that I don't think about where my life is going. I spend a great amount of time evaluating the dynamics of living and how it affects me. The people I have met, the experiences that I've had, the events that have shaped who I am will ultimately determine who I will become. In the desert Lt. Col. Randy Gordon always remarked that "destiny has brought us all together." The more I think about that statement, the more I realize how right he was. No planning went into my decision to join the ranks of the U.S. Army. It just happened. No planning took place prior to my soldiers and I being in the same platoon to fight on a modernized battlefield. It just happened. No planning could have prevented innocent lives from being taken on the battlefield. It just happened. No planning took place prior to my meeting a very special person who lately entered my life. It just happened. Some events in life are destiny. These are the events that shape us. We find out what we are made of, define what we believe in; they tell us who we are. The Gulf War did that for me.

It is the people whose lives have touched mine and whose lives I have touched, though, that have made my journey worth remembering: my dad, who would not allow me to let my fears make decisions for me; Staff Sergeant Deem, whose courage embodied the warrior spirit and who inspired me to always lead from the front; and most recently Leona, who has rekindled the burning ember inside me to search for the happiness that I know awaits me. The people that I've met have done this for me.

ALEX VERNON
(Army Commendation Medal with V-Device for valor in combat)[4]

President Bush's hasty 1991 declaration that the Persian Gulf War had "closed the book on Vietnam" insulted the American participants of both conflicts. For Gulf War veterans, our war became an epilogue, our newly dubbed "Southwest Asia campaign" the final campaign of Southeast Asia, the one in which the nation won back its pride. But Vietnam veterans never heard the book thump shut: That same year, Lt. Lewis B. Puller, Jr., USMC, published his Pulitzer-winning memoir *Fortunate Son: The Healing of a Vietnam Veteran*, describing his vanquishing of the ghosts of Vietnam; in May 1994, nine months after his only visit to Vietnam since the war, he found those ghosts reborn. "May God forgive him": for his suicide, one article prayed. But Lieutenant Puller's tragedy was that, unable to forget Vietnam, he could not forgive God. A year before, on Memorial Day at the Vietnam Memorial and amid anti-Clinton jeers, the legless Lieutenant Puller had wheeled forward to shake the president's hand. I imagine you can still spy his shadow, there — where officially his name cannot appear — on the obsidian wall. At Puller's memorial service, orange cones decorating the Fort Myer chapel parking lot reserved an additional twenty spaces for the disabled.

We know the plight of the Vietnam veteran. What do we know about veterans of the Gulf War? A 1995 Memorial Day editorial in *The New York Times* reported that "they may have more in common with Vietnam-era soldiers than World War II troops," that in fact they "are experiencing higher rates of unemployment, divorce, and alcohol abuse than Vietnam-era vets."[5] I would never assert any general parity between the horrors of the Gulf War and those of a Vietnam, Korea, or World War. Other soldiers of our generation have seen fiercer fighting, suffered greater tragedies, and been deployed away from home for longer periods, in places like Panama, Somalia, Haiti, and Bosnia (and Beirut and Grenada before).

We can mitigate the *Times's* statistics easily enough. Gulf War veterans returned to a nation with a worse economy and higher divorce rate than did the Vietnam vets, and to a society more sensitive to and more quick to diagnose posttraumatic stress disorder and alcohol abuse. We could argue that much of the to-do from Gulf veterans may be these twenty- and thirtysomethings growing up, growing older, yet with somewhere to point a finger. They can be victims. They can slough responsibility. The only angst the Gulf War veteran feels is a lack of Vietnam-angst angst, as a friend of mine has similarly surmised that the contemporary southerner pines for the angst of his postbellum forebears. In many cases these various arguments likely sit close to the truth.

None of the lives of those veteran friends of mine with whom I stay in touch have fallen apart — all officers, and no Gulf War Syndrome among them. If they suffer any, their sufferings are neither apparent nor discussed. I suspect that, like me, their ongoing self and the one left in the desert collide only sometimes, and it is easy enough to get on. One of our responses to the war has been belittlement. My West Point class's first captain (the ranking cadet), also a 24th Infantry Division Desert Storm veteran, in those first months home and trying, I suppose, to conciliate those classmates who did not deploy to the war, called it the "Beach Party" — as if, whereas Kurtz has become strangely symbolic of Vietnam, Ferris Bueller did the Gulf. I too have joked about my war, about "Purple Hearts for broken nails," as I once wrote. How dare a Gulf vet, after all, mope down like a dropped sack onto a barstool next to a veteran of a real war?

Yet how dare we dismiss our experience. Because for my soldiers, during Desert Shield's six-month wait on the mother of all battles, poetry was a jocoserious cadence about going home in a freezer-proof Ziploc sandwich bag. Because we did see the mangled dead and the mangled living. Because some of us saw friends wounded and killed, some of us did the wounding and killing. Because my division's after action review observed that "soldiers must be additionally 'hardened' to death and dying. Many reacted with what appeared to be symptoms of mild battle fatigue especially when faced with civilian deaths on the battlefield."[6] Because, as Alfred de Vigny reminds us, "the soldier is both victim and executioner."[7]

We tankers and grunts pulled the trigger and watched enemy vehicles stop and small buildings collapse and people crumble. We platoon leaders ordered others to pull the trigger. We drove our seventy-ton Abrams tanks over bunkers.

And I did all of this knowing that the thirty-nine-day air war and the artillery barrage rolling just ahead of me — streaking overhead shaking the earth beneath my track and setting the horizon aglow — that this extensive preparation of the battlefield was executed to make my mission easier, less painful. All that blind killing, for me. Dear Mom, My spoiling didn't end when I left home.

After our commander in chief pronounced Vietnam's death by the Gulf's one hundred-hour coup de grâce, we came home to the hoopla, to the parades and the cameras that constituted the national embrace. I remember feeling dubious about the outpouring, feeling that the group hug would amount to little more. Over the summer the parades became fewer, smaller, and not at all.

"Remember the Gulf War?" asks Bruce Cumings in his 1992 book *War and Television*. "Or was that last season's hit show?"[8] Cumings's hyperbolic rhetoric, if a jerked, cocky hip shot, at least lands in the engagement area. Some people's reaction upon learning about my involvement in the war:

"Cool."

"But you were an officer, right? You didn't, like, have to work with enlisted men."

"I met another guy, a tanker too, said he led the whole attack" (this one a dozen times now).

And not two years after the war: "Oh yeah, I remember that."

For Cumings, the Gulf War was "fought in the interest of forgetting." He charges that President Bush waged this "first 'television war'" to purge the nation of its Vietnam complex, "thus stubborn memory propels an unnecessary war to necessity."[9] If we even partially accept this thesis, then the forgetability of the Gulf War should not surprise: Drinking of Lethe works only when you forget kneeling on the river's bank and lowering your cupped hands into its waters.

Thinking about the war's forgetability, and television, and the *New York Times* report on Gulf War veterans, I am reminded of Robert O'Donnell, a thirty-seven year old who killed himself with a shotgun on 23 April 1995. Eight years earlier, he had pulled the eighteen-month-old Jessica McClure out of a well. According to journalist Lisa Belkin's account of O'Donnell's life,

he had saved a little girl's life, as the whole world watched, and, for a while, he was the center not only of his small universe, but of the real, known universe, the new one that sees everything simultaneously on CNN. There was a parade, countless television appearances, a letter from the president, a handshake from the Vice President, a made-for-TV movie. But eventually, the cameras went away, the world's attention moved on and he was left alone — a man so changed by fame that he no longer belonged in his world, but not changed enough that he could leave that world behind.

Postheroic O'Donnell had drug problems. He and his wife divorced. He lost his job. Baby Jessica's parents also divorced, and "others who helped to save the child found themselves drinking, or in marriage counseling, or in legal tangles, all because of the fickle, seductive, burning spotlight." O'Donnell's hometown paper ran an obit only. "What did he have to be depressed about?" Belkin quotes the paper's managing editor: "I could see if he found her down there dead, and he was haunted by that the rest of his life. But this was a success."[10] Our rescue of tiny Kuwait, too, was a success.

Thinking about Vietnam, I remember T. S. Eliot's *The Waste Land.* "Stetson!" the narrator of the first section of Eliot's 1922 poem cries to another on London Bridge: "You who were with me in the ships at Mylae!" The narrator has recognized a fellow World War I soldier, but he refers to a battle fought in 260 B.C. during the First Punic War. Some commentators have remarked that this line signifies the universality of war; a professor in graduate school pointed out Mylae's phonetic prescience of My Lai and the wasteland that was Vietnam.

But no war is the same. The wars of two veterans of the same war are not even the same war — veterans who write about war inevitably use the first person possessive. Were I not a veteran of the Gulf, had I not discussed my war with Vietnam veterans, I might imagine them resenting the support and welcome-home America showered on Gulf War soldiers. Maybe some do, though the ones I have spoken with are instead delighted that America has changed its ways. On some level war veterans bond with most other military veterans, whether they fought at all. The particulars of the service do not matter, as they belong to Providence. The willingness to serve is everything. I think the bond is tighter among war veterans — in the way we look in the other's eye, the way we shake hands. We know our wars were different, but we, from having been, know. In this sense, we did all stand in the ships at Mylae.

As for what may be the Gulf War's enduring legacies, I look to the myth from where this book's title comes. In naming the cause of Orion's death, the ancient storytellers diverge: In one version, the goddess Artemis, mistaking Orion from a distance for a villain, lets fly a shaft from her bow, its kinetic force penetrating the skull of her hunting partner — an honest accident. I imagine the spalling from his shattering skull making mush of his brain. In another version of the tale, the scorpion with repeated blows from its toxic tail stings Orion to death; we might imagine the constellation still receiving those blows, still voicing his unanswered pleas, crying his pain, expressing his ongoing suffering. It is as if these two versions of the tale, persisting in the stars, express the two persistent issues of Desert Storm, fratricide and the Gulf War Syndrome.

For the army, one immediate effect of the Gulf War and the nearly simultaneous end of the Cold War was the number of young officers who fled the service.

We can readily imagine the reasons. One lieutenant had never planned to stay past his five-year commitment anyway. "Five and fly" we had called it as cadets. Another decided he could not put his family through another lengthy and dangerous deployment. Yet another, perhaps a young captain, had a smart, ambitious wife who lately received admission to Stanford medical school. For him she had spent years in a dumpy Texas or Kentucky town outside a remote army installation; it was his turn to sacrifice. The old army paradigm — the old American paradigm — of the wife following the husband's career has been superseded. A fourth officer, as ambitious as anyone who ever made general, looked ahead to a twenty-five-year career with at best only five of those years spent in command. He leaves because he sees more opportunities for leadership outside the army. His similarly spirited friend would rather be rewarded for his proven abilities, not wait on a timescale to be promoted to the same rank and pay with several hundred of "roughly" the same caliber. A sixth has satisfied his curiosity about combat and perhaps finally quieted the shades of his father's war; a seventh decided that the violent life does not become him, that once is enough for being shot at and for killing. An eighth did not deploy to the Gulf and presumed the career of an officer who had missed the big one had a limited future. Women officers left for the same reasons plus one: motherhood. I imagine a larger percentage of women have left; those still in are likely either unmarried or married to another soldier.

And how can the army wince? During my days at West Point, the Academy changed its mission from inspiring in its graduates a "lifetime of service to the army" to a "lifetime of service to the nation." Not that our Academy experience had ever been about becoming generals. Being a platoon leader was everything. It was all that our officer instructors ever talked about — best job, only job, in the army, some of them said. So still another lieutenant leaves because he had realized his fullest career expectations. Yet the army *should* wince from the smarting of good leaders lost, and in truth there are as many explanations for young officers leaving the service in the years after the Gulf War as there are young officers who left the service in the years after the Gulf War.

I phoned Pat Hoy, a friend and former West Point professor, during one of my last opportunities to call home before the ground war. In my allotted fifteen minutes on the phone bank phone, I spent the first ten failing to reach Maria, my parents, then both my brothers. I got through to Pat with five minutes to talk.

"Your letters are full of anger," he challenged.

"It's the damn weather," I quipped, "freezing cold rain in the middle of the desert." Returning to the company, riding in the back of the Humvee, I realized I had dismissed him because I did not care to own up to my rage.

For the entirety of Desert Shield I privately protested our presence. To my fellow lieutenants, I complained that the Middle East had been a bloody mess for thousands of years; our moral crusade, and the American lives to be lost in the upcoming war, would change nothing. And what did rescuing Kuwait have to do with defending our Constitution, the mission to which I had sworn? To my soldiers, with whom I could not share these feelings, and to accustom them to the possibility of waiting and the possibility of dying, I explained how I would rather sit in the sand for eighteen months than risk their lives fighting the mother of all battles. To Maria I swore I would not vote for a Republican presidential candidate until I was out of the army. "If you and everyone you know aren't writing every politician you know and demanding American troops come home," I wrote to her on 27 October, "do it now. Please?" Matt Hoagland, Bravo Tank's Third Platoon leader, laughed my anger away. "You're too close to it. You can't be objective. Whatever we think now is bound to be revised when the war's over." He was right, and I knew it — but I was incapable of responding to the war politically or philosophically, or even rationally. This was personal. Hard facts can't check the momentum of emotional turbulence.

For the most part I managed to keep my feelings hidden, even from myself — to "tuck my soul away," as Hoy, a Vietnam veteran, would say — and continue the mission. Charlie Mike, as we said back then. My soul did break out a few times, usually in my letters, only rarely publicly. Anger, yes, and confusion, and bafflement, and supreme diffidence: a dust-devil whirling havoc on my insides.

In World War II, soldiers used booze and women to escape. In my more chaste war, I escaped through writing letters and reading books, only two with arguable pertinence: Paul Fussell's *Wartime* and T. E. Lawrence's *The Seven Pillars of Wisdom.* Along with the me who permitted his soldiers to go to war with a buffoon for a platoon sergeant, the me who escaped the desert through letters and books I can today hardly bear. Much of the time he spent in his Lotus-land of letters and books should have spent in thought on the enemy and fighting. He was pretentious, arrogant, and immature. His letters too often did not talk about the desert, the training, or his soldiers — "I will not describe what happened these last few days" — choosing instead to prattle about Jungian overtones in *Zen and the Art of Motorcycle Maintenance* and to relay to Maria every time he thought about other women, or about not marrying her. No, I do not care much for him.

On a late summer Friday afternoon, 1991, Jeannie Novak, the lieutenant who had seen us off to Saudi at Hunter Army Airfield, called from her new office at division headquarters with the news that the Defense Department was offering my Year Group '89 an early release from our remaining service. The local rock station played songs for its "electric lunch" on the theme of freedom. I jammed to the music in my car, the convertible I had bought with the money saved during the war. Top-down euphoria. Wind in my hair, Georgia sun on my face. I was free.

Five and fly, that old cadet expression, became *three and free.* Year Group '88 had received the word for their release months earlier; anticipating my early out, I had already finished my resignation paperwork by using a copy of Greg Jackson's. Other lieutenants who decided to leave the service came by my apartment to enter their information into the letters on my computer and print them. I also wrote Jan Myers, the congresswoman from Kansas who had provided my nomination for admission to West Point, and told her my plans to leave the service. Her reply praised my service and blessed my decision. I included that letter in my resignation packet until a major at brigade hazed me for its removal.

My mother labeled my eagerness to resign "crazed desperation." I was the first lieutenant of our year group at Fort Stewart to submit my papers. Rob Holmes gave me the nom de guerre of "the tip of the spear" after one of the 24th's own appellations. Mom wanted me to stay in the army for job security until I reminded her of the life insecurity. While before the war I might have entertained notions of remaining in the service, returning to graduate school on Uncle Sam's dollar, and balancing my life between the active and contemplative worlds of field duty and academia, after the war I could not wait a day to be a civilian studying English literature. West Point, the deployment, and the war rattled my psyche and kept it rattling for years. Sometimes you can still hear it.

I resigned to take back control of my life. Reflecting on my visits to Father Mike before we deployed, I suspect that they had much to do with an unconscious need to assert self: to expose the opportunity for not deploying so that the decision to deploy would be a decision, a volitional act. While as a young man before the deployment I believed, as young men do, my destiny mine, ever since the war I struggle to feel the course of my life mine rather than the end result of impersonal and invisible historical, cultural, political, economic, strategic, operational, and tactical machinations.

I resigned because, having trained for years and fought in combat, having witnessed others doing the same, I knew I did not have the stuff to command troops. Especially in combat. American soldiers deserve better leadership than I could ever provide. They deserve the likes of more committed leaders like Paul Kern, Dave Hubner, Dave Trybula, and officers no longer in the army, like Randy Gordon, Rob Holmes, Neal Creighton, and Greg Downey, whose reasons for leaving had nothing to do with any lack of talent for combat leadership. During Desert Shield, my fellow Bravo Tank platoon leader Matt Hoagland regularly joked, "you'll be a hero in spite of yourself"; meanwhile Eric Strong, a West Point classmate who did not deploy, called me in letters "Alex of Arabia, the Accidental Tanker." Because of my years in uniform and despite my resignation I remain a soldier, but I never was, never could have been, a warrior.

Second Brigade's new commander at the time I submitted my resignation, Col. Paul Kern's replacement, had to approve my request. He summoned me to his office. I stood locked at attention while he lectured me with raised voice on how I did not yet appreciate what it meant to sacrifice for my country, and how I would live to regret my decision. Then he told me he was going to ask that my termination date be delayed until after the brigade's next NTC rotation — he was terrified that he would not perform well at the NTC because so many of his experienced young officers were leaving the service. I went to my first Fort Stewart company commander, Capt. John Hadjis, for advice. "Don't fight him," he said, "unless you are plain sick of the shit."

I *was* plain sick of the shit. Before I had known I could resign, in the first months of being a first lieutenant and Alpha Tank's XO, I heard of an opening for a lieutenant with Division Protocol. I applied. Lieutenant Colonel Gordon counseled me against it and sent me from his office to reconsider; I returned two days later to tell him I wanted the job. In my mind, organizing VIP visits would advance a civilian career further than any more practice of my tanking skills. And I was tired of going to the field. Maj. Ken Boyd, 1-64's former executive officer and at the time on division staff, rejected my application "to protect the combat arms career of a solid young officer." Flash Gordon knew better, knew the instant I saluted and left his office the second time that whatever tanker bellyfire I might have had was extinguished.

I returned from the war selfish. The world had robbed me, and now it owed me. I bought the convertible, gave Maria up, chased skirts, then spent the three months after my resignation unemployed, making and breaking and making and breaking an engagement to another woman. The next three years, finally in graduate school at the University of North Carolina at Chapel Hill, were very much a recovery from the war and postwar period of my life. That period peaked in January 1994 after I watched the mediocre Kenneth Branaugh film *Dead Again,* a film about the persistence and resurrection of past violences. I sobbed, I gusted, for hours. My soul had come untucked and then some. It was the knowledge of my participation in the infliction of suffering and death that undid me that night. Recovering alcoholics — who are forever recovering, never recovered — stand up at meetings and declare: *I am an alcoholic.* That night in like fashion I stood up inside myself and declared: *I am a killer.* A taker of human life.

Three years after the war and I was just then coming home. I had recently fallen in love with a woman from the English Department who had no connections to the war. Letting go of my heart for Michelle may have done something to prompt the tearful letting go that night; over the next years she unquestionably helped guide me back to myself. My mother even sent her a card telling her as much. I do not suffer minor spells of depression as I did (though movie and newscast violence continues to muck with my insides). I did have one bout with depression that drove me out of school, and for the past three years I have worked for small software development companies specializing in education and training. But I am returned now to school, on my way to a Ph.D. and a career teaching writing and literature, and maybe publishing a little of my own work along the way.

I do miss elements of the army and army life, but I do not regret my decision to leave. Nor do I harbor any doubt that I shorted the country's investment in me. West Point exists to produce lieutenants the country can depend on to lead its citizen-soldiers into battle. The summer after the war, I participated in a Fourth of July parade in my hometown, a suburb of Kansas City, Kansas. As soldiers rode one per car past the reviewing stand, an announcer read their names over a loudspeaker. When it was my turn — I stood on the sedan's front seat, my body poked out through the sun roof, the car doors bore my name, and Maria rode in the back seat holding my leg — the parade announcer read my name, then offered an additional comment, something he hadn't done for the others, not even the captains and one major: "Thank you lieutenant, for bringing our boys home." That is what the office I held and what West Point are all about. That and nothing else.

The opportunity to coauthor and edit this book could not have come at a better time. I have reached a point, six years after the war, of having achieved enough emotional distance to write about it, but not so much temporal distance that my memory of the events has faded too much. For my survival in the desert, and for this book, I can only thank the stars, my commanders, my soldiers, and my friends.

A year after my homecoming, I attended a high school friend's wedding in Manhattan, Kansas. Driving from Kansas City to Manhattan, I was struck by the strangeness of cattle. Returned over a year, yet I found the common Kansan cow less real, less familiar, than an albino dromedary.

War for me will always be the color and texture of Persian sand, and the M1 tank.

Appendixes

A: Army Rank Structure, Abbreviations, and Slang

OFFICERS

Gen.	General	O-10	"four stars"
Lt. Gen.	Lieutenant General	O-9	"three stars"
Maj. Gen.	Major General	O-8	"two stars"
Brig. Gen.	Brigadier General	O-7	"one star"
Col.	Colonel	O-6	"full bird"
Lt. Col.	Lieutenant Colonel	O-5	"light colonel"
Maj.	Major	O-4	
Capt.	Captain	O-3	
1st Lt.	First Lieutenant	O-2	"LT"
2d Lt.	Second Lieutenant	O-1	"LT," "butterbar"

NONCOMMISSIONED OFFICERS (NCOS)

Cmd. Sgt. Maj.	Command Sergeant Major	E-10	
Sgt. Maj.	Sergeant Major	E-9	
1st Sgt.	First Sergeant	E-8	"Top"
M.Sgt.	Master Sergeant	E-8	
Sfc.	Sergeant First Class	E-7	
S.Sgt.	Staff Sergeant	E-6	
Sgt.	Sergeant	E-5	
Cpl.	Corporal	E-4	

ENLISTED SOLDIERS

Spc.	Specialist	E-4	"Spec 4"
Pfc.	Private First Class	E-3	"PFC"
Psc.	Private Second Class	E-2	"mosquito wings"
Pvt.	Private	E-1	

NOTES

Except in the case of the sergeant major, compound titles are often truncated in informal usage. So lieutenant colonels are referred to and addressed as "colonel," all sergeants of whatever rank are referred to and addressed as "sergeant," etc.

The letter-number listing indicates pay grade and is often used instead of a soldier's rank (but never when addressing a soldier). Pay grades across service branches match: a navy O-6 is a captain, the equivalent of an army colonel.

Noncommissioned officers are technically enlisted soldiers; the term either connotes both NCOs and the lower-ranking soldiers or just the latter (context dictates).

Corporals and specialists have the same pay grade (E-4), although corporals are considered noncommissioned officers because they hold a leadership position and so outrank specialists.

A first sergeant is the senior NCO in a company; the special nature of the position warrants it a distinct rank, even though it is the equivalent pay grade as master sergeant.

Unit commanders (captain for a company, lieutenant colonel for a battalion/task force, colonel for brigades and regiments, and general officers for divisions and higher) are commonly referred to as "the CO" or "the old man" by members of his or her command. A unit's second in command, the executive officer, is similarly referred to as the XO.

B: Glossary

AA: Assembly Area, a unit's home in the field

AOBC: Armor Officer Basic Course, a four-month course at Fort Knox for second lieutenants in the armor branch

ATACM: Army Tactical Missile System

BC: Bradley Commander, the soldier in command of an individual Bradley IFV or CFV

BDU: Battle Dress Uniform, the army's green camouflage uniform.

BP: Battle Position

CFV: Cavalry Fighting Vehicle, the M3 version of the Bradley used by scouts, with more firing ports than the M2 Infantry Fighting Vehicle

CG: Commanding General (Maj. Gen. Barry R. McCaffrey for the 24th; Lt. Gen. Gary Luck for the Eighteenth Airborne Corps; etc.)

CINCCENT: Commander in Chief, Central Command (Gen. H. Norman Schwarzkopf)

CO: Commander, usually used for a company commander

CP: Checkpoint ("Charlie Papa"), a graphic control measure for coordinating movements and communicating location information; also Command Post

CPX: Command Post Exercise, a training and coordination exercise conducted by and for unit commanders and their staffs

CTLT: Cadet Troop Leadership Training, a program whereby cadets from the Military Academy and ROTC units spend several weeks the summer before their senior year training with an active-duty unit

DCU: Desert Camouflage Uniform

Desert Laager: Variation of *laager*

DMAIN: Division Main, field headquarters for the 24th Infantry Division

EPW: Enemy Prisoner of War

FIST-V: Fire Support Team Vehicle, a modified M113 PC used at the company level by the fire support officer and his team; the FIST-V has a lazing device that can lock on a target and electronically transmit target data to the firing artillery units

FRAGO: Fragmentary Order, an unprepared or unplanned order issued/received; called fragmentary because it is very short, lacking the detail of an Operations Order

FSGCO: Family Support Group Coordination Office, an organization established at Fort Stewart by Major General McCaffrey to provide information to and otherwise assist families while a family member was deployed with the 24th Infantry Division

FSS: Fast Sealift Ship

FSO: Fire Support Officer, the artillery officer attached to an infantry or armor unit who advises the commander on using artillery and who communicates with the artillery units

GIRS: Grid Index Reference System, a graphic control measure on maps for coordinating movement and communicating location information by assigning alphanumeric identifiers to map grid coordinates

HET: Heavy Equipment Transport, used to move tracked vehicles along paved roads

IFV: Infantry Fighting Vehicle, the M2 mechanized infantry version of the Bradley, but with fewer firing ports and more room for transporting soldiers

Internal Look: A biennial CPX for CENTCOM, used for testing contingency plans and improving coordination among participating units

IP: Improved Product; the M1IP is the second generation of the M1 Abrams main battle tank

KTO: Kuwait Theater of Operations

Laager: Slang for a unit's Resupply on the Move (ROM) procedures

LBE: Load Bearing Equipment, the suspender and belt system worn over the BDU or DCU and used for carrying canteens, ammunition pouches, first aid pouch, compass, and/or other gear

LC: Line of Contact, a graphic control measure drawn on a map used to indicate the point in offensive operations after which the unit should expect to make contact with the enemy

LCE: Load Carrying Equipment, another term for LBE

LD: Line of Departure ("Lima Delta"), a graphic control element drawn on a map and used to coordinate the initial movement in offensive operations (e.g., several units cross the LD at a scheduled time); colloquially used as a verb, *to LD:* Ex: Delta Company LD'd at 0600 hours

LD/LC: Line of Departure/Line of Contact, one graphic control measure indicating both the LD and the LC

LOGPAC: Logistics Package, the delivery of supplies such as fuel, water, food, and sometimes mail

LT: Slang for lieutenant, as in *Hey, LT!*

LZ: Landing Zone, for helicopters

Mech: Mechanized, descriptor for an infantry unit, to distinguish it from light, Airborne, or other kinds of infantry

MLRS: Multiple Launch Rocket System

MOPP: Mission-Oriented Protective Posture, four posture levels define what soldiers wear for protection against the chemical weapons threat: MOPP I, chemical overgarments; MOPP II, chemical overgarments and rubber overboots; MOPP III, chemical overgarments, rubber overboots, and rubber gloves; MOPP IV, chemical overgarments, rubber overboots, rubber gloves, and mask

MRE: Meal Ready to Eat, preprocessed meals (often dehydrated) packaged in airtight brown plastic bags

NTC: National Training Center, Fort Irwin, California; brigades from Stateside units travel here to train for two weeks in the Mojave Desert against the OPFOR (Opposing Force), an American unit using Soviet tactics

OBC: Officer Basic Course (every branch has an OBC course), the several-month course teaches new lieutenants the essential skills and knowledge for their branch; the Armor Officer Basic Course (AOBC) is conducted at Fort Knox

OP: Observation Post, where guards pull duty for unit security

OPFOR: Opposing Force, the unit playing the enemy during simulation exercises; the National Training Center has a permanent OPFOR

OPLAN: Operations Plan

PL: Phase Line, graphic control measure used on maps to coordinate the movement of advancing units during an offensive operation

PT: Physical Training

REDCON: Readiness Condition, defined in four levels: REDCON 1, ready to execute the assigned mission on order with no notice; REDCON 2, ready to execute on fifteen minutes' notice; REDCON 3, ready to execute on sixty minutes' notice; REDCON 4, ready to execute on two hours' notice

RG: Republican Guard, the Iraqi military's elite army units

ROE: Rules of Engagement, the guidelines provided to American soldiers for when they can fire on the enemy

ROM: Refuel on the Move

SOP: Standard Operating Procedures

TAA: Tactical Assembly Area, a unit's home during hostilities, temporary and often serving as the unit's launch point

TAC: Tactical Assault Command (a subset of the TOC), the forward element of a battalion, brigade, or division headquarters; in the offense, the TAC travels with the combat units, while the TOC remains with the logistical supply trains

TC: Tank Commander (also Track Commander), the soldier in command of an individual tank or tracked vehicle

TF: Task Force, a task-organized battalion with both infantry and armor companies

TIRS: Terrain Index Reference System, a graphic control measure on maps for coordinating movement and communicating location information by assigning alphanumeric identifiers to terrain features

TOC: Tactical Operations Center, the TOC is the main headquarters for a battalion, brigade, or division

TOW: Tube-launched, optically tracked, wire-guided missile, an antitank missile system with both a dismounted and mounted versions (the Bradley is armed with one); infantry battalions have a fifth company, Echo Company, equipped with modified M113 personnel carriers called ITVs (Improved TOW Vehicles) armed with a TOW

Trains: A maneuver unit's inherent logistical support that trails the main fighting body several kilometers

UMCP: Unit Maintenance Collection Point, a battalion's "motor pool" in the field where vehicle and equipment maintenance is performed

XO: Executive Officer, second in command of a unit

Notes

Preface and Acknowledgments

1. Historical Resources Branch, U.S. Army Center of Military History, "XVIII Airborne Corps in Operations Desert Shield and Desert Storm: An Annotated Chronology" (hereafter "Annotated Chronology").

Introduction

1. Samuel Hynes, *The Soldiers' Tale,* pp. 4–5, 8 (emphasis added).
2. Norman Schwarzkopf, *It Doesn't Take a Hero,* photo caption. Earlier in his career Schwarzkopf had commanded the 24th: "I would have given anything to be with Barry McCaffrey and my old unit, the 24th Mechanized Infantry Division, which was about to mount a tank charge into Iraq" (452). When he retired with four stars in 1995, McCaffrey was the nation's most decorated soldier on active duty. James Kitfield's *Prodigal Soldiers* features him.
3. Joe Galloway, "The Point of the Spear," *U.S. News & World Report,* 11 Mar. 1991, p. 32; "Division Commander's Post-Attack Letter," 12 March 1991, *24th Mechanized Infantry Division Combat Team Historical Reference Book,* item 76 (hereafter *HRB* followed by item number).
4. The 24th's record slightly differs from the American total, in which more soldiers died during Desert Shield than Desert Storm. Norman Friedman, *Desert Victory,* p. 5.
5. Maj. Gen. Barry R. McCaffrey, Oral History, 28 Feb. 1991.
6. Rudyard Kipling, *The Irish Guards in the Great War,* pp. v–vi.

1. Operation Desert Shield, Part 1

1. Paraphrase of McCaffrey in Lt. Col. Richard J. Quirk, Oral History, 16 April 1991, p. 7.
2. Ibid., pp. 1–2.
3. Ibid., p. 6.
4. Initially, the Eighteenth Airborne Corps tasked only one brigade from the 24th Infantry and another from the 82d Airborne. Our commanders in short order decided that the situation required the entire corps. McCaffrey, Oral History, 24 Oct. 1990 (p. 2); and Maj. Jeff Bruckner, Oral History, 16 Mar. 1991 (p. 15). Bruckner, the 24th's liaison officer to the Eighteenth Airborne, remembers that the preliminary concept included an 82d Brigade and at most an air transportable–sized unit from the 24th, maybe one tank and one mechanized infantry platoon. The warning order from

corps tasked one brigade from the 24th as an "on-order" mission, meaning it would deploy only if called upon.

Our 2d Brigade was the division's first to deploy, because the 1st Brigade was still returning from a trip to the National Training Center. One of 2d Brigade's three battalions, 4-64 Armor, had deployed the majority of its soldiers to Korea over the summer for a twelve-month mission, leaving only a skeleton chain of command. McCaffrey swapped 4-64 with 1st Brigade's 3-69 Armor to give us a full brigade. The 1st Brigade would deploy after 4-64 filled its ranks with volunteers from nondeployable training units from Fort Knox. Meanwhile, the division gained the 197th Infantry Brigade from Fort Benning, since its assigned third brigade was a Georgia National Guard "round-out" unit that could not muster and move out prepared to fight quickly enough. After Desert Storm the 197th was permanently assigned as the 24th's third brigade, although it remained at Fort Benning.

5. "Annotated Chronology."

6. I am guessing Greg spoke with 1st Sgt. Burns, who served as 3-15's Delta Company first sergeant for the first month or so of Desert Shield and who had served in Vietnam.

7. Michael Shaara, *The Killer Angels,* p. 239.

8. Quirk, Oral History, p. 10.

9. Ibid., pp. 11–12.

10. A marine brigade with M60 tanks, army Apache attack helicopter units, the air force's 1st Tactical Fighter Wing, and navy aircraft carriers, according to Col. (Ret.) Richard M. Swain, Ph.D. Letter to John Hubbell, Kent State University Press, 7 Dec. 1997. In an email correspondence with me Col. Gordon confirms that after the 82d came "the Marines in Brigade strength with pre-po[sitioned equipment] from Diego Garcia" and then the Eighteenth Airborne Corps's Attack Aviation Brigade, followed by the 24th and the 101st.

11. McCaffrey, Oral History, 24 Oct. 1990, p. 3.

12. According to James Blackwell of the Center for Strategic and International Studies, two of the fast sealift ships broke down, one of which "took so long to repair that it arrived after the slow boats" (*Thunder in the Desert,* p. 98).

13. McCaffrey, Oral History, 24 Oct. 1990, pp. 14–16.

14. "Humvee" is the pronunciation for the acronym HMMWV, which stands for High-Mobility, Multipurpose Wheeled Vehicle. The Humvee replaced the old Jeep. It is also popularly called "Hummer."

15. Col. Paul J. Kern, "Operation Desert Shield [and] Operation Desert Storm," p. 2 and map.

16. "September 1: 0600 2nd Squadron (-), 4th Cavalry (24th Infantry Division), task force closes into Assembly Area CAVALRY with: Headquarters and Headquarters Troop; Troop C; Team D, 3rd Battalion, 15th Infantry; Battery A (MLRS), 13th Field Artillery; and Stinger section of Battery B, 1st Battalion, 5th Air Defense Artillery." "Annotated Chronology."

17. The two light divisions "aren't equipment-oriented the way we are. Particularly in the case of the 82nd, they are a little light on staying power or the ability to just sit

for a very long period of time, which they didn't see as a primary mission for themselves. For those reasons and whatever reasons I do not know, they moved into hard sites. I didn't visit the 101st, but I did visit the 82d. Their facility was a nicer place than where they live at Fort Bragg by far. It was beautiful. They set themselves in there and did their training just outside the gates or in the area." Quirk, Oral History, pp. 12–13.

18. 1st Lt. John A. Ford and 2d Lt. William Lockard, "Company Fire Support Operations," *Field Artillery* (Oct. 1991): 22–24.

2. Desert Shield, Part 2

1. "Annotated Chronology"; also Kern, "Operation Desert Shield [and] Operation Desert Storm," p. 1.

2. Gordon was perhaps prompted in his thinking by a memorandum from McCaffrey of 12 September 1990: "Under certain circumstances, METT-T [Mission, Enemy, Terrain (and weather), Troops, and Time] analysis may reveal we have to fight in company or battalion (pure) configuration versus fighting as company/teams or battalion task forces" (*HRB* 3). Maj. David R. Apt describes McCaffrey's thinking: "You don't break companies apart if possible. . . . He doesn't tell the brigade commander what to do but his philosophy is you don't need [to task organize companies] if you're in a wide open area where field of fire are great. For maintenance purposes, [too]. . . . Why break [companies] down for the sake of the school book solution? . . . The smartest thing was the logistically simplest to maintain over the long distance we will travel" (Oral History, 6 Feb. 1991). Admirably, McCaffrey trusted his battalion commanders to decide.

3. The contest was sponsored by U.S. Army Community and Family Support Center (USACFSC), and the winning entry for the short poem category was Capt. Gregory M. Smith's "The Soul of Armor" (*Feedback*, April 1994, p. 3):

> I have seen the dust of 59 tanks
> Ghost-like, illuminated
> By the blood-red predawn sky
> And I've felt the rumbling of their track
> Reverberating in my bones.
> The clang of steel on steel, and the anticipation
> Of upcoming contact.
> A clash of voices guiding me, as I guide others
> To the rhythm of the turret's whine.
> I've coughed and choked on diesel fumes
> Acrid in the morning air
> And I've smelled the unwashed bodies of my crew,
> The weariness etched in dusty lines
> Around their tired eyes.
> Yet I've been thrilled with the tracers arcs
> As they danced across the starlit night

And I've gloried in every main gun round
That tore apart the very sky.
The soul of Armor lies within
The crews of these leviathans
Who work and sweat and struggle on
All day, all night, 'till the bitter dawn.

4. Kern, "Operation Desert Shield [and] Operation Desert Storm," p. 4.
5. Prince, "The Arms of Orion," from *Batman* (Warner Bros., 1989).
6. " . . . track on the fleet of M1IPs will need to be upgraded to at least 500 miles of track life before crossing the LD. . . . Retention of the M1IPs is not 'free.' The ARCENT and Corps logistics burden to provide engines, track, and rounds capable of defeating Iraqi armor will be significant." Memo from Brig. Gen. Joe Frazar, *HRB* 13.
7. *HRB* 14.
8. *HRB* 13 (McCaffrey note); "Annotated Chronology" (3d ACR).

3. Desert Storm: The Air War

1. On 18 February, six days before the ground war, "the last equipment departed the Saudi ports for the VII Corps' tactical assembly areas." Frank N. Schubert and Theresa L. Kraus, eds., *The Whirlwind War*, p. 118.
2. Indeed, most of the Gulf War's twenty-eight incidents in which U.S. forces engaged friendly forces occurred during periods of limited visibility. "There were a total of 615 U.S. military battle casualties — 148 were killed in action, of which 35 were killed by friendly fire; there were 467 wounded, of which 72 were by friendly fire." Department of Defense news briefing, 13 Aug. 1991.
3. Apt, Oral History.
4. Gordon is "still convinced" that we did not need the Seventh Corps, as is General McCaffrey: "Obviously I think it now, I just think it would have been a lot less risky than I thought at the time." McCaffrey, Oral History, 28 Feb. 1991.
5. Robert H. Scales, Jr., *Certain Victory*, pp. 126–28; Schubert and Kraus, *The Whirlwind War*, pp. 106–7. In my limited research, I found no evidence that the 24th's initial one-corps plan, Southern Storm, received any attention by CENTCOM. Schwarzkopf's offensive planning team made its first formal briefing of its one-corps concept to the CENTCOM joint operations and plans officer on 25 September, the same day Major Apt presented Southern Storm to McCaffrey. Scales, *Certain Victory*, pp. 125–26. And both Apt and Maj. Jason Kamiya suggest that Southern Storm was intended only as an exercise to get the staff thinking about offensive operations. Apt, Oral History. Nonetheless, the revised two-corps Operation Desert Storm attack plan preserved critical elements of the 24th Infantry's one-corps Southern Storm vision. The difference is primarily one of degree. Southern Storm involved one corps; Desert Storm used two. Southern Storm called for a forty-eight-hour air war preceding the ground assault, during which time the ground units would move to their attack positions; Desert Storm extended the air war for forty days. In Southern Storm, a fixing force of U.S. Marines would launch the operation up the coast prior

to the main attack in the west; in Desert Storm a similar marine fixing force, including the Arab multinational Joint Forces Command, preceded the main attack in the west (Southern Storm did not add the Arabs to the battle until G+3). Six hours after the initial attack fixed Iraqi forces and their commanders' attention in the east, Southern Storm's main attack would commence, swinging around the western edge of Iraq's Kuwaiti defensive lines and penetrating the Iraqi rear; twenty-six hours after Desert Storm's fixing attack, its main attack would commence, swinging out even further west (into Iraq). And both plans called for marines to conduct a diversionary "demonstration" off the Kuwait coast. One difference between Southern Storm and Desert Storm was the established H-hour. Southern Storm would have kicked off in the evening for a night fight, whereas Desert Storm commenced in the morning. The working title for the initial two-corps plan was "Operation Desert Sword."

6. According to the 24th Infantry's operations officer (G-3), Colonel Lamar: "The soldiers did not know what they were training for, they did not know what they were rehearsing for. That was not told to them until the last minute, only because of an OPSEC [operational security] concern. . . . They did not know the type mission they were going to do, they did not know where they were going, and they did not know the importance of their mission. Now the commanders knew, and the commanders were put on board early on with the charter to maintain as much operational security as feasible while you were trying to train your soldiers. . . . The units themselves never knew what the mission was until approximately two days before we actually got the word to go," around 22 February, about three weeks after I had told my soldiers the plan. Lt. Col. Patrick Lamar, Oral History, 28 Feb. 1991.

7. I have in my possession thirty-one sheets. A brigade memorandum of 23 January 1991 authored by Maj. Garth T. Bloxham states that the brigade "will issue overlays and operate off of 4 sets of maps . . . which will consist of 8 1:50000 mapsheets," for a total of forty-eight sheets; the memo, however, lists thirty-six maps, while its diagram shows thirty-three. A diagram attached to the memo, presumably demarcating the division's operational area, shows between seventy-three and ninety-six mapsheets. (It has two different, overlapping outlines.) I received my maps from Captain Baillergeon on 25 January, the morning my Bravo Tank loaded the HETs for the move west. He gave me two sets, each a monstrously thick roll of nearly three hundred sheets held together by rubberbands. My set was incomplete, and some maps were black-and-white photocopies. Dave Trybula also received two incomplete sets on the twenty-fifth.

8. "Division leadership . . . believed that 1:100,000 scale was good enough. That is 25% as expensive as a 1:50,000 scale. We ended up with 1:50,000 because that's what was available . . . largely because that's what the light divisions wanted." Quirk, Oral History, p. 18.

9. Nothing about the battle for Khafji is reported in the "Annotated Chronology" even though it includes many other notable events from other units throughout the theater. While Scales's *Certain Victory* does confirm the initial report I received of three distinct attacks, it does not mention the fratricide or the number of U.S. casualties

(p. 190). Schubert and Kraus's *The Whirlwind War* gives the battle one sentence in a paragraph celebrating American defense agencies' "impressive" ability to quickly "answer demands from Central Command for new products," in this case for antifratricide methods: "The successful allied counterattack on the city of R'as al Khafji in the first week of February was marred when American support fire killed several CENTCOM troops" (p. 204).

10. McCaffrey, Oral History, 28 Feb. 1991.

11. Norman Friedman, *Desert Victory*, p. 15.

12. 2 Tim. 1:7: "For God has not given us a spirit of timidity, but of power and love and discipline." Rom. 8:28–38: "If God is for us, who is against us? . . . Who shall separate us from the love of Christ? Shall tribulation, or distress, or persecution, or famine, or nakedness, or peril, or sword? Just as it is written, 'For thy sake we are being put to death all day long; we were considered as sheep to be slaughtered.' But in all these thing we overwhelmingly conquer through Him who loves us."

13. "0235 Battery A, 3d Battalion, 41st Field Artillery . . . in support of Task Force 3-15 Infantry, fires one 155mm Copperhead round at border post (MT 885302), destroying the building; site subsequently swept by dismounted patrol from Company A, 1st Battalion, 64th Armor. [24th Infantry Division SITREP; . . . Eighteenth Airborne Corps Tactical Command Post Journal says that the COPPERHEAD was fired by Battery A, 1st Battalion, 41st Field Artillery at a building at MT 881609]." "Annotated Chronology."

4. Desert Storm: The Ground War

1. "24th Mechanized Infantry Division Combat Team: Operation Desert Storm Attack Plan OPLAN 91–3."

2. *HRB* 53. The document is marked classified until 1 March 1991, either expecting a G-Day after 1 March or releasing it from classification only well after the attack had begun.

3. The "Annotated Chronology" reports that our 2d Brigade had "two mechanized infantry company teams along Phase Line Opus." I am aware of TF 3-15's Alpha Tank, an armor company-team, and TF 1-64's Delta Tank, an armor pure company that had one infantry platoon attached to it for the PL Opus mission.

4. According to the "Annotated Chronology," ARCENT initially issued a warning order to the Corps at 0910 to have the 24th and the 3d ACR prepared to attack at 1200; the order from ARCENT to attack at 1500 came at 1300. *The Victory Book* says McCaffrey received the order from corps "around noon" (p. 86). The chronology also records that the corps's lead elements did have some minor engagements with the enemy.

5. The division crossed the LD with an amazing 95-97 percent equipment operational readiness rate. McCaffrey, Oral History, 28 Feb. 1991.

6. Per all plans and memories, 1-64 and 3-15 crossed the LD abreast, though the chronology specifies that the 2d Brigade was "led by Task Force 3-15 Infantry." Captain Swisher confirms that 3-15 was initially "the main attack," at least through Attack Position Dallas. Capt. Jeff B. Swisher, Oral History, 30 Apr. 1991, p. 7.

7. "The instructions to the [combat trains] maintenance crews was if you can fix it in thirty minutes, do so. We figured in thirty minutes . . . they should be able to catch up [with the main body]. And if not, go ahead and abandon that piece of equipment for follow-on maintenance crews in our field crews. . . . six hours behind us, . . . at the worst case a day or two behind us" Maj. Steven Tate, Oral History, 26 Apr. 1991, p. 8.

8. "1930 24th Infantry Division halts both attacking brigades to establish forward operating base and ROM sites." "Annotated Chronology."

9. "0600 24th Infantry Division reports that . . . 2d Brigade is at Objective GRAY. . . . 0900 24th Infantry Division reports that . . . 2d Brigade is still at Objective GRAY. . . . 1330 2d Brigade, 24th Infantry Division secures Objective GRAY. [Also see 24th Infantry Division SITREP, 26 Feb. 1991, which reports that on 25 Feb. Task Force 1-64 Armor suffered two killed in action and two wounded in action; Eighteenth Airborne Corps SITREP, 25 Feb. 1991, says attack began at 0800Z and objective secured at 1000Z and further specifies that Task Force 3-15 Infantry led the attack, with Task Force 1-64 Armor engaging a battalion command post at NU 210310 capturing fifty enemy prisoners of war]. . . . 1400 2d Brigade, 24th Infantry Division, secures Objective GRAY with fire support of 24th Infantry Division Artillery and 212th Field Artillery Brigade; Task Force 1-64 Armor engages suspected battalion command post at NU 210310 with indirect fire and captures about 50 enemy prisoners of war. [24th Infantry Division SITREP, 25 Feb. 1991, which does not give a time; Eighteenth Airborne Corps Tactical Command Post SITREP 181 (25 Feb. 1991), which gives time as 1400 and says 100 enemy prisoners of war; Eighteenth Airborne Corps Tactical Command Post Journals specify that the objective was seized and reported at 1400 but that it was occupied beginning at 1330 and that 100 enemy prisoners were captured and that a confirming report was also filed at 1501]. . . . 1800 24th Infantry Division forward line of own troops has . . . 2d Brigade on Objective GRAY." "Annotated Chronology."

10. Soldiers killed: Pfcs. Marty R. Davis and Corey L. Winkle. According to Lt. Col. Raymond Barrett, TF 3-15 commander, he received the initial incident report and Medevac request from Captain Schwartz around 1600 (Oral History, 1 Mar. 1991). Capt. Eric C. Schwartz adds that the Medevac took "a long time" to arrive, and that he later lost another soldier when "his leg was caught underneath the breach of the [tank] main gun and as the gun elevated it crushed his leg" (Oral History, 30 Apr. 1991, pp. 14–16). "1820 Two soldiers from Company B, 2d Battalion, 15th Infantry (24th Infantry Division) are killed and two wounded at NU 857337 when a grenade falls off a protective vest and explodes. . . . 2300 24th Infantry Division reports that Battle Positions 101, 102 and 103 have been secured respectively by the 197th Infantry Brigade, 1st Brigade and 2d Brigade." "Annotated Chronology."

11. "I know we got in formation at 0400. So I think it was a 0500 LD." Swisher, Oral History, p. 10.

12. In response to a question of mine, Col. Randy Gordon remarked that the "the original plan had 2d Brigade attacking Tallil Air Base at an earlier stage of the battle.

When the French were given that particular axis the plan changed. From what we knew about Jalibah at the time of planning, yes [it required more than a single task force]. The plan correctly gave the mission to the entire brigade. I believe we should have updated the plan as we gained information, but in the end it was okay." It does not appear that the plan had ever called for Task Force 1-64 to attack the objective alone. Email, 2 Sept. 1997.

13. Swisher's Oral History (pp. 12, 19) and a phone conversation with Greg Jackson confirm this company configuration in the task force box formation.

14. "*2300* 2d Brigade secured Battle Position 103 (PU 2380) and began preparations for attack on Objective ORANGE." "Annotated Chronology."

15. Swisher confirms a 0500 artillery prep and a 0600 LD time (Oral History, p. 12).

16. This initial diamond formation, with the two mech companies setting in a support by fire position, was confirmed by Colonel Gordon. Email, 26 Apr. 1998.

17. Dave Trybula's oral history interview, conducted by S.Sgt. Warren B. Causey, is very brief, and in the duplicate I have (copied from the one held at the Center of Military History's Oral History Activity), Dave's voice suffers the chipmunk effect of an improper recording speed.

18. Swisher confirms that TF 3-15 "hit the airfield a little bit farther north than what we originally intended, so my company hit the western fence and then very quickly, after several hundred meters, my northern platoon, which was Third Platoon, was pushed out the northern fence of the airfield because we had been pushed so far north." Swisher, Oral History, p. 14. Alpha Tank commander Eric Schwartz similarly remarks that "we ended up kind of — the two tank companies I think kind of became the main effort for the sweep across the northern portion of the airfield. . . . I didn't [see the link-up with 1-64 on the right flank]. I ended up losing contact with 1-64 after we started to make our northern turn. We never really came into contact with them." Schwartz, Oral History, pp. 21–24.

19. Two were killed, according to Colonel Gordon: "Pfc. John Hutto . . . and Spc. Andy Alaniz who had an eighteen-month-old daughter." Greg actually recalls the friendly fire incident occurring at the beginning of the battle, as the assault on the airfield began, not at the end, as Rob remembers. Captain Hubner and Colonel Gordon agree with Greg, the latter writing that "it happened when we were within 2,000–3,000 meters of the perimeter fence. . . . On the voice tape [of the battalion radio net] made by the medics, the second aid station moved to the three Bradleys just as Charlie and Delta Tank were assembling at the west end of the airstrip and beginning the assault. I had already sent [Maj.] Jim Diehl to take charge of [Charlie Mech] while we waited for 3-15 to show up at the airfield. The evacuation of dead and wounded was completed after we got to the other side." The commander of the company that suffered the friendly fire casualties, Capt. William Hamowitz, also recalls the incident happening prior to the assault. Additionally, he records receiving friendly mortar fire as well as friendly direct fire (Oral History, 5 Mar. 1991). Gordon flatly disagrees, asserting that all incoming mortar rounds were Iraqi. Gordon also recalls (differently from Downey) that the

failed scout link-up occurred with 3-69 and cites that failure as a contributing factor in the fratricide. Greg's version, in which the failed scout link-up occurred with 3-15, makes sense to me as a partial explanation for my failure to link up with 1-64's assault force.

20. *Victory Book*, pp. 100, 140, 144; *U.S. News & World Report* Staff, *Triumph Without Victory*, p. 377. Joe Galloway, a contributor to this book, traveled with the 24th Infantry during Desert Storm and is acquainted with both General McCaffrey and Colonel Kern.

21. "There were several reports . . . [of about] fifty armored vehicles . . . moving west." Swisher, Oral History, p. 25.

22. "[*0600*] 24th Infantry Division commences attack on Objective ORANGE with 1st Brigade firing artillery preparation followed by supporting ground attack and consolidation on objective. . . . *0600* 2d Brigade, 24th Infantry Division, attacks to Battle Position 104 and Jalibah Air Field (PU 555796), overcoming light resistance from airfield guards; Task Force 3-69 Armor destroys ten fixed wing aircraft (including MiG-29s), eight helicopters, and fourteen T-55 tanks at a cost of ten wounded in action; then carries out main effort attack on Objective ORANGE. . . . *0300Z* [0600] 1st Brigade, 24th Infantry Division, initiates supporting attack on Objective ORANGE; 2d Brigade then follows with the main attack, supported by AH-64 Apaches. . . . *0700* Company C, 3d Battalion, 15th Infantry (24th Infantry Division) has ten wounded in action when an M-2 Bradley is struck by an artillery round near Basrah. . . . *0725* Objective ORANGE secured by 24th Infantry Division. [Also see 24th Infantry Division SITREP, 27 Feb. 91, which says that AH-64 support during attack on ORANGE accounted for one tank, two MTLBs, one BDRM, one artillery piece, six trucks, two fuel trucks, and ten enemy killed in action; Eighteenth Airborne Corps Tactical Command Post SITREP 183 (27 Feb. 91), says that at 0715 the division's 1st and 2d Brigades encountered light resistance from infantry bunkers at ORANGE and destroyed four towed artillery pieces, fourteen supply trucks, two fuel trucks, one helicopter and one fixed wing airplane]. . . . *0900* 24th Infantry Division initiates attack to sweep Objective ORANGE oriented on Jalibah (PU 5580). [Eighteenth Airborne Corps Tactical Command Post SITREP 183 (27 Feb. 91)]. . . *1000Z* [1300] Objective ORANGE secure; reported damage to Iraqis of 58 tanks, 8 helicopters, 10 fighters, 2 BMPs, 77 heavy equipment transporters, 2 fuel trucks, 2 BDRMs, 2 MTLBs, 100 artillery tubes, 6 trucks, and 200 enemy prisoners of war. . . . *1300* 2d Brigade, 24th Infantry Division, continues attack to Phase Line AXE." "Annotated Chronology."

23. "We received an intelligence report . . . that indicated that the Hammurabi had approximately four infantry battalions moving northwest along Highway 8. That came in yesterday morning on the 27th. Subsequent other reports . . . seemed to confirm this. . . . Based on the information that was available, there were 200 tanks. . . . As of right now, we are facing elements of one infantry brigade — one battalion reported deployed north of the highway in 3-15's sector, one battalion deployed south of the highway in 1-64's sector. Approximately ten kilometers behind

those lead battalions is found the division counter-attacking force at sixty percent strength." Maj. Mark Rodriguez, Oral History, 28 Feb. 1991. "At least two brigades . . . though this is not totally confirmed." Anonymous, Oral History, 28 Feb. 1991.

24. "*27 February (C+204; D+41; G+3) 0920Z [1220]* ARCENT FRAGO #67 to OPORD DESERT STORM 001 announces a temporary cease fire effective at 0200Z [0500] on 28 February. . . . *2000Z [2300]* Eighteenth Airborne Corps FRAGO 79 to OPORD DESERT STORM gives the commander's concept for defensive and security operations in sector, but directs the Eighteenth Airborne Corps to be prepared to resume offensive operations. Additionally sets forth rules of engagement to be followed during the cease fire. [Note: Issued out of sequence.] *28 February (C+205; D+42; G+4) 0145* Eighteenth Airborne Corps receives notification of a possible cease fire to go into effect at 0200Z [0500]. . . . *0515* ARCENT FRAGO 68 directs attacks to continue until 0800C at which time a cease-fire will begin. . . . *0320Z* Eighteenth Airborne Corps FRAGO 78 to OPORD DESERT STORM announces that a cease-fire will begin at 0500Z [0800] on 28 February, but specifies that units are to continue offensive operations to destroy enemy armored vehicles with a maximum use of AH-64 helicopters and Air Force aircraft. Additionally specifies that the cease fire does not prohibit the destruction of bypassed equipment and facilities. Also directs a maximum effort to be made in refitting the force and planning for on order offensive operations after the cease fire. . . . *0800* CEASE-FIRE GOES INTO EFFECT. . . . *0800* At cease-fire, 24th Infantry Division poised along Phase Line AXE to engage Hamurabbi Division at Phase Line CRUSH, with 1st Brigade positioned on left, 2d Brigade in center, 3d Armored Cavalry on right, and 197th Infantry Brigade in center after completing refueling at Objective ORANGE; 2d Squadron, 4th Cavalry, in position behind 1st Brigade. NOTE: 24th Infantry Division Artillery with support of 212th and 196th Field Artillery Brigades fired up until cease-fire." "Annotated Chronology."

25. According to Swisher, the artillery barrage ceased at 0458 (Oral History, p. 29). The official theaterwide cease-fire actually did not commence until 0800; I have heard that the fact that the 24th understood that it was to begin at 0500, thus losing three hours of operational time, was no small point of anger for McCaffrey. Swisher also notes that at the time of the cease-fire, Task Force 3-15 was at the PU95 north-south gridline (about 47° 02' E, 30° 30' N). Swisher, Oral History, pp. 29, 26.

After the war McCaffrey characterized the cease-fire as a time of "tremendous" (*HRB* 70), "enormous" (*Victory Book*, p. 108), and "careful restraint" (*HRB* 77). The division recorded eight "post cease-fire incidents." Only one of these involved the 2d Brigade: on 01 March at 1104 hours, "2nd Brigade reported that enemy artillery and mortar fire impacted in their assigned sector. The brigade secured the site of a downed 101st Airborne Division helicopter." *Victory Book*, p. 109; *HRB* 77.

26. "There were reports of incoming [artillery] picked up on the radar, that incoming rounds were spotted, and we did have some counter[battery] fire approved to shoot. Later there was a report of activity within the sector, aggressive acts toward us. Several rounds were fired, and then we discovered that in fact the activity that

we saw were elements from the 3rd ACR forward within our sector as well as elements from one of our southern units moving across one of the battalion boundaries. No one was injured from the few rounds of artillery that were fired before a check fire was called." Anonymous, Oral History.

27. "0800 Eighteenth Airborne Corps assesses all Iraqi divisions in the Kuwaiti Theater of Operations to be combat ineffective. . . . 24th Infantry Division establishes Phase Line KNIFE screen line to enhance force protection with each brigade placing three company teams as the screen." "Annotated Chronology."

28. "We found a Chinese armored ambulance — it had a big crescent on it — that our Delta Company 1st. Sgt. was running around in. I finally made him quit before he got shot. We also found about three 113 ambulances and a 577, which we took the final drives out of. I think we took the engine out of one of them, and put it in [one of our] vehicles." Tate, Oral History, p. 51.

29. "0330 Military negotiations are postponed until 1100C on 3 March." "Annotated Chronology."

30. Colonel Gordon: "I was less than one kilometer behind Greg when the tomato-laden truck got in the way of Greg and another target. I was moving up to accompany the scouts as I thought we would be moving into the rear of 4-64 within a couple of hours. . . . It was definitely on the 2nd of March and was just south and west of the Rumaylah complex. . . . The man dying was unfortunate. . . . I still cannot believe that Greg thought I would be upset with him — those guys must have thought me to be such a tyrant." Email, 15 Sept. 1997.

31. On 3 March at 1355 hours, "GEN H. Norman Schwarzkopf meets with senior Iraqi representatives to negotiate cease-fire" ("Annotated Chronology"). On 3 March, Captain Swisher reports finding a crashed American F-16, with no ejection seat (Oral History, p. 34). The pilot may or may not have been one of those whom Hussein captured and chained to a potential air strike target as an air defense measure. I am reminded of the Gulf War's first downed pilot, Lt. Cmdr. Michael Speicher, whose fate "remains unknown." Tim Weiner, "Gulf War's First U.S. Casualty Leaves Lasting Trail of Mystery," *New York Times*, 7 Dec. 1997, p. 1.

32. Swisher reports that the company's position along the DMZ was roughly at the QU35 north-south gridline (about 47°27' E, 30°27' N). He also notes that "we saw the firefights between the Iraqis. . . . At night we could see the flashes on the horizon over Basra from the fighting" (Oral History, pp. 37, 40). My letter covering this period records that my day securing the road through the DMZ was 6 March; it may or may not correspond to this entry in the Eighteenth Airborne Corps Annotated Chronology for 7 March: "2d Brigade, 24th Infantry Division, establishes outposts at QU 351727 and QU 355692 to observe high speed avenues of approach."

33. McCaffrey, Oral History, 28 Feb. 1991.

34. "The idea from the very start was, Don't let them know we are here. Go where he is not. Move very quickly. . . . Interrogation of some of the EPWs indicated they had no idea that we were in Iraq. . . . They had no idea that American forces would come this way. None at all. They all suspected that the American forces would come

up the east coast into Kuwait. We know for a fact that the Iraqis tried to find us for the last six months we were in theater, and never were successful in figuring out where the 24th really was. As a matter of fact every [intelligence] report from captured intelligence sources indicate the Iraqis were convinced that we were on the east coast of Saudi Arabia. In reality, when they made that assessment, we were actually sitting on the Iraqi border west [of the Neutral] Area, waiting to go across the line." Lamar, Oral History. Many of the enemy tanks and BMPs destroyed by the 24th were riding down the highway on the back of HET transport trucks.

35. During the war, some of our refuel and resupply arrived just in time. Once the division Assault CP lost communication with its maneuver brigades for four hours (Lamar, Oral History). Additionally, "aspects of our logistical structure . . . were never tested, as result of the brevity of the war. . . . [C]ommanders in the field never had to ration their consumption. . . . [W]e never had to test our maintenance capabilities nor our medical facilities in any serious way." William G. Pagonis, *Moving Mountains*, p. 149. "Long distances for resupply in Iraq put a heavy strain on division/COSCOM transportation assets" (HQ, 24th ID, Operation Desert Storm AAR — Executive Summary para 2.D.20). On the route out of Iraq, "things did start breaking down. Again some of the tanks because of fuel problems with the fuel pumps. . . . Some of the 577s went down, and some of the 113s went down. . . . We burned up at least one [M88 Recovery Vehicle] just trying to [tow an M1]. . . . I started to have some track breakdowns on the 88s as well. . . . We pulled all of our broken equipment over on the side of the road across the berm because I would tell crews just to drag it across the berm, get it into Saudi Arabia, and we will figure out a way to get it on home from there" (Tate, Oral History, pp. 59–62). "Adequate communication assets were not available for requesting and controlling MEDEVAC aircraft. . . . Battalion aid stations were unable to communicate with supporting medical units" (JULLS 51553-19973); and "medical companies were inadequately equipped and staffed to complete the medical mission" (JULLS 51563-23896).

36. Scales, *Certain Victory*, p. 315.

5. After the Storm: Redeployment and Reflections

1. Bad weather forced the division's first convoy from Jalibah to King Khalid Military City to turn around on 5 March; the division's "token redeployment element led by Brig. Gen. [Terry] Scott" departed Dharhan Airport at 0700 on 7 March and arrived at Hunter Army Airfield at 0840 on the eighth. Another division redeployment flight departed Dhahran with 411 personnel at 1830Z on 7 March, landing at Hunter at 1920 hours on the eighth." "Annotated Chronology."

2. The "Annotated Chronology" records an additional half-dozen such incidents.

3. Greg Downey recalls boarding the plane on 19 March, and Rob Holmes at 0600 on the twenty-first. All of us were on the same flight.

4. Part of this has been adapted from an essay originally published as "Bridging the Gulf" in North Carolina's *Independent Weekly*, 14–20 Feb. 1996. Thanks to Bob Moser for his editorial talents and patience.

5. Eric Schmitt, "Victorious at War, Not Yet at Peace," *New York Times*, 28 May 1995, sect. 4, pp. 1, 4.

6. Pagonis, *Moving Mountains* (HQ, 24th ID, Operation Desert Storm AAR — Executive Summary, para. 2.A.8.

7. Paraphased by John Keegan and Richard Holmes in *Soldiers*, 87.

8. Bruce Cumings, *War and Television*, p. 103.

9. Ibid., 1–2.

10. Lisa Belkin, "Death on the CNN Curve," *The New York Times Magazine*, 23 July 1995, pp. 19–23, 32, 38, 41, 44.

Bibliography

This bibliography only lists works referenced. If quoted material does not have a source citation, it most likely comes from a personal conversation, letter, or email correspondence. A detailed chronology of Operations Desert Shield and Desert Storm can be found in the September 1991 *Military Review*. This chronology of international political and strategic events covers the period of 20 February 1990 through 9 April 1991, to include the beginning of Operation Provide Comfort.

The Center of Military History (www.army.mil/cmh-pg) has on-line a lengthy, if not comprehensive, Gulf War bibliography; the "XVIII Airborne Corps in Operations DESERT SHIELD AND DESERT STORM: An Annotated Bibliography", a select list of available oral history interviews; a full text version of Schubert and Kraus's *The Whirlwind War;* and a developing list of key personnel, with the goal of eventually naming every officer, warrant officer, and noncommissioned officer down to the platoon sergeant and armored vehicle track commander.

At the time of this book's publication, the Gulf War Declassification Project was concentrating its initial efforts on examining evidence of chemical weapons exposure and the Gulf War Syndrome. The other major army organization holding primary documents used for this book is the Center for Army Lessons Learned, Fort Leavenworth, Kansas.

Primary Sources and Postwar Narrative Accounts

Anonymous. "Oral History Interview." 28 Feb. 1991. Interviewer not identified, but probably S.Sgt. Warren B. Causey (317th Military History Detachment), in the Euphrates River Valley. Not transcribed. Tape duplicate obtained from the Center of Military History Oral History Activity, Washington, D.C. Interviewee not identified, though very possibly it is Maj. Walt Holton, executive officer of 2d Brigade 24th I.D., whose name appears on the tape label. The tape includes an interview with Maj. Mark Rodriguez (Bde S-2) and a Bde command and staff meeting conducted by Colonel Kern.

Apt, Maj. David Richard. "Oral History Interview." 6 February 1991. Center for Army Lessons Learned, Fort Leavenworth, Kans. It's believed that Maj. William H. Thomas III conducted the interview. A handwritten note to Major Apt on the first typed text page bears a signature partially lost in photocopying. "Bill" survived the copying; and Maj. Bill Thomas, commander of the 317th Military History

Detachment, was assigned by the Eighteenth Corps's historian to record the 24th Infantry Division (see Wright, Oral History, p. 39).

Barrett, Lt. Col. Raymond D. "Oral History Interview" 1 Mar 1991. Conducted by S.Sgt. Warren B. Causey (317th Military History Detachment) in the Euphrates River Valley. Not transcribed. Tape duplicate obtained from the Center of Military History Oral History Activity, Washington, D.C.

Barto, Maj. Joseph C. III. *Task Force 2–4 Cav — "First In, Last Out": The History of the 2d Squadron, 4th Cavalry Regiment during Operation Desert Storm.* Fort Leavenworth, Kans.: Combat Studies Institute, U.S. Army Command and General Staff College, 1993. Barto's book is essential for anyone concerned with the operational history of the 24th Infantry Division in Desert Storm. Barto did not join the squadron until a few weeks before the ground war; his book, therefore, only briefly treats Operation Desert Shield.

Bloxham, Maj. Garth T. "Map Sheets for Operational Graphics." Memorandum, 23 Jan. 1991. Center for Army Lessons Learned, Fort Leavenworth, Kans. In CALL database under "24ID 2D BDE MEMO, OPS GRAPHICS 910123."

Bruckner, Maj. Jeff. "Oral History Interview." 16 Mar. 1991. Conducted by Maj. Robert K. Wright at the Eighteenth Airborne Corps Main Command Post, Rafha, Saudi Arabia, Oral History Interview DSIT-AE-066. U.S. Army Center of Military History, Washington, D.C.

Department of Defense. News Briefing Transcript (unclassified), Tuesday, 13 Aug. 1991 at 1200. By Mr. Bob Taylor. Transcript dated 15 August 1991 (1336Z hours).

"XVIII Airborne Corps in Operations DESERT SHIELD and DESERT STORM: An Annotated Chronology." 21 Nov 96. Historical Resources Branch, U.S. Army Center of Military History. Obtained on-line from the U.S. Army Center of Military History. Compiled by the corps's command historian, these "files were initiated during the DESERT SHIELD/DESERT STORM deployment and completed after redeployment by carefully cross-referencing the official corps records before they were retired. The preliminary draft of this chronology was submitted as the documentation in the package recommending the XVIII Airborne Corps for the Presidential Unit Citation (Army). That award was never approved."

Ford, 1st Lt. John A., and 2d Lt. William Lockard. "Company Fire Support Operations." *Field Artillery* (Oct. 1991).

Hamowitz, Capt. William. "Oral History Interview." 5 March 1991. Conducted by S.Sgt. Warren B. Causey (317th Military History Detachment) in the Euphrates River Valley. Not transcribed. Tape duplicate obtained from the Center of Military History Oral History Activity, Washington, D.C.

JULLS Long Report No. 51553-19973 (00005). Submitted by Division Surgeon, 24th ID, 19 June 1991. Obtained through Gulf War Declassfication Project.

JULLS Long Report No. 51563-23896 (00008). Submitted by Division Surgeon, 24th ID, 19 June 1991. Obtained through Gulf War Declassfication Project.

Kamiya, Maj. Jason. *A History of the 24th Infantry Division Combat Team During Operation Desert Storm: "The Attack to Free Kuwait" (January through March 1991).*

Fort Stewart, Ga.: Headquarters, 24th Mechanized Infantry Division, 1991. One of a three-volume set compiled after the war by the division staff under Major General McCaffrey's directive.

Kamiya, Maj. Jason. "Oral History Interview." 8/9 Feb. 1991. Conducted by Maj. William H. Thomas III (317th Military History Detachment) in Saudi Arabia. Not transcribed. Tape duplicate obtained from the Center of Military History Oral History Activity, Washington, D.C.

Kern, Col. Paul J. "Operation Desert Shield [and] Operation Desert Storm." Center for Army Lessons Learned, Fort Leavenworth, Kans. In CALL database under "24ID 2D BDE HIST COL KERN."

————. "2nd Brigade After Action Review Briefing." Center for Army Lessons Learned, Fort Leavenworth, Kans. In CALL database under "24ID 2D BDE AAR BRIEFING COL KERN, VANGUARD BDE."

————. "2nd Brigade After Action Review Comments." Memorandum, 9 Mar. 1991. Center for Army Lessons Learned, Fort Leavenworth, Kans. In CALL database under "24ID 2D BDE AAR COMMENTS COL KERN 910309."

Lamar, Lt. Col. Patrick. "Oral History Interview." 28 Feb. 1991. Conducted by Maj. William H. Thomas III (317th Military History Detachment) in the Euphrates River Valley. Not transcribed. Tape duplicate obtained from the Center of Military History Oral History Activity, Washington, D.C. Lt. Col. Lamar was the 24th Infantry Division Operations officer (G-3).

McCaffrey, Maj. Gen. Barry R. "Oral History Interview." 24 Oct. 1990. Conducted by Maj. Larry Haystek and Dr. (Maj.) Robert Wright in eastern Saudi Arabia. Oral History Activity Catalog Number DSIT-A-006. U.S. Army Center of Military History, Washington, D.C. According to the oral history interview of Dr. Wright (see below), this interview occurred "where the main command post of the 24th Infantry Division was set up, vaguely in the vicinity of a dot on the map called As Sihaf" (p. 15).

————. "Oral History Interview." 28 Feb. 1991. Conducted by Maj. William H. Thomas III (317th Military History Detachment) in the Euphrates River Valley. Not transcribed. Tape duplicate obtained from the Center of Military History Oral History Activity, Washington, D.C.

"Operation Desert Storm After Action Review — Executive Summary." Headquarters, 24th Infantry Division (Mechanized), Fort Stewart, Ga., 8 June 1991. Obtained through the Gulf War Declassfication Project.

Pagonis, Lt. Gen. William G. *Moving Mountains: Lessons in Leadership and Logistics from the Gulf War.* With Jeffrey L. Cruikshank. Boston: Harvard Business School Press, 1992.

Quirk, Lt. Col. Richard J. III. "Oral History Interview." 16 Apr. 1991. Conducted by Maj. William H. Thomas III (317th Military History Detachment) at the 24th Infantry Division Headquarters in Saudi Arabia. Obtained from the Center for Army Lessons Learned, Fort Leavenworth, Kans.

Rodriguez, Maj. Mark. "Oral History Interview." 28 Feb. 1991. Interviewer not identified, but probably S.Sgt. Warren B. Causey (317th Military History Detachment), in the

Euphrates River Valley. Not transcribed. Tape duplicate obtained from the Center of Military History Oral History Activity, Washington, D.C.

Schwartz, Capt. Eric C. "Oral History Interview." 30 Apr. 1991. U.S. Army Center of Military History Oral History Activity Catalog Number DSIT-AE-121a. (For place and interviewer, see Swisher, below.)

Schwarzkopf, Gen. H. Norman. *It Doesn't Take a Hero: The Autobiography.* With Peter Petre. New York: Bantam Books, 1992.

Swisher, Capt. Jeff B. "Oral History Interview." 25 Apr. 1991. Interviewer not identified, but is probably S.Sgt. Warren B. Causey. Most likely conducted at Fort Stewart, Ga. Mr. Stephen Everett of CMH OHA agrees: "A lot of the interviews were conducted after the MHD returned to CONUS, while the detachment worked out of the PAO (or perhaps the museum)." Not transcribed. On the same tape with Maj. Tate's interview. Tape duplicate from the Center of Military History Oral History Activity, Washington, D.C.

Tate, Maj. Steven T. "Oral History Interview." 26 Apr. 1991. Interviewer not identified, but is probably S.Sgt. Warren B. Causey. Most likely conducted at Fort Stewart, Ga. (See Swisher, above). Not transcribed. On the same tape with Captain Swisher's interview. Tape duplicate from the Center of Military History Oral History Activity, Washington, D.C.

"24ID 2D BDE SYNCHRONIZATION MATRIX AND MAPS." Center for Army Lessons Learned, Fort Leavenworth, Kans.

24th Mechanized Infantry Division Combat Team Historical Reference Book: A Collection of Historical Letters, Briefings, Orders, and Other Miscellaneous Documents Pertaining to the Defense of Saudi Arabia and the Attack to Free Kuwait. Fort Stewart, Ga.: Headquarters, 24th Mechanized Infantry Division, 1992. One of a three-volume set compiled after the war by the division staff under Major General McCaffrey's directive.

24th Mechanized Infantry Division Combat Team: Operation Desert Storm Attack Plan OPLAN 91-3. Fort Stewart, Ga.: Headquarters, 24th Mechanized Infantry Division, 1992. One of a three-volume set compiled after the war by the division staff under Major General McCaffrey's directive.

U.S. Army. FM 17-15, *Tank Platoon.* Washington, D.C.: Department of the Army, 3 Apr. 1996.

———. FM 100-5, *Operations.* Washington, D.C.: Department of the Army, 5 May 1986.

———. FM 101-5-1 (or MCRP 4-2A). *Operational Terms and Graphics.* Washington, D.C.: Department of the Army and U.S. Marine Corps, 30 Sept. 1997. This is a joint U.S. Army/Marine Corps publication.

———. "Rules of Conduct: Victory Land." TASC 243-81, Fort Stewart, GA (undated).

Vernon, 2d Lt. Alex C. Unpublished correspondence during Operations Desert Shield and Desert Storm. Aug. 1990–March 1991. In author's possession.

The Victory Book: A Desert Storm Chronicle. Ed. Margaret C. Hall. Fort Stewart, Ga.: Headquarters, 24th Mechanized Infantry Division, December 1991. Published by

Josten's, *The Victory Book* was offered for sale to the division's soldiers. Its text is almost entirely the text of Kamiya's *History*.

Wright, Dr. Robert K., Jr. "Oral History Interview." 13 Dec. 1991. Conducted by Mr. Stephen Everett at Building 159, Southeast Federal Center, Washington, D.C. Oral History Interview DSIT-C-082. U.S. Army Center of Military History Oral History, Washington, D.C. Dr. Wright served as the Eighteenth Airborne Corps historian during Desert Shield and Desert Storm and conducted a number of oral history interviews of corps personnel. He was also a major in the Virginia National Guard. He commanded the 116th Military History Detachment.

Secondary Sources

Belkin, Lisa. "Death on the CNN Curve." *The New York Times Magazine,* 23 July 1995, pp. 19–23, 32, 38, 41, 44.

Blackwell, James. *Thunder in the Desert.* New York: Bantam Books, 1991.

Cumings, Bruce. *War and Television.* London: Verso, 1992.

Foote, Shelby. *Shiloh.* New York: Vintage Books, 1980.

Friedman, Norman. *Desert Victory.* Annapolis: Naval Institute Press, 1991.

Galloway, Joseph L. "The Point of the Spear." *U.S. News & World Report,* 11 Mar. 1991 (Gulf War issue), pp. 32–43. Joe Galloway accompanied the 24th Infantry Division during Desert Storm.

Gehring, Stephen P. *From the Fulda Gap to Kuwait: U.S. Army, Europe, and the Gulf War.* Washington, D.C.: Center of Military History, Department of the Army, 1998.

Helprin, Mark. "At Rest Between the Wars." *The Assembly* 51 (Mar. 1993). *The Assembly* is published by the Association of Graduates, United States Military Academy, West Point, N.Y.

Hoy, Pat C. II. *Instinct for Survival.* Athens: University of Georgia Press, 1992.

Hynes, Samuel. *The Soldiers' Tale: Bearing Witness to Modern War.* New York: Allen Lane/Penguin Press, 1997.

Keegan, John, and Richard Holmes. *Soldiers: A History of Men in Battle.* With John Gau. New York: Vintage, 1986.

Kipling, Rudyard. *The Irish Guards in the Great War.* Vol. 1. London: Macmillan, 1923.

Kitfield, James. *Prodigal Soldiers.* New York: Simon and Schuster, 1995.

Scales, Brig. Gen. Robert H. Scales, Jr. *Certain Victory: The U.S. Army in the Gulf War.* Washington, D.C.: Office of the Chief of Staff, United States Army, 1993. Dr. Robert Wright of the Center of Military History remarks that this project "was conducted at Fort Monroe at the direction of General Sullivan specifically to keep it clearly distinct from the Center or any other historical program. It was designed to be a fast-release volume, not a definitive study, and to be completed before the masses of records could be assembled. A superb job given the conditions the team had to work under. General Scales really got the most out of the limited materials available to him." Email, 12 Feb. 1998. In his foreword, Gen. Gordon Sullivan notes that "'certain victory' was not assured during the long autumn of 1990." One of General Sullivan's three enumerated themes of this book is to show how the American victory "vindicates the tireless and often unheralded work of a generation of Army leaders who forged a new Army from the dispirited institution that emerged from Vietnam" (p. iv). I wonder if this book's title was a rebuff of Denis Warner's *Certain Victory: How Hanoi Won the War* (Kansas City: Sheed, Andrews, and McMeel, 1978).

Schmitt, Eric. "Victorious at War, Not Yet at Peace." *New York Times*, 28 May 1995, sect. 4, pp. 1, 4.

Schubert, Frank N., and Theresa L. Kraus, eds. *The Whirlwind War: The United States Army in Operations Desert Shield and Desert Storm*. Washington, D.C.: United States Army Center of Military History, 1995. According to Dr. Robert Wright of the Center of Military History, "*The Whirlwind War* volume by Schubert and Krause (Mr. Charlie Anderson wrote the combat chapter) was a hasty project prepared in the first sixty days after the cease-fire. It got hung up in the security review process because of the Title V Report controversy and the resulting roles and missions arguments. Therefore, the footnoting is a bit confusing, since the vast majority of the records had not yet arrived back in CONUS when the book was written. The authors tended to make telephone calls, ask specific questions, and then ask for a source which could be cited (knowing that by the time the book was in print, there would be something someone could find). The footnote to the interview of me actually was a very brief call to Fort Bragg by Mr. Anderson; it was never recorded." Email, 12 Feb. 1998.

Seton-Watson, Christopher. *Dunkirk-Alamein-Bologna* (1993). In Hynes, pp. 139–40.

Shaara, Michael. *The Killer Angels*. New York: Random House, 1974.

Smith, Gregory M. "The Soul of Armor." *Feedback*, Apr. 1994, p. 3.

Stern, Lt. Col. Sir Albert G. *Tanks 1914–1918: The Log-Book of a Pioneer*. London: Hodder and Stoughton, 1919.

"Tracking the Storm." *Military Review* no. 9 (Sept. 1991).

Tripp, Nathaniel. *Father, Soldier, Son: Memoir of a Platoon Leader in Vietnam*. South Royalton, Vt.: Steerforth Press, 1996.

Trudeau, Gary. "*I'd Go With the Helmet, Ray*." Kansas City: Andrews and McMeel, 1991.
————. *Welcome to Club Scud!* Kansas City: Andrews and McMeel, 1991.

U.S. News & World Report Staff. *Triumph Without Victory: The History of the Persian Gulf War*. New York: Times Books, 1993. The "Preface to the Paperback Edition" is signed by Peter Cary, Brian Duffy, and Joseph L. Galloway. Joe Galloway accompanied the 24th I.D. during Desert Storm.

Vernon, Alex. "Bridging the Gulf." *Independent Weekly*, 14–20 Feb. 1996.

Weiner, Tim. "Gulf War's First U.S. Casualty Leaves Lasting Trail of Mystery." *New York Times*, 7 Dec. 1997, p. 1.

Index

Burton, Specialist, 238, 244

Bush, President George, 92; and cease-fire, 236; on Desert Storm and Vietnam, 281, 283; on liberation of Kuwait, 152; soldiers' opinion of, 12; ultimata to Iraq, 164, 168, 171, 173

Camels, 42, 47, 56

Capella (transport ship), 16, 33

Carrol, Private, 38–39, 196: in attack on Jalibah, 219; firing on truck, 246; speaking Arabic to POWs, 198

Casualties, 260; from friendly fire, 161, 227, 228, 304n.19; from grenade accident, 199; Iraqi, 191, 193, 205–6, 220, 246–47

Cavalry. *See* 2-4 Cav

Cease-fire, 242–43, 306n.24, 307n.31; ambiguity of, 245–46; correctness of, 251

Censorship of mail, 81

CFVs. *See* Bradley CFVs

Chain guns, 191; on Bradleys, 50; against Iraqi helicopters, 212; *vs.* Abrams's weapons, 102

Charlie Mech: in attack on Jalibah, 216, 226; at BP 1-64, 232–33; taking prisoners, 206

Charlie Tank, 182; approaching Basra, 235, 238–39, 245; in attack on Jalibah, 209, 215, 216–18, 222–23; first days in desert, 39–40; in initial attack, 183–85

Chem lights, 174

Chemical weapons: alarms for, 58; fear of, 159; preventive measures against, 98, 180. *See also* Mission Oriented Protective Posture

Cheney, secretary of defense, 152

Children, Arab: injured at Rumaylah, 244; love of chem lights, 174; soldiers' relations with, 66

Civil war, in Basra, 249

Civilians: Iraqi, 243–44, 307n.30; Saudi, 54, 66, 85, 88–89; U.S., 253, 260, 262–63, 265, 266; visitors to 2-4; at AA Augusta, 61–62

Close air support, in ground war plan, 150–51

Cluster bombs, 254. *See also* Artillery, unexploded

Combat lifesavers, 40

Commendation Medals, 254–55

Company teams: formation of, 33; in wedge formation, 184

Compass: inaccuracies in tanks, 104; in maneuver drills for scouts, 100; Neal's skill navigating with, 36–39

Constellations, 110–11; use in navigating, 37, 54

Counseling, as officer's job, 10–11

Creighton, Lt. Neal, Jr., 3–4, 39, 111, 143, 157; during air war, 147–48, 169; in attack on Jalibah, 199–200, 213–14; attack on Objective Gray, 198–99; and cease fire, 245–46; evaluation of platoon, 103–4; fall on tank, 196; family of, 4, 120, 270; friendships of, 164, 276; homecoming of, 264–66; in initial attack, 183; leadership by, 105–7, 120; navigation skill of, 36–39; postwar reflections, 267–71; raiding Iraqi supplies, 240–42; at Ranger School, 3, 19–20; sickness from local food, 75; tanks of, 31, 133, 144. *See also* Alpha Tank

Creighton, Mary, 7, 20, 78, 83, 110–11, 269–70

Cross-border operations, 168–75

Dammam, Saudi Arabia: arrival in, 26–29; moving out of, 34–35, 44; redeployment from, 260–61; transition to M1A1 heavies at, 132–34

Davis, Sergeant, 37; in attack on Jalibah, 213, 214, 219; in attack on Objective Gray, 198; in raid on Iraqi supplies, 241–42

Day trips, from AA Hinesville, 91, 94–95

Day *vs.* night attacks, 150, 176, 180; artillery for, 233; on Jalibah, 206–7

Decoy tanks, 60

Deem, S.Sgt., 233; and attack on Jalibah, 211–12; on beginning of air war, 146; and contact with enemy, 190, 191; during friendly fire incident, 172; roles of, 106, 131

Defense budget cuts: effects of, 7–8; McCaffrey protecting 24th from, 267. *See also* Downsizing, army

Defense/offense, 55; briefing on ground war plan, 149–51; change from defense, 107; correctness of stopping at cease-fire, 251; General Defense Plan, 76–78, 105–7; at Iraqi border, 158; offensive planning banned, 106; training in, 98, 105–7

Dehydration, 40

Delta Mech: Al's platoon with, 159, 247; and attack on Jalibah, 200–201, 208, 224, 228; at beginning of ground war, 171, 177, 186–88; friendly fire on, 234–35; in last engagement with enemy, 239–40; leaving Dammam, 44; life-style of, 56; moving through Iraqi fields, 233–34; at Objective Gray, 197; POWs taken by, 237; in task organization, 33, 46, 64, 76

Delta Tank, 135; at AA Hinesville, 67; in attack on Jalibah, 209, 215, 216–17, 218, 223, 227; at beginning of ground war, 152, 173–75, 181–83; in diamond formation, 182; and friendly fire, 227, 231; hasty resupply, 184; preparing for attack on Jalibah, 206–7

Demilitarized Zone (DMZ), 248–49, 307n.32

Deployment, 20–22; alerts, 10–11; of 2d Brigade, 10–11, 297n.4; fear of, 12–13, 15–16; preparing for, 12–14, 21–22; of Seventh Corps, 300n.1, 300n.4; of 24th Infantry, 2, 297n.4

Desert: causing increased breakdowns of vehicles, 50, 52; first days in, 39–42; soldiers' memories of, 271; in spring, 258. *See also* Terrain

Desert Shield: as defense mission, 76; effects of, 140; training during, 97, 213, 277

Desert Shield writing contest, 87, 299n.3

Desert Storm: effects on soldiers, 255–56, 270, 280–81, 283, 288; end of, 235–36; lessons from, 270, 275, 278; mission of, 153, 260; plans for, 189, 300n.5, 301n.6. *See also* Air war; Cease-fire; Ground war

Desert Storm OPORD, 153

Dharhran, Saudi Arabia, 249–50

Diamond formation: of Task Force 1-64, 182, 209, 231; of Task Force 3-15, 108

Diehl, Maj. Jim, 152, 158, 182; and Underberg, 66–67

Disciplinary measures: extra duty as, 72; withholding mail as, 84

Division Intelligence, 54, 231

Dock, Sgt. Randy, 83, 161, 197, 247; and attack on Jalibah, 218, 219, 225; and Egyptians, 257; fight with Boss, 62–63; and Freight, 163, 225; and HET accident, 115–16; and Iraqis, 201, 234; in last engagement with enemy, 239–40; and tanks, 136, 144, 187

Downey, Lt. Greg, 7–8, 14–15, 45, 93, 111, 166; at AA Augusta, 48–54; in attack on Jalibah, 202, 209–13; and battle plans, 77, 153; at beginning of air war, 146, 148; and cease-fire, 238, 255; and Chaplain Bedsole, 154–55; on combat, 2–3, 137–38, 143; concerns over vehicle condition, 13–14, 31; in cross-border operations, 169–75; family of, 14–15, 120; at Fort Stewart, 7–8; and fratricide, 172, 226, 228, 304n.19; friendships of, 8; on Gordon's leadership, 125–26; on homecoming, 261, 265; and incompetent platoon sergeant, 130–31; on just-get-it-done mentality, 157–58; lack of support group, 119, 137; at LD time, 177, 181; leadership by, 8, 31–32, 49, 71, 120; missions of, 157, 189–90, 229–31; moving through Rumaylah,

Hoagland, Lt. Matt, 22, 23, 248; and Al, 118, 286–87; on combat, 138; leadership by, 120

Holidays: meals, 91–92; packages, 93–94

Holmes, Kelli Barker: mail to Rob, 85, 94, 140; wedding, 271

Holmes, Lt. Rob, 2–4, 81, 111–12, 146, 155, 254; arrival in Saudi, 29–30; and attack on Jalibah, 206–7, 208, 214–16, 220–22, 226–27; on briefing on battle plans, 152; crews of, 31, 66; in cross-border operations, 173–75; decamping for combat, 140–42; and deployment, 12, 21; desert life, 40–44, 54–55, 72; and Downing, 112–14, 202–3; on end of Desert Storm, 235–36; family of, 4, 84, 120, 263–64, 273; and friendly fire, 105–6, 231; friendships of, 8, 24, 116–18, 133, 164, 168; on holidays, 93–94; on homecoming, 261–64; in initial attack, 152–53, 177, 181–83; on leadership, 8, 126–27; leadership by, 32, 84, 120, 122, 272; and Lorans, 191–92; orders to fire, 192–93; postwar reflections by, 271–76; and support platoon leader position, 123–25; and transition to M1A1 heavies, 133, 135; and women, 25, 261

Howard, Spc. Arthur, 222; and Arab children, 88–89; on return home, 263

Howitzers, 190, 205

Hoy, Pat, 285–86

Hubner, Capt. Dave, 191, 195, 261; and attack on Jalibah, 206–7, 220–21, 226; in cross-border operations, 173–75; on end of Desert Storm, 235–36; and fratricide at Jalibah, 227, 304n.19; and friendly fire, 231, 232; at LD time, 181–83; leadership by, 122, 135; recon by, 78; and Rob, 122–25, 272–73, 274

Hunter Army Airfield (Savannah): deployment from, 22–23; return to, 253, 264–65

Hussein, Saddam: and Iraqis, 249; plans to attack into Saudi Arabia, 249–50; reasons

for cease-fire, 236–37; and UN proscriptions, 164, 173

Hygiene: at AA Hinesville, 72, 73–74; in Dammam Tent City, 28; during initial attack, 188

Infantry, 50, 199; in attack on Jalibah, 217, 222, 225; drills on clearing trenches, 108–9; formations for, 182, 184; handling prisoners, 194, 200, 206; Iraqi, 216, 220–21, 245–47; in task organization with armor, 32–33, 58

Insects, 56

Intelligence, 29; about Republican Guards, 197, 305n.23; on enemy locations, 165, 167, 216, 231; during initial attack, 186; on Iraqi vulnerabilities, 164–66; from Iraqis, 249, 307n.32; on Jalibah Airfield, 199–200, 202, 216; on Khafji action, 160–61; from Long Range Surveillance Detachment, 190; Neal and Greg working in, 278–79; task force, 186, 232

Internal Look 90, 9

Iraq, 185, 226, 248, 307n.34; attacks on Saudi Arabia by, 64, 78, 160–61; capture of military trailer of, 249–50; deadline for withdrawal from Kuwait, 137, 139, 171, 173; defenses of, 153, 238–39, 250; locations of troops, 165, 167; losses of, 232, 233, 243–44, 260, 305n.22; map of, xxiii; military strength of, 23, 31, 32, 164–66; poor condition of soldiers, 190, 191, 194, 200, 227, 237, 249; soldiers of, 54, 56, 241, 249; U.S. ground attack into, 175, 176, 180, 183–85; U.S. planning about, 8–9, 106. See also Civilians; POWs

Irrigation, 65

Jackson, 1st Lt. Greg, 23, 68–70, 130; and Al, 118–19, 131; and Al vs. Freight, 144, 148–49; and HET accident, 115–16; on homecoming, 258, 265; and tanks, 144, 189, 250

Vernon, Lt. Alex, 75, 248, 269; in attack on Jalibah, 200–201, 208, 218–19, 221, 223–25; background of, 2–3, 7, 26–27, 96–97; briefing platoon on ground war plans, 158–59; and cease-fire, 236–37, 242–43; correspondence of, 82, 83–84, 138, 267, 285; decamping from AA Hinesville, 143; deployment of, 12, 21–23; evaluation of platoon, 104–6; family of, 21–22, 26–27, 82–83, 119–20, 145, 264–65, 287; and Freight, 18–19, 143, 148–49, 162–63, 178–80, 266; friendships of, 68–70, 118–19, 164; and HET accident, 115–16; homecoming, 264–66; during initial attack, 186–88; leadership by, 32, 130, 131, 287; moving through Iraqi fields, 233–34; moving toward Basra, 239–40; and Objective Gray, 197; postwar reflections, 281–89; rejoining Bravo Tank, 68–71, 247; souvenirs, 237, 239; and storage site, 228; and superior officers, 126, 256–57; transition to M1A1 heavies, 136; trip to staging area, 156–57. *See also* Ward, Maria Ketner Garnett
Veterans: bond among, 284; Gulf War, 281–82; Vietnam, 262, 265, 281
Victory Division, 22, 260
Victory Homecoming Team, Dave in charge of, 266
Vietnam War, Desert Storm as finale to, 23–24, 281, 283

Wadis. *See* Terrain
Walker, Sergeant ("Top"), 195, 227
Wannamaker, Sgt. Tom, 146
Ward, Maria Ketner Garnett, 27, 87; on Al's return, 264–66; letters from, 82, 83–84; letters to, 138, 286
Water: enforcing consumption of, 30, 40, 49; shortage of, 51–52, 240–42
Watkins, Spc. Forbes, 36, 37
Weapons: capturing Iraqi, 237, 245; as contraband souvenirs, 258, 260–61

Weapons systems: in attack on Jalibah, 219, 222–23; on Bradleys, 102–3, 212; on M1A1s, 135–36, 193
Weather: on arrival in Saudi Arabia, 27, 28, 30; during attack on Objective Orange, 200; cold and rain, 72, 157, 168; effects of, 56, 308n.1; on first days in desert, 39–42; during initial attack, 181, 186
Wedge formation: in attack on Jalibah, 214, 215, 225; infantry company-team in, 184
West, Pfc., 185; attachment to vehicle, 51; in CFV fire, 169–70; on combat, 138; effect of Desert Storm on, 256; during friendly fire incident, 172; and Iraqi artillery, 203–4, 230; and Iraqis, 244; and Lowther, 102, 103
West Point, 3, 8; alumni of, 93, 268; Dave teaching at, 276; early release of graduates, 286–87; mission of, 285; motivation to attend, 26–27; reunions at, 269; value of, 273–74
White, 2d Lt. Jeff ("Bambi"), 24, 85, 94, 140, 261; in attack on Jalibah, 221; in initial attack, 183; visiting other lieutenants, 164, 168
Wiggins, 172–73, 212
Wildermuth, John, 34
Willis, Mike, 62
Wills, before deployment, 21
Wilson, Sfc., 36–37, 39, 245–46
Wingate, Sergeant, 162
Wingman: importance of, 187; in tank platoon organization, 58
Winkler, Capt. Steve, 133, 153
Wynn, 2d Lt. Paul, 258

Yocum, S.Sgt. Joey, 47

Zero defect mentality, 274, 277
Zone recons, 202, 232; cross-border, 169–74; speed of, 106, 189